Patronizing the Public

Critical Media Studies

Series Editor

Andrew Calabrese, University of Colorado

This series covers a broad range of critical research and theory about media in the modern world. It includes work about the changing structures of the media, focusing particularly on work about the political and economic forces and social relations which shape and are shaped by media institutions, structural changes in policy formation and enforcement, technological transformations in the means of communication, and the relationships of all these to public and private cultures worldwide. Historical research about the media and intellectual histories pertaining to media research and theory are particularly welcome. Emphasizing the role of social and political theory for informing and shaping research about communications media, Critical Media Studies addresses the politics of media institutions at national, subnational, and transnational levels. The series is also interested in short, synthetic texts on key thinkers and concepts in critical media studies.

Titles in the Series

Global Communications: Toward a Transcultural Political Economy edited by Paula Chakravartty and Yuezhi Zhao

Governing European Communications: From Unification to Coordination by Maria Michalis

Knowledge Workers in the Information Society edited by Catherine McKercher and Vincent Mosco

Democratic Communications: Formations, Projects, Possibilities by James F. Hamilton

Hegemony in the Digital Age: The Arab/Israeli Conflict Online by Stephen Marmura

Punk Record Labels and the Struggle for Autonomy: The Emergence of DIY by Alan O'Connor

From the Labyrinth of the World to the Paradise of the Heart: Science and Humanism in UNESCO's Approach to Globalization by Vincenzo Pavone

The Laboring of Communication: Will Knowledge Workers of the World Unite? by Vincent Mosco and Catherine McKercher

Cultural Studies and Political Economy: Toward a New Integration by Robert Babe

Patronizing the Public: American Philanthropy's Transformation of Culture, Communication, and the Humanities edited by William J. Buxton

Patronizing the Public

American Philanthropy's Transformation of Culture, Communication, and the Humanities

Edited by William J. Buxton

LEXINGTON BOOKS

A division of
ROWMAN & LITTLEFIELD PUBLISHERS, INC.
Lanham • Boulder • New York • Toronto • Plymouth, UK

LEXINGTON BOOKS

A division of Rowman & Littlefield Publishers, Inc.
A wholly owned subsidary of The Rowman & Littlefield Publishing Group, Inc.
4501 Forbes Boulevard, Suite 200
Lanham, MD 20706

Estover Road
Plymouth PL6 7PY
United Kingdom

British Library Cataloguing in Publication Information Available

Library of Congress Cataloging-in-Publication Data

Patronizing the public : American philanthropy's transformation of culture,
communication, and the humanities / edited by William J. Buxton.
        p. cm. — (Critical media studies)
    Includes bibliographical references and index.
    ISBN 978-0-7391-2305-8 (alk. paper) — ISBN 978-0-7391-2306-5 (pbk. : alk.
paper)
    — ISBN 978-0-7391-3836-6 (electronic)
    1. Rockefeller Foundation—History. 2. Charities—United States—History. 3.
Cultural industries—United States—History. I. Buxton, William, 1947–
    HV97.R6P37 2009
    001.306'073—dc22   2009007251

Printed in the United States of America

∞™ The paper used in this publication meets the minimum requirements of
American National Standard for Information Sciences—Permanence of Paper
for Printed Library Materials, ANSI/NISO Z39.48-1992.

To Darwin H. Stapleton and Thomas Rosenbaum
for your passionate commitment to the study of philanthropy;
for your steadfast support of archival researchers

Contents

Preface

William J. Buxton

This collection had its origins in a workshop titled "American Philanthropic Support for Culture, Communications, and the Humanities" that was held at the Rockefeller Archive Center (Sleepy Hollow, New York) from August 19 to August 20, 2004. Given the increasing number of archive-based studies on the workshop's theme that had been produced in the preceding two decades, the participants were eager to share their findings, to explore interconnections, and to mark out common ground. Workshop members were subsequently invited to submit revised versions to be considered for inclusion in an edited volume. All did so, and all of the submissions were accepted. Aside from the first chapter, no other works have been added.

Neither the workshop—nor the edited volume that grew out of it—would have been possible without the support of the Rockefeller Archive Center. The Center not only fully underwrote the initiative through its conference and workshop program, but also made its unrivaled facilities available to us. Our spirited sessions were enriched by a tour of the archival vaults, by a visit to the room featuring John Rockefeller Jr.'s original office furnishings, as well as by our informal musings against the backdrop of the enchanting Pocantico Hills. We owe a debt of gratitude to the staff of the Center, in particular, to Dr. Darwin Stapleton, Dr. Jack Myers, Tom Rosenbaum, Kenneth W. Rose, Norine Hochman, Camilla Harris, Roseann Variano, Erwin Levold, Mindy Gordon, James Washington, Robert Battaly, and Mary Ann Quinn. The Rockefeller Archive Center, in line with its generous support for researchers, has also provided a subsidy for the publication of this volume. Belying the claims (advanced by ourselves and others) about how foundations shape and control the production of knowledge, the officers of the RAC have never made the slightest effort to steer this collection in any particular direction.

In addition to receiving assistance from the staff of the Rockefeller Archive Center, the contributors to this volume have benefited from the wise counsel, dedication, and generosity of many archivists, including Kacey Page, Rachel Borchard, Linda Severe, and Jena Whipking of the Archives of the Buffalo Museum of Science; Elaine M. Doak of the Pickler Memorial Library at Truman State University; Ron Magliozzi and Charles Silver of the Film Study Center, Department of Film, the Museum of Modern Art; Jane Gorjevsky of the Columbia University Rare Book and Manuscript Library; Daniel J. Linke of the Seeley G. Mudd Library at Princeton; Christine Roussel of the Rockefeller Center Archive Center; Marcy Goldstein and Idelle Nisilla-Stone of the Ford Foundation Archives; Christine Pelletier of the Canadian War Museum; and Joan Miller, Wesleyan Cinema Archives.

I also wish to gratefully acknowledge the support provided by Concordia University and by the Department of Information and Communication at Laval University.

Finally, Joseph Parry, Matthew McAdam, Michael Wiles, and Andrew Calabrese of Lexington Books have unfailingly supported this project from the beginning, and an anonymous reviewer of the manuscript provided us with valuable commentary. We are honored to have our volume published as part of the Critical Media Studies series.

William J. Buxton
Québec City, Québec
Canada

1

Civil Society and its Discontents: Bringing Culture, Communication, and the Humanities into the History of Philanthropy

William J. Buxton

This collection is a modest effort to provide a preliminary mapping of how large philanthropic foundations have transformed the realm of culture, communication, and the humanities. With some spillover, the chapters in the volume span the period from the late 1920s through to the late 1970s. This period was a crucial one for the development of philanthropic practice. It was ushered in by the consolidation of the various Rockefeller philanthropies into a new streamlined structure, grounded in divisions dealing with specific—but interrelated—realms of knowledge. This organizational realignment made it possible for Rockefeller philanthropy to strengthen its traditional programs in the natural and medical sciences, as well as nurture the developing areas of the social sciences, education, and the humanities. By virtue of its reconfigured structure, Rockefeller philanthropy not only became the major force in the foundation field, it provided the organizational template for general-purpose philanthropic bodies that subsequently emerged.

Arguably, this philanthropic world—as dominated by large foundations pursuing their own agendas—was in place until the mid-to-late 1970s. At that time, as a result of the growing recognition by philanthropies that their lack of concerted action was rendering them unable to withstand attacks from both the government and the public, their advocates began to conceive of, inter alia, foundations, philanthropies, charities, nongovernmental organizations, and nonprofit groups as comprising what was called the "independent" or "third sector." As with the earlier reconfiguration of Rockefeller philanthropy into a new and more efficacious structure, the

1

realignment of nonprofit organizations into a single realm had important implications for the sorts of fields that received funding. In particular, the emergent cooperative ethos made it possible to provide unprecedented levels of support for the arts, an area that had been largely overlooked and ignored by general-purpose foundations.

The period from the late 1920s through to the late 1970s was both defined by how American philanthropy was organized and practiced as well as marked by an increasing shift of philanthropic support toward culture, communication, and the humanities. Within this broad area, one can discern notable shifts in how the three constituents were interpreted and how they articulated with one another.

The chapters in this volume explore various aspects of how philanthropy has intersected with these changes in the sphere of knowledge and practice. The contributors are critical and independent scholars, working in a variety of academic fields including education, history, communication studies, film studies, musicology, humanities, and cultural studies. What they share in common is a strong commitment to theoretically informed research grounded in the careful study of archival documents.

PHILANTHROPIC PERSPECTIVES ON COMMUNICATION, CULTURE, AND THE HUMANITIES

Since the chapters in the volume rely heavily on archival material in order to capture the interplay between funders and recipients, the notions of culture, communication, and the humanities that are used correspond closely to those that have informed philanthropic thinking over the years, tracking the shifting meaning of the terms from the 1920s through to the 1970s. The humanities, considered by many to be "the "heart of the university," referred to the community of scholars whose main concern was interpreting manifestations of society's "spiritual existence."[1] They initially found institutional form in the American Council of Learned Societies (ACLS). Established in 1919, this body was the beneficiary of Rockefeller funding almost from the outset[2] and was an important area of concern for both Rockefeller and Carnegie philanthropies during the 1930s.[3] Since culture was a key component of society's "spiritual existence," its importance to the humanities cannot be understated. It not only generally referred to the way of life of peoples and communities, but more narrowly to particular forms of artistic and symbolic expression, the purview of areas such as music, art, drama, and literature.[4] Communication overlapped considerably with both broad and narrow views of culture, but emphasized the process of mediation rather than content per se. Formerly referring to interpersonal communication through language on the one hand, or to the connections provided by transportation on the other,[5] by the 1930s it was increasingly used to refer to the dissemination of messages and information from centralized sources through technological means.[6] Since it was thought to play the role of spreading ideas to a mass public, it also was referred to as "mass communication."[7] Radio broadcasting and film were of particular interest, but other phenomena were included as well, such as newspapers, print media, sound recordings, microphotography, museums, libraries, and the dramatic arts.[8]

In turning their attention to this overlapping set of concerns, there was more at stake for philanthropy officials than fondness for the phenomena per se. Operating within their mandates of improving human well-being, they supported initiatives that sought to bring about positive change in a broad range of areas, such as public health, public administration, industrial relations, and education. As a number of commentators have noted, this drew the philanthropies into the realm of public-policy issues.[9] However, it could be argued that philanthropies had an equal interest in helping constitute a new form of public life itself, based on knowledge of what was considered to be more enlightened social practice. Humanities, culture, and communication were critical in this regard, as they articulated knowledge, mediation, and aesthetics together in a new way,[10] constituting a mediated public sphere—the site of public opinion—grounded in communication technologies. This emergent public sphere differs somewhat from that described by Karl and Katz.[11] Their emphasis is upon how and to what extent the American government sought to establish nationally relevant programs of social reform. The public sphere, as they describe it, could best be seen as an extension of the state, comprising the arena in which state policy was implemented. In their view, the foundations came to aid and abet the state officials in the policy process. Our evidence suggests, however, that the sphere in question was not simply an extension of the state, but was relatively autonomous from it, was much more extensive than policy per se—and was grounded in culture, communication, and the humanities. It comprised the broader area of shared beliefs, knowledge, and values that formed the basis for broad deliberations—not only about policy issues, but about issues of significance and relevance to the collectivity.

This form of public sphere also departs from the bourgeois public sphere as analyzed by Jürgen Habermas (although it contains elements of what he described as the "refeudalization of the public sphere" of the twentieth century).[12] It was not comprised of citizens deliberating in sites such as salons, taverns, and coffee houses, but was a combination of interest-laden individuals, corporate bodies, and government officials—not to mention representatives of philanthropic bodies—whose process of deliberation was mediated by emergent mass communications. This entailed an elite-dominated world, in which government and foundation officials circulated.[13] The sphere was by no means self-contained but was inflected with other concerns. While it was biased by the interests working within it—particularly those of big business—it nonetheless retained some degree of open-endedness. Moreover, departing from the rationally based communicative model presented by Habermas, this realm was suffused with images, rhetoric, and display[14] with deliberative processes determined as much by emotions and sentiment as they were by reason.[15] This form of public, highly mediated by foundations and nonprofit groups, involving voluntary associations, cultural institutions, as well as universities and schools, began to take form during the 1920s, grew thereafter, and became the point of reference for philanthropic self-understanding (as well as consolidation) in the United States and abroad beginning in the 1970s.[16]

DISCUSSIONS OF PHILANTHROPY

Given the increasing importance that philanthropy accorded to the key constitutive features of the public—namely culture, communication, and the humanities—starting in the 1920s,[17] it is somewhat surprising that these areas received so little attention in the accounts of philanthropic work that were published with increasing regularity from the 1930s onward.[18] A number of these works fail to mention these areas at all.[19] Others allude to various ventures pertinent to culture, communication, and the humanities, without exploring what these initiatives were in any detail.[20] Some, in fact, give accounts that are not born out by evidence.[21]

The lack of attention to the humanities, communication, and culture is to some extent an artifact of the categories that were used by some foundation officials beginning in the 1920s. While the field of the humanities was recognized, those of culture and communication were largely bound up with the broader area of education and thus tended to be overlooked by both commentators and historians. In order to understand the neglect of the humanities, communication, and culture in historical accounts of philanthropy, one needs to look more closely at how histories were commissioned and produced. For the most part, those close to the foundations—often sponsored by the funding bodies themselves—largely conducted the historical work on philanthropies. The purpose of these histories was to present the philanthropy in question in the best possible light and to favorably impress the economic and political elites, who, as Hollis notes, had little interest in the humanities.[22] Above all, the failure of historians to give adequate attention to the humanities, communication, and culture could be attributed, at least in part, to the accessibility of sources. Foundations only made their papers available to carefully chosen "house historians." Others had to limit themselves to whatever other material was available.[23] As a result, the histories produced tended to be celebratory, impressionistic, biased, and quite uneven in their coverage of foundation activities.

Arguably, a shift occurred beginning in the mid-1950s, ushering in a period of better cooperation between foundation officials and historians.[24] In the subsequent three decades, more documentary material became available to researchers, as a number of major archives containing documents on philanthropy were established.[25] In addition, researchers in the history of philanthropy could avail themselves of the new resources that were becoming available to scholarship on philanthropy as a whole, which included new research centers,[26] new networks,[27] research tools,[28] publication outlets dedicated specifically to the study of the nonprofit sector,[29] and more funding sources.[30]

One might have expected that the quantity and quality of scholarship on philanthropy would have made a quantum leap as a result since it was now much more possible for independent scholars to undertake detailed historical research on foundations. Certainly this was in the case for work on some of the leading practitioners of philanthropy within the context of their immediate and extended families.[31] Some path-breaking, synthetical works also appeared.[32] However, on the whole, the gains were of a modest and gradual nature and were quite unevenly distributed across the scholarly domain. This state of affairs could be attributed, at least in part, to the reluctance of historians to work on the history of philanthropic foundations. Sealander notes that "historians are scarce among analysts of philanthropy,"[33] perhaps because the subject did not fit readily into the reward structure of the field.[34] Along the same lines, Lawrence Friedman observes that "historians constitute a small minority within ARNOVA and ISTR" (the large bodies involved with research on charities and foundations). He goes on to say that "cooperative, focused and closely coordinated research efforts by those trained in the historical profession have been almost nonexistent."[35] This left the scholarship largely to writers as well as academics working in other fields. As a matter of course, the histories they wrote on the impact of philanthropy were reflective of their own disciplinary concerns. In particular, perhaps because the history of science was institutionalized separately from history per se,[36] it became the site of a flood of impressive works in the field[37]—particularly in relation to medicine—leading to a number of fascinating debates. By the same token, histories of how philanthropies have shaped the field of psychology were well represented, not only because psychology has a strong presence within the history of science, but also because those interested in the history of psychology have been able to develop their own reference group in the form of CHEIRON.[38] Those working within the various social sciences,[39] as well as education,[40] also produced influential works, with pertinence to their particular disciplines. Given the extent to which the study of philanthropy was linked to practical issues facing foundation administrators,[41] historical work, at least to some extent, was shaped by how it might make current philanthropic practice more effective.[42] Arguably, archive-based historical work on the impact of philanthropy on the realm of culture, communication, and the humanities did not materialize in this period because none of these areas had corresponding institutionalized forms that would serve as a point of reference for research studies.[43] While the humanities were of course pervasive, they hardly could serve as a disciplinary point of reference. Communication and culture, while emergent objects of study, were only weakly developed as fields, with little sense of academic identity. Because those involved with the study of culture, communications, and the humanities lacked a disciplinary point of reference, it meant that when the history of these fields came to be written in a more serious way, the role of philanthropy was ignored, downplayed, or misunderstood. Two of the more notable historical treatments of the field of communications, namely those of Everett Rogers and Christopher Simpson, are cases in point, as they offer inadequate accounts of the role that philanthropy has played in the development of communication studies.[44] The same could be said for two recent substantial edited collections that largely fail to address the extent to which philanthropic foundations have shaped the field.[45]

Accordingly, while the post-1970s wave of research on the history of philanthropy contained numerous insights into its relationship to culture, communication, and the humanities, these areas were largely treated as peripheral rather than as a direct object of concern.[46] Given that the study of philanthropy is, for the most part, rooted in the here and now of making the third sector work more effectively, it is not surprising that historical studies of culture, communication, and the humanities—or historical work in general for that matter—have not been present to any great extent.

To be sure, there are recent signs that more attention is being given to these areas. At the time that the pioneering volumes edited by Kathleen D. McCarthy[47] and Paul DiMaggio[48] appeared, little had been written about philanthropic support for the arts and media; the same could be said for philanthropic support for humanities. However, subsequent to the publication of these texts, numerous articles and books have appeared pertinent to both areas, spanning a broad range of topics including the humanities,[49] cultural activities,[50] visual art,[51] radio,[52] film,[53] drama,[54] dance,[55] folklore,[56] libraries,[57] and the study of public opinion or propaganda.[58] In addition, some attention has been given to philanthropic family members (with linkages to foundation interests) as private patrons of the arts; Abby and Nelson Rockefeller immediately spring to mind in this regard.[59]

However, what has noticeably been lacking within this body of work has been the emergence of a central frame of reference for philanthropic support for the arts-humanities along the lines of what has taken place in the medical-natural-social sciences area. Aside from the work of DiMaggio, McCarthy, and Ellen Lagemann,[60] there is nothing that can compare to the contributions of authors such as Jonas,[61] Kohler,[62] Cueto,[63] and Fisher and Richardson.[64] It is hoped that *Patronizing the Public* might stimulate more attention to the area, raising fresh issues and opening up new lines of debate (akin to discussions about philanthropic support for molecular biology,[65] for the social sciences,[66] and for the area of public policy).[67] To this end, the collection may help to correct the bias of contemporary philanthropic scholarship against historical studies, and within historical work, may help to correct the bias against studies of the humanities, communication, and culture. It also can be seen as a challenge to mainstream scholarship on philanthropy as a whole—historical or otherwise—which is very much slanted toward accepting the status quo and to eschewing critical studies in favor of providing knowledge serving the needs and interests of nonprofit sector managers and administrators.

THE CRITICAL STUDY OF FOUNDATIONS

The volume speaks to issues that have been raised over the years by what has recently been identified as the critical study of foundations.[68] The first major effort to collect and systematize research informed by this approach was the collection *Philanthropy and Cultural Imperialism: The Foundations at Home and Abroad*, edited by Robert Arnove, which appeared in 1980 (hereafter *Philanthropy/Cultural Imperialism*).[69] Based largely on dissertations written in the 1970s, many of its chapters draw on historical material to ground their claims about the impact of philanthropy. While the contributors did not subscribe to a "uniform ideological framework," they shared in common a structural approach, and a concern to examine how foundations functioned in terms of their "organizational characteristics, modus operandi, and substantive decisions for control and social change." Their stance in relation to foundations was decidedly a critical one. As "relatively unregulated and unaccountable concentrations of power and wealth," these organizations were taken to task for corroding democracy, imposing their own agendas on society, keeping radical transformation at bay, and maintaining "an international and political order, international in scope, which benefits the ruling-class interests of philanthropists and philanthropoids." The organizing theme for the volume, according to the editor, was that of "cultural imperialism," which referred to the ethnocentrism of elites "from a particular class and cultural background" who take it upon themselves to "determine public policies in critical areas of culture" both in the United States and abroad, and to spreading "values and habits of a foreign culture at the expense of a native culture." This involved the exercise of "cultural or ideological hegemony" through the control of ideological structures by the dominant group.[70] Based on this line of analysis the contributors gave particular attention to "public education, professional training, and research activities, both at home and abroad."[71]

As a comprehensive and provocative text, *Philanthropy/Cultural Imperialism* has presented subsequent researchers with the opportunity to address its arguments, question its premises, and to examine the rigor and pertinence of its claims. By virtue of its grounding in historical material, the collection could have potentially served as a point of departure for clarifying issues about the workings and trajectory of philanthropy. However, while the text has been identified as the embodiment of the critical approach and respectfully cited, there has been very little engagement with its tenets, assumptions, and claims.[72] This has been unfortunate for critical historical scholarship on foundations, for it seems to have been assumed that the volume is the "last word" on the subject, meaning there is little need to go over the same historical ground drawing upon pertinent archival sources. Rather, it has been used as an Archimedean point for considering more contemporary issues.[73] Since the arguments and claims of *Philanthropy/Cultural Imperialism* in relation to the history of philanthropy are persuasive, yet have not been carefully scrutinized, what follows is an effort to critically examine its framework and major assumptions with a view to exploring the issues raised by the chapters in *Patronizing the Public*.[74]

Philanthropy/Cultural Imperialism effectively chronicled the work of foundations in a number of areas prior to the 1980s. However, its title notwithstanding, the chapters in the volume say very little about issues related to culture per se.[75] While the chapters on the impact of philanthropy on black higher education—both in the United States and in Africa—quite convincingly demonstrate the biases of the programs involved, their cultural aspects are not addressed in any detail.[76] Moreover, the related areas of communication and the humanities, which have long been central to foundation programs, receive almost no attention.[77] Yet prima facie, it would seem that the humanities (as a field responsible for producing the stock of ideas in a society), communication (as the means of mediating and circulating ideas), and culture (as the realm of aesthetic and symbolic expression) have great bearing on cultural domination or hegemony.

In their examination of American philanthropic support for communication, culture, and the humanities, the contributions to *Patronizing the Public* speak—albeit not always directly—to issues of cultural imperialism.

The chapters by Brison, Cramer, and Wrenn discuss how American philanthropy supported programs seeking to further American interests in relation to Canada and Latin America, as well at to Germany and Japan. Other chapters (such as those of Acland and McCarthy) explore how American foundations funded projects that aided and abetted cultural domination on the domestic front during the cold war, in a manner echoing the issues explored in *Philanthropy/Cultural Imperialism*.

By contrast, some of the essays in *Patronizing the Public* challenge the assumption that American philanthropies exercised cultural imperialism on behalf of American interests as a matter of course. As both Buxton and Wasson note, the Humanities Division (HD) of the Rockefeller Foundation (RF) sought to transform American cultural life in the 1930s and 1940s by adapting British cultural institutions (such as the BBC) to the United States, by bringing British cultural figures (such as Charles Siepmann, Geoffrey Gorer, and Paul Rotha) to America to provide advice and counsel, and by sending Americans (such as Lloyd Free) to Britain for specialized training, with a view to help strengthen U.S. cultural practices and institutions upon their return. In relation to Germany, Niquette and Buxton underscore how the HD looked favorably upon the circulation of German racial hygiene exhibits in the Buffalo Museum of Science and the New York Museum of Science and Industry; Gall examines how the HD sought to use improved film-music composition by supporting the research of Hanns Eisler; and Wasson notes how the Museum of Modern Art, by virtue of HD funding, was able to support Siegfried Kracauer's work on film criticism. Surely, if cultural imperialism on behalf of American foundations was an inherent feature of American philanthropic activities, how can one account for the RF support for what amounted to a British and German cultural invasion in the 1930s and 1940s? If anything, the RF could be accused of helping to further—at least in some measure—the cultural domination of the United States by forms of thought and expression originating in other countries.

Given that the patterns of cultural domination varied depending on the specific projects at issue and the period in question, this underscores the need to examine foundation activities in terms of the particularities of time and space. By extension, questions can be raised about which foundational entities represent the most appropriate objects for analyzing various projects, programs, and initiatives. For *Philanthropy/Cultural Imperialism*, those chosen were the largest "general-purpose" philanthropies, namely the so-called big three of Rockefeller, Carnegie, and Ford (along with a few others).[78] While this approach has a certain heuristic value, it assumes that the lines of policy are determined by the larger corporate body and then are translated into specific programs and projects. For the most part, while the chapters in *Philanthropy/Cultural Imperialism* do make mention of which philanthropic body was responsible for what program, the organization in question is often treated as incidental to the discussion, with little said about its origins, orientation, characteristics, and modus operandi.[79]

However, as a number of the chapters in *Patronizing the Public* demonstrate, the bodies that implemented and monitored projects were often not one of the big three per se, but rather lesser known, "specific-purpose" philanthropic entities. Hence, the chapters dealing with Rockefeller philanthropy in the 1930s and 1940s focus on the Humanities Division of the RF as well as the General Education Board. To be sure, as Richardson and Buxton both discuss, one needs to examine the activities of the these organizations within the context of the division of labor that informed Rockefeller philanthropy as a whole.[80] But it is impossible to adequately examine the nature and impact of Rockefeller philanthropic practices by confining oneself to the activities of only the Rockefeller Foundation. Moreover, by examining the particularities of lesser-known philanthropic bodies we are also obliged to discuss the larger philanthropic entities not only in terms of what they share in common, but what differentiates each of them from the others.[81]

Moreover, by examining foundational work "on the ground" within the lower-level philanthropic body responsible for coordinating projects and initiatives within broader programs, one is able to better understand the important role played by officers, the complex and delicate negotiation process between funder and recipient, as well as the interplay between the various projects underway. Examining them in this fashion means that the instrumentalist approach of many of the essays in *Philanthropy/Cultural Imperialism* can be challenged. A number of the chapters in that volume discuss the activities of foundations in terms of the general programs that they choose to support, with emphasis upon the amount of funding allocated for particular ventures. It is assumed that particular outcomes and effects, in line with the designs of the foundations, are the result of the injection of funds into particular projects.[82] While the essays in *Philanthropy/ Cultural Imperialism* provide a good account of the general intentions behind particular initiatives, much less attention is given to how specific ventures emerged and developed, and what their consequences were for the various constituencies involved.

What is largely missing, then, is an exploration of the *process* through which projects are enacted. This involves giving attention not only to levels of funding and the broader goals of projects, to the negotiations between officers and grant recipients,[83] but also to the monitoring and evaluating of projects.[84] One also needs to take into account the role played by outside experts, business interests, government officials, and public opinion in affecting how particular initiatives developed and what changes they engendered.[85] More broadly, it is important to consider how particular projects were interconnected, the extent to which envisaged elite networks emerged as a result of the philanthropic process, and the institutions and forms of discourse that began to take shape.[86] In this regard, it is crucial to examine the various components of funding programs (including research projects resulting in publications such as monographs, reports, and surveys) as well as workshops, conferences, internships, consultations, visits, equipment purchase, and the development of facilities. One must also give attention to how these various endeavors were coordinated in an effort to attain particular results.[87]

By putting questions of agency and process front and center, the chapters in *Patronizing the Public* call into question what has been described as the "left functionalism" that pervades *Philanthropy/Cultural Imperialism*.[88] That is to say, it is argued that given their size and durability the large foundations *must* be serving some sort of function for society. And since societies are characterized by inequality and domination, foundations *must* be contributing to these features, since these organizations are made up of elite members and represent large collections of wealth. While such a line of analysis is seductive, it means that one has already determined one's conclusions in advance; all actions taken by foundations by their very nature serve ruling-class interests.[89] Since the functional nature of foundational activities is assumed, it implies not only that the claims cannot be upheld or falsified by evidence, but that those involved in the philanthropic process are not considered to be agents. The contributions to *Patronizing the Public* for the most part do not deny that foundations can and do support the interests of the dominant elites. However, rather than assuming this as a matter of course, they seek to examine the extent to which particular projects reflect patterns of domination. To this end, in stressing the agency of those involved in the philanthropic process, it becomes possible not only to shed light on relations of power, but to examine the contradictions of foundational activities, including the unintended consequences of how counterhegemonic tendencies may have been unwittingly engendered.[90] By examining in more detail not just the contours of philanthropic power but the processes through which that power has been enacted, it is hoped that this collection will reinforce and amplify the critical study of philanthropy's history.

NOTES

I wish to thank Charles Acland and Theresa Richardson for their helpful comments on an earlier draft of this chapter.

1. Ernest Victor Hollis, *Philanthropic Foundations and Higher Education* (New York: Columbia University Press, 1938), 256.

2. Whitney J. Oates, "Humanities," in *U.S. Philanthropic Foundations: Their History, Structure, Management, and Record*, ed. Warren Weaver (New York, Evanston, & London: Harper & Row, 1967), 301.

3. Hollis notes that by the mid 1930s, 95 percent of the funding for the humanities came from Rockefeller and Carnegie philanthropies (*Philanthropic Foundations,* 277–78). That Rockefeller philanthropy accorded it great significance is evident by the fact that a separate Humanities Division (hereafter HD) was created within the Rockefeller Foundation [hereafter RF] during the realignment of the late 1920s.

4. Initially, culture—in the sense of specific forms of aesthetic expression—was supported quite unevenly, with some areas generously funded and others almost totally neglected. It was not until the 1950s that forms of cultural expression were supported more broadly. For discussions of why it took so long for foundations to recognize the arts, see Foulkes's chapter in this volume, and various chapters in Weaver, *U.S. Philanthropic Foundations.*

5. An encyclopaedia entry on the subject of the period emphasized communication as "understandings which prevail between [society's] members," giving secondary importance to "extending the physical conditions allowing for communication." Edward Sapir, "Communication," *Encyclopaedia of the Social Sciences,* vol. 4 (New York: Macmillan, 1931), 78–80.

6. Both Rockefeller and Carnegie philanthropies recognized that the spread of ideas and symbols to the masses could take place not only through their mass dissemination to a dispersed audience, but also through spatially specific cites in which the audience physically came to the institution in question.

7. Peters and Simonson trace the first use of the term (which was used interchangeably with broadcasting) to former NBC president David Sarnoff in the late 1920s. They note that by the late 1930s, it had become part of the part of the vocabulary of Rockefeller officers. John Durham Peters and Peter Simonson, eds., *Mass Communication and American Social Thought: Key Texts, 1919–1968* (Lanham, MD: Rowman & Littlefield, 2004), 9, 11.

8. During the 1930s, as Rockefeller philanthropy expanded its program in the humanities, one can detect a shift in the meaning for culture in relation to communications. While Carnegie philanthropies conceived of culture as an elitist sphere largely uncontaminated by commerce, Rockefeller philanthropy saw commercial mass media as framing culture. This meant that commercial and educational interests could then work together in a common cause. Moreover, rather than emphasizing support for cultural practices and products per se, Rockefeller philanthropy stressed the generation of a knowledge base within the humanities for the nurturing of culture and for making communication toward this end more effective.

9. Judith Sealander, *Private Wealth & Public Health: Foundation Philanthropy and the Reshaping of American Social Policy from the Progressive Era to the New Deal* (Baltimore & London: Johns Hopkins University Press, 1997).

10. These terms were arguably rearticulated during the cold war, as they became part of the American strategic offensive in what has been called "the cultural cold war," as evidenced in the activities of the Congress of Cultural Freedom. Frances Stonor Saunders, *The Cultural Cold War: The CIA and the World of Arts and Letters* (New York: New Press, 2000). The field of mass communication, as Simpson notes, developed into what could best be described as a "science of coercion" with the onset of the cold war. Christopher Simpson, *Science of Coercion: Communication Research and Psychological Warfare, 1945–1960* (New York: Oxford University Press, 1994). Once the cold war was underway, the American Council of Learned

Societies made an inventory of the personnel in the humanities to determine what intellectual resources were available for the national purpose. Charles E. Odegaard and Richard L. McCormick, *A Pilgrimage through Universities* (Seattle: University of Washington Press, 1999), 132.

11. Barry D. Karl and Stanley N. Katz, "The American Private Philanthropy and the Public Sphere, 1890–1930," *Minerva* 19, no. 2 (Summer 1981): 236–70.

12. Jürgen Habermas, *The Structural Transformation of the Public Sphere: An Inquiry into a Category of Bourgeois Society*, trans. Thomas Burger with the assistance of Frederick Lawrence (Cambridge, MA: MIT Press, 1989).

13. Eduard C. Lindemann, *Wealth and Culture: A Study of 100 Foundations and Community Trusts, and Their Operations During the Decade 1921–1930* (New York: Harcourt Brace, 1936).

14. John Durham Peters, "Distrust of Representation: Habermas on the Public Sphere," *Media, Culture & Society* 15, no. 4 (1993): 541–71.

15. This realm is very much in line with Gramsci's notion of a "civil society" that was advanced around the same time that the large foundations were beginning to orient themselves toward building social control within the public. For Gramsci, the notion of civil society was doubled-faceted. On the one hand, it was the "'spontaneous' consent given by the . . . masses . . . to the general direction imposed on social life by the dominant fundamental group" in the form of the hegemony of ideas. But on the other hand, it was the "ensemble of organisms commonly called private." Antonio Gramsci, *Selections from the Prison Notebooks of Antonio Gramsci*, ed. and trans. Quintin Hoare and Geoffrey Nowell Smith (London: Lawrence & Wishart, 1971), 12.

16. This is in line with what John Gardner termed the "independent sector" (IS) or the "third sector," namely, "the space between the state and the market economy." Katz maintains that the third sector, or at least "civil society," is now a central social-science concept in the analysis of democratic societies. Stanley Katz, "Where Did the Serious Study of Philanthropy Come From Anyway?" *Nonprofit and Voluntary Sector Quarterly* 28 (1999): 76, 78. See also Stanley Katz, "Grantmaking and Research in the U.S., 1933–1983," *Proceedings of the American Philosophical Society* 129, no. 2 (March 1985): 1–2; Jon Van Til, *Growing Civil Society: From Nonprofit Sector to Third Space* (Bloomington: Indiana University Press, 2000); Brian O'Connell and John William Gardner, *Civil Society: The Underpinnings of American Democracy* (Lebanon, NH: University Press of New England, 1999).

17. That foundation officials were quite aware of the growing importance of culture is evidenced by the Carnegie Corporation president's coauthoring of a volume in the *Recent Social Changes* series. Frederick P. Keppel and Robert L. Duffus, *The Arts in American Life* (New York, London: McGraw-Hill, 1933). Based on empirical data summarizing foundation grants to various forms of "nonprofessional education" between 1921 and 1934, Hollis notes that "contributions since 1921 to scholarly purposes of the humanities, while small when compared to the totals for the natural and social sciences, have accounted for an increasing proportion of the total of foundation gifts." Hollis, *Philanthropic Foundations and Higher Education*, 240.

As Lashner notes in relation to educational broadcasting, "Rockefeller, Carnegie, Payne, and Sloan funds contributed monies for internships and fellowships in educational radio, for formation and support of educational broadcasting associations, and for experimental projects. In particular, contributions from Rockefeller and Carnegie funds assisted in the formation of the National Advisory Committee on Education by Radio and the Association of College and University Broadcasting Stations (ACUBS); a $200,000 grant for the Payne Fund inaugurated the National Committee on Education by Radio (NCER); and Rockefeller money, in 1938, supported the Rocky Mountain Radio Council, a cooperative broadcasting project involving 22 educational institutions." Marilyn R. Lashner, "The Role of Foundations in Public Broadcasting, Part 1," *Journal of Broadcasting* 20, no. 4 (Fall 1976): 531–32. Reflective of its broad concerns with the effects of new communication technologies, in 1927 the Payne Fund earmarked $65,800 for the study of the effects of movies on children. Garth S. Jowett, Ian C. Jarvie, and Kathryn H. Fuller, *Children and the Movies: Media Influence and the Payne Fund Controversy* (Cambridge: Cambridge University Press, 1996), 33.

18. Indeed, the *Encyclopedia of the Social Sciences* has no entry for philanthropy per se. Rather, a reader looking for information on philanthropy is referred to the entry on "Charity," which does not even mention the large, American-based philanthropic bodies of the twentieth century. Kenneth L. M. Prat, "Charity," *Encyclopedia of the Social Sciences*, vol. 3 (New York: Macmillan, 1930), 340–44.

19. Armand C. Marts, *Philanthropy's Role in Civilization: Its Contribution to Human Freedom* (New York: Harper & Brothers, 1953); Joseph C. Goulden, *The Money Givers* (New York: Random House, 1972): Fritz Heiman, ed., *The Future of Foundations* (Englewood Cliffs, NJ: Prentice-Hall, 1973).

20. Raymond B. Fosdick, *John Rockefeller Junior: A Biography* (New York: Harper & Brothers, 1956); Ben Whitaker, *The Foundations: An Anatomy of Philanthropy and Society* (London: Eyre Methuen, 1974); Merle Curti and Roderick Nash, *Philanthropy and the Shaping of American Higher Education* (New Brunswick, NJ: Rutgers University Press, 1965); F. Emerson Andrews, *Philanthropic Foundations* (New York: Russell Sage Foundation, 1956); Robert H. Bremner, *American Philanthropy* (Chicago: University of Chicago Press, 1960); Oates, "Humanities."

21. Waldemar R. Nielsen, *The Big Foundations* (New York & London: Columbia University Press, 1972), 59–60.

22. Hollis, *Philanthropic Foundations*, 293.

23. John Ettling, *The Germ of Laziness: Rockefeller Philanthropy and Public Health in the New South* (Cambridge, MA: Harvard University Press, 1981), 256. The first collection of archival material available to researchers was a library opened by the Russell Sage Foundation in the 1920s. It eventually evolved into the Foundation Library Center (established in 1956 and shortened to the present-day Foundation Center in 1968).

24. Particularly important in this regard was a conference organized by F. Emerson Andrews of the Russell Sage Foundation to discuss how research on the history of American philanthropy could best be planned. Held at Princeton University on February 3–4, 1956, it resulted in the publication of the *Report of the Princeton Conference on the History of Philanthropy in the United States* (New York: Russell Sage Foundation, 1956). Peter Dobkin Hall claims that the impact of the conference was substantial, leading to the publication of numerous volumes. "The Work of Many Hands: A Response to Stanley N. Katz on the 'Serious Study'

of Philanthropy," *Nonprofit and Voluntary Sector Quarterly* 28 (1999): 524. A year after the Princeton conference, the chair of the meeting, Merle Curti, published a plea for more work to be done on the history of philanthropy in the United States. In addition to outlining the sorts of issues historians might examine, Curti stressed the need for members of the philanthropic community to provide their support for this endeavor. "The History of American Philanthropy as a Field of Research," *American Historical Review* 62, no. 2 (1957): 352–63. Likely guided by what he wrote in his 1957 article, Curti helped to found the University of Wisconsin History of Philanthropy Project in 1958, funded by the Ford Foundation. The subject chosen for particular attention was American higher education, which ultimately led to a coauthored volume on the subject, written with the support of the Ford Foundation. Merle Curti and Roderick Nash, *Philanthropy in the Shaping of American Higher Education* (New Brunswick, NJ: Rutgers University Press, 1965). Other notable works that were written within the purview of the project were Merle Curti, *American Philanthropy Abroad. A History* (New Brunswick, NJ: Rutgers University Press, 1963), and Daniel M. Fox, *Engines of Culture: Philanthropy and Art Museums* (Madison: State Historical Society of Wisconsin for the Department of History, University of Wisconsin, 1963).

25. The Rockefeller Archive Center was established on January 15, 1974, and opened its doors to researchers in August 1975. The center housed not only the extensive papers of Rockefeller philanthropies and family members, but a number of other non-Rockefeller collections as well (including the records of the Russell Sage Foundation, the Commonwealth Fund, and the Social Science Research Council). See http://www.rockarch.org/about/ (accessed October 21, 2008). Other major archival collections of philanthropic material that became available included Carnegie Corporation of New York papers (held in the Columbia University Rare Book and Manuscript Library), the Ford Foundation Archives (in New York City), the Western Reserve Historical Society (in Cleveland), and the Minnesota Historical Society (in St. Paul).

26. The Program on Nonprofit Organizations (PONPO), founded at Yale University in 1974 by John Simon, was the first academic unit in the United States to focus on philanthropic issues. Other ventures along the same lines include the Center on Philanthropy at Indiana University (founded in 1987 as part of the Indiana University School of Liberal Arts at Indiana University–Purdue University Indianapolis), and the Heyman Center for Philanthropy and Fundraising at New York University (founded in 1999).

27. The Association of Voluntary Action Scholars (AVAS), founded in 1971, evolved into the Association for Research on Non-profit Organizations and Voluntary Action (ARNOVA), which formed in 1991. David Horton Smith, "A History of ARNOVA," *Nonprofit and Voluntary Sector Quarterly* 32 (2003): 458–72. The International Society for Third-Sector Research was founded in 1992 with the aim of "promoting research and education in the fields of civil society, philanthropy, and the nonprofit sector," http://www.istr.org/about/mission.htm (accessed 12 August, 2008).

28. Since 1960, the Foundation Center has been publishing the Foundation Directory. Joseph C. Kiger, *Historiographic Review of Foundation Literature: Motivations and Perceptions* (New York: Foundation Center, 1987), 17.

29. ARNOVA has published the *Nonprofit and Voluntary Sector Quarterly* since 1989, along with the ARNOVA NEWS, ARNOVA ABSTRACTS, as well as an occasional paper series. *Voluntas,* the official journal of the International Society for Third-Sector Research (ISTR), was founded in 1990. The ISTR also publishes a report and a conference working-papers series. Other publication outlets include the philanthropy series at the Indiana University Press, as well as the *Research Reports of the Rockefeller Archive Center.*

30. Philanthropic foundations themselves—such as the Carnegie Corporation of New York and the Lilly Foundation—began to provide research funds on the history of philanthropy. The Rockefeller Archive Center has also developed an extensive program in support of researchers using material in its collections.

31. See Peter Collier and David Horowitz, *The Rockefellers: An American Dynasty* (New York: Holt, Rinehart & Winston, 1976); John Ensor Harr and Peter J. Johnson, *The Rockefeller Century: Three Generations of the Rockefeller Family* (New York: Scribner's, 1988).

32. See, for instance, Robert Kohler, "Science, Foundations, and American Universities in the 1920s," *OSIRIS,* 2nd series, vol. 3 (1987): 135–64.

33. Sealander, *Private Wealth & Public Health,* 7.

34. Karl notes acerbically that the arguments of Curti's 1957 article "have not convinced many history departments that philanthropy and foundations constitute subject matter worth tenure." He goes on to observe that "historians of foundations find themselves trapped between foundations that don't want to fund them and history departments . . . that don't want to hire them." Barry Dean Karl, "Going for Broke: The Historian's Commitment to Philanthropy," in *Philanthropic Foundations: New Scholarship, New Possibilities,* ed. Ellen Condliffe Lagemann (Bloomington: Indiana University Press, 1999), 292.

35. Lawrence Friedman, "Philanthropy in America: Historicism and its Discontents," in *Charity, Philanthropy, and Civility in American History,* eds. Lawrence J. Freidman and Mark D. McGarvie (Cambridge: Cambridge University Press, 2003), 3.

36. Numerous departments specializing in the history of science and the related areas of medicine and technology have been established over the years in the United States and abroad.

37. See for instance, E. Richard Brown, *Rockefeller Medicine Men: Medicine and Capitalism in America* (Berkeley: University of California Press, 1979); E. Richard Brown, "Rockefeller Medicine in China: Professionalism and Imperialism," in *Philanthropy and Cultural Imperialism: The Foundations at Home and Abroad,* ed. Robert F. Arnove (Boston: G. K. Hall & Co. 1980), 123–46.

38. See, for instance, Fritz Samuelson, "Organizing for the Kingdom of Behavior: Academic Battles and Organizational Policies in the Twenties," *Journal for the History of the Behavioral Sciences* 21, no.1 (January 1985): 33–47.

39. David M. Grossman, "American Foundations and the Support of Economic Research, 1913–29," *Minerva* 20, nos. 1–2 (Spring/Summer 1982): 59–82; Donald Fisher, *Fundamental Development of the Social Sciences: Rockefeller Philanthropy and the United States Social Science Research Council* (Ann Arbor: University of Michigan Press, 1993).

40. Ellen Condliffe Lagemann, *Private Power for the Public Good: A History of the Carnegie Foundation for the Advancement of Teaching* (Middletown, CT: Wesleyan

University Press, 1983); Ellen Condliffe Lagemann, *The Politics of Knowledge: The Carnegie Corporation, Philanthropy, and Public Policy* (Middletown, CT: Wesleyan University Press, 1989); Theresa R. Richardson, *The Century of the Child: The Mental Hygiene Movement and Social Policy in the United States and Canada* (Albany: SUNY Press, 1989).

41. Peter Dobkin Hall recounts the extent to which academic researchers in the Yale program were subject to unremitting "pressures to pursue a more focused agenda—one that would yield 'useful' results and contribute to the [independent] sector's advocacy concerns." Peter Dobkin Hall, *"Inventing the Nonprofit Sector" and Other Essays on Philanthropy, Voluntarism, and Nonprofit Organizations* (Baltimore: Johns Hopkins Press, 1992), 250.

42. See, for instance, David C. Hammack, "Historical Research for the Nonprofit Sector," *Nonprofit Management & Leadership* 16, no. 4 (Summer 2006): 451–66.

43. Exceptions include Lashner, "The Role of Foundations in Public Broadcasting, Part 1"; Marilyn R. Lashner, "The Role of Foundations in Public Broadcasting, Part 2: The Ford Foundation," *Journal of Broadcasting* 21 (Spring 1977): 235–54.

44. Everett M. Rogers, *A History of Communication Study: A Biographical Approach* (New York: Free Press; Toronto: Maxwell Macmillan Canada, 1994); Simpson, *Science of Coercion*. For a review essay on these works, see William J. Buxton, "The Emergence of Communication Study: Psychological Warfare or Scientific Thoroughfare?" *Canadian Journal of Communication* 21, no. 4 (1996): 473–84.

45. Elihu Katz, John Durham Peters, Tamar Liebes, and Avril Orloff, eds., *Canonic Texts in Media Research. Are There Any? Should There Be? How About These?* (Cambridge, MA: Polity Press, 2003); John Durham Peters and Peter Simonson, *Mass Communication and American Social Thought: Key Texts, 1919–1968* (Lanham, MD: Rowman & Littlefield, 2004). For a review essay of these works, see William J. Buxton, "Forging the Canon of Media Studies: Should We Heed the Plea for Timeless Texts?" *Canadian Journal of Communication* 32, no. 1 (2007): 131–37. Recently, however, the volume edited by Pooley and Park provides a rigorous and perceptive account of how Rockefeller philanthropy influenced the field of communication, drawing on a wide range of sources. David W. Park and Jefferson Pooley, eds., *The History of Media and Communication Research: Contested Memories* (New York: Peter Lang, 2008).

46. Kathleen McCarthy, "The Short and Simple Annals of the Poor: Foundation Funding for the Humanities, 1900–1983," *Proceedings of the American Philosophical Society* 129, no.1 (March 1985): 3–8; Lagemann, *Philanthropic Foundations*; Mark Dowie, *American Foundations: An Investigative History* (Cambridge, MA: MIT Press, 2001).

47. Kathleen D. McCarthy, ed., *Philanthropy and Culture: The International Foundation Perspective* (Philadelphia: University of Pennsylvania Press, 1984).

48. Paul DiMaggio, *Nonprofit Enterprise in the Arts: Studies in Mission and Constraint* (New York: Oxford University Press, 1986).

49. Charles R. Acland and William J. Buxton, "Continentalism and Philanthropy: A Rockefeller Officer's Impressions of the Maritime Provinces," *Acadiensis* 23, no. 2 (Spring 1994): 72–93.

50. Kathleen D. McCarthy, "From Cold War to Cultural Development: The International Cultural Activities of the Ford Foundation, 1950–1980," *Daedalus* 116, no. 1 (Winter 1987): 93–117.

51. Mary Ann Meyers, *Art, Education, and African American Culture: Albert Barnes and the Science of Philanthropy* (New Brunswick, NJ: Transaction, 2004).

52. See, for instance, Ludovic Tournes, "Mass Communications and the Foundations: Rockefeller, Ford, and the Role of Radio," in *Grant-giving Policies, Cultural Diplomacy, and Trans-Atlantic Relations, 1920–1980*, eds. Giuliana Gemelli and Roy McLeod (Brussels: P. I. E. Peter Lang, 2003), 129–44.

53. See, for instance, Haidee Wasson, *Museum Movies: The Museum of Modern Art and the Birth of Art Cinema* (Berkeley: University of California Press, 2005).

54. See, for instance, Bruce King, "West Indian Drama and the Rockefeller Foundation, 1957–1970: Derek Walcott, the Little Carib and the University of the West Indies," *Massachusetts Review* 35, no. 3 (1994): 493–508.

55. See, for instance, Julia L. Foulkes, *Modern Bodies: Dance and American Modernism from Martha Graham to Alvin Ailey* (Chapel Hill: University of North Carolina Press, 2002).

56. See, for instance, Ian McKay, *The Quest of the Folk: Antimodernism and Cultural Selection in Twentieth-century Nova Scotia* (Montreal/Kingston: McGill-Queens University Press, 1994).

57. See, for instance, William J. Buxton and Charles R. Acland, *The Politics of Knowledge and Information: American Philanthropy and Canadian Libraries* (accompanied by Charles F. McCombs, "Report on Canadian Libraries" originally submitted to the Rockefeller Foundation in 1942). (Montreal: McGill University, The Centre for Research on Canadian Cultural Industries and Institutions and the Graduate School of Information and Library Studies, 1998.)

58. See, for instance, Brett Gary, *The Nervous Liberals: Propaganda Anxieties from World War I to the Cold War* (New York: Columbia University Press, 1999).

59. See, for instance, Kathleen D. McCarthy, *Women's Culture* (Chicago: University of Chicago Press, 1991); Kathleen D. McCarthy, *Lady Bountiful Revisited: Women, Philanthropy, and Power* (New Brunswick & London: Rutgers University Press, 1990); Cary Reich, *The Life of Nelson A. Rockefeller: Worlds to Conquer, 1908–1958* (New York: Doubleday, 1996).

60. Lagemann, *The Politics of Knowledge.*

61. Gerald Jonas, *The Circuit Riders: Rockefeller Money and the Rise of Modern Science* (New York: Norton, 1989).

62. Robert E. Kohler, *Partners in Science: Foundations and Natural Scientists, 1900–1945* (Chicago: University of Chicago Press, 1991).

63. Marcos Cueto, *Missionaries of Science: The Rockefeller Foundation and Latin America* (Bloomington: Indiana University Press, 1994).

64. Theresa Richardson and Donald Fisher, eds., *The Development of Social Sciences in the United States and Canada: The Role of Philanthropy* (Stamford, CT: Ablex, 1999).

65. See, for instance, the exchange between Abir-Am and Fuerst, which generated considerable discussion: John A. Fuerst, "The Role of Reproductionism in the Development of Molecular Biology: Peripheral or Central?" *Social Studies of Science* 12, no. 2 (1982): 241–78; Pnina Abir-Am, "The Discourse of Physical Power and Biological Knowledge in the 1930s: A Reappraisal of the Rockefeller Foundation's 'Policy' in Molecular Biology," *Social Studies of Science* 12, no. 3 (1982): 341–82; John A. Fuerst, "The Definition of Molecular Biology and the Definition of Policy:

The Role of the Rockefeller Foundation's Policy for Molecular Biology," *Social Studies of Science* 14, no. 2 (1984): 225–52.

66. Donald Fisher, "The Role of Philanthropic Foundations in the Production and Reproduction of Hegemony: Rockefeller Foundations and Social Science," *Sociology* 17, no. 4. (1983): 206–33; Martin Bulmer, "Support for Sociology in the 1920s: The Laura Spelman Rockefeller Memorial and the Beginnings of Modern, Large-scale Research in the University," *American Sociologist* 17, no. 4 (1982): 185–92; Donald Fisher, "Philanthropic Foundations and the Social Sciences: A Response to Martin Bulmer," *Sociology* 18, no. 4 (1984): 580–87.

67. Sealander, *Private Wealth & Public Health*; Barry Dean Karl, "The Troublesome History of Foundations: Correcting a Contentious History," *Reviews in American History* 25, no. 4 (1997): 612–18.

68. This term was chosen to describe the leitmotif of a special issue of *Critical Sociology*: "Note on this Special Issue of Critical Sociology," *Critical Sociology* 33 (2007): 387. Other works in this vein include Volker R. Berghahn, *America and the Intellectual Cold Wars in Europe: Shepard Stone Between Philanthropy, Academy, and Diplomacy* (Princeton, NJ: Princeton University Press, 2001); Edward H. Berman, *The Influence of the Carnegie, Ford, and Rockefeller Foundations on American Foreign Policy: The Ideology of Philanthropy* (Albany: State University of New York Press, 1983); Soma Hewa and Philo Hove, eds., *Philanthropy and Cultural Context: Western Philanthropy in South East and Southern Asia in the 20th Century* (Lanham, MD: University Press of America, 1997); and John H. Stanfield, *Philanthropy and Jim Crow in American Social Science* (Westport, CT, and London: Greenwood, 1985).

69. Arnove, *Philanthropy and Cultural Imperialism.*

70. Arnove, *Philanthropy and Cultural Imperialism*, 1–2.

71. Arnove, *Philanthropy and Cultural Imperialism*, 2.

72. To be sure, Karl and Katz provide a balanced and probing exploration of the extent to which a Gramscian line of analysis, as developed in *Philanthropy/Cultural Imperialism*, could shed light on the historical relation between the ruling class and foundations in the United States. Barry D. Karl and Stanley N. Katz, "Foundations and Ruling Class Elites," *Daedalus* 116, no. 1 (Winter 1987): 1–40. Aside from this article, there is little evidence that DiMaggio's thoughtful commentary on the deficiencies of the collection, intended to provide guidelines for "future work in this neglected field," has been taken up in any great measure. Paul DiMaggio, "A Jaundiced View of Philanthropy," *Comparative Education Review* 27 no. 3 (October 1983): 442–45.

73. This certainly is the case for the set of articles representative of the critical study of foundations in *Critical Sociology* 33 (2007): 387–588. Moreover, Joan Roelofs, for whom the Arnove volume is an important point of reference, largely relies on secondary sources rather than archival material. This, in part, explains her very limited analysis of philanthropy and culture, devoting all of seven pages to the subject in her study of foundations and public policy. With her emphasis on how artistic practices were shaped by the "cultural cold war," she fails to examine how philanthropic support in this area prior to 1945 provided the foundation for post-war initiatives. Joan Roelofs, *Foundations and Public Policy: The Mask of Pluralism* (Albany: SUNY Press, 2003).

74. The text, along with Edward Berman's *The Influence of the Carnegie, Ford, and Rockefeller Foundations on American Foreign Policy*, are cited by many histories

of philanthropy. However, more often than not, they are invoked as exemplars of a beyond-the-pale radical approach, whose arguments, by implication, need not be addressed. See, for instance, Lagemann's *Philanthropic Foundations*, which lists these works in the annotated bibliography, but only alludes to them briefly in one of the chapters. Richard Magat, "In Search of the Ford Foundation," in Lagemann, *Philanthropic Foundations*, 300.

75. Indeed, a number of the chapters in the volume appear to be inspired—directly or indirectly—by the work of power-elite theorists such as C. Wright Mills and William Domhoff. See, in particular, the contributions of David E. Weischadle, Frank A. Darknell, Mary Anna Culleton Colwell, and Robert Arnove (on the transfer of knowledge). This might explain the volume's emphasis upon describing the designs and motivations of "big three" foundation executives as rooted in interlocking elite networks to the neglect of examining in detail the workings of specific projects.

76. See the chapter by James D. Anderson and the two by Edward Berman.

77. While there are scattered references to communications throughout the volume, these are largely in reference to the use of media and communications in foundation activities, rather than to the support of foundations for initiatives in media and communications per se.

78. This distinction was made in Arnove, *Philanthropy and Cultural Imperialism* and reiterated more recently in Robert Arnove and Nadine Pindede, "Revisiting the 'Big Three' Foundations," *Critical Sociology* 33 (2007): 389–425. See also Berman, *The Influence of the Carnegie, Ford, and Rockefeller Foundations*, and Inderjeet Parmar, "American Foundations and the Development of International Knowledge Networks," *Global Networks* 1, no. 2 (2002): 13–30.

79. See, for instance, Russell Marks's invocation of the General Education Board in his discussion of philanthropic support for individual differences research (which also mistakenly claims that the GEB was funded by the Rockefeller Foundation).

80. As Richardson describes it, Rockefeller philanthropy is a collection of institutions metaphorically described "as a 'fleet of ships,' the objectives and projects of which operate in tandem and with common interests." Theresa Richardson, "The Rockefeller Boards: The Organization of Philanthropy and the Origins of the Social Sciences," in Fisher and Richardson, *The Development of Social Sciences*, 37. By focusing on just one of these vessels, namely the Rockefeller Foundation, Arnove is not able to capture the synergy, dynamics, and tensions that have come to characterize Rockefeller philanthropy.

81. For instance, Sutton calls attention to the degree to which the Ford Foundation was guided by the detailed prescriptions of the Gaither Report. This stood in contrast to both the Rockefeller and Carnegie philanthropies, which took their cues more from the vague statements of the original donors. Moreover, as Sutton notes, the Ford Foundation developed a policy of creating particular funds (such as the Fund for the Republic) as a way of providing large bloc grants. In both instances, the recipient had considerable latitude to spend the grants. This stood in contrast to the Rockefeller philanthropies, which kept the recipients on a much shorter leash. Francis X. Sutton, "The Ford Foundation: The Early Years," *Daedalus* 116, no. 1 (Winter 1987): 41–92.

82. For a challenge of this view see Stephen Turner, "Does Funding Produce Its Effects: The Rockefeller Case?" in Fisher and Richardson, *The Development of Social Sciences*, 213–26. The amount of funding in and of itself does not guarantee success and influence, as Martin Wooster underscores in *Great Philanthropic Mistakes* (Washington, DC: Hudson Institute, 2006). On the other hand, modestly funded projects can have significant impact—though perhaps neither immediately nor in line with the effects intended. The film-music project of Hanns Eisler discussed in Gall's chapter provided the foundation for what eventually became the highly influential text on the subject by Eisler and Adorno. Theodor W. Adorno and Hanns Eisler, *Komposition für den Film* (München: Rogner & Bernhard, 1969); Theodor Adorno and Hanns Eisler, *Composing for the Films* (London & Atlantic Highlands, NJ: Athlone Press, 1994). And as Cramer points out in her contribution to this volume, the Pan American radio project, while seemingly small and relatively unsuccessful at the time, had the unintended consequence of raising the profile of the shortwave radio station WRUL, helping it to become a major player on the broadcasting scene.

83. Brison, for instance, in his contribution gives close attention to the give-and-take between American foundation officials and members of the Canadian cultural elite.

84. Wasson's chapter in this volume traces the extent to which the ventures of MoMA were closely monitored by the officers of the Humanities Division.

85. Wrenn's chapter in this volume, for instance, demonstrates the degree to which government officials were involved in the post-war, foreign-journalist program funded by the Humanities Division of the Rockefeller Foundation.

86. Acland's chapter in this volume shows in some detail the efforts of the Ford Foundation—through its Fund for Adult Education—to create the Film Council of America.

87. The relationship between the film-music project (discussed by Gall) and the broader radio and film programs (discussed by Buxton and Wasson, respectively) provides insight into how projects were intended to be inserted into the emergent networks in which new projects were beginning to take shape in the late 1930s.

88. DiMaggio, "Jaundiced View of Philanthropy," 443.

89. DiMaggio notes, for instance, that Arnove's dismissal of "the Ford Foundation's courageous support for Marxist intellectuals in authoritarian third-world states" as "an effort at co-optation" blinds him to be inserted into the extent to which "foundations have sometimes been politically progressive relative to other institutions." "Jaundiced View of Philanthropy," 444.

90. A case in point is the Henry Ford Bau, the main building (housing a library, offices, and classrooms) of the Free University of Berlin, which was built with support from the Ford Foundation as part of its program to promote American style "free institutions" in West Germany. The building was the site of the first sit-in to take place in West Germany (June 22–23, 1966), "Kleine Geschichte der FU," http://www.astafu.de/inhalte/artikel/a_2002/geschichte (accessed September 22, 2008). During the 1960s and 1970s (as the author can attest), the main amphitheater (Auditorium Maximum or "Audimax") of the Henry Ford Bau was not only the main site for packed lecture courses on Marxist political economy, but was also one of the primary gathering spots for meetings of student radicals.

2

From the Rockefeller Center to the Lincoln Center: Musings on the "Rockefeller Half-Century"

William J. Buxton

As noted in the preceding chapter, *Patronizing the Public* spans the period from the late 1920s through to the late 1970s, a timeframe that began with the consolidation of the Rockefeller philanthropies and ended with the formation of the so-called independent or third sector, comprised of charities, nonprofit organizations, and philanthropies. Given that the lineage of Rockefeller philanthropy (as linked particularly to John Rockefeller Jr. [Junior] and his son, John D. Rockefeller 3rd [hereafter JDR]) was of such significance for the broader trajectory of philanthropy in relation to communication, culture, and the humanities, this era could be characterized as the "Rockefeller half-century."[1]

THE ROCKEFELLER CENTER IN CONTEXT

At almost precisely the same time that the realignment of the Rockefeller philanthropies occurred,[2] Junior embarked on the building of Rockefeller Center in mid-town Manhattan.[3] This complex not only was intended to redefine business and cultural life in New York—if not the entire nation—but also was the site of the administrative headquarters for the new divisions of the Rockefeller Foundation along with a number of other Rockefeller philanthropies, including the General Education Board (GEB), the Spelman Fund of New York, and the China Medical Board.[4] The Rockefeller Foundation (RF) had particularly spacious quarters in the Rockefeller Center, taking "the entire fifty-fifth floor, half the fifty-fourth, and a dining room and lounge on the sixty-fourth."[5] The entire floor above the main RF offices was occupied by the family enterprises. Identified as "Room 5600" and listed as "Rockefeller, Office of the Mssrs" the complex housed the office of Junior, suites for his sons, along with "his associates, clerks, and messengers, and other functionaries of his family empire."[6] Moreover, the Rockefeller Center at various times accommodated a number of family-related businesses and organizations,[7] recipients of Rockefeller philanthropic funding,[8] and spin-offs of Rockefeller initiatives.[9] This meant that the Rockefeller business and philanthropic interests, though separate in theory, were not only cheek and jowl with one another, but also closely intersected with family ties and personal networks.[10] Over the course of the subsequent fifty years, the Rockefeller Center served as the nerve center for Rockefeller philanthropies, as linked to the extended family's social, political, and economic interests.

This era arguably came to an end with the untimely death of John D. Rockefeller 3rd on July 10, 1978,[11] effectively bringing to a close the period that had begun with the consolidation of Rockefeller philanthropies and the building of Rockefeller Center. Of all the six children of Junior, it was his eldest son, JDR, who best carried on the tradition of philanthropy—as linked to business and commerce—that had been established by his father and his grandfather, John Rockefeller Sr. While JDR pursued a number of other interests, he gradually gravitated toward philanthropy.[12] But there was also a strong line of continuity between the two Rockefellers in terms of their interest in contributing to public life through investing—and generating investments in—sites of cultural production and the built environment.[13] In the case of Junior, the centerpiece of his passion for building was undoubtedly the Rockefeller Center. To be sure, with the Radio Corporation of America (RCA) as its main tenant flanked by commercial theaters and other corporate interests, the center did not correspond to Junior's original intent to have the Metropolitan Opera and the Philharmonic Orchestra at the center of the complex.[14] As a number of commentators have suggested, it was a desire to complete the vision of his father that led JDR to take an important leadership role in the development of what was one of the major cultural developments of the 1960s, namely the Lincoln Center of the Performing Arts, located on Manhattan's Upper West Side.[15]

THE ROCKEFELLER CENTER AND
THE LINCOLN CENTER COMPARED

Aside from the fact that both ventures were spearheaded by pillars of the Rockefeller dynasty, they shared a number of features in common.[16] Both were linked to controversial urban-renewal schemes in so-called slum neighborhoods and were hotly contested. Both were described as a "city within a city" and as cultural meccas. Both were sites of cultural diffusion and transmission, albeit in rather different ways.[17] Both made effective use of public-relations schemes. Rockefeller Center had its own magazine (*Rockefeller Center Weekly*) and public-relations department (directed by Merle Crowell, who had succeeded Ivy Lee). Lincoln Center, from the outset, sought to create a desire by New Yorkers to attend events at the complex through a "Public Participation Campaign," launched in 1960 under the voluntary direction of advertising mogul, David Ogilvie with the support of "a committee of 31 major advertising executives."[18]

If both centers are viewed not simply as built environments, but, rather, as broad ventures that integrated philanthropy, knowledge, and commerce, as well as family connections[19] and personal networks, then further continuities can be noted.[20] But in order to understand this trajectory properly, one needs to add into the equation another venture that materialized almost exactly at the same time as the Rockefeller Center, namely the Museum of Modern Art (hereafter MoMA) founded by Abby Aldrich Rockefeller (the wife of Junior) and two of her friends (Lillie P. Bliss and Mrs. Cornelius J. Sullivan) in the spring of 1929. While initially Junior did not look favorably upon it, by the end of the next decade—in part because of his reluctant support—it had established itself as an important center for modern art.[21] Indeed, the Museum of Modern Art became a key part of a project by New York Mayor Fiorello LaGuardia (elected in January 1930) to establish a municipal art center and conservatory. When the Municipal Art Committee (of the city of New York) encountered difficulties in finding a suitable site for the Art Center, Nelson Rockefeller, in his capacity as executive vice-president of the Rockefeller Center, suggested that it be located on a private street extending from Rockefeller Plaza through to the Museum of Modern Art located two blocks to the north on West Fifty-third Street. The extended plaza was to be flanked by a new home for the Metropolitan Opera, a projected museum of nonobjective painting, as well as the headquarters of the Columbia Broadcasting System.[22] While a shortage of funds kept the scheme from materializing, some aspects of the plan were eventually acted upon.[23] And, as Krinsky maintains, "The art center itself was substantially realized at Lincoln Center, not under public sponsorship alone, but with the essential support of John D. Rockefeller 3rd."[24] The MoMA not only provided one of the initial fulcrums for the development of the municipal art center, it was also a resource, cultivating an anti-traditionalist sensibility for a number of figures who came to figure prominently in the development of the Lincoln Center.[25]

More generally, the MoMA formed part of the broader network of Rockefeller institutions and personnel that John 3rd drew upon when he became involved with the Lincoln Center.[26] Indeed, a number of the initiatives of the Lincoln Center bore a strong resemblance to earlier ventures of

Rockefeller philanthropy. The Lincoln Center Student Program, supported by the Fund for Education, was very much in line with various outreach programs of the Progressive Education Association, supported by the GEB.[27] The Juilliard School, in this respect, with its emphasis upon the training of music performers, echoed the HD's 1930s program of supporting the training of museum and media practitioners through fellowships.[28] Like a number of projects sponsored by the GEB, the program worked in cooperation with the Education Program of the State of New York. The support for the branch of the New York Public Library was akin to the program of support given by the RF Humanities Division (HD) for the Film Library of the Museum of Modern Art,[29] as well as for the history of theater collection at Yale. The Film Society of Lincoln Center, founded in 1969, grew out of the New York Film Festival, which was first held in 1962, and drew in part on the expertise of the Rockefeller-funded Museum of Modern Art.[30] Finally, the Repertory Theater at the Lincoln Center (which was eventually to evolve into the Lincoln Center Theater) was an initiative that resonated with the extensive program of Rockefeller support for amateur drama.

At first blush, of course, there was a fundamental difference between the two ventures. The Rockefeller Center was, from the outset, a commercial enterprise, albeit one that sought to bring commerce and the public together in a mutually reinforcing manner. While the initial planning was to include the arts, it became, rather, a mecca of mass culture comprised of commercial broadcasting and entertainment venues, such as the Radio City Music Hall. On the other hand, the Lincoln Center was a nonprofit endeavor, funded largely by foundation funds, private donations, and government support, which made up for the inevitable deficit incurred by constituent members, Arguably, it was not the for-profit versus nonprofit status that was crucial for understanding the two ventures; they could be better seen as differing forms of articulation between private capital, philanthropy, public life, and culture. In this sense, they were representative of their respective eras, with the Lincoln Center, in some sense, evolving from what was put in place with the Rockefeller Center.

ORGANIZING ARTWORK IN ROCKEFELLER CENTER

While Junior bore the ultimate responsibility for Rockefeller Center, the day-to-day construction of the complex was under the direction of John R. Todd, founder of the firm Todd, Robertson, and Todd Engineering Corporation. This involved a contract with three different architectural firms, eight architects from which were recruited by Todd to form Associated Architects, the group responsible for developing the designs for the Rockefeller Center.[31] This approach, which could best be described as "architecture by committee," was analogous to the division of a large business into departments headed by specialists who could pool their ideas.[32] Hence, particularly at the outset, the Rockefeller Center was designed in an organic manner. This involved not only the effort to harmonize the buildings that were to comprise the Rockefeller Center,[33] but also to plan for "convenient access and expeditious traffic flow."[34] The entire complex was to work as a structural whole, as a network.[35]

The decorative features of Rockefeller Center were chosen in the same integrated manner. To this end, Associated Architects enlisted the services of philosopher and anthropologist, Hartley Alexander to coordinate the works of art. The unifying theme he chose was "Homofabor—Man The Builder." As he described the intent of his proposal, "Civilization is . . . what Man adds to Nature . . . by their handiwork and arts [they] reshape it, . . . Rockefeller City . . . has . . . the chance of becoming the first clear expression of a new social idea . . . of human welfare and happiness as centering in the work that we do. . . . [If] a whole population, such as Rockefeller City will possess, can be lifted into a finer life in their working hours, then the economic democracy of America will have begun its answer to the Bolshevist challenge."[36] Frustrated perhaps by the rather arcane and nebulous nature of Alexander's proposal, Junior asked a number of eminent persons to suggest other themes for Rockefeller Center. It was on the basis of their commentary that the center's director of public relations, Merle Crowell, distilled the theme "New Frontiers and the March of Civilization" that was to be embodied in its art work.[37]

Alexander has been dismissed as "possibly the worst hiring decision in the Center's history" whose proposal was so bizarre and outlandish that it could hardly provide the overarching thematic framework for the artwork of Rockefeller Center.[38] However, in the view of Balfour, "His proposals did have a major influence." Well before Junior's intervention, "Alexander's specific suggestions for several of the major decorative projects had been approved by the architects and the artists had been commissioned."[39] Guided by Alexander's vision, these works were informed by a tension between classical narratives and the current machine age, thrusting the visitor into this tension.[40] Through the use of texts and images, the viewer was provided with hints of how to see through the art into a higher realm, which was available to all through the new means of technology. The performative aspect of the spectatorship was heightened by the ambient and collective motion of the visitor since the artwork was located in places such as over entrances or in outer foyers. The effect of the Alexander-inspired artwork, then, was very much tied into the ambulatory character of the Rockefeller Center, which, in addition to having numerous points of entry, was interconnected by an underground concourse, extending for over two miles in length. The decorative work of the Rockefeller Center served to mark the boundaries of the buildings with the intention of drawing the visitor into the theme of progress, thereby—at least at some level—transforming him or her in the process. The Rockefeller Center, befitting its major tenant's devotion to mass communication, not only communicated communication at every turn but also implicated the visitor in the process of communication. The individual artworks, largely by relatively unknowns, were secondary to the total ensemble and the overall effect.

The creation titled "Wisdom with Sound and Light," by Lee Lawrie, can be seen as the purest and most powerful embodiment of Alexander's vision. Moreover, the process by which it was constructed sheds a good deal of light on how Alexander's vision for the Rockefeller Center intersected with that of Junior and those involved with selecting its artwork.

Lawrie's sculpture, composed of carved Indiana limestone, cast glass, polychrome, and gilding (with Leon V. Solon responsible for the coloration), was installed over the main entrance to the RCA (now the General Electric) Building, on the eastern (Fifth Avenue) side of the Rockefeller Center. It consists of the large imposing figure of *Wisdom* (sometimes called *Genius*) flanked on the left by a figure symbolizing *Sound*, on the right by a figure symbolizing *Light*, and with a brilliant glass screen in a continuous panel recessed below the exterior of the masonry. Wisdom is portrayed as a deity-like figure holding in his right hand a golden compass pointing downward toward the glass panel. Between the figure of Wisdom and the glass panel (at the same level as the two flanking figures) is an inscription (partly obscured by the compass in Wisdom's right hand) in capital letters with some of the words separated by stars.

Obviously, there is a vast range of interpretations that a visitor or a passerby can give to this set of images. The meaning given to the artwork by the observer, if not directly congruent with the intended meaning, was nevertheless circumscribed by a specific set of interpretive precepts. What is particularly instructive about the sculpture is the extent to which it followed Alexander's guidelines, as set out in the proposal he submitted to Associated Architects. Given that the west door of the RCA Building was the major entrance to the entire Rockefeller Center, the sculpture was intended to convey the overarching theme of his proposal.

The general theme he proposed for the sculpture—"Voice Speaking through Time and Space"—was to be accompanied by an inscription from *Proverbs 8*, elaborating the creations of *HIM* as *Master Workman*.[41] As Balfour convincingly argues, the deity corresponded to the Homofabor, "symbolizing the Demiurge in Platonic philosophy, the Deity as creator of the material world."[42] Moreover, Alexander specified that the lateral images should symbolize "LIGHT and SPACE" on the one hand, and "SOUND and TIME" on the other. They were to convey "not only cosmic suggestion of the passage from *Proverbs*, but also developments of human understanding that

"Wisdom" (1934) by Lee Lawrie, located over the main entrance
to the GE Building (formerly the RCA Building), 30 Rockefeller Plaza, New York City (©
Christine Roussel 2009).

are being aided by radio and by television." Addressing the location and intended effect of the sculpture, Alexander added, "Since these entrances should be as brilliant as possible, serving as the illuminated initial to the whole city, glass mosaic relief would give the maximum effect."[43]

Lawrie (who had previously worked with Alexander on a project for the Nebraska State capitol) produced a sculptural work that was very faithful to Alexander's proposal. While most of the key elements were retained, the voice was now called "Wisdom," and Time and Space were decoupled from Sound and Light to be integrated in the glass panel. However, the major element missing from Alexander's proposal was the inscription, which had been dropped, likely because Alexander had been officially dropped as well: "The sculpture was completed in early 1933, wordless."[44]

However, as we have noted, the sculpture in its final form was accompanied by an inscription related to Wisdom and Knowledge. The decision to use this particular text was reached after a protracted negotiation involving John R. Todd, Merle Crowell, and Junior. The inscription that was finally used represented a compromise between Junior's wish to have the text convey (quite literally) that "even Time himself has to yield to the bridging influence of Light and Sound" and the desire of Junior's staff to deploy an inscription that was more open-ended.[45] While the final inscription chosen ("Wisdom and Knowledge Shall be The Stability of Time") accorded with Junior's evident wish to have it based on scripture (it is from the *Book of Isaiah* 33:6), it also spoke to more contemporary issues in line with the center's theme of "new frontiers and the march of civilization."[46]

Aside from the extent to which the sculpture was related to Alexander's original designs in relation to the desires of Junior and his staff, it also needs to be examined within the context of the broader ensemble of the decoration of the Rockefeller Center. With its emphasis upon new media forms (radio, film, television) and by virtue of its location over the main entrance of the Rockefeller Center's most important building, it served as a leitmotif for the many artworks in the center that represented media of communication. They were not only present in Alexander's proposal,[47] but also were chosen by the arts committee in line with the new theme for the Rockefeller Center. To some extent this could be attributed to the fact that the major tenants of the center were media-related—including RCA, RKO, and Time-Life. But the suffusion of the center with communication themes spoke to a broader recognition of the power and potential of the new communication media and a desire to have the visitor to the center partake in its civilizing mission. What made this possible was its large and well-integrated collection of public art coupled with accessibility to the public through numerous points of entry and an extensive concourse system.

The Rockefeller Center, as a powerful site for the new communications media, was thoroughly communicative in its organization and layout. This orientation was reflected in some of the Rockefeller philanthropies (particularly the HD and the GEB), which featured robust programs in the theory and practice of communication. While these programs were oriented toward culture, this was primarily in terms of how shared values and beliefs could be cultivated, in line with the international orientation of the Rockefeller Center (which featured French and British pavilions with Italian and German pavilions projected).[48] However, consistent with the Rockefeller dictum to support the development of knowledge rather than creative production per se, virtually no support was given to the arts in general or to the performing arts in particular. Indeed, within the Rockefeller Center, aside from the extensive decorative arts and the rampant mass culture disseminated by NBC radio and the Center's movie theaters, culture—as aesthetic creation and expression—had relatively little presence.

PERFORMING ARTS AND ARTWORK AT THE LINCOLN CENTER

This stood in contrast to the Lincoln Center, which began to take shape around a quarter century after the Rockefeller Center opened. Not only were the performing arts the focal point for the new complex, but philanthropy was slated to be one of the primary sources of support for the myriad forms of cultural expression that were housed in Lincoln Center. This sudden willingness of philanthropies and moneyed interests to underwrite the arts in the late 1950s reflected a shift in the cold war that followed the launching of Sputnik by the Soviet Union in 1957. In this escalating climate of tension, culture (as aesthetic expression) became increasingly viewed as another weapon in the American arsenal to counteract what was perceived to be a growing Soviet menace. As Lincoln Center director C. D. Jackson observed, "Culture today is emerging as a great element of East-West competition. Culture . . . is no longer a sissy word. Today it is a word of immense world-wide political significance."[49] As part of this mobilization of cultural resources, the Lincoln Center was assigned a leading role. As the center's board of directors claimed,

> "The Lincoln Center for the Performing Arts can be the greatest cultural development of our times that would not only symbolize cultural maturity to American citizens, but announce America's cultural maturity to the world. . . . [It] will draw the eye of the world to the American artist, the singer, the dancer, the player, and to the masses of American citizens who enjoy these arts."

Moreover, the fact that foundations were now embracing the cause of culture signified that philanthropic maturity was on the horizon as well: "Once the great object of American philanthropy was medicine; more recently, education. Now the arts and their relation to the contemporary American are coming into focus, just as the problem of his physical health did a half-century ago[50]. . . . As a symbol before the world, Lincoln Center will be all the better because it will be built and supported by the freely given gifts of private individuals, foundations, and corporations."[51]

This elevation of the performing arts, however, came at a price. While the Lincoln Center became known for its high aesthetic standards, it also was criticized for its inaccessibility, remoteness, and its isolation from the Upper West Side community.[52] In comparing the Lincoln Center to Times Square, Jans perceptively notes, "Unlike those who created the decorated fronts on the commercial theatres of Forty-second Street, these architects designed stark, monumental buildings that turned away from the sidewalk."[53] This isolation from the surrounding neighborhood (with implications for its relation to its public and visitors) could be attributed in large to the ethos and organizational approach that underpinned its original design.

Unlike the unabashedly commercial Rockefeller Center, the Lincoln Center was organized on a nonprofit basis, largely in recognition of the fact that the performing arts were not intrinsically profitable. It was assumed that it would operate at a loss, with the shortfall to be made up by foundations and wealthy donors. From the outset, Lincoln Center, as "a huge performing arts complex," has been composed of constituent members, representing various branches of the performing arts,[54] who are housed in buildings at the center. It has been run by Lincoln Center for the Performing Arts that serves as landlord, administrator, fundraiser, as well as concert organizer and producer for its resident organizations. While the constituent groups are managed autonomously, they are represented on the Lincoln Center's board of directors and share in the funding that the center raises.[55]

By virtue of this organizational structure, the early planning process for the Lincoln Center differed dramatically from that of the initial phase of the Rockefeller Center. Unlike the Rockefeller Center where John R. Todd, in conjunction with Associated Architects, developed an integrated plan (including artwork) for the entire complex, the Lincoln Center did not feature the same degree of integrated planning. Rather, the planning committee, as chaired by JDR, left it up to each constituent member to select its own architect and to come up with its own design, within the parameters of the Lincoln Center's overall budget.[56] This meant that while the planning for Rockefeller Center was organic and integrated, that of the Lincoln Center was individualistic and segmented. This difference might be attributed to the fact that the Rockefeller Center had a top-down structure, while the Lincoln Center, as a decentralized, nonprofit initiative, was obliged to make decisions through an ongoing negotiation between the managing committee and the center's constituent members. To be sure, the architects who were chosen met on several occasions to coordinate their designs and to decide on locations. But by all accounts this process was not entirely successful, leading to a design that was not noted for its harmony, albeit subscribing to an overall aesthetic based on "neoformalism," an offshoot of the international style, which combined classicism with modernism.[57]

The same principles of organization applied to the acquisition of artwork by the Lincoln Center. While the Lincoln Center had a committee for arts acquisition (chaired by Frank Stanton), the process involved each committee working with its architect to choose works deemed appropriate.[58] A number of the works were donated by benefactors, such as the gift by Mr. and Mrs. Howard Lipman of a work by Alexander Calder "because they considered [the Lincoln Center] the proper setting for the works of outstanding American artists of our time."[59]

There was a tendency of the artwork of the Lincoln Center to have been chosen not for its substance, but rather for how its lines fit in with that of the architectural designs. For instance, Philip Johnson chose "two female figures by Elie Nadelman (twice the size of the originals in his possession), because their curved surfaces offset the rectilinear lines of the New York State theater."[60] The art of the Lincoln Center was not only much less copious than that of the Rockefeller Center, but was also largely produced by high-profile figures such as Alexander Calder, Jasper Johns, Henry Moore, and Marc Chagall. Their artwork, for the most part, was placed in large interior spaces and was to be contemplated once one had entered one of the center's buildings. Unlike the decorative work of the Rockefeller Center, the art of the Lincoln Center was not immediately accessible to all. It not only required familiarity with the significance of the artist in question, but also an awareness of the interpretive codes that would allow meaning to be bestowed upon it.[61]

THE TWO CENTERS, THE PUBLIC, AND THE ROCKEFELLER PROJECT

By juxtaposing the two centers, one gains insights into how public life in relation to philanthropy, private interests, and the state evolved from the late 1920s through to the late 1970s. For the Rockefeller philanthropies of the 1930s, the Rockefeller Center not only provided them with physical space, but also helped to link them into networks of experts and potential recipients. The Lincoln Center was not the site of philanthropies per se. But given that it was dependent on foundations and wealthy donors for its survival, philanthropy—in particular the disbursement of funds—was an essential feature of its organizational structure. In this regard, JDR was the central figure.[62] As a departure from working within the Rockefeller network of philanthropies,[63] he was obliged to closely work in concert with a broad range of charities, foundations, and donors. What this suggests is that JDR's work with the Lincoln Center helped him to become more aware of the broader sphere of philanthropic endeavor.[64]

Indeed, at the same time as he was involved with the Lincoln Center, he was instrumental in the formation of two major investigative bodies dealing with foundations, the Commission on Foundations and Private Philanthropy (1969–1970), chaired by Peter Peterson and the Commission on Philanthropy and Public Needs (1973–1977), chaired by John H. Filer.[65] JDR's advocacy on behalf of the nonprofit sector, as manifest in his work with the two commissions not only was inflected by his work with the Lincoln Center, but also reflected his previous experience with Rockefeller philanthropy going back to his early work in the family offices at Rockefeller Center. His directorship of the Lincoln Center and the two commissions led him to become increasingly involved in extensive lobbying activities and fund-raising activities. In his efforts to convince lawmakers and potential donors of the worthiness of the causes he championed, he drew on the Rockefeller tradition of producing studies by experts that could be used as the basis for solving problems.[66] And like his Rockefeller forbears who drew on experts to shift public opinion, JDR took it upon himself to develop the support of the public for his ideas.[67]

Overall, JDR's work with the Lincoln Center and the defense of philanthropy could be seen as strikingly similar activities. In the same manner that he brought together donors and corporations of different stripes, and helped bring diverse arts together within a single rubric, he also sought to unify philanthropies together into what came to be known as the "third sector" or the "independent sector."[68] Indeed, the realm of high art (supposedly transcending commerce and politics) that was embodied in the Lincoln Center could be seen as an aesthetic variant of the third sector. Indeed, what made the remote and isolated nonprofit art complex of the Lincoln Center possible was the emergence of the third sector, whose interests very much included support for the arts.

The third sector—as the realm of philanthropies, charities, and nonprofit thought to be separate from market and state—harks back to the public that so preoccupied the early general-purpose philanthropies beginning in the 1920s. However, while the earlier Rockefeller philanthropies sought to mediate competing interests within this public, what JDR and his colleagues sought to accomplish was much more ambitious. Rather than accepting the makeup of civil society as a given, their aim was to reconstitute this realm along particular lines, which involved creating what amounted to a new "vital center" consisting of philanthropies, charities, and donors. These in turn would provide the lifeblood for not only various voluntary associations, but also the realm of cultural expression, which in the United States had largely been ignored by the government. Some progress has been made in carving out this area as a separate sphere—as evidenced in the explosion of activity in this area during the three decades that have elapsed since the death of JDR. But this has come at the expense of emptying civil society of the Gramscian tension and contestation that confronted philanthropic groups in the early years of the Rockefeller half-century.

NOTES

I am indebted to Theresa Richardson and to Julia Foulkes for their thoughtful and insightful comments on an earlier draft of this chapter.

1. This designation derives, of course, from the title of John Ensor Harr's and Peter J. Johnson's definitive study, *The Rockefeller Century: Three Generations of America's Greatest Family* (New York: Scribner's, 1988). The framing of my discussion in this manner, I should point out, is not to deny the importance of other non-Rockefeller–related developments in philanthropy; it is intended to call attention to a particular lineage within the broader transformation on American philanthropy from the late 1920s to the late 1970s.

2. See chapter 4 on the "New Humanities" and "New General-Education Programs" in this volume as well as that of Richardson.

3. The original project had been centered on the building of a new home for the Metropolitan Opera Company on land (known as the "Upper Estates") owned by Columbia University in the area bordered by Fifth and Sixth avenues and by Forty-eighth and Fiftieth Streets. Representatives from the company approached Junior (through his trusted advisor Ivy Lee) with a request to acquire the land from Columbia and donate it to them so that they could build the new opera house. While Junior was attracted to the prospect of contributing to the civic and cultural life of New York through such a deed, he also saw the possibilities of considerable financial gain in the transaction; he had been assured by a reputable real-estate assessor (Todd & Brown) that he could realize as much as $5.5 million a year in rent from the property. Accordingly, after an intense period of negotiation, he signed a contract with Columbia in October 1928, leasing the property for a twenty-four-year period (with the help of a sizable mortgage from Metropolitan Life). However, when the stock market crashed in 1929, the Metropolitan Real Estate Company pulled out of the deal, leaving Junior with a lease of $3.8 million a year on a property that was generating only around $300,000 annually in rent. Carol von Pressentin Wright, *Blue Guide: New York* (London: A & C Black Ltd., 1983), 285.

4. Daniel Okrent, *Great Fortune: The Epic of the Rockefeller Center* (New York: Viking, 2003), 259.

5. Okrent, *Great Fortune*, 259.

6. Okrent, *Great Fortune*, 259; "The Rockefeller Clan: A Public Family," *Time* (September 2, 1974).

7. These included the Chase National Bank (which had three branches in the Center), Eastern Airlines, the American Society for the Control of Cancer, Transit Advertisers, and the Standard Oil Company of New Jersey, which occupied "175,000 square feet spread through eight floors of the RCA Building." Okrent, *Great Fortune*, 262.

8. Notable examples are the New York Museum of Science and Industry, which opened in February 1936, as well as the short-lived American Film Center.

9. Perhaps the best known of these was Industrial Relations Counselors, founded in 1926.

10. As Brilliant points out, the family's business and philanthropic interests were closely bound up with one another. Eleanor L. Brilliant, *Private Charity and Public Inquiry: A History of the Filer and Peterson Commissions* (Bloomington & Indianapolis: Indiana University Press, 2000), 28.

11. He died in an automobile accident in Westchester County at the age of seventy-two. Nelson Rockefeller, his younger brother, died shortly thereafter, on January 26, 1979, of a heart attack.

12. Harr and Johnson, *The Rockefeller Century*, 555.

13. Junior's building ventures included Colonial Williamsburg, the restoration of the Palace of Versailles, the Cloisters Museum of gothic sculpture and medieval tapestry. Less successful building projects included an upper-class housing and golf community in Forest Hills, Cleveland, the Bayonne, New Jersey, worker housing project for Standard Oil of New Jersey, and "Negro" housing (called the Paul Laurence Dunbar Apartments) in north-central Harlem. JDR was the chief fundraiser for Japan House (home of the Japan Society), which opened in 1971. He also had donated the site upon which it was built (located on East Forty-seventh Street and First Avenue near the United Nations). I am grateful to Theresa Richardson for bringing these to my attention.

14. Josephine Young Case and Everett Needham Case, *Owen D. Young and American Enterprise: A Biography* (Boston: David R. Godine, 1982), 488.

15. Wayne Jans, "Theaters of Power: Architectural and Cultural Production," *Journal of Architectural Education* 50, no. 4 (May 1997), 232. See also Myer Kutz, *Rockefeller Power* (New York: Pinnacle Books, 1974), 95.

16. Junior was honored by the Rockefeller Center with a bronze plaque bearing some of his words, as was JDR by the Lincoln Center.

17. The Rockefeller Center was the home of RCA and NBC, which, initially at least, had a commitment to educational broadcasting. Walter Damrosch was responsible for the *NBC Music Appreciation Hour*, broadcast from 1928 to 1942 (and from Studio 8-H at NBC in the Rockefeller Center beginning in 1933). Intrigued by its significance, the Rockefeller Foundation funded a study of its impact. (Damrosch Park in Lincoln Center is named after Walter Damrosch. His brother Frank was co-founder of the Juilliard School of Music, which became a constituent member of the Lincoln Center.) Sondra Wieland Howe, "The NBC Music Appreciation Hour: Radio Broadcasts of Walter Damrosch, 1928–1942," *Journal of Research in Music Education* 51, no. 1 (Spring 2003): 64–77. *Live from Lincoln Center*, which began in 1976 to broadcast performances from the Metropolitan Opera for a television audience, carried on the RF's interest of using broadcasting for cultural uplift and was in line with the intermittent use of the Rockefeller Center for educational radio transmission.

18. Jans, "Theaters of Power," 234–35.

19. Hall has remarked upon the extent to which the family played a significant role in Rockefeller philanthropic endeavors. Peter Dobkin Hall, *Inventing the Nonprofit Sector and other Essays on Philanthropy, Voluntarism, and Nonprofit Organizations* (Baltimore: Johns Hopkins University Press, 1992), 189–99.

20. Family, philanthropic, and business interests intersected in property acquisitions, sales, and donations in the area north of Rockefeller Center. As Okrent notes, "By the end of the decade [the 1920s] the Rockefeller family owned fifteen separate lots (and their buildings) at the Fifth Avenue end of West 54th Street, thirteen more on the adjacent stretch of West 53rd, another six on West 55th, and a stately row of parcels marching up the west side of Fifth between 52nd and 55th Street" (Okrent, *Great Fortune*, 47). While Okrent maintains that these acquisitions had the aim of protecting the family properties from encroachment, it might be argued that, at least to some degree, speculation was at work, given the obvious impact the building of the Rockefeller Center had on real estate values in the area. Nelson Rockefeller proposed the extension of Rockefeller Plaza north to the Museum of Modern Art and built the two-towered Rockefeller Apartments (designed by Wallace Harrison) "one on 54th Street, the other on 55th Street, with a private garden in between." Junior had assented to its construction. Cary Reich, *Nelson A. Rockefeller: Worlds to Conquer* (New York: Doubleday, 1996), 137.

21. In 1939, the MoMA moved into a permanent home on this site in a building that was New York's first example of the "international" Bauhaus style. Fittingly, the new president of MoMA was Nelson Rockefeller (Reich, *Nelson Rockefeller*, 143, 144). The original family home located at 10 West Fifty-fourth Street was razed to make way for MoMA's Abby Aldrich Rockefeller Sculpture Garden (Okrent, *Great Fortune*, 377).

22. Krinsky, *Rockefeller Center*, 86–87; Kutz, *Rockefeller Power*, 95; Okrent, *Great Fortune*, 378–80.

23. They included the conversion of the Mecca Temple in 1942 into the City Center of Music and Drama, "offering low-priced operas and ballets." In 1965 CBS finally did build its headquarters near the site that had been suggested by Nelson Rockefeller (Krinsky, *Rockefeller Center*, 87).

24. Krinsky, *Rockefeller Center*, 87. There was a direct linkage between the never-to-be-completed municipal art center and the Lincoln Center within the city administration. Robert Moses, in his capacity of parks commissioner, was chosen by Mayor La Guardia to coordinate the planning for the art center. During the 1960s, as chair of the Committee on Slum Clearance, Moses was responsible for overseeing the federally funded Lincoln Square Project of clearing the Lincoln Square area "slums" and replacing them with a branch of Fordham University, middle-income housing, and a performing arts center. It was Moses who invited his old friend Wallace K. Harrison to become involved in the Lincoln Center project. Harrison was eventually chosen by the Exploratory Committee for a Musical Arts Center (chaired by JDR) to be its coordinating architect. He also was the architect for the Metropolitan Opera House. Harrison had been a member of the Associated Architects that designed the Rockefeller Center and had established a reputation as the Rockefeller "house architect" because of the numerous commissions he was given by Rockefeller family members. Krinsky, *Rockefeller Center*, 87; Edgar B. Young, *Lincoln Center: Building of an Institution* (New York & London: New York University Press, 1980), 35–43, 79; Okrent, *Great Fortune*, 152.

25. A number of figures that were instrumental in the development of Lincoln Center had originally cut their aesthetic teeth at the Museum of Modern Art, shortly after it was established. Both Nelson Rockefeller and Lincoln Kirstein as "charter members of the museum's Junior Advisory Committee" helped to organize an

exhibition in the spring of 1932 titled "Murals by American Painters and Photographers" (Okrent, *Great Fortune*, 224). In his later capacity as governor of New York, Nelson Rockefeller found a way for the state of New York to provide support for the Lincoln Center by integrating the New York State Theater into the 1964 New York World's Fair (Young, *Lincoln Center*, 132–37). Kirstein, as managing director of the New York City Ballet, was a member of the building subcommittee for the New York State Theater (Young, *Lincoln Center*, 155). Philip Johnson, the acclaimed architect who designed the New York State Theater, also had been closely involved with the MoMA in its early years. Like Nelson Rockefeller and Kirstein he was a member of the Museum's Junior Advisory Committee as well as "first director of the new department of architecture of the Museum." With cocurator Henry-Russell Hitchcock, he organized a show titled *Modern Architecture: International Exhibition*, which is widely recognized as having put the emergent international style (of which the Lincoln Center is arguably an offshoot) on the map (Okrent, *Great Fortune*, 158).

26. These included Edgar Young (retired president of Rockefeller Center), Victor Borella (Rockefeller Center director), Frank Stanton, George D. Woods, and Devereux Josephs (all Rockefeller Foundation board members), not to mention Nelson Rockefeller, who provided support for the Lincoln Center after becoming governor of New York in 1958.

27. It evolved into the Lincoln Center Institute, founded in 1975.

28. See chapter 8 by Niquette and Buxton in this volume.

29. See Wasson's chapter 6 in this volume.

30. Young, *Lincoln Center*, 230. In 1972, "the Society, with the help of the Rockefeller Brothers Fund and the co-sponsorship of the Museum of Modern Art's Film Department—instituted its New Directors/New Films Series." Stephen Stamas and Sharon Zane, *Lincoln Center: Promise Realized, 1979–2006* (New York: John Wiley, 2007), 16.

31. Okrent, *Great Fortune*, 108–9.

32. Krinksy, *Rockefeller Center*, 47–48.

33. This was true of the early phase, for which the RCA building was the centerpiece. The buildings constructed after 1936 largely reflected the emergent international style, closer to what one found in the Lincoln Center (Okrent, *Great Fortune*, 340).

34. Krinsky, *Rockefeller Center*, 48.

35. Eric Gordon, "Toward a Networked Urbanism: Hugh Ferriss, Rockefeller Center, and the 'Invisible Empire of the Air,'" *Space and Culture* 8, no. 3 (2005): 258.

36. Hartley Burr Alexander, "Rockefeller City—Thematic Synopsis," 1932, Rockefeller Family Archives, quoted in Alan Balfour, *Rockefeller Center: Architecture as Theater* (New York: McGraw-Hill, 1978), 137.

37. Balfour, *Rockefeller Center*, 138–39. Subsequently, as an art critic of the day noted, "A committee consisting of five museum directors [was] in charge of decisions touching matters of Art interest in Rockefeller Center." Louise Cross, "The Sculpture for Rockefeller Center," *Parnassus* 4, no. 5 (October 1932): 2. Donald Deskey was given the responsibility of choosing the decorative arts for Radio City Music Hall. (Krinsky, *Rockefeller Center*, 78).

38. Okrent, *Great Fortune*, 183–85.

39. Balfour, *Rockefeller Center*, 139. These included the great mural in the Music Hall foyer, "Quest of the Fountain of Eternal Youth" (painted by Ezra Winter), "Intelligence Awakening the Public," which became the mosaic "Intelligence Awakening Mankind," fashioned by Barry Faulkner on the wall of the Sixth Avenue entrance to the RCA buildings, as well as Diego Rivera's notorious fresco and Hildreth Meiere's allegorical roundels on the exterior of the music hall (Okrent, *Great Fortune*, 230).

40. The many artworks that were guided by the more diffuse theme of "New Frontiers," such as those of Lee Friedlander and Robert Garrison, reflected these tendencies in varying degrees.

41. Balfour, *Rockefeller Center*, 142.

42. Balfour, *Rockefeller Center*, 143.

43. Alexander, quoted in Balfour, *Rockefeller Center*, 143.

44. Balfour, *Rockefeller Center*, 143.

45. It is not clear whether or not Lawrie was called back to fashion the statement that was finally chosen.

46. The style of script chosen for the statement on the frieze very much reflected this fusion between antiquity and the modern. As Jonathan Hoefler of Hoefler & Frere Jones (Typeface Foundry) observes, the lettering represented a collision between "the Art Deco vogue for anything streamlined" such as "geometric sans serifs like Futura (1927) or Erbar (1929)" and the ancient Greek tradition, as embodied in "the Pericles typeface, designed by Robert Foster for the American Type Founders company in 1934—an especially masterful expression of that decade's vogue for the Greek lapidary style." E-mail to the author, 22 September, 2008 (cited with permission of Mr. Hoefler).

47. See note 34.

48. Reflecting the changing world circumstances in the late 1930s, the German pavilion was never built. In its place, an international pavilion was constructed. It was joined by a number of other buildings with an international orientation including the Time & Life Building and the Eastern Airlines Building (Okrent, *Great Fortune*, 381–82, 398–99).

49. C. D. Jackson, "Culture: A Status Symbol of the World," *Performing Arts* 1, no. 1 (March 12, 1959): 2–3, quoted in Jans, "Theaters of Power," 232.

50. Consistent with this shift of emphasis by foundations toward the arts, the Ford Foundation around this time largely abandoned its development projects abroad in favor of support for culture at home. Kathleen McCarthy, "From Cold War to Cultural Development: The International Cultural Activities of the Ford Foundation, 1950–1980," *Daedalus* 116, no. 1 (Winter 1987): 101.

51. "Text of Statement by Lincoln Center," *New York Times* (12 September, 1957): 28.

52. Goldberger likens the Lincoln Center to an "empty hole in the middle of a doughnut," which, with its indifference to the streets of New York, "is the exact opposite to . . . Carnegie Hall . . . enveloped in the swirling energy of the city streets." Its plazas, he maintains, "are . . . cold and uninviting, and do not function as destinations in themselves, the way public space in a city ought to." Paul Goldberger, "West-Side Fixer-Upper: New Ideas for Lincoln Center that don't involve dynamite," *New Yorker* (July 7, 2003), http://www.newyorker.com/archive/2003/07/07/

030707crsk_skyline_goldberger (accessed October 22, 2008). See also chapter 13 by Foulkes in this volume.

53. Jans, "Theaters of Power," 238.

54. The Film Society of Lincoln Center is an exception, as its subject matter fits more readily into the visual arts.

55. Hoover's Profile: Lincoln Center for the Performing Arts, http://www .answers.com/topic/lincoln-center-for-the-performing-arts-inc (accessed September 24, 2008).

56. The frame of reference was largely a "neo-formalist" one, and most had connections to Rockefeller interests. As Jans points out, there was a definite pecking order among the architects, which made for a good deal of conflict (Jans, "Theaters of Power," 238). The new formalism of the architecture was meant to highlight the high cultural standards of an American-based movement that had evolved out of the new internationalism.

57. It has been noted that "the complex explicitly recalls the formal order of Michelangelo's Piazza del Campodoglio in Rome," http://www.musiccenter.org/ about/index.html (accessed 13 September, 2008).

58. Kutz points out that many of the architects involved with the Lincoln Center had Rockefeller connections (*Rockefeller Power*, 95–96).

59. Young, *Lincoln Center*, 212.

60. Young, *Lincoln Center*, 206.

61. The two complexes illustrate principles of "Distinction" as outlined by Bourdieu. The aesthetic of the Lincoln Center was based on form, codes, and good taste (differentiated from the sensibilities of the popular classes) while that of the Rockefeller Center was based on what would be immediately intelligible to the masses, the subordination of form to function, clearly defined characters and situations, and the promise of a better future. Pierre Bourdieu, *Distinction: A Social Critique of the Judgment of Taste* (Cambridge, MA: Harvard University Press, 1984).

62. JDR, as one might expect, was instrumental in raising support from Rockefeller sources. This included funding from the Rockefeller Brothers Fund as well as a $10 million bequest in 1971 from the estate of Martha Baird Rockefeller, the widow of John Rockefeller Jr. (Stamas and Zane, *Lincoln Center*, 158). JDR gave $11 million of his own money to the Lincoln Center ("The Rockefeller Clan").

63. These included the Rockefeller Foundation, the Rockefeller Brothers Fund, and the Population Council. JDR was the chief fundraiser for Japan House (home of the Japan Society), which opened in 1971.

64. Mirroring JDR's experience, Edgar Young describes his history of the Lincoln Center as "a case study of how the 'Third Sector,' the voluntary, nonprofit sector, and functions in American life" (Young, *Lincoln Center*, 3). Young's book was dedicated to the memory of John D. Rockefeller 3rd.

65. JDR's role in these two commissions are discussed in Brilliant, *Private Charity*, and in John Ensor Harr and Peter J. Johnson, *The Rockefeller Conscience: An American Family in Public and Private* (New York: Scribner's, 1991).

66. In the case of the Filer Commission, ninety-one of the papers written for it were published in a five-volume series (Brilliant, *Private Charity*, 121). Recognizing the need for sustained and systematic research on the nonprofit sector, JDR provided a small planning grant for the "development of a nonprofit research center" at

Yale (Brilliant, *Private Charity*, 138), which led to the establishment of the Program on Non-Profit Organizations, under the direction of John G. Simon, founded in 1978. Flowing out the Lincoln Center initiative, a study of the performing arts in America was undertaken, funded by the Rockefeller Brothers Fund. See *The Performing Arts: Problems and Prospects: Rockefeller Panel Report on the Future of Theatre, Dance, Music in America* (New York: McGraw-Hill, 1965).

67. For the Lincoln Center, this involved enlisting the services of David Ogilvie to orchestrate a publicity campaign, as well as the sending of frequent press releases through the office of JDR (who also served as the center's spokesperson at public events). In order to make his thoughts on philanthropy better known to the public, JDR not only gave numerous talks and interviews, but also outlined his emergent views on the "third sector" in a text whose publication was supported by the JDR 3rd Fund. See John D. Rockefeller 3rd, *The Second American Revolution: Some Personal Observations* (New York: Harper & Row, 1973).

68. As Brilliant points out, the tax status of the Lincoln Center in pending legislation was one of the issues that propelled JDR to become active politically on behalf of foundations (*Private Charity*, 32). Moreover, subsequent to his involvement with the Peterson Commission, it was suggested that he form another "corporate commission" along the same lines, given that his work with the Lincoln Center had "prepared him well for pulling together a business commission" (Brilliant, *Private Charity*, 108).

3

Transformation and Continuity in Rockefeller Child-Related Programs: Implications for the Emergence of Communications as a Field of Concern

Theresa Richardson

> There is a hunger in the world which economists and political scientists cannot relieve. As they have in all ages, men turn today for their ultimate satisfactions to humanism—to the philosophers, the teachers, the historians, the artists, the poets, the novelists, the dramatists—all those who fashion ideas, concepts, and forms that give meaning to life and furnish patterns of conduct. It is they who really construct the world we live in, and it is they who with sensitive awareness of human perplexity and aspirations can speak effectively to a distracted age.[1]

Rockefeller-related philanthropies began to seriously fund communication technologies in the late 1930s as part of a program to adjust society and especially youth to the effects of the Depression in what can be called a distracted age. Rockefeller support for communications as aspects of its educational, humanities, and social-science programs was critical to the development of this new field, which took off with the onset of World War II.[2] A critical understanding and an ability to interpret and manipulate meaning and patterns of conduct seemed essential if human civilization was to survive in a changing world. The objective of this chapter is to examine the role of Rockefeller philanthropic support for the social sciences and humanities in the 1920s and 1930s and how its focus on promoting the health of children contributed to Rockefeller interest in the development of a new field in communication studies in the 1940s.

The first great Rockefeller philanthropy, the General Education Board (GEB), was established in 1903 to conduct a general-education campaign in the southern states. Between 1903 and 1917 the GEB successfully established a system of public elementary schools in the South. The schools were also used to gain access to the general population in order to promote public health. Under the direction of Wallace Butterick, the GEB, with its partner Rockefeller fund the Sanitary Commission for the Eradication of Hookworm Disease, led by philosopher Wickliffe Rose, demonstrated three lessons: (1) Philanthropies could successfully establish and shape civic institutions such as schools in the name of the public good. (2) Schools in turn with their captive youthful subjects also provided access to a larger public constituency through families, and (3) Knowledge grounded in scientific research could be demonstrated and applied with dramatic result beyond the classroom. The dominant Rockefeller philanthropy, the Rockefeller Foundation (RF) founded in 1913, elevated these lessons to a national and international level. While the arts and humanities were recognized as viable areas of support, Executive Secretary Jerome Greene of the RF pursued education and public health almost exclusively. It is important that the mandate for medical advancement included mental health from the earliest days of the Foundation. Socializing children into good habits of mental stability and thus preserving social stability became a rationale for a second general-education campaign in the 1930s. In the 1930s, the educational and public-health missions of the General Education Board and Rockefeller Foundation added a focus on child development that emerged from a third philanthropy, the Laura Spelman Rockefeller Memorial (LSRM) founded in 1918.[3] Communication studies as supported by Rockefeller philanthropy, in part, grew out of the perceived usefulness of applied versions of the social sciences and humanities in the effort to adapt personality development in children to cultural change through the use of media as an educational technology.

ROCKEFELLER PROGRAMS IN SOCIAL SCIENCE
AND THE HUMANITIES IN THE 1920s

The Laura Spelman Rockefeller Memorial became the primary vehicle (within the Rockefeller network of philanthropic organizations) for developing the social sciences that had a research focus on the socialization and development of children with an outreach to families.[4] The Memorial did not find this niche until Beardsley Ruml became its director in 1922. Ruml held a doctorate in psychology from the University of Chicago. He was interested in the potential of science to formalize a better understanding of social organization through research and its systematic application in social policy.[5] His assistant, Lawrence K. Frank, held a doctorate from Columbia University in economics, but his interests tended toward social psychology with a focus on the study of child development and parenting.

Under Ruml and Frank, the LSRM established a three-pronged approach to creating a technology of social change through research and application. The objective was to produce a "technical science" of parenting and public administration through the development of the social sciences and related research on children and youth.[6]

In 1922, Lawrence K. Frank began this effort by conducting a survey of the social-science fields associated with the welfare of women and children. The survey was used to formulate a plan of action for the development of an applied social science in which the fourth and last stage was disseminating knowledge, or communication.[7] The first stage was to concentrate on classes of related problems as "opportunities for coordinated effort" in interdisciplinary inquiry. The second stage was to promote institutions that already demonstrated their capacity for successful projects. This included the presence of "a range of professional opinion, the existence of scholarly and professional standards," as well as the potential to secure "intimate contact of the social scientist in the university with concrete social phenomena." The third stage was to "increase the highly visible able men working in the field," a reference to graduate-level training and fellowship programs. Communication was the fourth and final phase where the development of the social sciences was linked to the traditional role of the humanities in creating and monitoring various means of communicating knowledge. "The most fundamental truths will automatically get into textbooks, and will effect [*sic*] in some cases the teaching context in elementary and secondary schools."[8] The mandate to include the dissemination process became an essential part of social control associated with the field of communication. The first "tentative" steps toward the dissemination and control of information were taken through the "preparation of teaching materials for use in connection with secondary commercial instruction" and the advance of libraries internationally.[9]

In the booming 1920s, the LSRM experimented with child-study and parent-education research and demonstration through fifteen projects. Seven major research centers were funded including the Iowa Child Welfare Research Station; the Institute of Child Welfare at the University of California, Berkeley; the Institute of Child Welfare at the University of Minnesota; the Clinic for Child Development at the Institute for Human Relations at Yale University; the Child Development Institute at Teachers College, Columbia University in New York; the Institute for Child Study at the University of Toronto; and the American Association of University Women's child study projects at Cornell University.[10] Communicating and applying research findings to general as well as to specialized audiences were early aspects of these experimental demonstrations of the relevance of scientific research to social improvement. The Child Study Association became the core of a national parent-education outreach program that dealt with the dissemination of child-study research including the preparation of bibliographies for study groups, the publication of books and pamphlets and child-study magazines, as well as articles in magazines.[11] The interest in and experimental use of media as vehicles for outreach was not limited to print. In 1924, fourteen radio broadcasts were used to give talks on numerous topics that generated between thirty and fifty letters a week. The questions were answered by mail or through the *Women's Home Companion* magazine.[12]

The University of Iowa Child Welfare Research Station is a good example of early experimentation with applying research to practice through demonstration and media outreach. The Station initiated parent-study groups at the university and it also sent mobile mental-hygiene and parent-education teams to rural areas. By 1924, radio technology and public access to radio transmission was rapidly increasing. The Iowa Child Welfare Research Station initiated radio talks as a two-year project (1924–1926) "to find out whether people would study systematically about children; to make available for the people of the state the best thought about children; to induce parents to look at their children objectively as well as subjectively; and, to work from the standpoint of quality not quantity."[13] The potential of communication by distance via radio broadcasting was recognized in that it solved the problem of making on-site contact in the winter months. If people had access to receivers, radio transmissions could be heard regardless of the condition of the roads. The lessons of the Station's mobile units could reach, via the airwaves, distant communities and isolated farms.

Rockefeller support for the humanities was largely informal until the mid-1920s. In 1923, Wickliffe Rose, head of the original Sanitary Commission and director of the International Health Division of the RF, took over the presidency of the General Education Board when Wallace Butterick, its long-time secretary and executive officer, retired.[14] Rose was known for his profound belief in the potential of scientific methods to solve human problems and to perfect human knowledge as well as social organization. Rose chose the sciences and humanities as "fields for special development."[15] Abraham Flexner, an early Rockefeller philanthropic advisor and officer, was made the chief executive of a new Division of Studies and Medical Education. He was also made director of educational studies on the International Education Board (IEB), established in 1923. Between 1924 and 1928, the year of his retirement, Flexner set about developing a program in the humanities where serious scholars and students could pursue classical scholarly research. Flexner's projects were the "first significant humanities programs undertaken by the Rockefeller enterprises."[16] Flexner's interests extended to the promotion of rigorous scholarship in high schools and the articulation of the high-school curriculum with real university work.[17] Flexner's promotion of the humanities as purely academic did not escape criticism but it prevailed until a reorganization of the Rockefeller Boards opened new possibilities for an applied approach to the humanities.[18]

THE 1928 REORGANIZATION OF THE ROCKEFELLER BOARDS

In 1925 an internal report cited an overlap of personnel and interests among the multiple Rockefeller philanthropic boards. The report concluded that the "constituent boards and divisions might . . . look forward to a reorganization."[19] In 1926 and 1927 plans were drawn up that reconceptualized the Rockefeller philanthropies. Their intent was to bring all of the boards into the general framework of the Rockefeller Foundation's mandate to "advance human knowledge." On January 3, 1928, the LSRM was incorporated into the Rockefeller Foundation. LSRM programs in the social sciences, social technology, child study, and parent education were transferred to the GEB, RF, and a new fund, the Spelman Fund of New York (SF). The GEB was to continue LSRM's research in child development and socialization including parent education, but the focus was to be on adolescence and secondary education, beginning in 1927.[20]

The Rockefeller Foundation was internally reorganized in 1929 in order to assume new responsibilities. The Medical Education Division (organized in 1919) and the broader Division of Studies (organized in 1923) were collapsed into the Medical Science Division. A Natural Science Division was formed to carry on the work initiated by Rose's projects originally supported by the GEB. The Humanities Division was formed in recognition of Edwin Embree's and Abraham Flexner's argument that scholarship in these disciplines should be supported by Rockefeller philanthropies.[21] A Division of Social Science was created in order to carry out the development of the social sciences started by Beardsley Ruml and Lawrence K. Frank in the LSRM. The Division of Social Science also worked closely with the Rockefeller supported, but independent, Social Science Research Council (SSRC) that had been established in 1923 to promote the development of research in disciplines as diverse as psychology, sociology, economics, political science, geography, and anthropology. The Social Science Division was to continue to perfect applied social technologies and to professionalize experts in all forms of civic management. The Spelman Fund of New York was also a vehicle for this effort especially in the area of social technology.[22]

The reorganization precipitated a watershed in Rockefeller philanthropic leadership. In 1928 Flexner resigned. Wickliffe Rose reached mandatory retirement and also resigned from the presidency of the GEB. Trevor Arnett, secretary of the GEB between 1920 and 1924, succeeded Rose as president and at the same time joined the RF as a trustee. George Vincent, president of the Rockefeller Foundation from 1919 to 1929, retired, and Max Mason, who briefly directed the new Division of Natural Science (from 1928 to 1929), became president. Warren Weaver became director of the Division of Natural Science to replace Mason. Raymond B. Fosdick, who had been a trustee of the RF since 1921 and who had served as chairman of the Board of Trustees of the GEB, as well as advisor and friend of John D. Rockefeller Jr., succeeded Mason in 1932. In 1936 Fosdick became president of both the RF and GEB, positions he held until 1948.

Fosdick's tenure with Rockefeller philanthropies coincided with the optimistic and experimental 1920s where the social sciences in child-oriented research, parent education, and public administration were developed by the LSRM, while the GEB and RF explored alternative interpretations of educational studies, medical science, the humanities, and the natural sciences. The optimistic and experimental orientation of the 1920s turned to practical problems of survival and continuity in the early 1930s. While the reorientation was precipitated by the stock market crash of 1929, the problem was not interpreted as an economic one, but rather as evidence of unhealthy personal and cultural resistance to change. "This divergence between the natural sciences and social sciences, between machinery and control, between the kingdom of this world and kingdom of the spirit—this is where the hazard lies," declared Fosdick. "Science," he continued, "has exposed the paleolithic savage, masquerading in modern dress, to a sudden shift of environment which threatens to unbalance his brain.[23] In this view, social change had outstripped the capacity for human biological adaptation. Research needed to be applied to achieve practical solutions in restoring balance to the human psyche and thus to society in the face of change. Could the very mechanisms of change also be used as vehicles of restoration using new and expanding technologies for organizing and transmitting information through the radio, visual imagery, and faster means of printing newspapers, magazines, and other texts to a popular audience? This called for a new vision of the role of the humanities as encompassing all forms of exchange between human beings.

A MENTAL-HYGIENE MISSION FOR THE HUMANITIES

The arts and humanities were traditionally defined as "those studies that represent the accumulated heritage of mankind in literature, art and music." What if the humanities were not about accumulated knowledge so much as the contemporary exchange of knowledge? In 1929, Charles E. Merriam raised the question of the impact on social organization of different forms of communication. He asked: "What are the facts of the growth in extent and speed of communication and what social effects do this diffusion and invention produce?" Merriam went on to list what he meant by communication: "highways, automobiles, autobuses, steam locomotive passenger traffic, electric transportation, air travel and mail, moving pictures—news of the world, newspaper circulation, telephones, telegraphs, and radio."[24] The humanities in this view were to go beyond the contents of museums, libraries, parks, and theaters; literature, rhetoric, performance, and the academic study of related fields and texts. The new humanities in conjunction with the social sciences, and especially psychology, were to be concerned with the expansion of modes of interaction in order to save humanity from its own maladaptations.

William Fielding Ogburn, a leading quantitative sociologist at Columbia University and then at the University of Chicago after 1927, provided a theoretical analysis of the consequences of cultural imbalances in society, which he called "cultural lag."[25] Ogburn warned of an imbalance between the development of the natural sciences and social sciences where the normative sector of society lagged behind rapid changes in the technological and economic sectors. Ogburn argued that advances made in science created a gap between material developments and the capacity of social-control mechanisms to maintain continuity and order. New social-science knowledge was needed along with more sophisticated social-control agencies. The solution was to break down barriers between social disciplines so that they would become both more scientific and practical.[26] The support of Rockefeller philanthropy for the production of social and behavioral science competency was central to this mission.

Lawrence K. Frank likened cultural lag to an illness. He "pointed out that if nations had characters, then it made sense to think of society as the patient."[27] If the social body was in need of being cured, the cultural mechanisms that contribute to the development of the psychology of individuals and their collective behavior must be purged of maladjustments. The role of the new humanities was to facilitate mental health by teaching cultural tolerance as well as basic skills in communication and language. As new cultural interests and tastes developed, the "happiness of the individual and hence his (or her) value to society" would be enhanced. Individual satisfaction with life, it was thought, would be increased and conflicts decreased if individuals developed a "sympathetic point of view towards others through their vivid images of various national and social groups in contemporary society." This knowledge of the culture of others would promote self-understanding and better social relationships between individuals and groups.[28]

The stress on culture and cultural awareness utilized the language of anthropology in the social sciences but the stress on adjustment and socialization was grounded in child study, education, public health, psychology, and psychiatry. Training technicians in related fields to adjust maladaptations required social workers, psychologists, psychiatrists, and educators to work with children, adolescents, and adults in schools, clinics, and community

organizations. The arts and humanities were allies in the adjustment process. Adolescents in the transition from childhood to adulthood would
profit especially from a conscious use of the humanities to promote "an
objective attitude toward the self and that sympathetic interest in others that
is essential to the conduct of all human relations."[29]

STRATEGIES AND INTERSECTING
THEMES FOR ACTION IN THE 1930s

Areas of research and policy were addressed in a 1930 summer conference
held by the Policy and Programs Committee of the Social Science Research
Council.[30] A list of problem areas was created citing business and employment, international relations, urban life, personality and culture, and public
administration. It was recognized that these areas cut "athwart recognized
disciplines" in that they "represented areas of possible interest in scientific
research having to do with certain striking developments in our social system and emergence of fairly definite problems."[31] A Committee on Personality and Culture focused on "social types of personality," initiating research
on children and acculturalization, followed from the earlier work of Chicago
social scientist W. I. Thomas, funded originally by LSRM. A new orientation
in the humanities, it was thought, could further individual adjustment "by
giving an understanding of the cultural progress of the human race and appreciation of its achievements." The humanities were to "deepen the value
of daily life" and provide a "retreat from its exigencies."[32]

Another source of strategies for the 1930s came from the White House.
President Hoover asked the Rockefeller Foundation and the Social Science
Research Council to complete a survey and issue a report called *Recent Social
Trends* just before the stock market crash.[33] The RF appropriated $560,000
for the project with the SSRC as the fiscal agent and Edmund E. Day, a former chair of the Department of Economics at Harvard and dean of business
at the University of Michigan who became director of social sciences in the
RF in 1928, was given the leadership role with Sydnor M. Walker as his assistant. Lawrence K. Frank, formerly of LSRM, was given leave from the RF
from 1930 to 1931 to serve on the project as well. He later returned to the
GEB and its work with schools. Frank's chapter on childhood and youth in
the *Recent Social Trends* report stressed the plasticity of human nature and
the "growing belief in the possibility of directing and controlling social
life through the care and nurture of children." Walker, in her chapter on
"privately supported social work," argued for a "well-conceived" system of
public education where "public health, mental hygiene, eugenics and birth
control activities have potentialities for reducing dependency due to physical and mental disorder."[34]

When the *Recent Social Trends* report was conceptualized, the full impact of the stock market crash was not apparent but the escalating crisis of the Depression in the early 1930s heightened the pressure to find ways to turn the situation around. The subject of business cycles took on new meaning in a search for mechanisms of economic stabilization, but the roles of schools and family were also considered critical in terms of political stability. After the continuing fallout of the events of 1929, it became apparent that the present crisis struck at fundamental institutions and crossed with the most basic and evolving interests of Rockefeller philanthropy. One quarter of the labor force (some 13 million workers) was unemployed and by 1933 millions of families faced serious hardship.[35] The economic collapse and loss of jobs was felt as much by youth in their teens as by adult workers. Without the possibility of employment, adolescents who would have left school after the elementary grades continued their education in high schools that were unprepared for the rapid expansion of the student population. To make matters worse, the continuing students were considered intellectually and emotionally unfit for the advanced course work advocated by Abraham Flexner in his promotion of the humanities in the 1920s. A massive effort was needed to reconfigure high schools to meet changing demands. The Rockefeller boards joined in a concerted response to the crisis by initiating a general-education campaign directed at the reform of secondary education.

THE NEW GENERAL-EDUCATION CAMPAIGN, 1933–1941

In April 1933 the Rockefeller boards took up a mutual effort that envisioned their work as that of one body instead of three philanthropies. The General Education Board, the Spelman Fund, and the Rockefeller Foundation, including all of its four new divisions, were to work together. The "new" general education program was a massive undertaking to restore order to society through restructuring schools with attention to the emotional and social needs of the expanding teenage population now concentrated in high schools. The crisis demanded largess in Edmund E. Day's words, which echo Ogburn's vision of cultural lag: "Old beliefs are outmoded. New faiths must take their place. Meanwhile culture lags and individuals find no secure intellectual anchorage."[36] The major thrust of the project was built on L. K. Frank's child study and parenting demonstrations, and Ruml's experimentation with creating a technology or social science of public administration and control, which were now part of the Rockefeller Foundation and the Spelman Fund. The educational and public health focus of the early General Education Board and Sanitary Commission came together with the Rockefeller Foundation's long-term interests in psychiatry in medical science as well as its new-found concerns with applied knowledge derived from the humanities and the social sciences. The effort was to apply all of the previous research in interdisciplinary studies on human behavior to a kind of demonstration project using educational institutions as vehicles of advancement. Educating the next generation to be mentally healthy workers and citizens, it was argued, would ensure economic prosperity, political stability, and social harmony.

The new general-education program adopted a broad-based range of projects coordinated by the General Education Board, which had joint leadership with the Rockefeller Foundation and its divisions including the humanities and the social sciences. The Spelman Fund looked to the education of efficient and informed public managers and administrators. Both trajectories of the project required the handling and dissemination of data. Research was required on how new technologies could be used to socialize individuals and to organize social interactions in ways that would prevent economic and political disorder. As the political climate escalated with critiques of capitalism when the Depression continued on into the mid-to-late 1930s, controlling and shaping public opinion and social thought became essential, and Rockefeller philanthropies looked to expand and determine how to effectively use media technologies as educational tools.[37]

Edmund E. Day, as director of the Social Science Division of the Rockefeller Foundation, was also made director of general education in the General Education Board as coordinator of the general-education campaign.[38] When Day left the philanthropies in 1937 to become president of Cornell University, his assistant, Robert Havighurst, became the project director.[39] David Stevens and John Marshall in the Rockefeller Foundation Humanities Division were also responsible for the project and shared mutual appointments in the GEB and in the RF. Beardsley Ruml directed the Spelman Fund in public administration and Lawrence K. Frank, his former assistant in the LSRM, continued to work on child study and parent education through the GEB and the Spelman Fund.

Officers in the Rockefeller network of philanthropies had learned early on that direct intervention in social policy attracted controversy and that it was best to work through other established agencies. The new general-education program was put into action by funding projects conducted by the National Education Association (NEA), by the Progressive Education Association (PEA), by the American Council on Education (ACE), by the American Council of Learned Societies (ACLS), by the National Research Council (NRC), and by the Social Science Research Council (SSRC). The work also built on projects that were already underway. In 1930 the PEA began a study on college-entrance requirements and their articulation with the high school curriculum that seemed to echo Flexner's earlier interests in this area. A survey was conducted in 1931 to identify colleges that could potentially participate in a larger study. In 1932 the project became officially the Commission on the Relation between School and College. This commission and two other PEA commissions (the Commission on Secondary School Curriculum, and the Commission on Human Relations) joined the new general-education program with $1.622 million in Rockefeller grants. The most well-known experiment was the Eight-Year Study.

The Eight-Year Study was a longitudinal national project that investigated different forms of high school organizations and their efficacy. The outcome was to change the institution of the high school from one with a traditional academic mission to one with a popular mission that went beyond academics but could still articulate with universities and produce quality graduates. The study was to last eight years (from 1933 to 1941), hence the popular name. By 1933, 250 colleges willing to admit students who did not meet traditional qualifications had been identified. Thirty city systems of secondary education (the number was eventually reduced to twenty-nine) also agreed to participate by sending students with traditional credentials and some with unconventional qualifications for the longitudinal study. There were ten public schools or school systems.[40] There were thirteen private schools.[41] Six of the schools were laboratory schools affiliated with universities.[42] Half of the schools were identified as "shackled" in that they required students to take traditional precollege academic courses of study that emphasized memorization and expertise in the classics in a humanistic liberal-arts tradition. An equal group of schools were termed "unshackled" in that students in these schools to varying degrees adopted an untraditional or progressive curriculum and pedagogy. The colleges identified in the survey agreed to admit students from both shackled and unshackled schools so that their academic progress could be compared.

Concern over the monitoring of the records and data resulted in the establishment of a new working subgroup in 1934 called the Committee on Records and Reports under the direction of Ralph Tyler from the Bureau of Educational Research at Ohio State University. Researchers under Tyler came to be known as the "Evaluation Staff." In 1936 four college centers were selected to compare 150 graduates of cooperating schools with 150 graduates of noncooperating schools in a total of twenty-five colleges with 3,600 students. Tyler soon left Ohio State to succeed Charles Judd as chair of education at the University of Chicago, a move that elevated the prestige and visibility of the evaluation process.

With the input of $620,000 worth of Rockefeller support, the original 1930 project exceeded the purpose of the study to investigate the high school curriculum and college entrance: it became a way to demonstrate and actually change the structure and purpose of high school education. The more differentiated curriculum in the unshackled group was justified by the perception that not all students were mentally or emotionally suited for college attendance. The purpose of high school for those not destined for college was to create citizens and workers with good habits and healthy dispositions. The evaluation of the two types of schools was limited to students who did go on to colleges from both the shackled schools with its one college–oriented curriculum and the upper-level academic college-bound group in the unshackled high schools. The results were that the unshackled schools produced students equivalent or superior to shackled schools and that the more progressive the unshackled school were in terms of innovation, the more superior they were to traditional high schools.[43] The unshackled schools could successfully select and train superior students while they also served a more general and mundane student population. Shackled schools were much less flexible when faced with an expanded and more diverse student base where they had more difficulty meeting high standards. The results of the longitudinal aspect of the Eight-Year Study were published in five volumes between 1942 and 1951.[44] In spite of the poor timing of the first publications in the first year of World War II, the influences on secondary-school curricula were felt for more than two decades. Various forms of differentiated curriculum became a common feature of postwar high schools.

In the fall of 1933, the Commission on Secondary School Curriculum was established by the executive board of the PEA with a gift of $350,000 from the GEB. The purpose was to investigate the aims and objectives of the high school and college curriculum. V. T. Thayer of the Ethical Culture School was made chair. Thayer's research was concerned with the role of schooling in personality development and the significance of changes in pedagogical styles. In 1928 he wrote *The Passing of the Recitation*, a positive commentary on the superiority of lectures and active learning in the secondary school over the traditional recitation by students of memorized material.[45] After the stock market crash, Thayer became convinced that the schools were a significant factor in adjusting social change. "School functions," he wrote, "arise from changing conditions. As the community disintegrates and the home becomes confused, the school serves more and more as the focusing point for influences bearing upon the child. Upon it now rests the responsibility for developing the child's personality and for socializing the individual in the interests of the future. To meet this new responsibility the school itself is undergoing transformation."[46] Thayer's concerns were echoed by Edmund E. Day in a 1932 report.[47] The committee conducted a major survey of the secondary-school curriculum and literature that had identified innovative approaches to pedagogy and curriculum that might address changing schools in a changing world.

The Commission on Secondary Education identified major "personal-social needs" that they felt should be used to revitalize conventional courses. This included: (1) personal living issues such as health, self-assurance, workable philosophy of life, range of interests, and esthetic satisfaction; (2) personal-social relationship issues including mature relationships in the home and family, and with age mates of both sexes; (3) social-civic relationships in the need for responsible participation and social recognition; and (4) economic relationship in the need for emotional assurance of progress toward adult status, guidance in choosing an occupation, ability to choose goods and services, and the need for effective action in solving basic economic problems.[48] Suggestions for the curriculum might include budgeting in mathematics, human sexuality in biology, patterns of family life in world history, or careers in civics. The curriculum was also to cover broad topics rather than narrow subjects. English would replace grammar, spelling, or classical literature. History, geography, and civics were to be replaced by social studies. The Commission on Secondary Education recommended that learning be correlated around central themes within and among classes with cooperative planning between teachers. Courses should further parallel one another in schools and colleges—that is to fuse math and science, or social studies with English or a foreign language.

The idea of a core curriculum was stressed sometimes with either a special extra-long course or a main course called "general education," a "stem course," "basic course," or "core." Guidance and curriculum was blended into this course, which could be taught by a core teacher or teachers and could either be structured or unstructured. Core courses followed guidelines that closely resembled the "personal-social needs" framework so that students learned about themselves and living with others, as well as living in and understanding society. "Communication" is expressly noted as an important part of the core curriculum. Colleges were encouraged to experiment with interdisciplinary programs commonly identified with "the general education movement" to provide "integrative, common learning experiences that are significant to all students regardless of their fields of specialization.[49] Major publications came out in 1939 and 1940 that dealt with secondary curriculum and general education.[50]

Other groups that furthered the new general education project included the Committee on Human Development, funded with $220,000. The American Council on Education created the Committee of Twenty-one, which, with Rockefeller funding, provided $179,000 to study rural schools and programs of self-appraisal and evaluation. The American Youth Council was established under the American Council on Education in 1935 with a seven-year grant of $1.35 million to study specific problems of youth such as unemployment.

CHILD STUDY AND PARENT EDUCATION
WITH A FOCUS ON ADOLESCENTS

Adolescent research at the University of California, Berkeley, in conjunction with Oakland Public Schools, was one of the last child-study and parent-education projects negotiated by L. K. Frank funded through the LSRM in 1927. With the reorganization, Frank became director of GEB's child-development research with Robert J. Havighurst as his assistant. The research, which started with infants and young children, turned to adolescents. Research on adolescents fit well into the general-education program mandate to restructure secondary education through interdisciplinary studies. When Frank left the GEB, Havighurst assumed his role in the GEB, including the task of overlooking the adolescent studies in Berkeley. The Berkeley research was interdisciplinary. It utilized (1) the medical and natural sciences to study physical growth and mental health; (2) the social sciences to study behavior; and (3) the humanities to study ways to teach, learn, and understand social change and personal development.[51] Funding for this project not only survived the reorganization but continued to be supported though the Second World War ending in 1950.

The research identified and differentiated individuals in the twelve- to twenty-year-old school-age populations, who would have been in their early working years if the economy had been prosperous. This new extended school-age cohort was considered unstable and potentially a menace to social order. The prolongation of youth made it necessary to learn more about the physical and mental attributes of puberty and how to socialize the young so that they could best adapt to changing social and economic times. Robert J. Havighurst of the GEB and Alan Gregg, director of medical science in the RF, felt that the Berkeley and Oakland studies were a major contribution to knowledge on human development. The program sought to understand and manipulate the development of adolescents at a potentially unstable life stage. It also experimented with adult education and the use of media to teach parents, high school teachers, and administrators to understand the needs of this transitional age group. An aspect of the research was to study personality development in relation to culture and family life. Parents were interviewed and parent education was provided through study groups. NBC stations aired a radio program called *Unlimited Horizons*. The program used the longitudinal case studies conducted during the research and "glamorized" them in order to create object lessons.[52]

The GEB extended support for the Berkeley-related projects to midcentury in order to complete the compilation and analysis of data. Disseminating research findings became an increasingly dominant portion of the continued appropriations from 1938 to 1950.[53] In 1938 Havighurst sent a memo to RF president Raymond Fosdick requesting $6,000 to publish the Berkeley data.[54] Four thesis and two monograph series, including six publications, eleven articles, and seven other abstracts or papers from the Institute research were published from this fund.[55] Additional funds produced a *Yearbook on Adolescence*, and Herbert Stoltz's and Lois Meek Stoltz's work on adolescent growth titled, *Somatic Development in Adolescent Boys*.[56] Popular books were published through the Child Development Monograph Series. Journals provided advice to the public as well as to a variety of professionals in education, medicine, psychiatry, and the social sciences.[57]

In 1943 the GEB funded a Center of Documentation and Collaboration for the Study of Human Development and Behavior at the University of Chicago to collect all of the research on human development from infancy to old age. Robert J. Havighurst joined the Chicago faculty in 1941 to co-ordinate the center.[58] The Center for Documentation and Collaboration also continued the work of the Commission on Teacher Education of the American Council on Education that had been set up with GEB funds in 1938 with a grant of $250,000.[59]

USING THE HUMANITIES TO
EDUCATE FOR HUMAN RELATIONS

In the mid-1930s the humanities were intimately seen as responsible for defining American character and culture. The personality and culture field of concentration elevated the concept of "national character" in the mid-1930s. In 1934 and 1935, the general-education campaign supported Conferences on Human Relations.[60] The Commission on Human Relations was formed under the auspices of the Progressive Education Association headed by Alice Keliher. With a grant of $223,670 the group wrote books to address "the adolescent in terms of his personal and social problems." The commission also experimented with literature, drama, and film as educational tools. The Motion Picture Project made arrangements with Hollywood to portray human experiences and to "illustrate points of tension in human living, such as problems of the family, marriage, individual adjustment to life, group relations, and the relationship of the individual to society." Sixty-eight such films were made by 1939.[61]

Half a million dollars were spent in the production of films for educational purposes in the general-education program. Radio broadcasting had been an experiment of the parent-education program of LSRM in the 1920s and it continued to be an area of interest and possibility. The General Education Program directed $370,000 toward four educational radio projects. All of the funds went to projects that originated independently of the Foundations. The largest sum went to the very successful school broadcast *Ohio School of the Air* at Ohio State University, which first aired in 1929. The university hosted an annual Institute for Education by Radio in 1930 that brought together commercial broadcasters with academics interested in educational broadcasting. The University of Wisconsin initiated the first university-based radio station in 1916 and developed the Wisconsin School of the Air in 1931 and a Wisconsin College of the Air in 1933. The third group to receive funds was the Cleveland Board of Education efforts to use local stations to broadcast to public schools in the area.[62] The PEA, which had first shown an interest in radio in 1919, was also funded in radio to complement its active film project. The GEB in its 1936–1937 *Annual Report* hailed educational research projects in radio as a wave of the future but enthusiasm waned as radio took on other roles as war approached.[63] A series of grants to the World Wide Broadcasting Foundation was intended to support educational radio ventures such as a shortwave station in Boston with call letters W1XAL (changed to WRUL in 1938). The station was seized in 1942 for national defense purposes and was used to broadcast the *Voice of America*. The station resumed private broadcasting after the war. Other projects in radio were supported in Chicago and the Rocky Mountain Radio Council in Colorado and Wyoming.[64] The interdisciplinary, interboard General Education Program of the Rockefeller philanthropies in the late 1930s supported a variety of media including broadcasting, motion picture(s), music, drama, and handicrafts. Nearly $1 million was spent to advance communications projects in colleges and universities prior to the end of the program in 1940.[65] It furthered the work of institutions of common interests with schools and colleges devoted to public education such as museums and libraries. The program not only funded the traditional text as a form of communication but also addressed "special techniques" in printing and the creation of illustrated educational materials for school-age children, college, and university programs, as well as adult educators from parents to teachers and administrators.[66]

CONCLUSION: IMPLICATIONS FOR THE FIELD OF COMMUNICATION STUDIES

In 1939 and 1940, a series of seminars were held with Rockefeller support with the objective of establishing a new discipline to systematically study the dynamics and uses of the new technologies of mass communication. Communication, the fourth stage of the social sciences, encompassed the language arts of the humanities as a way to study and appease human nature and to reconcile it with social change. This effort to heal society through personality adjustment to culture as an aspect of mental health led to direct support for a fledgling new field in communications in the 1940s.

Communications in its earliest sense was part of the new secondary general-education campaign. The concern with child development turned toward human development in the form of using the media to inform the public and to shape mass views on issues central to the business of the state. This became more critical as war overtook Europe and engulfed the United

States in 1942. Communication took the form of intelligence for the military and propaganda for the people. To make these efforts successful, it was necessary to create experts well beyond the level of the original Rockefeller-family publicist Ivy Lee with his insight that the media of communication should be manipulated to shape public opinion while fundamental social issues were addressed. The social sciences and humanities as constituted did not address the process of how to understand the efficacy of different ways to manipulate the media, produce and transmit information for specific purposes to a range of audiences. The early experiments with secondary education did not grow as fast as the need for persuasion and propaganda for public consumption, which included manipulation and pacification in shaping leisure time. After the war the use of media such as motion pictures, broadcasting in radio and television, as it became commonly and personally available on a widespread basis, became even a larger concern for philanthropists, researchers, and government officials. The media continued the general-education agenda of the 1930s in creating the image of the postwar baby boom child and the new teenager in the 1950s. Along with the advance of media and mass communication was the study of the phenomena itself as a field of study.

NOTES

Unpublished material in this chapter has been quoted courtesy of the Rockefeller Archive Center, Sleepy Hollow, New York.

1. Raymond B. Fosdick, *The Story of the Rockefeller Foundation* (New York: Harpers & Brothers Publishers, 1952), 237.

2. William J. Buxton, "Reaching Human Minds: Rockefeller Philanthropy and Communications, 1935–1939," in *The Development of the Social Sciences in the United States and Canada: The Role of Philanthropy*, eds. Theresa Richardson and Donald Fisher (Stamford, CT: Ablex Publishers, 1999), 177–92.

3. Theresa Richardson, "The Rockefeller Boards: The Organization of Philanthropies and the Origins of the Social Sciences," in Richardson and Fisher, *The Development of the Social Sciences*, 37–58.

4. The Laura Spelman Rockefeller Memorial's (hereafter LSRM) total expenditure from 1918 to 1928 was $4,907,235.85. "LSRM Appropriations, Social Service and Welfare," October 18, 1918 to April 30, 1928. Rockefeller Archive Center (hereafter RAC), Rockefeller Foundation Archives (hereafter RF), Record Group (hereafter RG) 3, Series 910, Box 2, Folder 11.

5. Peter Collier and David Horowitz, *The Rockefellers: An American Dynasty* (New York: Holt, Rinehart & Winston, 1976), 143.

6. L. K. Frank, "Memorandum, Research in Social Science," 26 April, 1924. RAC, LSRM, Series II, Box 2, Folder 22.

7. Committee Review of Social Science, Lawrence K. Frank author, "The Status of Social Science in the United States, 1919–1920," Report 22. RAC, LSRM Series III, Subseries 6, Box 63, Folder 679. Frank, trained as an economist with a doctorate from Columbia University, served as business manager of the New School for Social Research in New York City before becoming affiliated with Rockefeller philanthropy. His interests in social science tended toward social psychology. His fascination with the problems of childhood reflected his mentors at Columbia, Wesley C. Mitchell, and his wife, Lucy Sprague Mitchell, an innovative educator and pioneer in community laboratory schools and the child-study movement in New York.

8. "Memorial Policy, Social Sciences, Extracts," October 1922. Spelman Fund of New York (hereafter SFNY), Series II, Box 3, Folder 108.

9. "Memorial Policy, Social Sciences, Extracts"; "Social Science–Library Assistance, 8 October, 1918 to 30 April, 1928." RAC, RF, RG 3, Series 910, Box 2, Folder 11.

10. Theresa Richardson, *The Century of the Child: The Mental Hygiene Movement and Social Policy in the United States and Canada* (Albany: SUNY Press, 1989), 129.

11. Sidonie Gruenberg, "The Child Study Association of America: Its Organization and Methods." RAC, LSRM Series III, Subseries 5, Box 27, Folder 284.

12. "Child Study Association of America, Inc., Summary of the Season's Activities, 1924–1925." RAC, LSRM Series III, Subseries 5, Box 27, Folder 285.

13. May Pardee Youtz, "Iowa State Program of Parent Education." RAC, LSRM Series III, Subseries 5, Box 27, Folder 284.

14. "Memoranda from the Old Man Butterick, Johns Hopkins Hospital, 17 January, 1924." RAC, GEB Series I, Subseries 2, Box 331, Folder 3485.

15. Raymond B. Fosdick, *Adventures in Giving: The Story of the General Education Board* (New York: Harper & Row, 1962), 226, 229.

16. Thomas Neville Bonner, *Iconoclast: Abraham Flexner and a Life in Learning* (Baltimore: Johns Hopkins University Press, 2002), 194–95, 198–99.

17. Bonner, *Iconoclast*, 194.

18. Anson Phelps Stokes to Abraham Flexner, 9 April, 1927, GEB files, quoted in Fosdick, *The Rockefeller Foundation*, 239; also Fosdick, *Adventures in Giving*, 235–39.

19. B. Ruml and R. M. Pearce, "Report of the Committee on the Interboard Conference, on Mental Hygiene, Psychology, and Psychiatry," India House, University of California Berkeley, 1 p.m., 18 December, 1925. RAC, RF, RG 3, Series 906, Box 2, Folder 17, Program and Policy Psychiatry, 1916–1940.

20. A program begun in 1927 centered at the University of California, Berkeley and the city of Oakland was followed by Lawrence K. Frank, as head of child-development research in the GEB, and Robert J. Havighurst, his assistant, a new officer in the GEB who had previously worked with Raymond B. Fosdick.

21. "Memorandum on the Conference at Gedney Farms, 10–11 October, 1924." RF files, quoted in Fosdick, *The Story of the Rockefeller Foundation*, 238.

22. See Division of the Rockefeller Foundation 1913–1984, Rockefeller Archive Center Source Materials, RAC.

23. Quoted from an interview with Raymond B. Fosdick in Daniel J. Kevles, *The Physicists: The History of a Scientific Community in Modern America* (New York: Knopf, 1978), 249, fn9.

24. Charles E. Merriam, "The Growth of Communication," transmitted by Wesley Mitchell to President Herbert Hoover, 21 October, 1929. *Report of the President's Committee on Social Change*, 6. RAC, RF, RG 1.1, Series 200, Box 326, Folder 3873.

25. William Fielding Ogburn, *Social Change with Respect to Culture and Original Nature* (New York: B. W. Heubsch, 1922).

26. Ogburn, *Social Change*. Also on cultural lag see Donald Fisher, *Fundamental Development of the Social Sciences: Rockefeller Philanthropy and the United States Social Science Research Council* (Ann Arbor: University of Michigan Press, 1993) 39, 44; Donald Fisher, "A Matter of Trust: Rockefeller Philanthropy and the Creation of the Social Science Research Councils in the United States and Canada," in Richardson and Fisher, *The Development of the Social Sciences*, 82–83; Hans Pols, "The World as Laboratory: Strategies of Field Research Developed By Mental Hygiene Psychologists in Toronto, 1920–1940," in Richardson and Fisher, *The Development of the Social Sciences*, 118, 130.

27. Quoted in Ellen Herman, *The Romance of American Psychology: Political Culture in the Age of Experts* (Berkeley: University of California Press, 1995), 35.

28. Herman, *Romance of American Psychology*, 35.

29. Herman, *Romance of American Psychology*, 35. See also Dennis Raymond Bryson, *Socializing the Young: The Role of Foundations, 1923–1941* (Westport, CT: Bergen & Garvey, 2002); and Richardson, *The Century of the Child*.

30. Robert Lynd to Sydnor Walker, 18 March, 1930, SSRC Summer Conference, 1930. RAC, RF, RG 1.1, Series 200, Folder 407 and Series 200S, Folder 4812.

31. "Staff Conference," 3 October, 1930, Program and Policy 1929–1930, 2–3. RAC, RF, RG 3, Series 910, Folder 1.

32. "Arts and Humanities." RAC, GEB Series I, Subseries 3, Box 363, Folder 3740 (see also Folders 3741, 3742, 3743).

33. Fisher, *Fundamental Development of the Social Sciences*, 101.

34. *Recent Social Trends in the United States; Report of the President's Research Committee on Social Trends*, vol. 2 (New York: McGraw-Hill, 1933), 752, 1223.

35. *Recent Social Trends*, vol. 2, 124; Arthur M. Schlesinger Jr., *The Crisis of the Old Order* (Boston: Houghton Mifflin, 1957); Arthur M. Schlesinger Jr., *The Coming of the New Deal* (Boston: Houghton Mifflin, 1959).

36. E. E. Day, "Cultural Adjustment to a Changing World," Draft Section of the Summary Report, 5 October, 1932, 2. RAC, GEB Series I, Subseries 3, Box 363, Folder 3742.

37. Wilber Schramm, *The Beginnings of Communication Study in America* (Thousand Oaks, CA: Sage Publications, 1977), 135.

38. E. E. Day to General Education Board Trustees, "Preliminary Report of the Program in General Education, 26 December," cited in Raymond B. Fosdick, *Adventures in Giving: The Story of the General Education Board* (New York: Harper & Row, 1962), 242–43.

39. Fosdick, *Adventures in Giving*, 242–43. Havighurst was trained in the natural sciences but became interested in education after teaching at the Laboratory School of Ohio State University.

40. Denver, Des Moines, and Tulsa. The single public schools included Altoona Senior High School in Pennsylvania; Bronxville High School in New York; Cheltenham Township High School in Illinois; Eagle Rock High School in Los Angeles; New Trier Township High School (Winnetka, Illinois); Radnor High School in Pennsylvania; and Shaker High School (Shaker Heights, Ohio).

41. Dalton of New York City; Francis W. Parker in Chicago; John Burroughs in St. Louis; and Tower Hill in Wilmington, Delaware.

42. Lincoln School and Horace Mann Schools of Teachers College, Columbia; the University of Chicago High School; the University of California's University High School in Oakland, California; the University School of Ohio State University; and the Wisconsin High School of the University of Wisconsin. Edward A. Krug, *The Shaping of the American High School, 1920–1941* (Madison: University of Wisconsin Press, 1972), 134–35.

43. Krug, *The Shaping of the American High School*, 259–60.

44. Dean Chamberlin et al., *Did they Succeed in College?* (New York: Harper & Brothers, 1942); Eugene Smith and Vivian T. Thayer, *Appraising and Recording Student Progress* (New York: Harper & Brothers, 1942); Dean Chamberlin et al., *Thirty Schools Tell Their Story* (New York: Harper & Brothers, 1943); Wilford M. Aikens, *The Story of the Eight-Year Study with Conclusions and Recommendations* (New York: Harper & Brothers, 1943); also see Frederick L. Redefer, "The Eight-Year Study: Eight Years Later," (EdD dissertation, Columbia University, 1951).

45. Vivian T. Thayer, *The Passing of the Recitation* (New York: Heath, c1928).

46. Vivian T. Thayer, "School and the Shifting Home," *Survey* 64 (1 September, 1930): 457, 486.

47. E. E. Day, "Cultural Adjustment to a Changing World," Draft of Summary Report, 5 October, 1932, 2. RAC, GEB Series I, Subseries 3, Box 363, Folder 3742.

48. Gordon F. Vars, "Curriculum in Secondary Schools and Colleges," in Association for Supervision and Curriculum Development (ASCD) 1972 Yearbook Committee, *A New Look at Progressive Education* (Washington, DC: ASCD, 1972), 233–55.

49. Vars, "Curriculum in Secondary Schools," 242–43.

50. Vivian T. Thayer, Caroline B. Zackery, and Ruth Kotinsky, *Reorganizing Secondary Education* (New York: D. Appleton-Century, 1939); Committee on the Function of English in General Education, *Language in General Education* (New York: D. Appleton-Century, 1940).

51. "Memorandum, Robert J. Havighurst to Robert B. Fosdick, 13 May, 1938." RAC, GEB 930, Series I, Subseries 3, Box 374, Folder 3910.

52. "Interview Memoranda to Flora Rhind from Harold E. Jones, 2 July 1942." RAC, GEB 930, Series I, Subseries 3, Box 375, Folder 3914.

53. R. J. Havighurst, "Memo Concerning the Guidance Study at the University of California," 19 January, 1938; W. W. Brierley to R. Sproul (president of the University of California) 16 December, 1938; R. J. Havighurst, "Publication of Results of Research at the California Institute of Child Welfare," 22 December, 1938. RAC, GEB 930, Series I, Subseries 3, Box 374, Folder 3911; R. J. Havighurst to E. Tolman (dean of education at the University of California, Berkeley), 9 September, 1940. RAC, GEB 930, Series I, Subseries 3, Box 375, Folder 3912.

54. R. J. Havighurst, "Publication of Results of Research at the California Institute of Child Welfare," 22 December, 1938. RAC, GEB 930, Series I, Subseries 3, Box 374, Folder 3911.

55. Jean W. MacFarlane, "Statement of Objectives, Points of View," 26 October, 1938. RAC, GEB 930, Series I, Subseries 3, Box 374, Folder 3911.

56. Stoltz's *Yearbook* was subsidized with a publication grant of $5,000 cited under "Grants-in-Aid to I 48049"; F. M. Rhind, "Interview with Harold Jones, re: Publication Yearbook," 4 May, 1943, and outline of "Yearbook on Adolescence." RAC, GEB 930, Series I, Subseries 3, Box 374, Folder 3911.

57. R. J. Havighurst, "Publication of Results of Research at the California Institute of Child Welfare," 22 December, 1938. RAC, GEB 930, Series I, Subseries 3, Box 374, Folder 3911.

58. F. M. Rhind, "Request from Dr. Tyler for Continued Support of the University of Chicago's Center of Documentation and Collaboration for the Study of Human Development and Behavior," 5 January, 1943; R. Hutchins to F. M. Rhind, 8 April, 1943; W. W. Brierly to R. Hutchins, 11 December, 1943; F. M. Rhind, "Interview of Chicago Child Development Center Collaborators, D. A. Prescott, and R. J. Havighurst," 17 November, 1943, 23 July, 1943, 16 August, 1943; R. J. Havighurst to F. M. Rhind, 11 October, 1943. RAC, GEB 930, Series I, Subseries 3, Box 375, Folder 3920. Also see Alice B. Smuts, "The National Research Council on Child Development, 1925–1933," in *History and Research in Child Development*, eds. A. B. Smuts and John W. Hagen, Monographs of the SRDC, Series No. 211, Vol. 50, Nos. 4–5 (1985): 108–25.

59. "Inter-University Collaboration to Further Research in Child Development and Behavior and to Extend the Use of Research Findings in the Education of Professional Persons." 15 March, 1944. RAC, GEB 930, Series I, Subseries 3, Box 375, Folder 3920.

60. "Aims and Objectives of a Course in Human Relations," and "Report on Study of Human Relations." RAC, GEB 930, Series I, Subseries 3, Box 376, Folder 3930. "Conference on Human Relations," August 1935, Report and Summary of Conference Proceedings, cited in Dennis R. Bryson, *Socializing the Young: The Role of Foundations* (Westport, CT: Bergen & Garvey, 2002), 177.

61. General Education Board, "Progressive Education Association—Commission on Human Relations Preparation of Teaching Materials," November 1940, two reports and list of publications. RAC, GEB Series I, Subseries 2, Box 283, Folder 2957; General Education Board, "Progressive Education Association—Motion Picture Project," Draft, January 1940, 1. RAC, GEB Series I, Subseries 2, Box 284, Folder 2962.

62. William J. Buxton, "GEB Support for School-Broadcasting Projects, 1937–1942," *Research Reports of the Rockefeller Archive Center* (Winter 2004): 8–14.

63. General Education Board, *Annual Report for the Year 1936–1937* (New York: General Education Board, 1937).

64. Fosdick, *The Story of the Rockefeller Foundation*, 245–46.

65. Theresa M. Richardson and E. V. Johanningmeier, "Educational Radio, Childhood, and Philanthropy: A New Role for the Humanities in Popular Culture, 1924–1941," *Journal of Radio and Audio Media* 13, no. 1 (2006): 1–18.

66. Rockefeller Foundation, "New Programs in the Humanities, April 10, 1935, ii." RAC, RF, RG 3, Series 911, Box 2, Folder 10; on radio and film see William J. Buxton, "Reaching Human Minds: Rockefeller Philanthropy and Communications, 1935–1939," in Richardson and Fisher, *The Development of the Social Sciences*, 177–92; on the use of educational films on children in Canada, see Brian J. Low, *NFB Kids: Portrayals of Children by the National Film Board of Canada, 1939–1989* (Waterloo, ON: Wilfrid Laurier University Press, 2002); and Brian J. Low, "The Hand that Rocked the Cradle: A Critical Analysis of Rockefeller Foundation Funding, 1920–1960," unpublished manuscript.

4

Communication Practice and Theory in the "New Humanities" and "New General-Education" Programs of Rockefeller Philanthropy, 1933–1940

William J. Buxton

REALIGNMENT AND SOCIAL CONTROL

During the late 1920s, Rockefeller philanthropy consolidated some of its major concerns into five Divisions (Medical Science, International Health, Natural Science, Social Science, and Humanities) of the expanded Rockefeller Foundation (RF). The new divisional structure suggested what long-time Rockefeller Secretary Frederick T. Gates would have called "scatteration." But the intent of the change was to bring about a "structural unity" to the various areas of Rockefeller philanthropic interest. As newly elected Foundation president Max Mason described the reorientation to the Board of Directors in the 1930s: "It was not to be five programs, each represented by a division of the Foundation; it was essentially one program, directed to the general problem of human behavior, with the aim of control through understanding."[1] This realignment was followed by a period of deliberation, during which each Division's goals and priorities were reformulated. The small and modestly funded Humanities Division was particularly affected by this reorganization.

As part of a thoroughgoing review, a "committee of three" on "appraisal and plan" was struck to examine the purpose and future direction of the various Rockefeller boards. In its section on the Humanities Division (HD), the committee implicitly criticized the "cloistered kind of research" that the Humanities Division had previously supported. This shift of emphasis "toward greater effect on contemporary society," meant a fundamental reorientation for the humanities program. Rather than focusing on "a few highly trained scholars as interpreters of the past," officers were to now take into account "those men and methods able to influence contemporary taste in large masses of population." Given that drama, film, radio, and popular print—"the obvious sources of influence on public taste of today"—are mediums of slight interest to scholars, the officers were to be "released from relations with much of the scholarly world. . . . Their new contacts were to be with men outside universities and colleges." By virtue of this shift toward the new communication media, the HD would help to find better means for reaching the public more effectively.[2] These concerns dovetailed with the "general education" movement in the 1930s, the concern of which was the "education of the great masses of people for life in a democracy, as distinct from the transmission of tradition to a small elite."[3]

The interest of the HD in communications embodied the overall concern with social control that underpinned the "structural unity" of the Rockefeller Foundation divisional realignment. The Medical Science Division, as its director Alan Gregg wrote in his annual report of 1932, was to "give special attention . . . to the field of psychiatry . . . and in general the whole field of psychobiology [which] may be immensely fruitful and [in which] further knowledge will be highly valuable."[4] Particular attention was given to the field of neurology, as it was held that through understanding and control of the nervous system "physical pain and mental stress" could be relieved. Similarly, the Division of Natural Science, in the hope of Max Mason, was to "shed new and revealing light on man and his problems of the mind."[5] In the same way that the Natural Science and Medical Science Divisions were to address issues of control in relation to the mind, the nervous system, and the microbiological processes of the human body, the Humanities Division was to turn its attention to how minds were reached and controlled externally, through the intricate web of communications. In this sense, the HD's concern with the cultural and communicative aspects of control was to complement the social or "human relations" aspects of control that had become the mandate of the Social Sciences Division under the direction of E. E. Day. The Humanities Division worked in tandem with the General Education Board, the area of concern of which overlapped to a considerable extent with that of the HD.[6]

This coordination of tasks was simplified by the fact that John Marshall, in addition to holding the position of assistant director for the humanities in the Rockefeller Foundation, was also assistant director in general education on the General Education Board.[7] Under the leadership of David Stevens (who was director of the HD as well as director of general education within the GEB) and Marshall, the HD began to encourage projects that helped to "reach human minds" with the "realities of the highest value to civilization," namely, "man's spiritual and intellectual experiences."[8] This was part of a general trend of "widening the area of public appreciation," and supporting work "with more direct applications to present-day needs."[9] This involved a shift away from the earlier program of support for the humanities, which was largely directed toward the traditional fields of inquiry within the universities, namely, the "seven major areas of knowledge and human experience—linguistics, literature, art, music, archaeology, religion, philosophy, and various phases of history."[10] In the view of the Rockefeller officers, "by holding to the traditions of polite learning and exact scholarship, humanistic scholars have kept their disciplines away from active life." Indeed, in their obsession with fact, and by eschewing interpretation and ignoring "their application of knowledge for social benefit," scholars of this persuasion "have hindered the normal growth of human thought and feeling." This limitation was rooted in the organization of universities into disciplines, of which the "modes of operation and their choices of material were determined by scholars of narrow social interests." Hence, "the old belief in a need to protect the fundamentals of tradition still dominates university disciplines so strongly that contemporary forces for humanistic development make slow progress in our institutions." In embracing antiquarianism, "the humanities miss their sole function to make mankind more humane by promoting the culture of the general mind."[11]

THE HD/GEB PROGRAM IN COMMUNICATION

The new program in the humanities (dovetailing with the new general-education program) not only represented a shift in content, it also marked a radical change in the process through which programs were chosen, developed, and monitored. Under the old system, funds were dispensed to trusted representatives of the elite universities that had been selected in consultation with the American Council of Learned Societies (ACLS). These representatives, in turn, decided which projects at their universities (most often their own) would be funded. However, with the onset of the new program in the humanities, Rockefeller officers—particularly Marshall and Stevens—were given enormous discretion in choosing programs to be supported, setting the criteria for their assessment, and determining their extent and duration. Moreover, by virtue of their capacity to select and oversee numerous projects simultaneously, they were able to give shape and direction to a variety of subfields, by encouraging grant recipients to interact, exchange ideas, and engage in common endeavors. The officers not only helped to secure funding for projects they considered to be worthy, they were also actively engaged in building communities of thinkers and practitioners who came to share similar goals and values as participants in the Rockefeller-sponsored initiatives.

The combined communications programs of the HD and the GEB encompassed a broad range of initiatives, practices, and research projects, including support for meetings, fellowships, publications, and research projects. Despite the strictures against involving itself in propaganda and direct political and social intervention, Rockefeller philanthropy was used to support media production. What is particularly striking about the Rockefeller programs in communication is that they were not confined to conventional media or mass communications, but comprised a variety of institutions and practices that were considered to be inherently communicative in nature. As these concerns were outlined in a planning document,

> The search for more direct ways of extending the area of public appreciation called for assistance from persons with intimate knowledge of the ways in which the American public now gains its culture. Such help was enlisted for reports on broadcasting, motion picture [sic], music, drama, and handicrafts: on institutions of community influence, as museums and libraries: and on special techniques used in printing and illustrating educational materials for adult groups.[12]

Specifically, the new program in the humanities prominently featured motion pictures and radio as the two key areas that were to be given emphasis. As John Marshall noted in a memorandum,

> Both radio and motion pictures are recognized as instrumentalities potentially of great importance alike for formal education and for the general diffusion of culture. But they have so far been exploited for the most part for purposes of entertainment. Since this exploitation has been commercial, the effort has been to entertain as large a section of the public as possible. The vested interests [do not take] chances with anything that does not have demonstrated "entertainment value" for the public at large. The result is . . . that the possibilities of radio and motion pictures have been explored only within a relatively narrow range.[13]

Marshall suggested that as long as explorations about radio and motion pictures took place within a commercial framework, their full possibilities could not be realized. What he proposed, then, was the need for "a period of experimental development" in order to "work out new techniques appropriate to purposes other than entertainment."[14] At the same time, Marshall by no means proposed that the HD should only support work in communications outside of the commercial framework. This ambivalence about commercial media characterized the HD programs in communication. While the projects it supported primarily took the commercial system as its point of reference, it also encouraged forms of "experimental development," which involved initiatives that departed from private-profit assumptions. Taken as a whole, the HD-funded ventures in the area of radio and film had as their aim the strengthening of the educational component, both inside and outside of the commercial sector.

It is evident from Marshall's comments—and those of other Rockefeller officers—that radio and film, as new media, were considered to play a vanguard role within the communications sector. With their penchant for innovation, they not only represented the possibility that change could take place within other cultural institutions, but they also offered the technical means that could be adapted to change the institutions in question. In particular, two of the "old" cultural institutions that had previously been well funded by Rockefeller philanthropy—namely, libraries and museums— were thought to be ripe for transformation drawing on the insights from the new media.[15] For the library program of the HD—which was primarily internationalist in nature—this meant an emphasis on microphotography, with a view to improving the storage, cataloging, and circulation of library materials. It also involved helping libraries become more proficient in dealing with audiovisual materials and to assist them in developing the means to organize and exchange this form of new media. Along the same lines, museums were considered by Rockefeller officers to be bastions of conservative thinking, which limited their ability to communicate to a mass public. Accordingly, pilot programs were supported that emphasized the development of new approaches of display and organization, drawing on advertising and the use of storylines to make museum exhibitions more accessible to visitors. Finally, both museums and libraries were increasingly considered to be sites where both radio and film could be deployed effectively to educate the mass public. Paralleling these developments in film, radio, libraries, and museums, the drama program—largely in the hands of David Stevens—sought to revitalize and enrich noncommercial theater by drawing on insights from the new media as well as through technical innovation in areas such as lighting and the use of photography.

Finally, the new program in the humanities not only emphasized communication in terms of particular media and institutions, but also as a broader method with an inherently international dimension. Hence, attention was given to "the need for an international language, language as the gateway to the far east, and interchange of materials in print." Concretely, this meant facilitating cultural exchange as well as supporting the efforts of C. K. Ogden to develop Basic English.[16] Overall, the two elements of practice and theory were ever present, the solid scholarly knowledge complementing the new practically based knowledge.

Beginning in 1935, the HD and GEB between them supported numerous ventures in communication centered on radio and film. These included not only well-known ventures such as the Princeton Radio Research Project and the Museum of Modern Art film library but also largely unrecognized initiatives such as the Evaluation of School Broadcasting project (ESB) at

Ohio State University and the American Film Center (AFC) in New York City. Moreover, the HB and GEB provided numerous fellowships for promising practitioners and researchers to hone their skills at venues such as NBC, CBS, the BBC, and the Brooklyn Museum. In addition to providing financial support for these various projects, the HD and the GEB also encouraged those who were receiving funding to meet with one another to exchange ideas. This effort by the HD-GEB to create a new community of practitioners was not confined to the United States. Marshall made full use of his biannual visits to the United Kingdom during the 1930s to encourage greater contact between American and British media figures with a view to forging a transatlantic cultural network.[17]

TOWARD GREATER INTEGRATION

In the late 1930s, there was a move to go beyond interaction toward integration with the emphasis upon organized multilateral meetings of interested parties in order to develop emergent communities of shared interests. This included conferences such as those on educational broadcasting,[18] on speech in radio and film,[19] and two conferences on the interpretation of the natural sciences for the general public.[20] In each case, those involved in similar ventures were brought together with a view to developing a coherent approach to the issue at hand.

Perhaps the best known of these endeavors developed out of the HD's efforts to give coherence and direction to the Princeton Radio Research Project. Marshall's lack of confidence in the administration of the Project had led him to consult with Robert Lynd, professor of sociology at Columbia University, who had been closely involved with the Project since its inception. It was Lynd's view that the director of the Project, Paul F. Lazarsfeld, needed to be "held to a *defined* program" and to be given more explicit "sailing orders."[21] The "sailing orders" materialized in the form of a series of seminars, which began in September 1939 and continued until June 1940. The purpose of the seminars was to channel Lazarsfeld's research along more systematic lines. Marshall recalled:

> We felt that Lazarsfeld's research for the first period was admirable, but that it was scattered and unfocused. With Lazarsfeld's agreement we therefore subjected him to a day's examination. We had a group of people and we sort of cross-examined Lazarsfeld all that day, trying to get him to define some focus for his work in the next period of his work. While we did get Lazarsfeld to agree to certain foresight to what he would go on to do, the work was still in a conceptual muddle. There was no sharpness to it whatsoever. So we came to agree in the spring of 1939 that we should hold this series of meetings at monthly intervals throughout the coming academic year.[22]

The first meetings of the committee took place on September 20 and 23, 1939. Dubbed the "Communications Group," it would subsequently meet on a regular basis throughout the academic year. These meetings led to the production of numerous memoranda, commentaries, and working papers, culminating in two summary documents, "Research in Mass Communications,"[23] and "Needed Research in Communications."[24]

Perhaps the most notable contribution of the seminar—as a number of commentators have pointed out—was to systematize "the job of research in mass communications,"namely "to learn what mass communications do in our society." This involved "getting evidence with which to answer four basic questions":

> What they do became a question of what effects do mass communications as a whole, or any single communication, have. What effects they have likewise inescapably involved discovering to whom what was said. How these effects occurred necessitated analysis of what was said. And that analysis . . . required answers to a fourth and final question—who said it and with what intention. In brief, then, the job of research in mass communications is to determine who, and with what intention, said what, to whom, and with what effects.[25]

This formula became well known through Harold Lasswell's use of it in an article written in the postwar period.[26] As such, it has become a standard point of reference for defining how research can or should be conducted in the field of communications. However, while it has been recognized that the formula was likely expressed for the first time in the communication seminar of 1939–1940, what has largely gone unexamined is the extent to which the formula was grounded in the HD-GEB program in communication during the period from 1933 to 1945. Arguably, the formula was more than simply a guide to research in mass communications; it articulated the emergent network of communications that the HD-GEB had sought to cultivate, beginning with the new programs in the humanities and general education launched in the early 1930s. In effect, the role of the "central agency" called for by the Communication Group was already being played by the HD-GEB directorship. In the same way that the new agency "was [to assign] responsibility, ensure the comparability of findings, and their pooling in some central formulation and reporting,"[27] the officers of the HD-GEB had sought to give direction and coherence to the emergent field of communication, with particular emphasis upon the generation and circulation of knowledge. In doing so, they deployed an approach that was strikingly similar to the formula enunciated by the Communication Group.

This was evident in both radio and in film—the two key sectors of the communication program. In relation to radio, the concern to develop coherence within a particular subfield could be seen in a conference on broadcasting for schools that was organized once all of the new projects addressing this issue were up and running.[28] Its purpose was to "effect a closer liaison" among these ventures in terms of their relation to general education. Representatives of the four main school broadcasting projects were invited to attend,[29] along with those involved in related RF ventures, namely, Lazarsfeld, Loring Andrews (representing the World Wide Broadcasting Foundation [WWBF]), Allen Miller (representing the University Broadcasting Council [UBC]), and Charles Hoban, an associate at the American Council (ACE) on Education Motion-Picture Project.

Given that the list of invitees was so carefully selected and that the conference itself was so tightly framed by the general-education agenda, it was evident that the GEB officers felt the need to build a more closely knit community among those involved in school broadcasting as well as others who had relevant expertise.[30] Judging by the limited duration of the projects and the emphasis placed upon interaction between them, it was evident that one of the main goals of the GEB was to quickly generate a network of committed activists that could make the school-broadcasting movement self-sustaining. Indeed, John Marshall was quite pleased that the emphasis of the workshop was on creating leadership in the field. The particular constellation of projects that were supported bore an uncanny resemblance to the model of communication that emerged around the same time at the RF-sponsored Communication Seminar of 1939–1940.

The members of this seminar (organized and led by John Marshall) viewed communication as an ongoing process linking media production with transmission and reception. Along the same lines, each of the various school-broadcasting projects funded by the GEB had an emphasis corresponding to particular aspects of the model. The Progressive Education Association projects were oriented toward production, as were the WWBF and the UBC. The Cleveland School Board and the Wisconsin projects focused on how transmission to specific audiences occurred, as did the Princeton Radio Research Project. Finally, the more broadly conceived ESB explored how the link between production and reception could be facilitated through effective evaluation—the same concern that was at the heart of the American Council on Education Motion-Picture Project. Along similar lines, an effort was made to develop a more clearly defined division of labor and working relationship among the GEB- and RF-sponsored projects in the area of film. Specifically, the GEB allocated $300 to defray the costs for a meeting of representatives from the various film initiatives, held at the RF offices in New York in February 1939. While there is little evidence that this meeting resulted in a more coherent film program, the very fact that it was held reveals the extent to which the different film ventures were thought to comprise an interrelated complex. Indeed, this set of projects embodied the HD's emergent priorities of elevating public taste, preserving and circulating cultural artifacts, developing a knowledge base for cultural practices, mediating between private, public, and state sectors, and "reaching men's minds" through the new mass media. It was through cultivating a community of practitioners that these goals were to be realized. GEB fellowships played an important role in this regard, as they allowed for the circulation of ideas that developed as a result of the visits to various institutions by GEB-sponsored fellows. In addition to helping those in the educational sector improve their skills by spending time with commercial film organizations (such as the March of Time), it also allowed for promising talent to become familiar with the work going on at such RF- and GEB-sponsored ventures as the American Film Center (AFC) and the Minnesota Visual Education project. Again, the division of labor among the various practitioners of educational film bore a striking resemblance to the framework for the study of communications developed in the communication seminar of 1939–1940. The Minnesota project, along with AFC—and to some extent a PEA project on film—were concerned with production. Projects of the Association of School Film Librarians (ASFL) and of the Museum of Modern Art (MoMA) were aligned with distribution. And finally, a project of the American Council of Education (ACE) and the PEA project were concerned with reception. In effect, the schema produced by the communication seminar can best be viewed as the articulation of the communicative strategy that had been deployed by Rockefeller officers—particularly John Marshall—to build a community within the emergent educational communication sector, the core of which was film and radio. Not only were attempts made to generate communities within each of these sectors, but broader efforts also were made to link radio and film together, and to connect the radio-film complex to other areas, such as libraries, museums, schools, and professional bodies (such as science-diffusion specialists).

THE DÉNOUEMENT OF THE
ROCKEFELLER COMMUNICATION PROGRAM

These interconnecting clusters were in place by around 1940, consolidated by the series of conferences and seminars that took place. This meant that any new project approved for funding was inserted into the burgeoning set of networks, taking its shape and direction from the broader designs of the communication program. The Film Music Project of Hanns Eisler serves as an exemplar of the extent to which particular ventures were defined by their interplay with other initiatives and expertise within the HD-GEB film-radio program as well as the broader Rockefeller family network.[31] However, this densely textured and methodically integrated program proved to be short-lived. With the onset of the war, in line with broader Rockefeller philanthropic priorities, the HD-GEB began to increasingly focus on matters considered to be of the greatest urgency, such as public opinion and propaganda.[32] Moreover, the emergent transatlantic community that had fuelled the communication program withered on the vine, supplanted by a broad-ranging effort to strengthen cultural regions of the Americas,[33] and to develop closer hemispheric ties with both Canada and Latin America.[34] The communication program began to wind down by 1942, and by 1945 was considered to be all but over.

To be sure, certain vestiges of the program continued on after the war, such as the support given to the Allerton House Conferences of 1949–1950 (at which the National Association of Educational Broadcasters was formed) and to the seminars for foreign journalists.[35] But the officers of the HD and GEB, responding to a whole new range of issues that emerged with the onset of the cold war and increasing global tensions, were quite happy to pass the communication torch on to other philanthropic bodies such as the Ford Foundation and the Fund for the Republic, which had come to view questions related to media and democracy as vital to the American national interest.[36]

NOTES

Unpublished material in this chapter has been quoted courtesy of the Rockefeller Archive Center, Sleepy Hollow, New York. This chapter draws on material from the following articles I have written: "The Political Economy of Communications Research," in *Information and Communication in Economics*, ed. Robert E. Babe (Boston/Dordrecht/London: Kluwer, 1994), 147–175; "From Radio Research to Communications Intelligence: and Rockefeller Philanthropy, Communications Specialists, the American Intelligence Community," in *The Political Influence of Ideas: Policy Communities and the Social Sciences*, eds. Alain-G. Gagnon and Stephen Brooks (Westport, Conn.: Praeger, 1994), 187–209; "Reaching Human Minds: Rockefeller Philanthropy and Communications, 1935–1939," in *The Development of Social Sciences in the United States and Canada*, eds. Theresa Richardson and Donald Fisher (Stamford, Conn.: Ablex, 177–192); "Rockefeller Support for Projects on the Use of Motion Pictures for Educational and Public Purposes, 1935–1954," *Research Reports Online*: Rockefeller Archive Center (April, 2001); "John Marshall and the Humanities in Europe: Shifting Patterns of Rockefeller Foundation Support," *Minerva* 41 (2003): 133–153;"GEB Support for School-Broadcasting Projects, 1937–1942," *Research Reports from the Rockefeller Archive Center* (Winter 2004) : 8–14.

1. Wilder Penfield, *The Difficult Art of Giving: The Epic of Alan Gregg* (Boston: Little Brown, 1967), 251.

2. Rockefeller Foundation, "The Humanities Program of the Rockefeller Foundation: A Review of the Period 1934 to 1939," 15. Rockefeller Archive Center (hereafter RAC), Rockefeller Foundation (hereafter RF), Record Group (hereafter RG) 3, Series 911, Box 2. Folder 11. It may be that the RF's burgeoning interest in mass

communications was related to it's relocation in May 1933 to the fifty-sixth floor of the newly constructed RCA Building, putting it in close proximity to the National Broadcasting Company (NBC), as well as to numerous other commercial-media interests.

3. Joan Ogden, "The Rockefeller Foundation and the Film," 1970, 4. RAC, RF, RG 3, Series 911, Box 5, Folder 52.

4. Penfield, *The Difficult Art of Giving*, 262.

5. Penfield, *The Difficult Art of Giving*, 254.

6. Indeed, while the HD and GEB were still considered separate entities, they in fact had become quite integrated by 1936. Thirteen out of sixteen trustees were common to both. They shared a common counsel, associate counsel, treasurer, assistant treasurer, comptroller, and board president. This integration in the form of "considerable functional consolidation" had been hastened when the two organizations began to share quarters in 1933, occupying offices on the same floor with a common waiting room. This led to a combination of a variety of functions including "information, fellowships and travel, purchasing, office service and library." Indeed the only function that remained separate was the maintenance of files. T. B. Appleget, "Foundation Organization-Report," 1936, 9–10. RAC, RF, RG 3, Series 900, Box 19, Folder 142.

7. This appeared to have been a temporary state of affairs. It was felt that "eventually Mr. Marshall should give full time either to the Humanities program in the Foundation or at the general education program in the General Education Board." T. B. Appleget, "Foundation Organization-Report," 10.

8. Rockefeller Foundation, "The Humanities Program," 2.

9. Rockefeller Foundation, "Statement of program presented at special Trustees conference, December 1936," 15. RAC, RF, RG 3, Series 911, Box 2, Folder 10.

10. Rockefeller Foundation, "The Humanities Program," 1.

11. Rockefeller Foundation, "The Humanities Program," 6–7.

12. Rockefeller Foundation, "New Programs in the Humanities," April 10, 1935, ii. RAC, RF, RG 3, Series 911, Box 2, Folder 10.

13. John Marshall, "Memorandum on Humanities Program," January 22, 1936. RAC, RF, RG 3.1, Series 911, Box 5, Folder 51.

14. Marshall, "Memorandum on Humanities Program," 1.

15. The new program in libraries—with particular attention given to the support for microphotography—is discussed briefly below. The new museum program is addressed more extensively in chapter 8 of this volume by Niquette and Buxton.

16. This was a simplified form of English with a core vocabulary of 850 words. Ogden intended that it become both an international auxiliary language as well as means to teach English as a second language. See Charles Kay Ogden, *Basic English: A General Introduction with Rules and Grammar* (London: Paul Treber, 1930).

17. These included Charles Siepmann, Geoffrey Gorer, and Paul Rotha coming to America to provide advice and counsel, and Lloyd Free going to Britain to study at the BBC staff college.

18. Two grants (of $500 and $1,000) were awarded to the American Council on Education to organize the second National Conference on Educational Broadcasting that took place from November 29 to December 1, 1937, in Chicago. "Humanities Review," 21. RAC, RF, RG 3, Series 911, Box 2, Folder 11. The first

National Conference on Educational Broadcasting had taken place December 10–12, 1936, in Washington, D.C.

19. The Conference on Speech in Radio and Film was held at the Rockefeller Foundation in New York City on October 11 and 12, 1937. RAC, RF, RG 1.1, Series 200, Box 226, Folder 2691.

20. These were the Conference on the Interpretation of the Natural Sciences for the General Public held at Rye, New York, June 15–16, 1938, and the Second Conference on Interpretation of the Natural Sciences for the General Public held at Rye, New York, June 16–17, 1939.

21. Quoted in David Morrison, "The Beginning of Modern Mass Communication Research," *Archives of European Sociology* 19 (1978): 356.

22. Quoted in Morrison, "The Beginning of Modern Mass Communication Research," 357.

23. Seminar Memorandum No. 7, March 15, 1940. RAC, RF, RG 1.1, Series 200, Box 224, Folder 2678.

24. Seminar Memorandum No. 9, April 12, 1940. RAC, RF, RG 1.1, Series 200, Box 224, Folder 2678.

25. Seminar Memorandum No. 7, 17.

26. Harold Lasswell, "The Structure and Function of Communication in Society," in *The Communication of Ideas,* ed. Lyman Bryson (New York: Institute for Religious and Social Studies, 1948).

27. Seminar Memorandum No. 9, 21.

28. It was held at the Westchester Country Club in Rye, New York, from January 27–29, 1938.

29. These were the Evaluation of School Broadcasts Project (ESB) located at Ohio State University, various projects organized by the Progressive Education Association (PEA), the Study of School Broadcasting organized by the Cleveland Board of Education, and the Research Project in School Broadcasting undertaken at the University of Wisconsin.

30. Grant-in-Aid, Conference on School Broadcasting, December 17, 1936. RAC, General Education Board (hereafter GEB), RG 918, Series 1, Sub-series 2, Box 359, Folder 3705.

31. See chapter 7 by Gall in this volume.

32. Brett Gary, *The Nervous Liberals: Propaganda Anxieties from World War I to the Cold War* (New York: Columbia University Press, 1999).

33. Charles R. Acland and William J. Buxton, "Continentalism and Philanthropy: A Rockefeller Officer's Impressions of the Humanities in the Maritimes," *Acadiensis* 23 (Spring 1994): 72–93.

34. See Cramer's chapter 5 in this volume.

35. See Wrenn's chapter 10 in this volume.

36. See Acland's chapter 11 and McCarthy's chapter 12 in this volume.

5

The Rockefeller Foundation and Pan American Radio

Gisela Cramer

This chapter explores a small, yet intriguing, undertaking funded by the Rockefeller Foundation's Humanities Division in 1937–1938: the Pan American Broadcasting Project. Written and produced under the responsibility of the Pan American Union, the Pan American Broadcasting Project consisted of a series of sixteen radio programs broadcast to Latin America over W1XAL, a Boston-based educational shortwave station operated by the World Wide Broadcasting Corporation. A Division record documenting the funding decision explained the objectives of the project. Although "originating in the United States," the programs were to be the product of a multilateral effort and "genuinely Pan-American in point of view." They were meant to stimulate "more general cultural interchange" and thus create "better mutual understanding among the countries of the three Americas." By providing inspiring programs of "cultural interest," moreover, the series was hoped to "set standards" and help raise the quality of both U.S. shortwave programming and of domestic broadcasting in Latin America.[1] Such objectives, of course, were long-term in nature and far too ambitious to be accomplished by a small series of broadcasts. Rather, as John Marshall, the leading Foundation officer concerned with this undertaking, explained elsewhere, the series was understood to be experimental in character. It was put on the air to test the water and "to determine the type of radio best suited for promoting better understanding and closer relations between the twenty-one republics of the western hemisphere."[2]

How to explain the Foundation's interest and involvement in the Pan American Broadcasting Project? The records just mentioned suggest this undertaking to be an outgrowth of the Foundation's general mandate to help improve international understanding and overcome national partisanship. At the same time, they suggest that this project may also be interpreted as an (albeit small) element in a larger program that came into being toward the mid-1930s as part of a major reorientation of the Foundation's Humanities Division.

The new humanities program is explained in greater detail elsewhere in this volume.[3] For our purposes here, it suffices to draw attention to the Foundation's *Annual Report* for 1935 that succinctly describes the direction the humanities program was to take in the future. It was now to be less concerned with the work of individual scholars engaged in the preservation and interpretation of the materials of culture, and more with the processes by which culture and education were diffused in modern society.[4] More precisely, the new program set out to explore ways and means by which the channels of mass communication could be enhanced in their ability to serve the general public by strengthening their role in the diffusion of knowledge, culture, and international understanding among wide audiences. Whereas traditional academia was now found wanting for its typically cloistered existence, the modern mass media, particularly radio and film, were seen to be reaching out to ever-increasing audiences, yet offering little beyond entertainment programs of a quality that fell far short of what John Marshall and his fellow officers deemed acceptable.[5]

The new humanities program led, among other things, to a profound interest in communications and to the funding of a number of path-breaking research institutes directed by Paul F. Lazarsfeld, Hadley Cantril, Harold D. Lasswell, and other social scientists.[6] Indeed, the Rockefeller Foundation came to be credited as having been a "midwife" to the establishment of communication studies as a discipline in the social sciences.[7] As is well known, toward the late 1930s these research institutes increasingly engaged in work related to national-security objectives. "Galvanized by the recognition that the Roosevelt Administration, hamstrung politically, could not adequately prepare for war on the propaganda front," Brett Gary explained, Rockefeller Foundation officers and communication scholars "took up the slack."[8] In order to prepare for a spiritual war against totalitarian propaganda both within and outside the United States, the Rockefeller Foundation helped to lay the groundwork for a wide range of monitoring and research institutions, including the Shortwave Listening Centers at Princeton and Stanford, the Totalitarian Communications Project at the New School for Social Research, or the Experimental Division for the Study of Wartime Communications, that were eventually absorbed by the state.[9]

Not surprising, by autumn 1937 when the Pan American Broadcasting series went on the air, fears about Axis propagandistic inroads into the hemisphere were very much on the minds of those involved in the project. Their attention was drawn, most of all, to the aggressive use of shortwave radio by Nazi Germany.[10] It is therefore tempting to read this project against the background of national-security concerns. Wasn't this project, in essence, meant to compete with rival and hostile powers for the hearts and minds of Latin Americans? Were the Pan American Union and the Rockefeller Foundation taking the initiative to build up defense mechanisms long before the Roosevelt administration was politically free to take decisive action?

Incidentally, when such decisive action came in August 1940, it was closely associated with a member of the Rockefeller family. Combating Axis propaganda and securing the allegiance of Latin Americans was made the task of a special government agency, the Office of Inter-American Affairs (OIAA).[11] Directed by Nelson A. Rockefeller, the OIAA engaged in massive propaganda campaigns and radio, including the Boston-based educational transmitter, became one of the major channels.[12]

In the following sections, I will explore the origins of the Pan American Broadcasting Project, its characteristics and contents, before discussing it against the background of the Humanities Division's new communication program and national-security concerns. The broadcasting series, I will argue, neatly reflects the underlying rationale of the Foundation's early communications program, in that it endeavored to induce an "upgrading" of radio programming to, and within, Latin America. At the same time, national-security concerns were clearly present among the architects and sponsors of the project. Such concerns, however, were addressed in a way that seemed compatible with the cultural and educational objectives of the early communications program. I will conclude with a short reflection on the difficulties the experiment encountered, contrasting it with the approach to radio programming developed by the OIAA.

THE ORIGINS OF THE PAN AMERICAN UNION'S RADIO PROJECT

Even as radio became, in the late 1920s and 1930s, a major weapon in the political arsenal of the world's greater and lesser powers, many observers, particularly among the, what Akira Iriye has termed, "cultural internationalists,"[13] continued to pin hopes on this medium as a possible means to further mutual understanding between nations. War and aggression, it was assumed, were to a large extent the product of a lack of familiarity and knowledge about other countries, their culture and customs, and hence might be avoided by increasing cultural and educational interchange among the peoples. Radio technology, it seemed, was ideally suited to serve toward this end. Shortwave broadcasts spanning the globe as well as the exchange of programs between stations, by relay or transcriptions, were ready and comparatively inexpensive devices to spread knowledge and mutual understanding among wide audiences throughout the world. Thus, Albert Einstein remarked in 1930 at the opening of the German Broadcasting Exhibition in Berlin, "Radio can easily contribute to eliminate that mutual feeling of strangeness (*Fremdheit*) that so easily degenerates into suspicion and hostility."[14]

In the Americas, the idea of radio as a medium for mutual understanding and cultural interchange had surfaced at various conferences, most notably during the Seventh International Conference of American States at Montevideo (1933) and again at the Inter-American Conference for the Maintenance of Peace at Buenos Aires (1936). Prodded by officials of the Pan American Union (PAU), the Montevideo, and later the Buenos Aires conference, had voted resolutions recommending to advance a multilateral effort of broadcasting. While delegating the general administration to the PAU, it proposed that every member nation should contribute individual programs to be jointly broadcast over the so-called Pan-American frequencies. These shortwave channels had been registered by the United States with the Bureau of the International Telegraph Union in Berne in the late 1920s and had subsequently been reserved for this purpose.[15] After 1933 PAU officials had strenuously sought to transform the Montevideo resolutions into a concrete plan for multilateral broadcasting. Yet like so many of the nonbinding resolutions resolved at international conferences, the project did not materialize. To begin with, PAU officials were unable to secure sufficient support in the United States for its radio project. They had hoped that the Roosevelt administration would supply a shortwave station toward this end as a tangible expression of the Good Neighbor policy in the communications and cultural field, yet the latter failed to commit itself.[16]

Time, moreover, was running out for the PAU's radio project. During the second half of the 1930s, the international scramble for shortwave frequencies intensified. In February 1938, an International Telecommunications Conference was to convene in Cairo, and it was widely assumed that competing powers would lay claim to the unused Pan American frequencies. Hence, in order to forestall the loss of these channels, government officials now decided to assign them, for the time being, to private broadcasters for immediate use. Toward this end, the Federal Communications Commission (FCC) scheduled hearings in the fall of 1937, by which time a number of applicants, including Walter Lemmon's World Wide Broadcasting Corporation in Boston, had handed in their applications for the frequencies in question.[17]

More than a technical detail, this issue was a major driving force behind the Pan American Broadcasting Project. For the Pan American Union, this project was a last-ditch effort to safeguard its claims to the frequencies. In a "frank discussion" on the matter, recorded in a memorandum of conversation by John Marshall, PAU officials applying for financial support explained how this project was to show the "feasibility and value of intercultural broadcasting for Pan America," and thus to "demonstrate and maintain the Union's ultimate right" to the frequencies.[18] The turn of events would prove them not altogether unsuccessful. In early 1938, the Pan American frequencies came to be assigned on a temporary basis and with a number of restrictions. Thus, the radio stations gaining the right of use were held to cooperate with the PAU and to allow for a transmission of broadcasts furnished by Pan American member states.[19]

While the Pan American Union tried to safeguard an "ultimate right," Marshall recorded, "Lemmon undoubtedly [hoped] to obtain use of one or more of these frequencies."[20] Lemmon's W1XAL had been directed rather toward domestic and European audiences and only recently had made steps to expand its programming to Latin America, most notably by collaborating with the PAU in the Pan American Broadcasting Project. Thus, the station's experience in inter-American broadcasting was rather limited. Moreover, W1XAL's financial solidity, engineering practices, and even safety standards left much to be desired, as the FCC was well aware.[21] Nevertheless, Lemmon was able to outdo a much larger competitor, who had also applied for the use of the Pan American channels: NBC.[22] He gained two of the four frequencies in question. (The remaining two were made available to a station operated by General Electric, which was about to greatly expand its transmitting facilities.) Whereas NBC had difficulties convincing the FCC that it was making sufficient efforts to produce suitable programs for Latin America,[23] Lemmon, before and during the hearings on the matter, presented the ongoing Pan American Broadcasting Project as a showcase example for things to come.[24] As such, his application was openly supported by the PAU.[25] Moreover, by pointing to the support the Rockefeller Foundation had invested into W1XAL's program development and by greatly exaggerating the Foundation's future commitments,[26] Lemmon seems to have calmed the FCC's manifest and well-founded doubts as to the financial solidity of the station.[27]

The Foundation's support for the Pan American Broadcasting Project thus helped to bolster the position of both the Pan American Union and Lemmon's World Wide Broadcasting Corporation (WWBC)[28] in the field of inter-American radio. This support came at a time when, for reasons discussed below, the large commercial broadcasters were preparing for an expansion of their shortwave programming to Latin America. While the Foundation's funding policy was not directed against the large commercial stations per se, it certainly aimed to carve out a larger role for educational and cultural programming in the expanding field of inter-American broadcasting.

CHARACTERISTICS AND CONTENTS
OF THE PAN AMERICAN RADIO SERIES

The Pan American Broadcasting Project consisted of a series of sixteen half-hour programs. Written and produced under the responsibility of the Pan American Union, these programs were arranged and broadcast by Walter Lemmon's shortwave station in Boston. Lemmon, a radio engineer and inventor, had invested sizeable sums of his own fortune in the early 1930s to launch W1XAL. As to program development, he relied on various sources, but mainly on the Rockefeller Foundation, for financial support. A considerable part of W1XAL's educational programs were written and produced with active and direct participation of scholars and educators from Harvard University and other institutions of higher learning in or close to Boston. By 1938 Lemmon's *University of the Air* had become the most important educational station in the United States, claiming small but growing audiences in the country, Britain, and in some parts of continental Europe.[29] An American "vest pocket version" of the BBC, as William Buxton has called it,[30] Lemmon's station was an important element in the Rockefeller Foundation's new communication program as far as radio was concerned.

For the new Pan American project, Lemmon hired a special program director, Philip Barbour, to manage the scripts and technicalities of the series by working closely with PAU officials and Latin American diplomats in Washington. A shortwave enthusiast and self-proclaimed expert in educational broadcasting,[31] Barbour had engaged in research and had only recently returned from an extended (ten months) tour through Central and South America. Funded by the Rockefeller Foundation, he had investigated the use of radio for educational purposes and the shortwave situation in general before landing a job with W1XAL.[32]

Hence, considerable fieldwork had been done before this project came up for funding in mid-1937. Comparatively little energy was employed, however, to reflect on the overall objective of the series. Like many other efforts destined to "better mutual understanding" by increasing the cultural and educational interchange among nations, project planners did not spell out clearly how such a program might actually work. To put it bluntly and raise but one out of many issues: increasing information and knowledge about foreign peoples and their culture does not necessarily produce sympathetic views, as public-opinion researcher Hadley Cantril was to point out a few years later in a confidential report prepared for Nelson Rockefeller's Office of Inter-American Affairs. Analyzing the attitudes of U.S. citizens toward Latin Americans, he found that the more information the respondents seemed to have about the nations south of the Rio Grande, the less sympathetic they were toward Latin Americans.[33]

Yet, while such issues were not explicitly raised, the design of the project shows that its producers and sponsors, most likely out of practical experience, were implicitly aware of at least some of its possible pitfalls. Thus, their selection of contents was anything but random. They shunned topics pertaining to the realm of contemporary politics, a sphere that would have been difficult to navigate if the series was to bring about *sympathetic* understanding.[34] The opening broadcast on October 15, 1937, featured Secretary of State Cordell Hull and Colón Eloy Alfaro, ambassador of Ecuador and vice chairman of the Pan American Union, giving stately speeches about the value of the program for inter-American relations.[35] Thereafter, the series focused on the culture and the intellectual achievements of Latin America, some of the talks being country- or author-specific, others dedicated to overarching treatments of the music and literature of the region. The series also included some subject matter of a more specifically Pan American character, featuring, for instance, a presentation on the Inter-American Court of Justice, and concluding with a talk on the Pan American Union by its director, Leo S. Rowe.[36]

Cultural topics, to be sure, could also, and easily, spin into unwanted directions. Hence, care had to be taken to select contributors who "would do a great deal to promote mutual understanding, if properly supervised," as a memorandum by Lemmon pointed out.[37] Prominent among the contributors were Latin American diplomats based in Washington, who for one reason or another, had developed an interest or expertise in literature, art, or music, and were eager to present their own achievements and national cultural heritage over the air. While these contributions could easily be gathered in Washington, a few others, featuring mostly academics and specialists in their field, were recorded in Havana and elsewhere for the series. A number of scholars based in the United States also contributed to the program by giving talks on their subject of expertise, for example, the music and literature of Latin America. Hence, although produced in the United States, the series was to feature (what Rowe called) "leaders of thought"[38] from all over the hemisphere and thus become, as a Foundation memorandum called it, "genuinely Pan-American in point of view."[39]

As so often is the case, music was considered a particularly propitious medium to further "mutual understanding," and the program's managers went into some effort to procure recordings of music from various parts of Latin America. Recordings of typical tunes were hoped to make the programs more attractive and authentic.[40] Music, of course, was as vital an ingredient for successful radio programming in Latin America as elsewhere. At the time, tangos, sambas, and other popular tunes were conquering mass audiences throughout the region. Such "mutual understanding" as could be garnered by *popular* music, however, was not exactly what the program's designers had in mind, as will be explained below.

The individual programs were produced mostly in Spanish,[41] hence reducing the possible audience to the Spanish-speaking regions of the Americas. Future translations into English and other languages, however, were mentioned as a possibility to widen their regional appeal.

It was well understood that the broadcasts from Boston would reach a rather limited audience. As elsewhere, most listeners south of the Rio Grande were tuning in to domestic broadcasting rather than international shortwave stations. To overcome the limitations of shortwave broadcasting, the series was recorded by electrical transcriptions to be offered free of charge to selected stations in Latin America, usually noncommercial government or university-based stations with an interest in cultural programs. These transcriptions, moreover, were to be employed to reach audiences in the southern regions of South America. As was the case with most of the U.S. shortwave stations at the time, W1XAL's signal strength was too weak to be clearly audible beyond the equator. The project, therefore, envisaged the use of transcriptions for the time being, contemplating the possibility of relay agreements with a sufficiently powerful South American station for the future, that is, once this type of programming got off the ground.[42]

At the same time, it was obvious that the subject matter and format of the Pan American series were not designed to reach mass audiences but instead aimed at a small, educated elite.[43] Assuming that the cultural elite throughout Latin America had similar educational backgrounds, interests, and tastes, the projects' advocates obviously hoped to be able to develop a type of transnational program that would appeal to small, yet influential audiences throughout the hemisphere.

THE PAN AMERICAN BROADCASTING PROJECT AND THE ROCKEFELLER FOUNDATION'S COMMUNICATIONS PROGRAM

Counting on the insights gained by Barbour's fieldwork, on the experience of the largest educational broadcaster in the United States and on the institutional expertise and connections of the Pan American Union, the Rockefeller officials were rather optimistic about the prospects of Pan American broadcasting. In an memorandum on the possible merits of the project, they expressed that this venture, once tested and dutifully revised after the initial experimental phase, would demonstrate how "broadcasting can become a medium of genuine cultural interchange for Latin America, and also between North and South America."[44] It was meant not only to serve an overarching goal of "international understanding" but also to induce an "upgrading" of radio broadcasting both at the local and the international level. At the local level, the use of transcriptions was expected to have, what an internal memorandum called, "a demonstration effect." On the international level, the series was hoped to reveal the feasibility of educational and cultural radio in general and to impress the larger short-wave broadcasters in particular. "Based as it is on a thorough knowledge of present conditions in South and Central America," the memorandum continued, this project should set "standards for such broadcasting in this country, at a time when the two principal chains [i.e., NBC and CBS] are initiating similar services."[45]

At first sight, it seems somewhat bewildering that such high hopes were attached to a small, experimental series, funded by a grant of a mere $12,800 (in today's terms, some $155,500). In order to understand such optimistic assessments, it is necessary to view the project as part of a larger program, that is, the communication program of the Humanities Division, and discuss some of the underlying assumptions and convictions that guided it.

There certainly was no blueprint available for philanthropic engagement in the mass-communications sector, and the Humanities Division's funding praxis, by supporting a multitude of projects both large and small, followed a rather experimental and somewhat scattered approach, as other contributions to this volume explain in greater detail.[46] The Division aimed to explore ways by which the channels of mass communication, both modern (radio, film) and more traditional (popular press, museums), could be enhanced in their ability to diffuse knowledge, culture, and international understanding among wide audiences. Assuming that there existed a considerable, albeit ineffective, demand for such contents that, by and large, was not being served by the media, the Humanities Division set out to study possible remedies. These included the funding of undertakings that immediately served to expand the cultural and educational supply available to the public (such as Lemmon's *University of the Air*); the establishment of links between the media, universities, and other centers of knowledge and culture[47]; the interchange "throughout the world of constructive radio programs"[48]; experiments to test the usefulness of modern media for educational purposes (such as documentary films or radio programs for classroom use); or communication research as a tool to reveal the needs and demand structure of broader audiences. Once the preferences of an increasingly educated and culturally literate audience were revealed and the means to draw upon knowledge and culture as a source for mass consumption were in place, it was implicitly assumed, even the deftest of commercial media could be induced to invest less into, what John Marshall called, a "pathology of substitutes" and more into "genuine knowledge."[49] Hence, the communications program, while not aiming at a wholesale restructuring of mass communications, aspired to induce processes toward an upgrading of the system that would eventually be self-sustaining and independent of the Foundation's aid.

An analysis of the Pan American Broadcasting Project against this back-drop may help to spell out some of the underlying assumptions and convictions that led the Foundation's officers to be optimistic about the project. Reviewing the current broadcasting situation in Latin America, a memorandum prepared by Lemmon and based on Barbour's field study pointed out to the "pathology of substitutes" to be found over there. A rapid expansion of radio broadcasting in Latin American was giving rise to some large and powerful stations. These, however, were found to devote themselves exclusively to "endless tangos, sambas, and whatnot, interrupted every two-and-a-half to three minutes by advertising." While not opposed to a transmission of cultural programs, these were unwilling or unable "to originate programs of such nature." The few stations found to produce "cultural programs of considerable interest" were largely owned by governments and universities operating with small, local transmitters and working in isolation from each other. Hence, Latin Americans had been left "woefully ignorant not only of what is being done culturally in the United States, but even of what is being done in the nearest Latin American republic."[50]

The Pan American Broadcasting Project went about to change this sorry state of affairs through essentially three steps: First, by producing an appealing series; second, by demonstrating that there existed a real demand for cultural programming as was to be measured, in this case, not so much by audience responses, which were difficult to come by, but by the reactions of local stations many of which, when previously approached by Barbour, seemed eager to cooperate; third, by inducing a cooperative effort, by which programs produced in one country would be recorded and made available for broadcasting elsewhere, in both smaller and larger stations. Latin America was viewed as a sufficiently homogenous region in cultural and linguistic terms[51] to allow a buildup of transnational audiences for the type of programs involved. Hence, once the feasibility and the technicalities of the project could be demonstrated, local stations (including the larger U.S. networks) were expected to pick up the idea and start cooperating by the exchange of programs. This cooperative effort, it was implicitly assumed, would lead to a self-sustaining process of cultural interchange that would serve the overarching objectives of international understanding and of a general upgrading of radio broadcasting.

THE PAN AMERICAN BROADCASTING PROJECT AND NATIONAL-SECURITY CONCERNS

When Philip Barbour toured Latin America in 1936 on a Rockefeller Foundation fellowship, "he found that the European programs came in with such power that they blanketed the ether."[52] Studies commissioned by U.S.

federal agencies came to similar conclusions. European programs, particularly those originating from Germany and Italy, seemed to drown the weak signals emanating from the United States.[53] Indeed, except for Liechtenstein, Monaco, and a few other minor states, the Europeans had invested heavily in international broadcasting,[54] and shortwave radio came to be viewed as a major weapon in the arsenal of foreign policy. Stirred by several studies on European radio incursions into the hemisphere and by rather alarming press reports about (what seemed to be) highly sophisticated propaganda techniques employed by Nazi Germany, a number of federal regulators and politicians in Washington revived the longstanding idea of establishing a powerful shortwave station to be run by the federal government and directed at Latin America. In 1937–1938, various bills were introduced into both Houses of Congress to force the matter.

None of these bills would be signed into law. They met stiff resistance from the broadcasting industry, found insufficient support among the general public, and failed to get backing from the White House. Yet, they served to increase the pressure on private broadcasters to expand their services to Latin America. Fearing that the government, by entering the shortwave sector, might eventually interfere with both international and domestic broadcasting, the radio industry now signaled a willingness to take programming to Latin America more serious. Whereas previously their shortwave programs were little more than rebroadcasts of shows produced for the domestic market, they now set out to expand the number of programs designed specifically for audiences south of the Rio Grande even though shortwave radio continued to be an unprofitable venture. New federal regulations, moreover, forced them to step up their transmission equipment to a signal strength comparable to that of their European competitors.[55]

Not surprisingly, when the Pan American Radio series went onto the air in autumn 1937, it was widely perceived as part of an American response to challenges posed by international competitors. "Highly tooted as expressions of good will toward Latin America," reported *Newsweek* in November 1937, these broadcasts "actually mark the entrance of the U.S. into competition with Japan, Britain, Italy, and Germany, all of which send short-wave propaganda well baited with entertainment."[56]

Walter Lemmon himself was quick to present the series—and other programs—in this light. Thus, he suggested, as a FCC memorandum recorded, that his *"University of the Air"* would "combat the prevailing opinion . . . in South America" that life in the United States was—in contrast to Europe—devoid of culture and dominated by "commercial and material aspects only."[57] According to the *Washington Post*, in early 1938 he proclaimed that his station might serve very much the same objectives as the proposed government station "without any cost to the taxpayer" while avoiding the political risks that a government-owned radio station would involve. Referring to the Pan American series presently on the air, he pronounced it to be successful in showing that "radio can become a great force in binding closer together the peoples of this hemisphere and even of the world." He continued to profess a special concern for creating goodwill in the "smaller Central American states . . . since they will make good buffer states for this country in case of war."[58]

Such utterances, of course, have to be interpreted in the context of a public and bitter confrontation between broadcasters and the advocates of a government station. They should, therefore, not carry too much weight in an inquiry into the origins of the Pan American Broadcasting Project. Yet, it seems that national-security concerns were indeed present and not just touted in public to ward off government incursions into broadcasting. Internal memoranda and papers on the project equally show evidence of a growing uneasiness about the "increasing intensity in the bombardment of propaganda" in the United States and in Latin America of "German, Italian, Russian, or other foreign origins."[59]

On a more fundamental level, we may assume that foreign-policy objectives could hardly have been absent in a radio project promoted by Leo S. Rowe and the Pan American Union. Though it proclaimed the absolute equality of its member states, the American Republics, this organization was so obviously dominated by Washington that outspoken critics referred to it as a "colonial office," just as they likened the Pan-Americanism promoted by the United States to Pan-Germanic, Pan-Slavic, and other imperial designs elsewhere.[60] Even without being a simple, let alone effective, tool of control for Washington, the Pan American Union was one of the instruments in place to exercise what Joseph S. Nye and Robert O. Keohane have called "soft power" or "the ability to achieve desired outcomes in international affairs through attraction rather than coercion."[61] Acceptance abroad of U.S. leadership could obviously be sought by different means, and Rowe had consistently argued in favor of "cultural exchange" and "mutual understanding" as means to create goodwill and maintain U.S. influence in Latin America.[62] Much to the liking of Rowe, a less coercive exercise in power politics had come to the forefront with the onset of the Good Neighbor policies.[63]

In a discussion with Rockefeller Foundation officials on the possible merits of the Pan American Broadcasting Project, he implicitly placed the project within the context of U.S. foreign policy and, more specifically, the Good Neighbor policy. According to a memorandum of conversation, he expected this project to help "provide a broad popular base for the present excellent inter-governmental relations." Except for Mexico, Rowe explained, the relations between the United States and the governments of Central and South America had taken a very positive turn, yet because of the "lack of knowledge on the part of the general population of the

Latin American states . . . these good governmental relations have as yet little popular support."[64] Such popular support, we may add, must have been deemed advisable if the hemisphere was to be effectively insulated against propagandistic intrusions from the outside.

In a guarded manner, an intermediate report of the Rockefeller Foundation on the radio project raised a related point. Contrasting the radio series currently on the air as a kind of antithesis to crude propagandistic maneuvers of other powers, the report maintained that this was "no conscious effort to beat the big drum for any special interest. The whole purpose and technique of the broadcasts are directed to the end of making the peoples of the Americas more aware of their common interests, better acquainted with the history, the music, the drama, the literature, and the other arts, institutions, and cultural achievements of our Western nations."[65] This set of ideas, indeed, sounds very much like one of the standard themes worked by American propagandists during the war, when Nelson Rockefeller's Office of Inter-American Affairs was beating a truly "big drum" to ponder the common history, destiny, and interest of the nations of the Western Hemisphere, in a very "conscious effort" to forge a united front against the Axis.[66]

Yet, in comparison to the massive and, at times, blunt exercise of radio propaganda later on by the OIAA,[67] the content matter and design of the Pan American series seem to have been grounded rather in an internationalist creed. The internationalist response to growing national-security concerns was trying to create goodwill south of the Rio Grande by expanding educational and cultural cooperation and interchange, as exemplified by the exchange of radio programs envisioned by the project. While such a response was compatible with, or even subservient to, national-security objectives, it shunned away from an overtly instrumental view of cultural and intellectual exchange as a vehicle for public diplomacy or even propaganda.

Not surprisingly, this approach did not satisfy all contemporary observers. Among the reactions to the program, we may discern a preview of the more visible conflicts arising during the war when internationalists and their critics exposed divergent views on how to approach Latin America in order to gain general goodwill and effective cooperation.[68] Whereas some observers praised the Pan American Broadcasting Project for not following the line of blatant propaganda supposedly employed by the Europeans,[69] others were left unconvinced. For the latter, radio shows featuring, for instance, the Mexican ambassador and poet Dr. Francisco Castillo Nájera reading from his own works and, with a musical background consisting of *corridos*, discussing Mexican poetry, did simply not seem the most propitious approach to garner goodwill for the United States.[70] Thus *Newsweek*, while crediting European and Japanese broadcasts to Latin America as propaganda "well baited with entertainment," lambasted the Pan American series as "containing mere expressions of international friendship" and thus "amateurish compared to the carefully planned German propaganda programs."[71]

EPILOGUE: THE RESULTS

As mentioned earlier, the Pan American Broadcasting Project was an experiment designed to "determine the type of radio best suited for promoting better understanding and closer relations between the twenty-one republics of the western hemisphere." It was hoped to induce far-reaching effects with respect not only to inter-American relations, but also to the quality of radio broadcasting in the Americas. The project was to work in essentially three steps. First, by producing an appealing series; second, by demonstrating that there existed a real demand for cultural programming, as measured by the response of local stations; and third, by inducing a cooperative effort, by which programs produced in one country would be recorded and made available for broadcasting elsewhere.

Evaluating the experiment, however, turned out to be more difficult than expected. In effect, for none of the three steps mentioned were the project's accomplishments clear. The series' appeal among audiences was difficult to gauge, since listener responses were difficult to come by, thus precluding any serious analysis of the reactions it produced. Due to W1XAL's rather sloppy handling of this phase of the project, even the Latin American stations' responses proved to be difficult to evaluate. With some prodding by the Rockefeller Foundation, Lemmon's crew in 1940 finally ascertained to which stations the electrical recordings had been sent, yet due to the lack of response, it remained unclear how often and how these had been used, let alone how the audiences had reacted.[72] What seemed obvious, nonetheless, was that local stations had not reacted with fervor to "advice and suggestions" from the United States as the project's architects had expected.[73] The precise reasons for this lack of enthusiasm were impossible to determine.

Was it simply that Lemmon's W1XAL lacked the necessary organizational capacity to run an experiment on this scale, as was suggested by Barbour who left the station rather disgruntled soon after the experiment was concluded?[74] Was it that the subject matter of the series, as Rowe seems to have suggested afterward, "lacked in interest"?[75] Did this program and other broadcasts by the University of the Air fail to elicit enthusiastic responses south of the Rio Grande for being "almost painfully intellectual and patronizing," as a contemporary observer suggested?[76] Or was it simply that both Lemmon's and Rowe's staffs had failed to sufficiently engage Latin American stations in their "genuinely Pan-American" design?

Whatever the reasons were, the failure of the experiment to deliver tangible results came as a clear disappointment to the Rockefeller officers. Not surprisingly, when Rowe applied for funding for a similar radio project in November 1938, he was turned down.[77] What did become clear during the course of the experiment, was that—as Rowe summed up the situation—none of the existing international broadcasters "can do the job alone." In order to establish a service "comparable to what other countries now are offering," John Marshall suggested, they would have to coordinate their programming among themselves.[78] To be sure, it would take a government agency, namely, Nelson Rockefeller's Office of Inter-American Affairs, to coordinate U.S. broadcasting to Latin America. By 1940, however, national-security concerns were outweighing any concerns for the use of radio as a medium to spread culture and knowledge. True, even under the pressure of war, the OIAA's programming did not completely lose sight of radio as a means to educate and to enlighten, but culture and education were now clearly subservient to national-security objectives. Thus, OIAA radio officers would develop programs on the history, as well as the cultural and intellectual traditions of Latin America—but such content matter was used primarily as a vehicle to convey other messages, namely how incompatible such traditions were with the *Weltanschauung* promoted by the Axis.[79]

If the Pan American Broadcasting Project itself was a far cry from the PAU's original plan to provide for a cooperative and multilateral use of the Pan American frequencies, it was still aiming at a cooperative and multilateral effort. By the time the OIAA came into existence, such an orientation seemed definitely outdated. Teaming American shortwave stations into a government-led campaign to spread goodwill and sympathy for the United States among mass audiences led to a style of programming that did not leave room for cooperative and multilateral endeavors. Nor did it leave room for "painfully intellectual" programs destined to impress slim minorities. Hence, as other shortwave stations, Lemmon's *University of the Air* was eventually taken over by government agencies, that is, the Office of Inter-American Affairs and the Office of War Information,[80] despite the station's resolute resistance against being "Goebbelized" as one of World Wide's trustees, Harvard professor and astronomer Harlow W. Shapley, chose to call the process.[81]

NOTES

Research for this paper was made possible by grants and fellowships from the Rockefeller Archive Center, the Roosevelt Presidential Library, and the German Historical Institute in Washington, D.C. I would also like to acknowledge comments and suggestions by the participants of the workshop on "American Philanthropic Support for Communication and Culture," August 2004, at the Rockefeller Archive Center. Unpublished material in this chapter has been quoted courtesy of the Rockefeller Archive Center, Sleepy Hollow, New York.

1. Resolved RF 27088, Pan American Union, Latin American Broadcasts, 18 June, 1937, 1–3. Rockefeller Archive Center (hereafter RAC), Rockefeller Foundation (hereafter RF), Record Group (hereafter RG) 1.1, Series 200, Box 266, Folder 3170. I am grateful to Bill Buxton for bringing this and the following sources related to the Pan American Broadcasting Project to my attention.

2. John Marshall to Leo S. Rowe, 7 June, 1937. RAC, RF, RG 1.1, Series 200, Box 266, Folder 3170.

3. Cf. the contributions of William J. Buxton (chapter 2) and Theresa Richardson (chapter 3) to this volume.

4. The Rockefeller Foundation, *Annual Report for 1935* (New York: Rockefeller Foundation, 1935).

5. For thorough discussion of these issues see William J. Buxton, "John Marshall and the Humanities in Europe: Shifting Patterns of Rockefeller Foundation Support," *Minerva* 41, no. 2 (2003): 133–53, and his "Reaching Human Minds: Rockefeller Philanthropy and Communications, 1935–1939," in *The Development of the Social Sciences in the United States and Canada: The Role of Philanthropy*, eds. Theresa Richardson and Donald Fisher (Stamford, CT: Ablex Publishers, 1999), 177–92.

6. For a biographical account of the foundation of communication studies see Everett M. Rogers, *A History of Communication Study: A Biographical Approach* (New York: Free Press, 1994).

7. Brett Gary, "Communication Research, the Rockefeller Foundation, and Mobilization for the War on Words, 1938–1944," *Journal of Communication* 46, no. 3 (Summer 1996): 125. Other scholars rather emphasize the preparation for psychological warfare during World War II as a pivotal moment in the consolidation of the research field. See, for instance, Christopher Simpson, *The Science of Coercion: Communication Research and Psychological Warfare, 1945–1960* (Oxford & New York: Oxford University Press, 1994).

8. Gary, "Communication Research," 125; on the political difficulties to establish propaganda and propaganda-control agencies in the United States, see Richard W. Steele, "Preparing the Public for War: Efforts to Establish a National Propaganda Agency," *American Historical Review* 75, no.6 (October 1970): 1640–53.

9. The most thorough analysis of these matters is Brett Gary, *The Nervous Liberals. Propaganda Anxieties from World War I to the Cold War* (New York: Columbia University Press, 1999), 85–173.

10. Contemporary American reports tended to exaggerate the effort, thoroughness, and care that was going into Nazi Germany's shortwave operations; for a more realistic view based on German archives see Willi Boehlke, *Die Macht des Radios: Weltpolitik und Auslandsrundfunk* (Frankfurt/M.: Ullstein, 1977).

11. The first official title Office for Coordination of Commercial and Cultural Relations Between the American Republics was changed a few months later to Office of the Coordinator of Inter-American Affairs. In 1945 the office was again renamed to Office of Inter-American Affairs (OIAA). The establishment of the OIAA and the role of Nelson Rockefeller are discussed in great detail by Claude Curtis Erb, "Nelson Rockefeller and United States–Latin American Relations, 1940–1945" (PhD dissertation, Clark University, 1982); Cary Reich, *The Life of Nelson A Rockefeller: Worlds to Conquer, 1908–1958* (New York: Doubleday, 1996), 165–261.

12. Some analysts, based on records available at the Roosevelt presidential archive, have concluded that U.S. radio programming during the war remained a rather weak endeavor; see Michael Fortmann and David G. Haglund, "Public Policy and Dirty Tricks: Two Faces of United States 'Informal Penetration' of Latin America on the Eve of World War II," *Diplomacy and Statecraft* 6, no. 2 (1995): 536–577. Yet a viewing of the pertaining record group (National Archives II, RG 229) would have shown otherwise. A comprehensive analysis of the truly massive propaganda offensive in Latin America during World War II, in both short- and standard-wave programming, is still lacking; for a pioneering account of the OIAA's activities in Mexico see José Luis Ortiz Garza, *La guerra de las hondas* (Mexico: Planeta, 1992).

13. Akira Iriye, *Cultural Internationalism and World Order* (Baltimore & London: Johns Hopkins University Press, 1997).

14. As quoted in Boehlke, *Die Macht des Radios*, 72 (my translation, G. C.).

15. The origins and possible use of the Pan American Frequencies are discussed in National Archives (hereafter NARA) II, RG 173, FCC, Entry 100A, General Correspondence 1927–46, Box 312, Folder 81–11, A. D. Ring, Chief, Broadcast Section, Memorandum to Broadcasting Division, Subject: Pan American Frequencies, 9/24/1937.

16. For a thorough discussion of the decision-making process within the Roosevelt administration and its failure to comply with the PAU's requests for a short-wave facility to make use of the frequencies see Bruce N. Gregory, *The Broadcasting Service: An Administrative History: The United States Information Agency Special Monograph Service* (Washington, DC: USIA, 1970), Part 1; Fred Fejes, *Imperialism, Media, and the Good Neighbor* (Norwood, NJ: Ablex, 1986), 81–95. Apart from general references to the matter in the Leo S. Rowe papers, the archives of the Pan-American Union (hereafter PAU), located at the Columbus Memorial Library in Washington, D.C., do not seem to hold specific materials that would shed light on the reasons for the failure to implement the Montevideo resolutions.

17. For further details on the Pan American frequencies and the impending Cairo Conference see NARA II, RG 173, FCC, Entry 100A, General Correspondence 1927–46, Box 312, Folder 81–11, T. A. M. Craven, Chief Engineer, Memorandum to the Broadcast Division, 11.08.1937; see also Gregory, *The Broadcasting Service*, Part 1; Fejes, *Imperialism*, 81, Howard S. LeRoy, "Treaty Regulation of International Radio and Short Wave Broadcasting," *American Journal of International Law* 32, no. 4 (October 1938): 719–37, especially 728–734.

18. John Marshall (hereafter JM) Interviews, 2 June, 1937, 1. RAC, RF, RG 1.1, Series 200, Box 266, Folder 3170.

19. The decision in the matter of the Pan American Frequencies is explained in NARA II, RG 173, Federal Communications Commission, FCC 25089, Docket Number 4843–4845, decided 1 February, 1938, 9.

20. JM Interviews, 2 June, 1937, 1. RAC, RF, RG 1.1, Series 200, Box 266, Folder 3170.

21. On engineering and safety standards, see, for example, NARA II, RG 173, FCC, Entry 100A, General Correspondences, Box 451, Folder 89–6: Inspector in Charge to Chief, Field Section, 29.12.2937. W1XAL's financial solidity was equally in doubt. Thus, before the hearings, the FCC enquired about the financial backing

W1XAL was receiving from the Rockefeller Foundation (RF), in view of the "situation regarding Pan American frequencies" (see JM Interviews, 2 June, 1937, 2. RAC, RF, RG 1.1, Series 200, Box 266, Folder 3170). When questioned during the hearings, Lemmon was unable to give details on revenues and operational costs and got away with flimsy references to the RF. NARA II, RG 173 Federal Communications Commission, Entry 120, Docketed Case Files 4843, Box 1299, Official Report of Proceedings Before Federal Communications Commission at Washington, D.C., 29.10.1937, 61–62. Lemmon's station remained in dire straits as the subsequent and, at times, frantic efforts to raise money show. Severe organizational shortcomings continued well into the war when Lemmon's station, as were other shortwave stations, was taken over by the government. Further information on this issue is to be found in the Franklin D. Roosevelt Library, Hyde Park, FDR Official File, 4425: Radio Station WRUL, 1940–42; FDR Library, Lowell Mellet Papers, Personal Files, 1938–1944, Folder Lemmon, Walter S.; and in World Wide Broadcasting Foundation, RAC, RF, RG 1.1, Projects Series 200R, Box 296, Folders 3524–5.

22. In an interim report on the progress of Pan American radio series to the Rockefeller Foundation, the director of the program, Philip Barbour, mentioned that the development of the program served to "justify the assignment" of the two frequencies to World Wide. See Interim Report on Progress in the Experimental Cultural Broadcasts to Latin America (Philip Barbour), 8; RAC, RF, RG 1.1, Series 200, Box 266, Folder 3171. The pertaining FCC records (see below) suggest likewise.

23. Not only the shortwave stations operated by NBC, but also by General Electric, were found to, by and large, transmit to Latin America regular chain materials that had been produced for domestic audiences. Since GE had put more effort into the experimentation with signal strength and reception conditions in Latin America and was about to install a more powerful transmitter, the FCC argued, the application submitted by GE was preferable to NBC's. For further details see NARA II, RG 173, Federal Communications Commission, FCC 25089, Docket Number 4843–4845, decided 1 February, 1938.

24. For the statements of Lemmon and his staff during the hearings see NARA II RG 173 FCC, Entry 120, Docket Section, Docketed Case Files 4843, Box 1299, Official Report of Proceedings Before Federal Communications Commission at Washington, D.C., 29 October, 1937.

25. NARA II, RG 173, FCC, Entry 120, Docket Section, Docketed Case Files 4843, Box 1299, Lemmon to FCC, 6 August, 1937; Rowe to Lemmon, 30 July, 1937.

26. Thus, for example, Lemmon insinuated that a "permanent endowment plan" would eventually be worked out with the RF and other philanthropic organizations; for further details see NARA II, RG 173, FCC, Entry 120, Docket Section, Docketed Case Files 4848, Box 1299, Official Report of Proceedings Before Federal Communications Commission at Washington, D.C., 29.10.1937, p. 14f, 61f. When alerted by the president of NBC, who complained about Lemmon's statements, John Marshall called on Lemmon to correct his position before the hearings would end (RAC, RF, RG 1.1, Series 200R, World Wide Broadcasting Foundation, Box 295, Folder 3518), Inter-Office Correspondence, Marshall to DHS (David H. Stevens), TBA (Thomas B. Appleget), 5 November, 1937, but this does not seem to have produced any results.

27. The FCC's own internal reports on W1XAL were extremely critical as to organizational, engineering and safety standards (see, for example, NARA II, RG

173, FCC, Entry 100A, General Correspondences, Box 451, Folder 89–6: Inspector in Charge to Chief, Field Section, 29.12.2937). W1XAL's financial solidity was equally in doubt. Thus, before the hearings, the FCC enquired about the financial backing W1XAL was receiving, in view of the "situation regarding Pan American frequencies" (see JM Interviews, 2 June, 1937, 2. RAC, RF, RG 1.1, Series 200, Box 266, Folder 3170).

28. RF support was technically not going to the World Wide Broadcasting Corporation (WWBC) but to the World Wide Broadcasting Foundation (WWBF), an organization founded within Lemmon's corporation to administer financial support by the Rockefeller Foundation and other philanthropic entities toward the development of educational programs. Since the station W1XAL (or, as it was later called, WRUL) was owned by the corporation, which in turn had rather unclear ownership structure but was largely controlled by Lemmon, I will continue to refer to the World Wide Broadcasting Corporation or simply to "Lemmon's station."

29. For a sympathetic portrayal of Lemmon's career and the WWBC see *Forum and Century* 99, no. 6 (June 1938): 321. To determine the size and nature of W1XAL's audiences, the Rockefeller Foundation had Princeton Radio Researchers look into it. While the latter were unable to ascertain the size, they suggested audiences to be rather small and consisting largely of three groups: (1) shortwave enthusiasts who listened to the programs on radio technology offered by the station, (2) Christian Scientists who were attracted to the station because it carried news programs based on the *Christian Science Monitor* and also broadcast religious services of interest to them, and (3) listeners belonging to highly educated and upper-income groups who made very discriminate use of radio. World Wide Broadcasting Foundation, Resolved 38056. RAC, RF, RG 1.1, Series 200R, Box 295, Folder 3513.

30. Buxton, "John Marshall," 149.

31. Barbour himself explained his background as a witness in the FCC hearings on the Pan American Frequencies in NARA II, RG 173 Federal Communications Commission, Entry 120, Docketed Case Files 4843, Box 1299, Official Report of Proceedings Before Federal Communications Commission at Washington, D.C., 29 October, 1937.

32. For the trips see NARA II Official Report of Proceedings; some of his findings were published in Philip L. Barbour, "Short-wave Broadcasting and Latin America," *Bulletin of the Pan American Union* (October 1937): 739–750, where he gives an overview of the number, location, broadcasting capacity, and strength of shortwave stations in Latin America. In his report for the Rockefeller Foundation, he specifically outlines the situation of cultural and educational stations in Summary of Present Situation of Broadcasting in Latin America, 17 June, 1937. RAC, RF, RG 1.1, Series 200, Box 266, Folder 3170.

33. Analyzing the data of various opinion polls conducted in 1940, Cantril found: "It is very obvious that an increase in information about the countries of Latin America does not produce more flattering characterizations of the people in these countries. On the contrary, many adjectives which, in our culture, are definitely derogatory and unfavorable are used much more frequently by well informed than by uninformed persons." Hadley Cantril, American Social Surveys Confidential Report. What People of the United States Think and Know About Latin America and Latin Americans, 18 January, 1941. NARA II, RG 59, Records of the Department of State

Relating to Political Relations Between the United States and the other American Republics, 1940–1949, M1276, roll 20, 710.11/2686/attachment.

34. Among the hotly debated topics of the day was, to mention but one example, the Mexican nationalization of foreign oil companies.

35. Further details about the inauguration can be found in the *Bulletin of the Pan American Union* (December 1937): 914–16.

36. A short listing of the program titles is provided in the article, "La Universidad Nacional Fija Programa y Horario," published in "Panamá-América." RAC, RF, RG 1.1, Series 200, Box 266, Folder 3171. Unfortunately, I have not been able to locate the original scripts for the program.

37. Memorandum Relative to a Projected Series of Educational and Cultural Radio-Broadcasts to Latin America, 5. RAC, RF, RG 1.1, Series 200, Box 266, Folder 3170.

38. Rowe to Marshall, 28 February, 1938. RAC, RF, RG 1.1, Series 200, Folder 3171.

39. Resolved RF 27088, Pan American Union, Latin American Broadcasts, 18 June, 1937, 2. RAC, RF, RG 1.1, Series 200, Box 266, Folder 3170.

40. The advantage of local recordings over the use of U.S. orchestras to play Latin American tunes is explicitly discussed in Lemmon's Memorandum Relative to a Projected Series of Educational and Cultural Radio-Broadcasts to Latin America, 4–5. RAC, RF, RG 1.1, Series 200, Box 266, Folder 3170.

41. Except for No. 12, which featured a talk (in French) on Haiti by the Haitian ambassador in Washington, E. Lescot, as well as Haitian music, the programs were in Spanish. Originally, the production plan had also envisaged programs in Portuguese, but these failed to materialize.

42. Lemmon to Marshall, 10 June, 1937. RAC, RF, RG 1.1, Series 200, Box 266, Folder 3170; The Americas on the Air, 12. RAC, RF, RG 1.1, Series 200, Box 266, Folder 3171.

43. JM Interview with L. S. Rowe, Director of Pan American Union, 22 July, 1938. RAC, RF, RG 1.1, Series 200. Box 266, Folder 3171.

44. Hot List—1 June, 1937. Humanities. Pan American Union. Pan American broadcasting. RAC, RF, RG 1.1, Series 200, Box 266, Folder 3170.

45. Hot List—1 June, 1937. Humanities. Pan American Union. Pan American broadcasting.

46. An overview can be found in the contributions of Theresa Richardson (chapter 3) and William Buxton (chapter 4) to this volume.

47. Thus, the RF funded the preparation of materials and programs produced by university professors and scholars to be broadcast over larger commercial chains or smaller educational stations. For a discussion of the Chicago Round Table and similar initiatives see Buxton, "John Marshall"; Buxton, "Reaching Human Minds"; and the Rockefeller Foundation, *Annual Reports* 1935–1939.

48. RF, *Annual Report 1935*, 279, this quote refers to a grant for the WWBF.

49. The quotes are from Gary, "Communication Research," 124f.

50. This assumption was supposedly based on an interview with the director of the Argentine-North American Institute of Culture in Buenos Aires, Argentina. Memorandum Relative to a Projected Series of Educational and Cultural Radio Broadcasts to Latin America, 6. RAC, RF, RG 1.1, Series 200, Box 266, Folder 3170.

51. See "Memorandum Relative to a Projected Series."

52. "The Americas on the Air," 9. RAC, RF, RG 1.1, Series 200, Box 266, Folder 3171.

53. U.S. Department of Commerce, Bureau of Foreign and Domestic Commerce, *Report of International Short-Wave Broadcasting Reception in Latin America* (Washington: GPO, 1937).

54. For an overview over the expansion of shortwave transmission facilities in the 1930s, see Boehlke, *Macht des Radios*, 28–70.

55. For a comprehensive discussion see Gregory, *The Broadcasting Service*, Part 2; Michael B. Salwen, "Broadcasting to Latin America: Reconciling Industry-Government Functions in the Pre-Voice of America Era," *Historical Journal of Film, Radio and Television* 17, no. 1 (1997): 67–89; Fejes, *Imperialism*, 63–114.

56. *Newsweek*, 29 November, 1937.

57. NARA II, RG 173, Federal Communications Commission, Entry 100A, General Correspondence 1927–46, Box 451, Folder 89–6, G. P. Adair, Acting Chief, Broadcast Section, Engineering Department, Memorandum to the Commission, 4 December, 1937, 3.

58. *Washington Post*, 9 January, 1938, B1, 7.

59. These quotes were taken from a short interim report from the Rockefeller Foundation titled "The Americas on the Air," from early 1938, 9. RAC, RF, RG 1.1, Series 200, Box 266, Folder 3171.

60. For a brief portrayal of the Pan American Union, its foundation, functions, and organizational features, cf. Gordon Connell-Smith, *The Inter-American System* (London: Oxford University Press, 1966), 44–61.

61. Robert O. Keohane and Joseph S. Nye, "Power and Interdependence in the Information Age," *Foreign Affairs* 77, no. 5 (September/October 1998): 81–94.

62. On Rowe's position and politics see Robert David Johnson, "The Politization of Cultural Diplomacy: Inter-American Relations between the World Wars," *The Cultural Turn. Essays in the History of U.S. Foreign Relations*, eds. Frank A. Ninkovich and Liping Bu (Chicago: Imprint, 2001), 131–55, particularly 139–48. During the war, the PAU would receive funding from Rockefeller's OIAA for a number of projects deemed promising in the propaganda war against the Axis, including the organization of essay contests with the title "What Inter-American Cooperation Means to My Country." For further details cf. NARA II, RG 229, Entry 1, General Records, Central Files, 3. Information, Science and Education, Contests, Scholarships, Box 382, Folder: Latin American Essay Contest CO–111, OEMcr–71.

63. This is not the place to engage in a discussion of such a complex issue as the Good Neighbor policy; for a general treatment of the matter see David Green, *The Containment of Latin America. A History of the Myths and Realities of the Good Neighbor Policy* (Chicago: Quadrangle Books, 1971); Frederick B. Pike, *FDR's Good Neighbor Policy: Sixty Years of Generally Gentle Chaos* (Austin: University of Texas Press, 1995); Irwin F. Gellman, *Good Neighbor Diplomacy. United States Policies in Latin America, 1933–1945* (Baltimore & London: Johns Hopkins University Press, 1979). Although his treatment of some of the issues involved appear outdated today, Green's insistence on treating the Good Neighbor policies as a form of power politics remains valid.

64. JM Interview with Rowe, 22 July, 1938.

65. "The Americas on the Air," 9–10. RAC, RF, RG 1.1, Series 200, Box 266, Folder 3171.

66. For a discussion of the contents of OIAA campaigns directed toward Latin America see Ursula Prutsch, *Creating Good Neighbors? Die Kultur- und Wirtschaftspolitik der USA in Lateinamerika, 1940–1946* (Stuttgart: Steiner, 2008); Uwe Lübken, *Bedrohliche Nähe. Die USA und die nationalsozialistische Herausforderung in Latein amerika, 1937–1945* (Stuttgart: Steiner, 2004).

67. For a rather sarcastic description of the blunt propaganda that pervaded some of the radio programming during the war, see Hernane Tavares de Sá, *The Brazilians. People of Tomorrow* (New York: John Day, 1947), 229–35. Tavares de Sá had been one of the foreign advisors to the OIAA.

68. The tensions between advocates of "internationalist," "national interest," and "aggressive national interest" approaches in the State Department and the Office of Inter-American Affairs are discussed in Frank A. Ninkovich, *The Diplomacy of Ideas. U.S. Foreign Policy and Cultural Relations, 1938–1950* (Cambridge: Cambridge University Press, 1981), chapter 2.

69. See, for instance, the *Washington Post*, 9 January, 1938, B1.

70. This was one of the earliest broadcasts in the Pan American series; for further details see "The Americas on the Air." RAC, RF, RG 1.1, Series 200, Box 266, Folder 3171.

71. *Newsweek*, 29 November, 1937.

72. Lemmon to Manger, 9 April, 1940. RAC, RF, RG 1.1, Series 200, Box 266, Folder 3171.

73. As had been suggested in Barbour's report on the findings of his trip to the Rockefeller Foundation, Summary of Present Situation of Broadcasting in Latin America, 17 June, 1937 (Philip Barbour). RAC, RF, RG 1.1, Series 200, Box 266, Folder 3170.

74. IAL (Irving A. Leonard) Interviews; Mr. Philip Barbour, 3 November, 1938. RAC, RF, RG 1.1, Series 200, Box 266, Folder 3171. Barbour's complaints should not be dismissed as that of a disgruntled employee. Thus, Robert E. Sherwood, the director of the Foreign Information Service, complained about the station: "The business affairs of this station has been conducted in such a weird and sloppy manner that the organization is now under investigation by the F.C.C." Sherwood to President, 7 May, 1942. FDR Library, OF 4425. Radio Station WRUL, 1940–42. During the war, Barbour would work for Nelson Rockefeller's OIAA.

75. JM Interview with L. S. Rowe, Director of Pan American Union, 22 July, 1938.

76. Beth Arlene Roberts, "United States Propaganda Warfare in Latin America," (PhD dissertation, University of Southern California, 1943), 382, as quoted in Fejes, *Imperialism*, 102.

77. Rowe to Leonard, 21 November, 1938; Marshall to Rowe, 17 March, 1939. RAC, RF, RG 1.1, Series 200, Box 266, Folder 3171.

78. JM Interview with Rowe, 22 July, 1938.

79. Among the staples of propaganda contents directed at Latin American audiences were, for instance, shows on the wars of independence, the national heroes and their struggle for liberty against foreign (i.e., European) oppressors. The documentation for these and other examples is to be found in NARA II, RG 229.

80. Rockefeller's OIAA came to control one-third of WRUL's station time for its broadcasts to Latin America, whereas the Office of War Information (OWI) controlled the remaining two-thirds for broadcasts directed at other parts of the world.

81. NARA II, RG 173, Federal Communications Commission, Entry 100A, General Correspondence 1927–46, Box 451, Folder 89–6, David C. Crockett, Executive Secretary, WWBF, to Charles Sumner Bird, 11 April, 1942, and attached news clips. Lemmon's resistance to the proposed leasing arrangements by which the government took over the nations' shortwave stations may have been motivated by disappointment about the financial compensation WWBC was to receive. Shapley, however, fought explicitly and publicly for the right to determine at least a part of the programming over World Wild's station.

6

Hollywood Bypass: MoMA, the Rockefeller Foundation, and New Circuits of Cinema

Haidee Wasson

In 1935 the Museum of Modern Art (MoMA), New York, announced the formation of a film library, a department tasked with saving and exhibiting films. At this point in American history the screen life of a typical film was extremely brief; the bulk of commercial features were rushed off of movie screens to make way for the next, new film. Their return to the screen was highly unlikely. Viewing art films, and what we today call movie classics, was an unusual activity, possible in major urban centers and only a small number of theaters. Not only was film culture predicated on the ephemeral life of particular films, it was also dominated by a relatively recent, but formidable, centralized force: Hollywood. The American Supreme Court's 1915 decision defining film as a "business pure and simple," legally enshrined the industry's primary organizing principle: film as commercial entertainment. This decision proved lasting and pervasive, securing the way for a functional oligopoly not just over film production but also over film distribution and exhibition. Alternative models for film culture, predicated on the idea that film making and film viewing might be free from the imperatives of profit and consumerism, participant in artistic, agitational, or minority formations, survived only on the margins of film culture. Such ideas took their earliest and fullest shape outside of the United States in nations seeking to protect themselves from Hollywood's imperial reach.

As such, when MoMA announced the marriage of film to art museum, there was widespread uncertainty about the pairing. The prominent and authoritative art museum seemed at odds with the commercial and popular medium. Questions persisted: what did a common and spectacular amusement have to do with the comparatively elite and sacral space of the museum? Why would anybody watch an *old film*? What did art have to do with movies? There can be no doubt that in the 1930s, museums were dramatically different from commercial movie theaters, art significantly distinct from main-street movies. Their content, themes, modes of exhibition, and social rituals—on the whole—represented distinct forms of cultural value and disparate socioeconomic constituencies. Movies were not accompanied by docent lectures, dates of origin, or didactic placards. Art was not generally host to raucous and polyglot crowds but to civilized and select viewers. American art museums brimmed with European paintings and sculptures; European films appeared infrequently, if at all, in American movie theaters. Art had pedigree; movies did not. To be sure, the worlds of movies and museums were notably different and at first glance mutually incompatible.

Early film screenings at MoMA confirm the oddity of the coupling. Visitors to the museum's auditorium demonstrated uncertainty about basic things, such as how to behave when watching movies in an art museum. The ideal art viewer observed in quiet, reverent concentration. By comparison, the ideal moviegoer engaged in a highly social and interactive event. Movie theaters entailed a diversified film program. Sing-a-alongs, animated shorts, feature films, and newsreels often invited audience members to participate in a dynamic mode of leisure. MoMA's filmgoers walked knowingly into a disjunctive mode of film-viewing and museum-going, one that operated on principles distinct from those overseen by Hollywood but also dissonant with those imagined by museum administrators. Confusion resulted. Despite what MoMA's programmers imagined as a new, enlightened, and serious film audience, viewers enacted precious little of the dignified and controlled behavior desired. They talked loudly during screenings. They argued aggressively over seats. They laughed at tragic heroes and weeping women, cackling with abandon at the sight of violent deaths. They arrived to films late and left early. It seems from available reports that the raucous movie viewer dominated the quiet art appreciator, importing behavioral norms and entertainment rituals straight from the world of popular amusement. Complicating this, the expansive network created by the Film Library, which not only showed films at the museum but also sent films to viewing groups throughout the country, functionally created hundreds of satellite museum movie theaters, multiplying the contextual factors bearing upon this novel cultural configuration. As the museum's audience expanded—and continued to both accept but also resist its institutional authority—museum administrators and curators scrambled to control its spiraling project.[1] Taking films seriously at MoMA was neither simple nor obvious; it required imposing persistent institutional discipline and entailed recognizing that the museum's sprawling film audience would, in fact, persist in misbehaving.

MoMA's film activities then constitute both a novel *idea* about cinema—film belongs alongside the other modern arts—and also a novel *material configuration*—films from all periods should be circulated and seen beyond and outside of the commercial movie theater. The Film Library's success can, in part, be traced to these now common-sense assertions. Its basic principles provide the foundation of the home theater, the art-house movie complex, and the public museum alike. Yet, during the 1930s there was no guarantee of its endurance, let alone its short-term survival. The film industry monitored the library's activities but only supplied minimal and token financial support. If the general public found MoMA's experiment unusual, MoMA's Board of Trustees demonstrated its own ambivalence. Denied museum funding in its earliest years, the library was in fact made whole by a few determined employees and made possible by essential support from the Rockefeller Foundation. Because it was the primary source of financial support, the Foundation exercised considerable influence on the formative shape and direction of the library itself, expanding the art museum into a film theater, and also catalyzing a mobile network of film programs and exhibition venues. This chapter identifies the importance of MoMA's Film Library for changing ideas and practices of cinema during the interwar period. It does so by examining its relationship to Rockefeller Foundation goals, considering the underexamined role of American philanthropy in the history of the first American film archive and film museum. This paper argues that the Rockefeller Foundation played a small but crucial role in shaping a key institution of cinema, and it helped to form a generative site for the basic idea that film could and should be seen outside of movie theaters with the purpose of studied contemplation and civic engagement.

MoMA OPENS

America's first museum of modern art opened in October 1929, just ten days after the stock market crash that signaled the beginning of the Great Depression. Founded by members of the established American elite, MoMA introduced a considerably new model of art and art institutions into the museum world. Abby Aldrich Rockefeller, Lillie P. Bliss, and Mary Quinn Sullivan, often referred to as "the ladies," acted as the driving force behind the museum's early formation. Their interests in modern art were, of course, made possible by their privilege. All three traveled extensively in Europe. Early discussions about the museum began in Egypt, on trans-Atlantic cruise ships, and during various salons, teas, and luncheons. Such encounters led directly to hiring Alfred Barr, the young maverick art historian, schooled at Princeton and Harvard, who became the museum's first director. Barr imported a then-unusual approach to modern art. In addition to his commitment to what is conventionally known as modernism (the paintings and sculptures of the impressionists, symbolists, constructivists, surrealists, and so on), he also understood art as a cross-formal dialogue. A good art historian, according to Barr, understood not just the painting or sculpture of a given era, but also the pottery, wall drawings, graphic design, and, if appropriate, reproducible forms and mechanisms. Thus, from the beginning, MoMA was organized to encompass all arts indigenous to the modern period, which included film, photography, design, theater, dance, and architecture. As a museum administrator, Barr also asserted his long interest in art education and was unafraid to make use of so-called mass media to forward his ideas about art, connoisseurship, and everyday life. Accordingly, MoMA was chartered as a national educational institution. It quickly became the most visible museum in the country, well known nationally and internationally. This was due in no small part to the museum's aggressive adaptation of the circulating exhibit and its enthusiastic embrace of relatively inexpensive and wide-reaching media forms. The museum's active public-relations campaigns ensured that its educational mission and advocacy for modern art appeared almost daily in middlebrow magazines, newspapers, and on radio programs.

By the early 1930s, MoMA constituted a daily national force, one that was frequently aided by the Rockefeller imprint. The museum's links to the Rockefeller name, fortune, and Rolodex constitute not only a steady presence in museum publicity but also in museum organization and gallery exhibits. In addition to Abby Rockefeller's initial work to form the museum, she served on the board of trustees throughout the museum's early years. She also made several donations of art to the museum. Such bequests include thirty-six oil paintings, and 105 watercolors, gouaches, and pastels in 1936, which culminated in a show titled *New Acquisitions: The Collection of Mrs. John D. Rockefeller* (1936). In 1939 she donated thirty-six sculptures, which became the basis of the sculpture garden now bearing her name. A year later she donated 1,600 prints, mostly by American artists. Upon her death in 1948, the Abby Aldrich Print Room opened, featuring these and other prints. Her personal collection also became the basis for several exhibitions, including *American Folk Art: The Art of the Common Man in America, 1750–1900* (1933).[2] She also contributed art to the infamous van Gogh exhibition in 1935. The museum, in short, provided regular exposure for her personal collection, which helps to explain why members of her family referred to MoMA as "Mother's Museum." Abby additionally provided cash donations to the museum, allowing Alfred Barr to purchase art during his European travels. In January 1938, she donated $20,000 to establish an acquisition fund for the museum.[3] It's worth noting that Abby's determined advocacy for the museum was inversely related to the disapproval of the modern arts expressed by her husband John D. Rockefeller Jr., who favored antiquities and classical European art forms.[4] Indeed, despite the family's ample wealth, he went so far as to limit her spending on art to no more than $25,000 per year, declaring this to her in the form of a dictated memo.[5] Barr once described John Jr.'s attitude toward modern art as "granite indifference."[6] Indeed, John Jr.'s support of the arts took a radically different path, most well known is his contemporaneous support for the Metropolitan Museum of Art's satellite museum, the Cloisters, dedicated to medieval art. Nonetheless, his feeling toward modern art did not prevent him from approving the donation of the very land upon which MoMA's signature building was constructed at West Fifty-third Street, opening its doors in 1939. Last, Nelson Rockefeller, one of Abby's favored sons and future governor, was elected president of the museum in 1939.[7] To be sure, the Rockefeller name was a constituent component of the museum's brick-and-mortar foundation, as well as its steel and glass aesthetic.

While other Rockefeller family members played varying roles throughout the museum's seventy-five-year history, Abby and Nelson occupied by far the most significant positions during the museum's first twenty years. In some ways surprising, both also participated to a degree in the formation of the film department. Abby served on the first museum committee to survey the possibilities of establishing a film department, along with Edward Warburg and John Hay Whitney.[8] But even before this, Abby kept an eye on the film activities of the museum. In 1933, working in the fledgling museum library, Iris Barry—who would later become the Film Library's first curator—began to publish the first issues of the museum's bulletin. On its brief pages, she began to include reviews for films playing in the New York area. Titles were surprisingly wide ranging from the bawdy to the experimental: *The Three Little Pigs* (Walt Disney, 1933), *Tarzan and His Mate* (Cedric Gibbons, 1934),[9] *The Private Life of Henry VIII* (Alexander Korda, 1933), *Queen Christina* (Rouben Mamoulian, 1933), *Thunder Over Mexico* (Sergei Eisenstein, 1933), and *Lot in Sodom* (J. Sibley Watson and Melville Webber, 1933). The very first of Barry's reviews discussed the sultry Mae West, calling her film *She Done Him Wrong* (Lowell Sherman, 1933) the "Hollywood product at its vital best—perfect pace, brilliant execution, robust approach to an attack upon a simple subject, and a perfect vehicle for that original screen personality, Mae West."[10] In doing so, Barry had succeeded both in discussing a controversial female film figure and in lending critical acclaim to *Variety's* top-grossing 1933 film in the museum's new bulletin.[11] The popular clashed with the properly artistic, ruffling some museum members' feathers. Mrs. Rockefeller took notice.

Sitting beside Barry's review of *She Done Him Wrong* was a review of Frank Lloyd's *Cavalcade* (1933), adapted from Noel Coward's stage play of the same name. *Cavalcade* was a middlebrow historical drama, documenting the multigenerational effects of war on one family. It was also winner of the 1933 Academy Award for Best Picture. Nonetheless, Barry dismissed the film as "theatrical where it should be cinematic, dense with false sentiment and inverted patriotism," and notably not a film that "calls for praise or imitation."[12] One internal document suggests that these film reviews stirred up "something of a hornet's nest." Abby Rockefeller received calls from her indignant friends, expressing outrage that the museum could, on the one hand, endorse such a "vulgar" film and on the other reject such an obviously high-minded and elevated play like Coward's. Barry explained to Rockefeller that while *Cavalcade* was entirely derivative of stage conventions, West was a uniquely cinematic personality and screen presence, true to the medium and therefore utterly original.[13] Apparently, the explanation was sufficiently persuasive, though the discussion would continue. The need to appease Abby further indicates the power and influence she held at the museum. Barr—a longtime advocate for film—understood this, and before securing Film Library success, regularly sent postcards to her, and to others, with recommendations of current films "which seemed works of art."[14] Film Library staff also kept Abby informed about key programming strategies and proudly announced healthy film attendance.[15] Abby Rockefeller eventually acquiesced to the idea of film art, though she continued to express concern about accepting films that contained sexual and therefore objectionable content, which she euphemistically termed "Freudian." Her friends, as we have seen, had similar opinions.[16]

Disagreements generated by MoMA's film plans resonate throughout internal museum documents; the clash between polite and affirmative films and those that were more overtly sexual, frankly gritty, and even vaguely propagandistic (e.g., Soviet or French) films appeared regularly. Nelson Rockefeller also felt the brunt of this conflict between the seemingly high and apparently low objects of culture that collided regularly at the museum. For instance, as museum president, Nelson was forced to defend the programs of the Film Library against a growing body of critics: film writers, politicized agitators, and even famed filmmaker D. W. Griffith. This last example is most interesting as it best embodies the pull between the American, internationalist elite, and the populist characters filling the American film scene. D. W. Griffith himself sent a rude missive to Rockefeller objecting to Iris Barry's position as curator and her plans to mount a landmark show dedicated to Griffith's films in 1940. In this letter, Griffith wrote that he and other film attendees were dismayed that Barry regularly expressed more enthusiasm for the recent spate of Soviet films shown at the museum than for Griffith's own homegrown American ones. Griffith conceded that this was understandable, given that Barry—born in the United Kingdom—herself was "foreign." His argument against Barry grew. He cited numerous conversations with unnamed people who also felt that she seemed consistently and notably unfriendly to American films in general. He continued:

> Now I don't pretend to be damn brilliant or dipped deeply in the wine of sophistication but I, as an American, made pictures mostly for the Americans and I believe on the whole the American people have liked my pictures very well.[17]

Griffith concluded the letter to Rockefeller with the suggestion that rather than Barry, his brother, Albert Griffith Grey, curate the show and that Seymour Stern write the film notes. He suggested that if this could not be arranged he would prefer that his films not be shown at all. He finished the letter: "Sorry to make all this trouble for you but you are young, good looking and have all that dough and on the other hand, I am an old and fading weed and don't want to work no more. So, on the whole, I think it is only right that I should give you at least a little trouble." He signed the letter "most insincerely yours." Griffith's Americanist populism and clear disaffection for Rockefeller wealth did not win out. Rockefeller responded politely but directly. In the end, Barry curated the show, from which a lasting and influential book was also written, a book that ironically helped to secure Griffith's place in an American film canon.[18]

Abby and Nelson Rockefeller hold important roles in the early history of the Film Library, in part, because of their general prominence both inside and outside of the museum. But their direct or even regular influence on the library appears minimal. By far the most important Rockefeller influence on the Film Library was that of the Foundation. To emphasize, when MoMA's Film Library formed, its future was by no means secure. Despite obtaining an official mandate from the museum, the Film Library had no consistent source of revenue or other financial support. Museum trustees were polite and tolerant but not forthcoming. Hollywood moguls were suspicious and kept their distance. The idea of "free movies" had long been known to cause waves of nausea among them. It was the funding supplied by the Humanities Division of the Rockefeller Foundation that made the project possible at all.

Support for the Film Library resulted from a marked shift in the Humanities Division's official mandate, which had recently been charged with reorienting their funding away from "cloistered" research and toward individuals and organizations interested in "the obvious sources of influence of public taste today."[19] Film, in addition to other mass media, fell cleanly within this mandate. The status of film research or what we might call "film knowledge" and education during this period was emergent, but still largely scattered and certainly far from centralized. Foundation officials were uninterested in practices and discourses of morality and censorship that typified the ongoing struggle between Hollywood and various religious and civic organizations. The Foundation seemed equally unpersuaded by effects-research that had been popularized by the widely circulated versions of the Payne Fund Studies, the most elaborate film-research project up to that time.[20] Rather, Rockefeller officers sought to effect change in the manner in which people watched and understood movies, seeking to engender discrimination in film viewing. This, it was believed, would provide a defense against the deleterious influences of so-called mass media and a corrective to the damaging effects of propaganda—commercial, foreign, and domestic.[21] The models for using film in this way were most fully developed outside of the United States and had yet to be adequately implemented inside its national borders. The ongoing work of John Grierson in London during the late 1920s and 1930s (and in Ottawa as of 1939) was considered an ideal model. Key here was not just Grierson's efforts to make particular kinds of films (documentaries), but deemed equally important was the construction of supporting distribution and exhibition circuits, crucial for fomenting the productive use of films by a network of engaged publics. Rockefeller officers considered this model necessary to, but distinct from, the dominant commercial modes enshrined by Hollywood.

John Marshall, the key Foundation officer here, consistently expressed interest in coordinating and furthering the civic possibilities of film education and educational film. He pursued these goals at MoMA, but also through several other projects. Among these was the American Film Centre (AFC), headed by Donald Slesinger, founded in 1938 and based in Rockefeller Center. The film center acted primarily as an information resource to educational-film exhibitors, filmmakers, and public-service agencies. In general, the AFC linked those who needed educational films with those interested in making them, serving as a coordinator in the educational film field. Its initial mandate was broad and included several major goals: (1) research into audience habits and preferences; (2) establishing cooperation among schools and adult education groups; and (3) assisting MoMA in forming a national network of film societies. Brett Gary reports, however, that the AFC primarily became deeply embroiled in assisting with the needs of state agencies during the war.[22] In addition to the AFC, the Rockefeller-funded General Education Board also supplied money to form the School Film Libraries Association and other projects to facilitate the use of films in public libraries as well as schools and universities.[23] Also important to note is Foundation support for film societies outside of the United States. Indeed, throughout the latter half of the 1930s, the Foundation funded the growth of Canadian film societies, established on principles similar to MoMA's Film Library.[24] Collectively, these projects should be understood as linked closely to Marshall's vision for new models that productively paired media with public and general education. This impetus irrefutably influenced the shape taken by MoMA's Film Library. Its exhibition programs as well as the scholarship conducted with its resources grew directly from Rockefeller mandates.

Marshall was the officer actively involved with MoMA's film project. Initially, he believed that MoMA provided the opportunity to fund an organization with aspirations of national significance that sought to link educational organizations and institutions and to better develop educational distribution channels. He was less interested in film art or in art films than in establishing film's civic place within projects to elevate standards of public engagement. His conception of film education included educating *with* film as well as *about* film.[25] Most important, Marshall was committed to generating a particular kind of film-viewing public. This audience was, he imagined, essential for eventually influencing the kinds of films available not just outside of movie theaters but inside them as well. Of the Film Library's project he wrote:

> If it succeeds, it will organize a new audience for films much as the Carnegie Library organized a reading public which was previously nonexistent. And, if such an audience exists for films that cannot now be shown theatrically, its existence should give substantial encouragement to the production of new films of educational and cultural value.[26]

Marshall relied here on a well-known and successful effort to integrate book libraries into an everyday common sense about the place of reading in American life. Here book libraries provide a metaphor and model for a fundamental transformation of film culture, one that was far more coordinated and integrated with an idea about the productive interface between celluloid and public life than had been previously realized.

THE FOUNDATION FUNDS FILM

When Alfred Barr initially began agitating for a Film Library at MoMA, his initial vision was significantly different from that which gradually evolved. Barr was influenced by the relatively small but highly engaged film societies that formed in major European cities during the 1920s and early 1930s. Such venues provided access to largely European films, and they provided a context for discussion that was charged with the intellectual and aesthetic debates characterizing the evolving modern arts in general. In short, Barr suggested that MoMA build a modest cinema salon, where hard-to-find titles by mostly European directors could be shown to a discerning if small public. The salon would feature amateur and avant-garde experiments, as well as include works by filmmakers now identified as comprising the canon of so-called narrative art cinema (Abel Gance, Mauritz Stiller, René Clair, E. A. Dupont, Jacques Feyder). Eisenstein, Pudovkin, and Chaplin "as director" also earned mention. Barr called attention as well to the decaying state of many of "the great films of the past quarter century." He suggested, consequently, that a curatorial as well as an exhibition division might also be considered for the museum. In its earliest formulations, however, the Film Library resembled a cine salon, designed to show accomplished works at the museum by great, primarily European artists.[27]

Less than three years later, in April 1935, Barry and John E. Abbott (Barry's husband and a former Wall Street financier) submitted what would become the foundational document for the establishment of a film department, then named the Film Library.[28] Two months later, the foundation of the Film Library was publicly announced, funded by a start-up grant supplied by the Rockefeller Foundation and matched with lesser funds by John Hay Whitney, an avid art collector, a museum insider, and a film-industry investor. Nelson Rockefeller was present at the signing. Barry presided as curator, Whitney was appointed president, and Abbott became director. The official mandate read:

> The purpose of the Film Library of the Museum of Modern Art is to trace, catalog, assemble, preserve, exhibit and circulate to museums and colleges single films or programs of all types of film in exactly the same manner in which the museum traces, catalogs, exhibits and circulates paintings, sculpture, models and photographs of architectural buildings, or reproductions of works of art, so that the film may be studied and enjoyed as any other one of the arts is studied and enjoyed.[29]

Sidestepping debates about high, low, or middlebrow cultural forms, the Film Library set out to include a comprehensive sample of "film art," a working category seemingly unrestricted by reformist, high-aesthetic, or Marxist critiques of Hollywood film or bourgeois concepts of art. Barr's Eurocentrism was radically expanded. "Film art" grew to include examples of modernist European cinema as well as narrative, documentary, spectacular, Western, slapstick, comedy-drama, musical, animated, abstract, scientific, educational, dramatic, amateur, and newsreel films.[30]

Like Barr's earlier pleas, the "Outline" asserted that the motion picture was the only great art peculiar to the twentieth century, significant not only for its "aesthetic qualities," but also for its effect on taste and the lives of the "large bulk of population."[31] Thus, the Film Library encompassed the sociological and populist functions of cinema as well. Moreover, Barr's revised cine salon combined with the ascendant modes of curation and educational practices at the museum; the library staff intended not only to collect such films but also to circulate them widely through the expanding exhibition circuit comprised of museums, schools, film societies, and civic clubs, making available "those films which the individual groups everywhere have found difficult to obtain."[32] Also included in the "Outline" was a plan to lend projectors, to compose and circulate film notes, to assemble a library of film literature, to act as a clearinghouse for information on all aspects of film, and to link interested groups to this information and to each other. Nourishing a nascent film culture was a conscious yet carefully designed goal, avoiding contentious claims that film was simply an art like all others and also avoiding the association of the Film Library programs with entertainment—the proverbial poor cousin of educational and art films. The sweeping nature of this plan reveals more than Abbott and Barry's enthusiasm; it also marks a clear shift away from the exclusive Euro ciné salon first envisioned by Barr. Amateur, avant-garde, and popular American films—old and new—would ideally take their place beside the works of European narrative art directors, in part so that American films could be more fully respected, and in part so that an increasingly diverse community could be supplied with the films it wanted.[33] Such acts constitute an expanded idea of institutional function, embodying a new ideal for museums and cinema.

The library grew quickly and soon found itself issuing daily press releases, earning international recognition, and circulating its programs widely. As these early years progressed, smaller Foundation grants continued to exercise influence on its shape. Given Marshall's interest in both generating a body of film knowledge and growing distribution and exhibition circuits, the Foundation approved special one-time grants to the Film Library to fund targeted programs. For instance, through 1935 and 1937, Jay Leyda was funded specifically on several distinct grants to (1) research and write film program notes, (2) to study the organization of film materials in the United States and Europe for loan and rental, and (3) to help with developing the circulating educational programs of the library.[34] This was in addition to his research on Soviet film that was also funded by the Foundation.[35] Indeed, a great deal of the research generated at MoMA reflects the Foundation's interest in documentary film, as well as its investments in understanding contemporary media more generally. Well-known documentarians such as Paul Rotha and Basil Wright were invited to take up research residences at the Film Library. Rotha accepted the invitation, delivering a series of lectures on documentary-film methods and "the creative presentation of facts as we find them in everyday life." He advocated that film could and should be used for combining aesthetic and civic experiments: fusing the cinematic with the citizen.[36] Marshall also brokered grants to Siegfried Kracauer (now-canonical film theorist) to study at the Film Library, which culminated in the publication of his seminal sociopsychological study of Weimar and Nazi cinema, *From Caligari to Hitler: A Psychological History of the German Film*.[37]

The initial money donated by the Foundation represented the bulk of library funds, and—more problematically—was intended as a temporary seed grant. As such, John Abbott and Iris Barry (director and curator respectively) needed to shape their future grant requests, and indeed the library itself, in accordance with Marshall's ideas, which depended heavily on increasing the accessibility to films and the means by which educational-film viewing might occur. Abbott and Barry continually documented their activities in this field by highlighting their circulating programs and their program notes. An appendix to a 1937 report on the library's activities, authored by Abbott, articulated a role for the Film Library that fashioned it primarily as a national coordinator for educational-film activities, with a view to growing a production house as well as a training school for filmmakers.[38] Throughout, Marshall pushed Barry and Abbott to target the creation of film-study circuits. Marshall was well aware that the difficulties of this were numerous and included the basic expense to museums, colleges, and study groups of both buying 16 mm equipment and also renting the library's programs. He nonetheless persisted.

By 1938 Marshall conceded that among all American organizations funded by the Rockefeller Foundation that the Film Library's activities were "the most visible and important for organizing specialized audiences with tastes for classics, documentaries or non-entertainment driven films," acknowledging their early success with creating an extensive specialized and educational service through traveling film programs.[39] Yet Marshall remained unsatisfied with this success, recommending that the library hire a field agent to further explore opportunities for film study and to resolve the distribution problems that continued to plague it. He also began to informally as well as formally pressure the library to gear its activities even more in this direction. Only two years into the Foundation's support for the library, he explicitly asked that money it gave in the future be channeled toward the library's services to distributing films to educational institutions.[40]

The library was encouraged to lower rental prices, to more actively work to form film societies, and to increase the number of touring lectures.[41] The Film Library, according to the Foundation, needed to increase its audience, partly, it reasoned, so that through film rentals it might become self-sufficient. Expanding the audience, it was believed, would also better ensure that the goals of fostering film appreciation and influencing the kinds of film produced would be more likely to succeed. The library politely agreed with Marshall, and made efforts to focus more on the "effort to organize its potential audience" and "to concentrate its efforts on educational work through course offerings in schools, colleges, and universities." This resulted in the hire of Douglas Baxter, who was tasked with assessing and resolving MoMA's distribution needs. His report indicated that the main barriers to increased screenings were lack of funds and equipment; objection to inability to charge admission (more on that below); and basic disinterest among the educational community.[42]

Important to note here is that the Rockefeller Foundation was notably adverse to sanctifying film art or in fortifying the Film Library as a singular site in which individual films would become cherished relics, practices inspired by the traditional model of the art museum. It primarily conceived of films less as objects and more as pedagogical activities that corresponded more effectively to the new mediated environments in which people lived. The Film Library was best conceived, according to the Foundation, as a method for mass education and as an early contributor to the formation of a national infrastructure to facilitate this. There is little evidence that either Marshall or any other Foundation officer assumed close scrutiny of film-library acquisitions in general or of individual films in particular, or that it took any clear steps to control its curatorial affairs or to limit its internationalism. The idea of the specialized and attentive audience was an idealized abstraction, posed against the similarly abstract mass, whose broad outlines seem to have been largely accepted by MoMA and the Foundation.

CIRCULATING PROGRAMS—LIBRARY SUCCESSES

During its first ten-year period, MoMA's film offerings expanded and its programming diversified. Yet there remained numerous impediments to library success. The agreement that the Film Library had struck with the industry governing exhibition of its films proved to have a lasting and sizable impact. This agreement stipulated that all user groups must qualify as educational and nonprofit—no admission could be charged. The effects of this were twofold. On the one hand, it was restrictive. It meant that anyone who wanted to see one of their films either had to become a museum member and live in New York, or he/she had to join or perhaps form a study group somewhere else. On the other hand, it served as a catalyst for further institutionalization of a particular ideal of cinematic engagement, providing a formative influence on the emergence of an American film-society movement. The founding of such groups was encouraged in film-library catalogs and brochures throughout the period.[43] Forming a film society made potential renters readily identifiable under the institution's remit. Closely linked to the emergence of a film-society movement is the marked increase of interest in university-level film study throughout the 1920s and 1930s. Film societies commonly—though not exclusively—formed under the aegis of established organs of higher education. It was these organizations that became crucial to MoMA's success, actively renting films and also lending legitimacy to their activities. In turn, film-library programs and film notes fundamentally changed the material conditions in which film study evolved in the United States.[44]

MoMA's film programs and program notes allowed a still-unusual idea—films could and should be studied—to shift from local, specific, and sometimes eclectic projects to a nationally-organized, highly-coordinated system that could be run with regularity and reliability. Film Library programs offered the advantage of expert curation, reliability, and authoritative sanction; they were based on a standardized set of films and also on regulated methods for analysis around which curriculum could be established and maintained. The didactic inter-titles, inserted by library staff to all of its circulating films, served as automated film lectures, inexpensively distributed and reproduced with each film projection. Screenings of MoMA programs were held not just by film societies, but were also hosted by university departments across the curriculum.[45] Indeed, MoMA's films were used in a surprising range of departments and programs, including visual education, drama, public speaking, art and archeology, fine arts, economics, and sociology. Library programs were also frequently shown in language departments. Film societies concurrently proliferated at many of these same institutions, fed almost exclusively by MoMA's programs.[46]

The use of MoMA's programs also spread to appreciation clubs, amateur and art associations, as well as to previously established educational groups, and museums throughout the United States and Canada. Despite what may seem a relative success for the new exhibitor, particularly given the prestigious venues in which its films appeared, the library as well as the Rockefeller Foundation remained dissatisfied with the comparatively small percentage of the film-going audience they attracted. Clearly one of the problems facing the library in its quest to generate a studious audience for cinema was material. Potential audiences and rental groups lacked some of the most basic requirements for participating in the study circuit. Many simply did not have access to a film projector. Additionally, those interested in renting or buying necessary equipment possessed widely varying kinds of spaces, with different seating arrangements, and unreliable power supplies. Voltages, frequencies, and amperages varied. Early on, the Film Library anticipated that such variables would present a problem. As such, they discussed supplying projectors along with their films and even generated a scheme to act as a broker for the purchase of adequate projection systems. Yet, these did not come to fruition. Well into 1940, technical problems combined with a general shortage of funds, continued to hinder groups interested in library programs.

The vast majority of Film Library programs circulated in 16 mm format. Yet, despite the spread of the 16 mm gauge nationally and internationally, penetration of the format was by no means complete. Further, the cost of 16 mm projectors was still relatively high during this period, taxing small groups and institutions with meager and even modest audiovisual budgets. For instance, in 1935 AMPRO sold a silent 16 mm projector for $135 ($2,153 in 2008). Victor sold its 16 mm sound projector for as much as $395 ($6,300 in 2008). Self-projection technology was itself developing rapidly, with various silent projectors and later sound projectors introduced throughout the period. Constantly improving machines adapted to continually discovered needs, new units were marketed throughout the decade. Such contraptions featured adaptable lenses and more powerful bulbs to accommodate viewing spaces of varying dimensions. In order to manage these complexities, Barry suggested early on that the library might circulate its own projector and screen with the programs, creating a self-contained theater impervious to constant changes and high costs. She estimated that this would cost the library $575 ($9,171 in 2008)—a sizable portion of their available budget.[47]

The cost of renting the programs themselves was also a problem. Initially, the library intended to work by annual subscription, charging a membership fee of $250 ($3,987 in 2008) per year for use of its services. Judging this to be utterly prohibitive, it began to charge per program: $25 ($332 in 2008) for a two-hour film program in either 35 mm or 16 mm gauge if booking the whole series; $40 ($638 in 2008) for the same program if not. After criticism from the Rockefeller Foundation, as well as reports from the field that its programs remained beyond affordability, the library lowered its prices, differentiating rental rates by film gauge, and making the structure of available programs more flexible. Despite this, total revenue for film rentals dropped during the following year in approximately the same ratio as the price reduction, possibly indicating that the price reduction was either inadequate or irrelevant.[48] Further, it became increasingly evident that film rentals, once held to be the primary method by which the library might wean itself from outside support, could simply never provide a self-sustaining source of income for the library. Barry estimated that the library was only able to earn somewhere between 5 and 10 percent of its operating costs back through income earned by film rentals.[49] In short, distributing and exhibiting films to small, specialized audiences was expensive.

CONCLUSION

MoMA disrupted some of the more staid and conventional aspects of traditional cultural institutions, particularly of museums. It did so by invoking the relatively novel and modern assertion that in addition to paintings and sculpture the material of everyday life—buildings, photographs, advertising, machine parts—constituted valuable sources of aesthetic, historical, and intellectual contemplation. By situating film within this institutional claim, the Film Library contributed directly and indirectly to a national, highly-mediated, and modern dialogue on the means by which elite, middlebrow, populist, and industrial logics of film's value might convene at the sites of art. The Film Library emerged seeking to blend, balance, and further inflect films with the institutional edicts of preceding cultural institutions. It sought to coordinate resources, circulate select films, and advocate for distinct modes of interpretation.

In short, the project to transform cinema from its status as a passing and mass entertainment to an edifying and educational activity grew out of the impulse to arrest the seemingly endless circulation of ephemeral images, securing them in time and space, moving them away from the location of commercial cinema and relocating them (sometimes the same images and sometimes not) elsewhere as part of an imagined and physical strategy of stabilization. This was neither an ideologically benign nor simple impulse. It was tied both to class-inflected projects to reform cinemagoers deemed ignorant or dangerous as well as to alternative models for cinema that sought to integrate movie watching with organized modes of cultural engagement that might be critical not just of industry, but also of middlebrow and religious moralizing. This included protection from the rising forces seeking to regulate film content according to spiritual and other ostensibly moral dictates, as well as from the raucous frisson of popular movie houses. Reworking the most basic material infrastructures in which films circulated and were seen was not achieved only by MoMA's efforts but also by an emergent network of individuals and organizations that long fought to adapt cinema to uses other than those allowed by commercial cinema. Yet MoMA became one of most authoritative and centralized forces seeking to broker this transformation. The Rockefeller Foundation made the library possible. Its philanthropic underpinnings are an underconsidered element in the history of this shift, a fundamental transformation of the conditions in which movies became institutionalized as modes of thinking, writing, and debating modern life.

NOTES

Unpublished material in this chapter has been quoted courtesy of the Rockefeller Archive Center, Sleepy Hollow, New York, and of the Museum of Modern Art, Department of Film Series, Special Collections, Film Study Center, New York City.

1. Such bad behavior occurred frequently enough that the library's first curator, Iris Barry, had a slide projector permanently installed in the museum's auditorium, equipped with a slide that read: "If the disturbance in the auditorium does not cease, the showing of this film will be discontinued." If, after stopping the film and

showing the slide, the audience still did not compose itself, the house lights would come up and the show would be declared over. Charles Turner, a regular member of MoMA's early audiences recalls that sometimes Barry's rebuke would come only ten minutes into the picture. To further ensure decorum, and to bolster her own disciplinary capacities, Barry reserved a permanent seat in the auditorium, alongside a phone connecting her instantly to the projectionist. She was a common fixture in the theater, regularly monitoring both image quality and audience comportment. For more on this see Charles L. Turner, "Witnessing the Development of Independent Film Culture in New York: An Interview with Charles L. Turner," interview by Ronald S. Magliozzi, *Film History* 12, no.1 (2000): 72–96.

2. Some of the objects in this show were given to the museum in 1939, and eventually they became part of another Rockefeller project, colonial Williamsburg in Virginia.

3. For more on the context in which Abby made these gifts to the museum see Russell Lynes, *Good Old Modern* (New York: Atheneum, 1973).

4. According to Laurence Rockefeller, John D. dismissed Abby's personal collection of modern art and her taste in general, considering the objects she collected "strange, irresponsible objects." Quoted in Daniel Okrent, *Great Fortune: The Epic of Rockefeller Center* (New York: Penguin, 2003), 100.

5. He did at least sign the memo "Affectionately, John"! Okrent, *Great Fortune*, 127.

6. Quoted in Okrent, *Great Fortune*, 126.

7. He had previously served and continued to serve on many museum committees as well. Nelson also made donations of cash and was a collector of art as well.

8. For more on Whitney, see E. J. Kahn Jr., *Jock: The Life and Times of John Hay Whitney* (Garden City, NY: Doubleday, 1981).

9. Barry was unafraid to celebrate the popular, bawdy, or low-budget film. She reverently described Tarzan as "a silly symphony gone mad." Barry, "Film Comments" *Bulletin of the Museum of Modern Art* 9 (May 1934): 4. Barry also favored *The Invisible Man* (James Whale, 1933), deeming it "a brilliant choice of subject, brilliantly executed by Claude Raines." Barry, "Film Comments," *Bulletin of the Museum of Modern Art* 5 (January 1934): 4.

10. Barry, "Film Comments," *Bulletin of the Museum of Modern Art* 1, no.1 (1933).

11. Despite the film's success, it was also quite controversial. For more discussion of the furor over West and Paramount's purposeful sidestepping of the Production Code, see Leonard J. Jeff and Jerold L. Simmons, *The Dame in the Kimono: Hollywood Censorship and the Production Code from the 1920s to the 1960s* (New York: Grove Weidenfeld, 1990), 17–32.

12. Barry, "Film Comments,"(see note 10), 1. A brief article in a museum bulletin published in February 1934 noted that among all the articles and notes in the publication, the "Film Comments" had by far elicited the greatest volume of correspondence. Reportedly, one of these letters was from John Ford, who upon reading Barry's review of *Doctor Bull* (1933) wrote to her: "I really must see 'Dr. Bull.' I directed it but I haven't seen it." Barry [attributed], "Films and the Museum," *Bulletin of the Museum of Modern Art* 1, no. 6 (1 February, 1934): 3.

13. Mary Lea Bandy reports that Abby Rockefeller's friends called her to complain about the museum's endorsement of the "vulgar" Mae West. Mary Lea Bandy,

"'Nothing Sacred': Jock Whitney Snares Antiques for Museum," in *The Museum of Modern Art at Mid-Century: Continuity and Change*, vol. 5, Studies in Modern Art (New York: Museum of Modern Art, 1995), 77. For more on Barry and her thinking about film see Haidee Wasson, *Museum Movies: The Museum of Modern Art and the Birth of Art Cinema* (Berkeley: University of California, 2005).

14. Alfred H. Barr Jr., "The 1929 Multi-departmental Plan for the Museum of Modern Art: Its Origins, Development and Partial Realization." Museum of Modern Art (hereafter MoMA), Department of Film Series, Special Collections, Film Study Center, 9.

15. Abbott, for instance, assured Rockefeller that they did not intend to show all of the films they collected, particularly controversial films such as *L'âge d'or* (Luis Buñuel and Salvador Dalí, 1930). Memorandum, John Abbott to Abby Rockefeller, 7 June, 1935. MoMA, Museum Matters, Film Library Committee, 1.7.

16. Barry briefly discusses the resistance to film at the museum, particularly of popular films in "The Film Library and How it Grew," *Film Quarterly* 22, no. 4 (Summer 1969):19–27; see also Alice G. Marquis, *Alfred H. Barr, Jr.: Missionary for the Modern* (New York: Contemporary Books, 1989), 128.

17. D. W. Griffith to Nelson Rockefeller, 27 August, 1940. Rockefeller Archive Center (hereafter RAC), Rockefeller Family Archives (hereafter, RFA), Nelson A. Rockefeller Papers, Record Group (hereafter RG) 4, Series 200, Box 139, Folder 1367.

18. Iris Barry, *D. W. Griffith, American Film Master* (New York: Museum of Modern Art, 1940).

19. William J. Buxton, "Reaching Human Minds: Rockefeller Philanthropy and the Social Sciences, 1935–39," in *The Development of the Social Sciences in the United States and Canada: The Role of Philanthropy*, eds. Theresa Richardson and Donald Fisher (Stamford, CT: Ablex, 1999), 177–92.

20. While the Payne Fund Studies were complex and diverse on the whole, the ideas that gained the most currency were those found in Henry James Foreman's *Our Movie Made Children* (New York: Macmillan, 1933). Foreman's book warned of the dangers of Hollywood movies and their tendency to spread vice and licentious behavior.

21. Quoted in Buxton, "Reaching Human Minds," 180.

22. Brett Gary, *The Nervous Liberals: Propaganda Anxieties from World War I to the Cold War* (New York: Columbia University Press, 1999), 109–14.

23. The Foundation also supported film projects at Yale University, University of Minnesota, and elsewhere. Additionally, in April 1940, the Rockefeller Foundation granted the American Library Association $5,500 to explore this question. The results are published as Gerald Doan McDonald, *Educational Motion Pictures and Libraries* (New York: American Library Association, 1942). Additional film-education projects were also funded by Rockefeller's General Education Board. These projects include healthy appropriations for the American Council of Education, the Progressive Education Association, and the Visual Education Unit of the University of Minnesota. For more on the funding of film see Buxton "Reaching Human Minds," 184–85. The Carnegie Corporation also funded experiments in setting up cooperative film circuits to help libraries cost-effectively integrate films into their services. These projects began in 1948. For more on this see Grace T. Stevenson, "Public

Libraries," in *Sixty Years of 16 mm Film, 1923–1983*, ed. Film Council of America (Evanston, IL: Film Council of America, 1954), 123–29.

24. The National Film Society of Canada (NFS) was established "to encourage and promote the study, appreciation and use of motion and sound pictures and television as educational and cultural factors in the Dominion of Canada and elsewhere." Quoted in Yvette Hackett, "National Film Society of Canada, 1935–1951: Its Origins and Development," in *Flashback: People and Institutions in Canadian Film History*, ed. Gene Walz (Montreal: Mediatexte Publications, 1986), 138. The NFS was established as a national organization. Local chapters followed. The NFS is an example less of a series of local and organic initiatives but more the efforts of a few who presumed themselves worthy and capable of speaking to questions of the national through film. It was also funded by the Carnegie Corporation. See Hackett, "National Film Society of Canada," 135–65. See also Charles Acland, "National Dreams, International Encounters: The Formation of Canadian Film Culture in the 1930s," *Canadian Journal of Film Studies* 3, no.1 (1994): 3–26.

25. "RF Aid to the Museum of Modern Art Film Library, 1935–1949." RAC, Rockefeller Foundation Archives (hereafter RF), RG 1.1, Series 200R, Box 251, Folder 2993.

26. John Marshall, "Inter-office correspondence," 28 March, 1938. RAC, RF, RG 1.1, Series 200R, Box 250, Folder 2986.

27. Chaplin provides the common exception to this. Yet Barr refused to fully acknowledge Chaplin's genius as a popular performer. For more on Barr's advocacy of film see "Notes on Departmental Expansion of the Museum," 1932. MoMA, Department of Film Series, Special Collections, Film Study Center, Department of Film Media.

28 John Abbott and Iris Barry "An Outline of a Project for Founding the Film Library of the Museum of Modern Art" (New York: Museum of Modern Art). Reprinted in *Film History* 7 (1995): 325–35. The Rockefeller Foundation supplied $500 ($7,972.00 in 2008) toward the expense of preparing this report. "Grant Action." RAC, RF 1.1 Series 200R, Box 250, Folder 2983.

29. Abbott and Barry, "Outline," 3.

30. Abbott and Barry, "Outline," 3, 13.

31. Abbott and Barry, "Outline," 1–2.

32. Abbott and Barry, "Outline," 21.

33. For more on the Film Library's inclusion of American films and their early relationship to the industry see Haidee Wasson, "'Some Kind of Racket': The Museum of Modern Art's Film Library, Hollywood and the Problem of Film Art, 1935," *Canadian Journal of Film Studies* 9, no.1 (Spring 2000): 5–29.

34. These grants totalled approximately $8,500 ($135,250 in 2008). "RF Aid to the Museum of Modern Art Film Library, 1935–1949." RAC, RF, RG 1.1, Series 200R, Box 251, Folder 2993.

35. Jay Leyda's previous research in Russia and his later work at the Film Library also resulted in the translation and publication of Sergei Eisenstein's *The Film Sense* (1942) and *Film Form* (1949), published together as: *Film Form and Film Sense*, trans. and ed. Jay Leyda (New York: Meridian Books, 1957). Also crucial was his book *Kino: A History of the Russian and Soviet Film* (New York: Collier Books, 1960). This book is dedicated to Barry and indebted to the Film Library's resources, as well

as a grant from the Rockefeller Foundation. Pieces of it first appeared in the film notes generated for the Film Library's traveling and in-house film programs. This grant was also brokered by Barry.

36. A lecture he gave at the National Board of Review during his stay was published as Paul Rotha, "The Documentary Method in British Films," *National Board of Review Magazine* 12 (November 1937): 3–9. His books up to the point of his visit included *The Film Till Now* (London: Jonathan Cape, 1930); *Celluloid: The Film Today* (London: Longman's Green, 1931); *Documentary Film* (London: Faber & Faber, 1935); and *Movie Parade: A Pictorial Survey of Cinema* (London: Studio Publications, 1936). It is worth noting that Rotha was only twenty-three when he published his first sweeping overview of world cinema. He was just thirty when MoMA invited him to be a visiting scholar. His first book influenced Alfred Barr during the latter's second major visit to Europe. He brought along a copy of Rotha's tome as a guide for films he ought to see.

37. (Princeton: Princeton University Press, 1947). Further grant money also enabled Kracauer to write two reports on Nazi propaganda: "Propaganda and the Nazi War Film" (New York: Museum of Modern Art, Film Library, 1942), and "The Conquest of Europe on the Screen: The Nazi Newsreel, 1939–1940," *Social Research* 10, no. 3 (1943): 337–57, which preceded Kracauer's well-known book.

38. One interesting thing to note is that this appendix is not a part of the Film Department's collection. Strangely, while the report is held in the Study Center's special collections, this particular section is only available at the Rockefeller Foundation Archives. While it is difficult to know for sure precisely why this is the case, it is tempting to speculate that it was not included in the report that was forwarded to trustees.

39. John Marshall, "Inter-office Correspondence," 28 March, 1938. RAC, RF, RG 1.1, Series 200R, Box 250, Folder 2986.

40. Marshall, "Inter-office Correspondence."

41. "The request to the Foundation is for general support, but it is recommended that the proposed grant of $70,000 ($1.116 million in 2008) be made toward the expenses of maintaining and extending the Library's collections and of making its services available to educational organizations." "Grant Action." RAC, RF, RG 1.1, Series 200R, Box 250, Folder 2983.

42. Douglas Baxter, "A Report on the MoMA Film library," 1940. RAC, RF, RG 1.1, Series 200R, Box 251, Folder 2998. It should also be noted that general lack of coordination plagued efforts at forging film-art circuits generally throughout this period. The film department's records are fittingly filled with Barry's letters to various distributors, collectors, and exhibitors trying to track down prints for library programs.

43. Such entities satisfied the legal agreement arranged with studios. No other formal institutional affiliation was necessary. See, for example, "Conditions of Rental," *Film Library Bulletin, Museum of Modern Art* (1940): 21–22.

44. For more on the history of film study during this period see Dana Polan, *Scenes of Instruction: The Beginnings of the U.S. Study of Film* (Berkeley: University of California, 2007).

45. Dartmouth, Stanford, Bryn Mawr, Mount Holyoke, Smith, William and Mary, Vassar College, and the New School for Social Research. Films were hired

by the Universities of Chicago, Pittsburgh, Washington, Minnesota, Missouri, and California-Berkeley. New York University, Princeton, Brown, Cornell, Colgate, and Indiana filled out the list. I would like to acknowledge Dana Polan for his assistance with sorting through this generative moment in the early history of American film study. For more see Polan's, *Scenes of Instruction*.

46. Film Library staff claimed success in catalyzing film societies in Buffalo, Los Angeles, and Washington and at Bryn Mawr, Haverford, Harvard, and Dartmouth, among others. *Film Library Bulletin*, 1938–39. MoMA, Department of Film Series, Special Collections, Film Study Center, Department of Film, 4.

47. Film Library, Museum of Modern Art, "Cost of Circulating a 16 mm Projector," [Appendix G] in *Report on the Film Library*. RAC, RF, RG 1.1, Series 200R, Box 251, Folder 2996. I have been unable to find evidence that this ever happened.

48. "Annual Report on the Film Library," 1939. MoMA, Department of Film Series, Special Collections, Film Study Center, Department of Film.

49. Iris Barry to Rockefeller Foundation [report], 1948. RAC, RFA, Nelson A. Rockefeller Papers, RG 4, Series 200, Box 139, Folder 1367.

7

An "Art of Fugue" of Film Scoring: Hanns Eisler's Rockefeller Foundation-Funded Film Music Project (1940–1942)

Johannes C. Gall

On Monday, August 5, 1940, the celebrated playwright Clifford Odets noted in his diary, which was to be published posthumously under the title *The Time is Ripe*:

> Hanns Eisler, wife, and technical assistant are going to California to do some work on a Rockefeller Foundation Project. In the afternoon I went up to a private projection room and saw some of Hanns's work, a musical score fitted to a series of nature shots. His plan is to fit music to every variety of stock shot, so making a sort of "Art of the Fugue" of musical accompaniment.[1]

This concise diary entry provides an insightful glimpse into the work of an ambitious project in its early, albeit already busy and productive, stage. In the center is Hanns Eisler, forty-two at the time, a gifted composer, and able mind, who could already look back on an eventful life. The son of the philosopher Rudolf Eisler,[2] he studied composition with Arnold Schönberg when the latter was developing his far-reaching twelve-tone technique. Eisler was a quick study and receptive to the ideas and techniques of his teacher. Nonetheless, his early works have a characteristic ironic tone that betrays a critical distance to the aesthetics of the Second Viennese School. In fact, Eisler increasingly took exception to his teacher's "art-for-art's-sake" stance, which culminated in 1926 in an often-cited quarrel with Schönberg, who reproached his student for his disloyalty. The discord marked a turning point in the early career of Eisler, who had moved from his hometown of Vienna to Berlin the year before. Henceforth, he endeavored to compose music for a social cause, namely for the working-class struggle to overcome capitalism. Whereas Eisler had been awarded the prestigious Art Prize of the City of Vienna in 1925 for avant-garde work following in Schönberg's footsteps, he subsequently acquired an international reputation as a composer of music for the proletariat. As Eisler wrote in his curriculum vitae for the Rockefeller Foundation (RF): "This proved . . . that the modern style and the people need not necessarily be enemies."[3] In 1930 his musical contribution to the controversial play *Die Maßnahme* (*The Measures Taken*) marked the beginning of a lifelong collaboration and friendship with the poet and playwright Bertolt Brecht.

Eisler's political viewpoint and engagement as well as his Jewish ancestry forced him into exile following the Nazis' assumption of power in 1933. In line with Brecht's aphorism "changing countries more often than shoes," Eisler spent the ensuing years on an odyssey in which he lent his musical skills largely to antifascist political action and to film production. In 1938, after shorter stays in Austria, France, the Netherlands, Denmark, England, the United States, Czechoslovakia, the Soviet Union, and Spain, he eventually sought permanent refuge from Nazi persecution and settled in New York at the invitation of Alvin Johnson, the indefatigable director of the New School for Social Research (NSSR), to teach courses in music composition as well as in music theory and history.[4]

The second person Clifford Odets mentions in the diary entry cited above is Eisler's second wife, Louise Eisler, née von Gosztony, a writer whose budding career was cut short by the Nazis' rise to power. The third person, to whom Odets refers as Eisler's "technical assistant," is the twenty-five-year-old sound engineer and editor Harry Robin. Odets became acquainted with Robin during the rehearsals of his recent play *Night Music*, for which Eisler composed the incidental music and Robin worked as a sound technician. Eisler, on the other hand, met Robin as a student at the NSSR. Born in Brooklyn to Russian immigrant parents, Robin graduated from Brooklyn College in 1936 and had subsequently gained his first experience in motion-picture soundtrack work during a two-year post as junior sound engineer at the Max Fleischer animation studio, noted for *Betty Boop* and *Popeye the Sailor*. At the NSSR, Robin sought to develop his musical knowledge and proficiency by studying with Lan Adomian and Marc Blitzstein, who introduced him to Eisler. They "'hit it off' right away,"[5] and before long Robin "was Eisler's assistant-driver-gofer."[6] The first film on which they collaborated was *Pete Roleum and His Cousins*—a stop-motion puppet two-reeler commissioned by the petroleum industry for screenings at the New York World Fair in 1939 and 1940.[7] Due to the innovative soundtrack of this film, which used stereophonic (or even quadraphonic) effects before the actual invention of stereophony,[8] Donald Slesinger, director of the RF-funded American Film Center (AFC) and the World Fair's education director,[9] became aware of Robin's skills and sponsored him for a RF fellowship. Robin was accepted and first visited the Visual Education Unit at the University of Minnesota in Minneapolis,[10] then moved on to the Stevens Institute of Technology in Hoboken, New Jersey, for a five-month stint on Harold Burris-Meyer's RF-funded project on sound in theater,[11] before he was assigned to work with Eisler.

The "private projection room" of which Odets writes, where he and Eisler went to view some of the composer's Rockefeller Film Music Project (FMP) work, was in the Preview Theater at 1600 Broadway, which appears to have been a top address for independent and innovative film production at that time.[12] Before eventually moving to Los Angeles in the spring of 1942, Eisler would go to this studio whenever the FMP necessitated the screening of film material or the use of a Moviola.

The "series of nature shots" that Odets reports to have seen in the projection room of the Preview Theater makes up the motion picture *White Flood*, an educational short on the silent and powerful force of glaciers.[13] *White Flood* was the fourth of seven films produced by the nonprofit company Frontier Films and, besides *History and Romance of Transportation*, the only nonpolitical one.[14] Eisler delivered a score for this documentary as part of a reciprocal arrangement through which he obtained suitable film material for his musical experiments and Frontier Films saved the related costs, since Eisler used the budget of the FMP for the production of the musical soundtrack.[15]

Odets's depiction of Eisler's work at the end of his diary entry as an "'Art of the Fugue' of musical accompaniment" captures with aphoristic precision a main idea of the FMP: the production of a variety of sound films and film sequences, each of which can serve as a model for film scoring—just as the pieces in the *Art of Fugue* by Johann Sebastian Bach can serve as a compendium of contrapuntal techniques. Thus, as an "Art of Fugue" of film scoring, the artistic results of the FMP can be appreciated for their aesthetic qualities, analyzed for their film-scoring techniques, and utilized for further study. Moreover, Odets's suggestion of an analogy to Bach's *Art of Fugue* is visionary in regard to how Eisler's film experiments might continue to function as an inspiring contribution to the art and craft of film scoring.

GENESIS AND CONCEPT

The FMP was approved at a meeting of the executive committee of the RF on January 19, 1940. The approval entailed a grant of $20,160 over the two-year period from February 1, 1940, to January 31, 1942. It was assigned to the NSSR, on behalf of whom Alvin Johnson had proposed the FMP. The purpose of the grant, as stated in the minutes of the RF for January 19, 1940, was "to enable . . . Eisler at the [NSSR] to devote the next two years to [experiments] which would indicate possibilities of music in film productions for the most part new and as yet untried."[16] The need for such an undertaking was brought about by the erratic development of the field of motion-picture music—a field that, as Eisler would argue, was usually regarded as playing a mere subsidiary role in film production and not given its due attention. Consequently, there was a "gap between the highly evolved technique of the motion picture and the generally far less advanced techniques of motion-picture music."[17] To explore and suggest ways of bridging this gap, the experimental work of the FMP was planned to comprise four half-yearly experimental demonstrations. John Marshall, then assistant director of the Humanities Division (HD) of the RF[18] and largely responsible for "orchestrating the Division's support for new forms of mass media,"[19] summarized the proposal of the FMP:

> Eisler's plan is to select for purposes of demonstration short sequences from existing films, . . . for which he will prepare and record on film alternative musical accompaniment. He will present the results of his work to small audiences of filmmakers in New York and in Hollywood, together with reports explaining his procedure. In this way, . . . Eisler will deal with four types of problem, each culminating in a final report: (1) the possibilities of utilizing new types of musical material in film production [also problems of musical form]; (2) problems of instrumentation; (3) problems of blending music and sound effect [and dialogue]; (4) the more general problem of music in relation to the content of the film—rudimentary esthetics of film music.[20]

Besides these specific fields of problems, the four demonstrations would also include all principle film types, as it was later announced by the NSSR in a press release: "Documentary films, animated cartoons, as well as feature films will be represented."[21] After their completion, the practical results of the FMP, altogether about eighty minutes of sound film, were to be deposited in the Museum of Modern Art (MoMA) Film Library, which had been set up with funds from the RF some five years before. As its curator Iris Barry, John Marshall, and Eisler agreed, the library would "make prints . . . available to qualified film makers and students of the film at a nominal charge."[22] That is, the MoMA Film Library would integrate the practical results of the FMP into its regular program of preservation and circulation. However, Eisler was not content with merely elaborating and explaining exemplary film-music demonstrations; he was also interested in ascertaining the unbiased audience reactions at these demonstrations. For this purpose, he proposed using the "questionnaire method . . . with an audience carefully selected from various groups in accordance with most recent practice in sampling."[23] Eisler intended to present the evaluation of the respective questionnaires in each of his biannual reports.

The amount of the grant, $20,160, was accounted for by the following yearly items: $3,000 for Eisler's salary, which was commensurate with the yearly salary of a married professor at the NSSR; $1,440 for his technical assistant, Harry Robin, conceived as a continuation of his stipend as a RF fellow in film production; $5,000 for the costs of two half-yearly demonstrations; $250 each for traveling expenses and the reproduction of reports; and a yearly contingent of $500 for the measurement of audience reaction, with the provision that beforehand Eisler was "to find means to characterize audience reactions."[24] Since Harry Robin's RF fellowship would last until July 1940, it was arranged that he would "be assigned for work with . . . Eisler until the termination of his fellowship . . . with the consequent reduction of $720 in the first year's budget."[25]

Given the context of this chapter, the conception of the FMP has been deliberately illustrated by means of John Marshall's recommendation for sponsorship rather than through Eisler's proposal submitted by the NSSR, in order to highlight the specific expectations that RF officials might have had regarding the FMP. However, this conception also corresponds to the actual prehistory of the FMP, for its materialization was to a large extent indebted to Marshall's vision, engagement, and perseverance. It was Marshall whom the young Joseph Losey, future famous film director, first sounded out about the possibility of RF support for Eisler. Joseph Losey was in contact with John Marshall since he had worked for an educational-film project carried out under the auspices of the Commission of Human Relations (CHR) of the Progressive Education Association and funded by a grant from the General Education Board (GEB), for which Marshall served as an assistant to its vice president, David Stevens.[26] Losey had met Eisler in 1935 during his visit to Moscow[27] and later commissioned him to score *Pete Roleum and His Cousins*, Losey's first film.

Marshall would certainly have been able to quash any hope of a grant for Eisler by laconically referring to the RF policy of not providing support for individual composers, or even film composers, however skillful they might be. Instead, Losey could inform Alvin Johnson on September 26, 1939: "Hanns' work on films, and so forth, will not qualify him as a scholar, but I believe the research he is doing for you might. Mr. Marshall also thought so."[28] Johnson then got himself in contact with Marshall. He suggested that the research Eisler could do under a grant from the RF would be on a book on modern music, for which Eisler was contracted by Oxford University Press.[29] However, apparently in a personal meeting, Marshall convinced Johnson that Eisler's research on film music would rather correspond to the objective of the RF, namely the new communication program of the HD, and thus have better prospects of support. Consequently, Johnson urged Eisler to work out a "Research Program on the Relation between Music and

Films,"[30] which he submitted to Marshall on November 1, 1939, along with a brief survey of "Eisler's Work as Composer for the Films."[31] Despite a few utopian elements, such as the production of "a number of opera shorts, perhaps using animated cartoons and puppets,"[32] Marshall was very impressed by this research program. In fact, as he confided to David Stevens, director of the RF's HD, he was "impressed to the extent of asking why we shouldn't make a small grant-in-aid to the [NSSR] on much the same basis as we made our original grant-in-aid to Stevens Institute for Burris-Meyer's work. If Eisler is as good as he sounds, such a small investment now, possibly followed up as we did with Burris-Meyer by some support over a longer period of time, might prove a surprisingly good investment."[33]

Thus it was Marshall who first contemplated the possibility of Eisler's research qualifying not only for "aid to a deposed scholar,"[34] but, following some initial support, for a full RF project of the NSSR.[35] After consultation with David Stevens, Marshall arranged for Eisler to call on him in order to discuss the possibilities of such a project. When they met, Marshall advised Eisler to specify an exact proposal, which should include "a concrete plan of work"[36] and a preferably modest budget. Moreover, it may also have been Marshall who gave Eisler the idea of tackling his laboratory experiments by rescoring existing motion pictures, as this idea seems to have been modeled on the modus operandi of the RF-funded CHR project, within the scope of which Hollywood footage was utilized to edit educational short films.[37] In any case, in the eventual proposal, which Johnson submitted on behalf of the NSSR on December 5, 1939, Eisler suggested for the first time using existing footage and abandoned, among other idealistic plans, his idea of tailor-made film material, which in any case would have conflicted with official RF policy.

However, after receiving the proposal and budget, Marshall did not simply let the usual application procedure take its course. Instead, he asked Iris Barry of the MoMA Film Library to provide him with references to Eisler's work in film. Barry then furnished Marshall with a list of "films for which Hanns Eisler [had] composed music,"[38] as well as references to his film scores in Kurt London's pioneering book *Film Music*,[39] and in an article penned by Eisler himself in *World Film News*.[40] Marshall later also arranged for Eisler to meet Barry in person to discuss the possibilities of cooperation with the MoMA Film Library, which led to the aforementioned agreement. Moreover, Marshall ensured "that Eisler [was] in close contact with Burris-Meyer" so that they could "collaborate whenever non-musical [sound] effects [would be] involved and in other phases of the study where Burris-Meyer's competence would come into play."[41] Likewise, Marshall contacted Paul Lazarsfeld, the director of the famous Radio Research Project (RRP), and asked him about his opinion of Eisler and whether the expertise of the RRP could be applied to the composer's plan empirically to study the effects of film music.[42] Finally, Marshall arranged a meeting between Alvin Johnson, Eisler, Eisler's technical assistant Harry Robin, and himself to go through the original proposal once again and outline the recommendation Marshall could give at the next meeting of the executive committee of the RF. This pertained particularly to the estimated budget, which was revised and simplified. Also, Marshall "tried to explore [the] plans which Eisler and Johnson have for assuring the effect of the [FMP]."[43]

So Marshall did not exaggerate at all in his following reply to Eisler's thank you letter on January 29, 1940: "I was . . . glad to do anything I could to bring this proposal into consideration here for I felt personally that it promised most useful outcomes."[44] In fact, it was Marshall who prompted Eisler to propose a project, which the composer would probably not have conceptualized himself, although it corresponded to his own theoretical and artistic interests. Marshall, moreover, steered the application in the direction of the communication program of the RF. Likewise, he endeavored to assure the success of the proposed FMP and make it derive benefit from, and be for the benefit of, some of the other RF and GEB–funded undertakings by carefully integrating it into the network of projects and scholarship supported by Rockefeller philanthropy.

Did the FMP, so thoroughly conceived, eventually fulfill its aims? Was it a success or a failure? The answer is "both" or rather "neither," which also reflects the current opinion of the FMP. Eisler biographer Jürgen Schebera inadvertently pinpoints the problem by describing the project as "legendary"[45]: though it enjoys some fame, it continues to be steeped in legend. The purpose of this chapter is to illustrate and explain the ambiguous outcome of the FMP.

THEORETICAL RESULTS

Among the actual achievements of the FMP, pride of place is held by the book *Composing for the Films*.[46] It was published almost five years after the end of the project, unpleasantly at the time when, as one of the first victims of the anticommunist witch hunt, Eisler was in the firing line of the House Committee on Un-American Activities (HUAC).[47] Eisler wrote the book together with Theodor W. Adorno, who, however, chose to withdraw his co-authorship so as not to get embroiled in the affair.[48] Despite being apparent from the style and content of many passages, Adorno's eminent contribution was thus not known to a broader public until 1969, almost seven years after Eisler's death, when Adorno decided to publish the original[49] German version under the names of both authors.[50]

Though it evolved from the research of the FMP (and for Adorno's part also from his experiences of the RRP), the book *Composing for the Films* goes well beyond the scope of the musical experiments of the project. The authors largely draw on their experiences with the Hollywood film indus-try,[51] which is taken as the epitome of the "cultural industry."[52] Within the "strictly delimited segment" of the production and reception of film music, they attempt to "show the interaction of [the] two factors [of mass culture]: the aesthetic potentialities of mass art in the future, and its ideological char-acter at present,"[53] that is, within the culture industry.

Some of the common prejudices about motion-picture music as well as bad film-scoring practices are exposed (chapter 1: "Prejudices and Bad Habits"); the sociological and aesthetic background of such practices is elu-cidated (chapter 4: "Sociological Aspects," chapter 5: "Elements of Aesthet-ics"). On the other hand, Eisler and Adorno address the "aesthetic poten-tialities" of film music by identifying and exemplifying models that, with regard to their musical dramaturgy or function, represent "critical ideas" to-ward a scoring practice beyond the patterns criticized (chapter 2: "Function and Dramaturgy").[54] Furthermore, the authors make an emphatic plea for employing "The New Musical Resources" (chapter 3), "because objectively they are more appropriate"[55] for film. This chapter can be largely under-stood as the response to the problem area that is listed first in the proposal of the FMP. The argument is excellent and still thought-provoking today. Also, the three other problem areas of the FMP are addressed in *Composing for the Films*: "the more general problem of music in relation to the content of the film" in the second and fifth chapter, the "problems of instrumen-tation," as well as "blending music and sound effect" in parts of the sixth chapter, "The Composer and the Movie-Making Process." Finally the artistic outcome of the FMP, that is, its film-music demonstrations, are presented and explicated in a special "Report on the Film Music Project." Eisler and Adorno originally conceived of it as the seventh chapter, but the editors of Oxford University Press chose to banish it to an appendix, which thus had the disadvantage of not being incorporated in the premises for the "Sug-gestions and Conclusions" in the last chapter of the book. Nonetheless, this report represents an impressive account of the FMP, which encourages further study. As the composer Antony Hopkins wrote in his review of the British edition[56] of *Composing for the Films*:

> It is when we get to the appendix that the book really comes to life. In it, we find a description of the work done by the [FMP] of the [NSSR]. I would rec-ommend this section to the notice of all film directors, for it might do much to renovate their ideas about the possible functions of film music. It also in-cludes the score of a sequence written to film by Eisler, one of *Fourteen Ways to Describe Rain*.[57]

It does not appear that many film directors or others in the field of film production followed the advice of Hopkins. In the United States, this may have been to some extent due to Eisler's conviction and deportation for alleged un-American activities, which hurt his artistic legacy for years to come.[58] Moreover, many Hollywood composers and filmmakers felt personally insulted by the devastating critique and polemical tone in many of the book's passages. It is therefore not surprising that they reacted defiantly to the constructive suggestions in *Composing for the Films*. It may also be assumed that many readers who earned their livelihood in the film industry cast the book aside before reading through to the appendix.[59] In the German Democratic Republic, where Eisler ultimately settled[60] after his deportation from the United States in 1948, such accounts and analyses as in the report on the FMP were not necessarily well received either. Instead, the experiments of the FMP were in danger of being viewed as esoteric and arousing suspicion of formalism. This can be inferred from the unappreciative and occasionally nonsensical deletions made in the first German edition, particularly in the chapter on the FMP.

Thus, Adorno's words in the postscript of his 1969 edition of *Composing for the Films* may be especially relevant to the elements pertaining to the FMP: "The book . . . had up until then led an apocryphal existence for political reasons both in the East and West, and had been read by very few of those people who could perhaps have been interested in it."[61] Regarding the book as a whole, its shadowy existence ceased after Adorno revealed his coauthorship. Although *Composing for the Films* continues to be controversial, it is considered a classic today. It has been reprinted many times (also in the *Collected Writings* of Adorno and the *Collected Works* of Eisler) and translated into several languages. It is largely because of this book that the FMP has not sunk into oblivion, but enjoys some renown.

In addition to the appendix in *Composing for the Films*, Eisler wrote two other reports on the experimental work of the FMP. The first report, "Film Music—Work in Progress," was published in 1941 in the periodical *Modern Music*,[62] and the second one was the "Final Report" of October 31, 1942. Both of these are informative and instructive, but do not systematically address the four problem areas outlined in the original FMP proposal. Instead, the 1941 interim report provides some cursory insights into the experimental work of the FMP as well as details about Eisler's score for the documentary *White Flood* and his ideas of rescoring selected sequences from the Hollywood features *The Grapes of Wrath* (by John Ford, Twentieth Century Fox, 1940) and *The Long Voyage Home* (by John Ford, Walter Wanger Productions, 1941).[63] The "Final Report," on the other hand, offers a brief overview of the practical results of the FMP, that is, the completed demonstrations, by outlining the musical methods employed in each demonstration and indicating the general dramaturgical methods that were taken into consideration. An in-depth theoretical analysis is put off until the publication of a special book, the future monograph *Composing for the Films*.

Whereas Eisler brought his 1941 interim report to wider public attention through its publication in *Modern Music*, the American forum for
the musical avant-garde at that time, he merely sent a single copy of his
"Final Report" to John Marshall. This final report was neither reproduced,
nor did it circulate. It was not published until 1983, when it appeared in
a volume of Eisler's *Collected Works*.[64] Still, Eisler did not refund the contingent of the grant that had been earmarked for the reproduction of four
biannual reports, in total $500. No protest came from the RF, just as there
were no queries about the other divergences from the original itemization
of the budget.

PRACTICAL RESULTS

The ambiguity of the FMP, as to whether it was a success or a failure, particularly stems from the character of the experimental demonstrations that
Eisler worked out within the scope of the project—the elements of what
Odets called the "Art of Fugue" of film scoring. First, these do not coincide
with the conception in the proposal of the FMP and the press release issued by the NSSR on February 21, 1940. Not all of the principle film types
were represented in the experiments. Documentary material predominated
and no animated films were included, nor was all of the footage that Eisler
worked with from already-completed motion pictures. Instead, Eisler wrote
the score for the educational documentaries *White Flood* (1940) and *A Child
Went Forth* (1941)[65] as part of the original production. This was, as previously mentioned, a reciprocal arrangement: as a countermove to his obtaining film material of high quality, Eisler waived his fee and paid for the production of the musical soundtrack from the FMP's budget. However, for *A
Child Went Forth*, Losey's second screen venture, Eisler also had a 5 percent
share in the profits.[66] There were also profits from this two-reeler portray-
ing "a model solution for the evacuation of children" in modern warfare.
"Distributed by the Rockefeller Committee on South American Relations
[i.e., the Office of the Coordinator of Inter-American Affairs (OCIAA) or, as
of March 1945, the Office of Inter-American Affairs (OIAA)] and the Office
of War Information, [the film] had been dubbed in twenty-four languages
by October 1945."[67]

Eisler also listed selected sequences from the motion picture *The Forgotten
Village* (1941)[68] among the artistic results of the FMP.[69] Aside from the fact
that he wrote the score for this cinematic fable about deep-rooted supersti-
tion in rural Mexico in between his work on the FMP, it was completely beyond its scope. Eisler was paid a regular composer's fee and no expenditures
from the RF grant were made on the production of the musical soundtrack
to *The Forgotten Village*. In addition, Eisler listed excerpts from newsreels

among the results of the FMP.[70] The surviving documents, however, reveal that, although the composer did intend to score a newsreel (apparently by March of Time), he never carried it out.[71] Instead, he seems to have fallen back upon some newsreel-like sequences from the documentary *The 400 Million* (1939), to which he had composed his first dodecaphonic film music.[72] This substitution with excerpts from Joris Ivens's cinematic indictment of the Japanese aggression against China is suggested by the details Eisler gives in the appendix of *Composing for the Films* and the "Final Report" (e.g., that the newsreel contained war scenes such as the aerial bombing of a city, the score was set for large orchestras and in an improvisation-like form, and the recording was conducted by Dr. Fritz Stiedry).

It may be assumed that Eisler included excerpts from *The Forgotten Village* and an alleged newsreel among the practical results of the FMP in order to meet both the proposed total running time of circa eighty minutes and the intended variety of film types. However, it should be noted that it was difficult for Eisler to obtain suitable Hollywood footage for his experiments. Unlike the CHR, he required film material that had to fulfill two other conditions: First, it was not to be in the final composite form but in the form of separate visuals and soundtracks in order that the composer's alternative score could be mixed anew with the dialogue and the noises of the respective sequences. Second, it had to be of outstanding quality, for the potential of film music is limited by the picture itself: "Good music accompanying hackneyed or idiotic action and meaningless chatter becomes bad and meaningless."[73] Initially, Donald Slesinger of the RF-funded AFC and Iris Barry of the MoMA Film Library sought to obtain on Eisler's behalf the requisite Hollywood footage, but to no avail.[74] Therefore, as noted in Odets's diary entry, Eisler, his wife, and his technical assistant traveled to Hollywood in August 1940 in order to get in contact with the heads of the film industry, introduce them to the work of the FMP, and gain their cooperation. For this purpose, Marshall arranged for Eisler and Robin to meet the staff of the Motion Picture Research Project (Leo Rosten's pioneering venture into the sociology of Hollywood), which, after initial support from the Carnegie Corporation, had just been awarded a grant from the RF.[75] Rosten readily made the premises and facilities of his office available to Eisler and Robin during their stay in Hollywood. He also helped introduce them to institutions and people with influence and decision-making power such as the Academy of Motion Picture Arts and Sciences and its then-president Walter Wanger. Their tour through major film studios including Metro Goldwyn Mayer, Paramount, Columbia, Twentieth Century Fox, RKO, and Disney, as well as institutions such as the Motion Picture Producers and Distributors of America. (MPPDA, also known as the Hays Office), obviously went well and, before long, several favorable contacts had been made.[76]

Unfortunately, Eisler had to leave Hollywood and ultimately return to New York before he could wholly reap the benefits from those contacts. In fact, his abrupt departure marks the moment after which the FMP appears to have been derailed from its original course. The reasons for this may be attributed to the visa and financial troubles Eisler was facing at that time.[77] Notwithstanding his five-year appointment as a professor of music at the NSSR, beginning in the fall of 1938, he had not yet succeeded in obtaining an immigration visa. Instead he was still residing in the United States on a temporary visa for business and pleasure. In 1938 Eisler took the first steps toward applying for an immigration visa under the German-Austrian quota, but was denied "because of his political views and affiliations."[78] Since he was also denied the extension of his visitor's visa, he even had to discontinue his lectures at the NSSR in mid-semester, spring 1939, and take asylum in Mexico City. There he could continue teaching music courses at the Conservatorio Nacional de Musica for the next five months until he reentered the United States on a new visitor's visa in time for the fall semester at the NSSR.

Around that time, Eisler and Johnson appear to have arrived at a daring strategy: Eisler would hold out on temporary visas until the fall of 1940, at which point he would have completed his second year of continuous teaching as a professor of music and hence be eligible for a nonquota visa.[79] However, continuing on as a professor without immigration status proved economically ruinous for Eisler. He had obtained his temporary visa on the condition that he was not paid a regular salary. Instead, he merely received a meager "compensation for his teaching in the form of one-half of the tuition fees of his students."[80] As a consequence, the composer was severely debt-ridden when the NSSR was awarded an RF grant for him to carry out the FMP. Moreover, Eisler's temporary visa expired on January 28, 1940. He applied for an extension, which was denied by the Department of Labor. Eisler ignored the department's demand to leave the country in the hope that he could somehow get by until September 1940, when he would be eligible for a nonquota immigration visa. In the meantime, he was able to twice elude arrest, the warrant for which was issued on July 17, 1940. The first time he was staying with a friend in Bucks County, Pennsylvania, and commuting to New York, when he was thought to be residing on New York's Upper West Side. The second time, when his new address had been investigated, he had just left for Hollywood. From there, Eisler and his wife went across the Mexican border on September 19, 1940, to secure nonquota visas. They were able to do this at the consulate without incident, but the Eislers were impeded from reentering the United States the following day by an outstanding warrant as well as misgivings and protests about Eisler's political character. His case was heard before a board of special inquiry, which debarred him and his wife from immigrating. Subsequently, Eisler appealed to the Immigration Board of Appeals in Washington, which eventually admitted him and his wife for permanent residence in the United States and quashed the warrant for arrest. The award, however, was delayed for almost a month, during which the Eislers were stuck at the Mexican-American border and precious time passed by. After his eventual admission, Eisler thus had no other choice than to return immediately to New York and fulfill the legal requirements of his nonquota visa, which were to fulfill his duties as a music professor at the NSSR.

To make matters worse, Harry Robin also left Hollywood shortly after Eisler's departure and traveled back to New York to get married. Upon learning of Eisler's visa debacle, he surprisingly refrained from returning to Hollywood (apparently on Johnson's advice) to conclude the project's business. Eisler repeatedly demanded the immediate resumption of work in Hollywood, but Robin did not concede. Into the bargain, Robin also asked Marshall for an increase in salary, because he was now married.[81] Marshall replied that this would be a question Robin would have to raise with the NSSR. Any increase in salary would, however, have to "be within the budget which the [RF's] grant provided for the [FMP]."[82] As Marshall suggested to Johnson, such a revision of the FMP's budget might entail $600 reallocated to an increase in Robin's yearly salary, since under the conditions of his previous RF fellowship, "his stipend would have been increased $50 a month if he had been married."[83]

For Eisler, the prospect of an additional burden on the FMP's budget may have been the last of a series of annoyances that led him to take harsh measures: he dismissed Robin by telegraph. Yet this dismissal, however understandable it might have been, was not to the project's advantage. Not only was Robin a skillful sound engineer and music editor whose collaboration had been invaluable, he was also the only fully employed technical assistant who had ever worked on the FMP. Later on, Eisler would enlist the services of technical assistants only as required. Again, nobody at the RF raised objections about the consequent reallocation of the FMP's budget. However indifferent RF officials appeared toward Robin's abrupt dismissal, his departure may have contributed to make Eisler gradually lose his standing with the RF and decrease his chances of further financial support. For John Marshall and other RF officers, Robin undoubtedly represented a link to their previous projects and commitments. They therefore may not only have been alarmed by the deviation of the FMP from its planned course, but also may have taken it as a sign that Eisler was all too ready to disregard the network into which the FMP had carefully been integrated in order to assure its effects along the lines of the communication program of the RF.

Close to the agreed end of the term of the FMP, on December 10, 1941, Alvin Johnson supportively submitted a memorandum by Eisler requesting another subsidy of $4,950, which would provide a salary for Eisler and an assistant as well as cover travel expenses for one more year. This, it was argued, would make it possible not only to conclude the experimental work of the FMP, but to expound "the theory and experience which this work [had] presented"[84] and thus bring the study to full fruition. Since John Marshall replied that he saw little chance of his "being able to get consideration for further support,"[85] Eisler resorted to merely requesting a nine-month extension of the grant, which was approved by the RF on January 29, 1942.[86] However, this extension entailed a significant reallocation of the budget of the FMP. During the remaining period, Eisler drew from the unexpended balance of the RF grant a salary for himself and an assistant,[87] which was effectively deducted from the original allocation for the other budget items. In other words, the experimental work of the FMP had to be carried out with fewer resources than had been originally conceived.

Defying these adversities and financial bottlenecks, Eisler succeeded in working out two more film-music demonstrations in addition to the educational shorts *White Flood* and *A Child Went Forth*. One was an alternatively scored version (or rather two versions) of an excerpt from the Hollywood feature *The Grapes of Wrath* (1940).[88] Eisler had the good fortune of securing the required material from this film classic through the contact he had made with Twentieth Century Fox during his visit to Hollywood as well as with the assistance of the New York office of the MPPDA—namely its assistant to the secretary Arthur DeBra.[89] For his experiments, Eisler chose the only sequence that also contains an original score by Alfred Newman, then director of the Twentieth Century Fox Music Department, and rescored it twice. The result was a remarkable assemblage of three versions of the same film excerpt: the original one with music by Alfred Newman and the two alternatives with music by Hanns Eisler. As stated in the appendix of *Composing for the Films*, "the purpose was to gauge the whole range of [musico-] dramatic possibilities" in feature films.[90] In addition, Eisler obviously paid particular attention to different ways of relating music, noise, and dialogue. The recording of the composer's alternative scores set for large orchestra was made in late 1942 in Los Angeles under the direction of Jascha Horenstein and apparently with members of the Los Angeles Philharmonics. Eisler was very much satisfied with this recording and "proud like a chicken [*sic*],"[91] as he wrote to Odets.

Another film-music demonstration was a new sound version of *Rain*, the much-admired cinematic poem by the great film auteur Joris Ivens, which had been released as a silent film in 1929 and had first been scored by Lou Lichtveld in 1932. With permission of Ivens, the film material requisite for this demonstration appears to have been borrowed from the MoMA Film Library[92] and was prepared for Eisler to (re-)score by the editor Helen van Dongen, Ivens's long-term partner and collaborator. Van Dongen was also part of the RF network as she had been working on the CHR project for a longer period of time, whereas Ivens had left within two months and been replaced by Joseph Losey.[93] Later, van Dongen collaborated on a project of Nelson Rockefeller and the MoMA on Latin American film.[94]

Eisler gave his new sound version the title *Fourteen Ways to Describe Rain* and considered it "the richest and most complete"[95] of all the demonstrations worked out under the auspices of the FMP. As he explained in the appendix of *Composing for the Films*:

> [The score] is composed in the twelve-tone style, [set] for . . . flute, clarinet, violin (alternating with viola), cello, and piano. The task was to test the most advanced resources and the corresponding complex composing technique in their relation to the motion picture. The picture about the rain seemed particularly suitable for this because of its experimental character and the lyrical quality of many of its details, despite its thoroughly objective treatment. Every conceivable type of musico-dramatic solution was considered, from the simplest naturalism of synchronized detail painting to the most extreme contrast effects, in which music "reflects" rather than follows a picture.[96]

First-rate musicians such as Rudolf Kolisch (conductor), Tossy Spivakovsky (violin), and Eduard Steuermann (piano) took part in the recording of this crown of the "Art of Fugue" of film music, the mastery and beauty of which would cause much awe among its listeners (and spectators) at the time.

The rescored excerpt from *The Grapes of Wrath* and Eisler's new sound version of *Rain* would provide ideal source material for empirical study, inasmuch as they represent alternatives to preexisting films and film sequences. However, an analysis of audience reactions such as conceived in the proposal of the FMP was never realized.[97] For a while, exiled art psychologist and film expert Rudolf Arnheim was under consideration to be invited to serve as a consulting expert to the FMP's empirical study.[98] Arnheim even formally offered Eisler his assistance in a letter of January 3, 1941,[99] but shortly afterwards he received a RF fellowship to work with Lazarsfeld's RRP in analyzing soap operas and their effects on American radio audiences. Eisler later sought to involve his friend, art historian and sociologist Joachim Schumacher as well as, in particular, Lazarsfeld and his RRP in the potential empirical study of the FMP. For the latter case, Adorno offered to undertake an analysis of the collected data.[100] Eisler apparently arranged a meeting with Lazarsfeld to discuss these possibilities over lunch, but it never came to pass.[101] Subsequently, no further efforts seem to have been made to measure audience reactions. Once more, this omission was accepted by the RF without objection, even though the contingent allotted for analyzing audience reactions was largely expended otherwise.

It was certainly in the interest of Marshall and the RF that the results of the FMP, upon its completion, would be well publicized. Thus, while the grant was supposed to permit experimentation free from the constraints of the film market, it was never intended that the FMP be regarded as the utopian venture of an enthusiastic idealist whose work would ultimately end up on the ash heap of history. Rather it was hoped that the outcome of the FMP could give impetus to innovation in, and the advancement of, the practice of film scoring and film production in general.

One may therefore be disappointed that there seems to have been little appreciation for the artistic results of the FMP at first. The demonstrations were never shown in their entirety nor were there many screenings at all. Certainly, the two educational shorts *White Flood* and *A Child Went Forth* were distributed and hence seen by a number of people, but it is unlikely that they were aware of the background and significance of the scores for these pictures. Eisler also does not appear to have ever publicly presented his alternate version of an excerpt from *The Grapes of Wrath*. He may have considered this experiment too controversial to be introduced to Hollywood, particularly since his alternate score highlights the controversial nature of the motion picture itself. Subsequent to the FMP, Eisler was able to establish himself in Hollywood as a freelance film composer and thus had good reason to shy away from openly antagonizing the music business in the film industry with alternative versions to Oscar-winning productions. Instead, Eisler would mainly show two sequences from *White Flood*, about which he, or sometimes even Adorno, would say a few words of introduction. These presentations at least met with great success, which can be inferred from the reviews and the composer's own account.[102]

In the "Final Report on the [FMP]," Eisler stated that the "whole practical results, that is to say film and music, [would] be put at the disposal of the [MoMA] after six more months," as arranged.[103] Unfortunately, this does not seem to have ever been the case. Instead, the respective film material was initially stored in vaults in both Hollywood (Moviola Company) and New York (Preview Theater), the rental for which was paid by the NSSR from the balance of the RF grant. On May 23, 1944, the financial department of the RF admonished the NSSR to send the overdue final statement in order to close the account.[104] This final statement engendered a lengthy correspondence between Eisler, Johnson, and the financial departments of both the NSSR and the RF concerning the expenditures that were incurred after the termination of the grant. In the end, it was agreed that the payments for vault rental made after November 1, 1942, would be refunded to the RF and that the scattered film results would be sent to the NSSR at cost. Interestingly, Marshall did not intervene by reminding all those involved about the original arrangement with the MoMA Film Library; he refrained from any comment.[105] Later, in 1947, Clara Mayer, dean of the School of Philosophy and Liberal Arts of the NSSR, asked Eisler in a letter what she was to do with his films, as the inflammable nitrate material of which they were composed appeared to violate insurance regulations.[106] What decision was then made remains an unanswered question. However, it is certain that Eisler showed his *Fourteen Ways to Describe Rain* in Los Angeles and in New York shortly before he left the United States for good in 1948. Since then this new sound version of *Rain*, as well as the alternative version of an excerpt from the *Grapes of Wrath*, have been lost without a trace. Only recently the corresponding autograph music to Eisler's *Grapes of Wrath* experiments[107] as well as the spectacular original sound recording of the *Fourteen Ways to Describe Rain*[108] have been rediscovered. With regard to those two precious pieces of Eisler's "Art of Fugue" of film music, this finally allows a reconstruction in the one case and a reproduction in the other.[109]

CONCLUSION

Adding to the ambiguity of the FMP is the lack of acknowledgement on the part of the RF regarding the significant accomplishment the FMP made on a relatively small grant. In telling *The Story of the Rockefeller Foundation*, Raymond Fosdick, president of the RF of many years standing, only vaguely refers "to half a dozen diversified experiments" in the field of film study.[110] Certainly, Fosdick had every reason to deliberately avoid an acknowledgement of the FMP after Eisler's deportation and in the era of McCarthyism: several newspapers had cited Eisler as evidence of alleged RF funding of communists.[111] Fosdick was thus not in a position to praise the RF for the stimulation and support of a study in mass culture that eventually resulted in the seminal *Composing for the Films* as well as a thought-provoking artistic compendium of film scoring. In fact, it may even be the case that, among others, the Eisler affair had a certain discouraging effect on the funding policy of the RF. Knowing of the composer's political conviction and his "radical past"[112] in (musico-)political action, John Marshall and the other officers of the RF had demonstrated remarkable open-mindedness in 1940 by assuming "that Eisler had no political interests and was entirely preoccupied with his music" and hence assessing his qualification for the proposed project solely "from a technical point of view."[113] Following the HUAC hearings regarding Eisler and his deportation, the RF appeared to have been wary about supporting leftist individuals and institutions. However, the likelihood that there would be devout Marxists such as Eisler among the applicants for sponsorship by the RF certainly dwindled with the onset of the cold war and the era of McCarthyism.

The ambiguous attitude that RF officers took toward the FMP and the ambiguity of the project's effects were not confined to the aftermath of the FMP. In fact, even though Marshall played a decisive role in the conception and materialization of the FMP, he was not able to bring himself to recommend the project for further financial support at the end of 1941, when it became evident that a broader scope of time and resources would be required to realize the study's full potential. The reasons for such reserve may have been twofold. First, some developments and omissions that had occurred in the previous course of the FMP—the missing biannual demonstrations and reports, the dismissal of the former RF fellow Harry Robin, as well as Eisler's precarious struggle for an immigration visa and his resulting financial troubles—certainly did not inspire Marshall to believe that the FMP was progressing well. Second, and presumably more important, there had been a shift in focus of the RF communication program, "mobilizing for the war on words,"[114] which made the purpose of the FMP appear less urgent, especially when the United States eventually entered the war following the Japanese attack on Pearl Harbor on December 7, 1941.[115]

So the ambiguity about the success or failure of the FMP is multifaceted. This ambiguity can be discerned in three areas—the course of the FMP, its outcome, and its appreciation and effects—and is determined by the choices of the following four participants and parties: Eisler himself, his actual and potential collaborators, the target group of the film-music study, and the RF. As far as the RF is concerned, aside from granting or declining financial support, the key role that the communication program of the foundation played in the whole of the FMP and thus also in the project's success or failure has long been overlooked.

NOTES

My special thanks go to William J. Buxton, Oliver Dahin, Richard P. Nangle, Barry Salmon, and Anne Sudrow for their critical proofreading of this chapter. Unpublished material in this chapter has been quoted courtesy of the following archives: Rockefeller Archive Center, Sleepy Hollow, New York; Archiv der Akademie der Künste, Berlin; the Raymond Fogelman Library of the New School, New York City; the Feuchtwanger Memorial Library, Special Collections, University of Southern California Libraries; and the Lilly Library, Indiana University, Bloomington, Indiana.

1. Clifford Odets, *The Time is Ripe* (New York: Grove Press, 1988), 237. I wish to thank Breixo Viejo for referring me to this quote. Viejo has been very committed to elucidating the history and aesthetics of Hanns Eisler's Film Music Project (hereafter FMP). In 2003 he presented a doctoral thesis on *Historia y Estética del Film Music Project* at the Universidad Autónoma de Madrid, published as *Música moderna para un nuevo cine. Eisler, Adorno y el Film Music Project* (Madrid: Ediciones Akal, 2008). The year before he completed a twenty-four-minute documentary on the FMP, *Stretta*, as a project thesis for a master's degree in media studies at the New School in New York. This project was encouraged and supervised by Barry Salmon, who likewise never tires of teaching and lecturing about the FMP in addition to furthering its creative impetus in his own work as a film composer.

2. Rudolf Eisler is renowned for several encyclopedic endeavors: Rudolf Eisler, *Wörterbuch der philosophischen Begriffe und Ausdrücke* (Berlin: E. S. Mittler & Sohn, 1899); completely revised and substantially enlarged edition, *Historisches Wörterbuch der Philosophie*, ed. Joachim Ritter (Basel: Schwab, 1971); Rudolf Eisler, *Philosophen-Lexikon: Leben, Werk und Lehren der Denker* (Berlin: E. S. Mittler & Sohn, 1912); Rudolf Eisler, *Kant-Lexikon: Nachschlagewerk zu Kants sämtlichen Schriften, Briefen und handschriftlichem Nachlaß* (Berlin: E. S. Mittler & Sohn, 1930; reprinted Hildesheim/Zürich/New York: Georg Olms Verlag, 1994).

3. Curriculum vitae of Hanns Eisler sent with letter from Alvin Johnson, 8 July, 1940. Rockefeller Archive Center (hereafter RAC), New School for Social Research (hereafter NSSR), Music Filming 1939–1941, Rockefeller Foundation Archives (hereafter RF), Record Group (hereafter RG) 1.1, Series 200R, Box 259, Folder 3095 (hereafter RAC Music Filming 1939–1941).

4. For an account of the important role played by the NSSR in supporting refugee musicians from Nazi Germany, see Werner Grünzweig, "'Bargain and Charity'?: Aspekte der Aufnahme exilierter Musiker an der Ostküste der Vereinigten Staaten," in *Musik im Exil: Folgen des Nazismus für die internationale Musikkultur*, eds. Hanns-Werner Heister, Claudia Maurer Zenck, Peter Petersen (Frankfurt/M.: Fischer Taschenbuch Verlag, 1993), 297–310. For a discussion of Eisler's courses as listed in the lecture timetables of the NSSR, see Tobias Faßhauer, "Kontrapunkt und Sozialtheorie: Hanns Eislers Kurse in den Vorlesungsverzeichnissen der [NSSR]—Teil 1: 1935–1938," *Eisler-Mitteilungen* 29 (June 2002): 18–21; "Music Rediscovered: Hanns Eislers Kurse in den Vorlesungsverzeichnissen der [NSSR]—Teil 2: 1938–1939," *Eisler-Mitteilungen* 30 (October 2002): 20–23; "A Beginning in an Evolving Field: Eislers Kurse in den Vorlesungsverzeichnissen der [NSSR]—Teil 3: 1939–1942," *Eisler-Mitteilungen* 31 (February 2003): 16–19.

5. Telephone interview with Harry Robin, conducted by Ted Cohen for WBAI, May 1982. Transcript located in the Archive of the Academy of Fine Arts in Berlin (Archiv der Akademie der Künste), Berlin (hereafter AdK), Hanns Eisler Archive (hereafter HEA) 7790. I thank the staff at the AdK, particularly Werner Grünzweig, director of the music archives, and Helgard Rienäcker and Anouk Jeschke, the former and present archivists in charge of HEA, for their help with my research.

6. Erica Robin-Clark, "Eisler Opened the Door: Harry Lewis Robin, 1915–2001—A Musical Remembrance," *Eisler-Mitteilungen* 29 (June 2002): 11.

7. Released 1939 by Petroleum Industries Exhibition; producer, director: Joseph Losey; script: Joseph Losey, Kenneth White; photography: Harold Muller (Technicolor); animation: Charley Bowers; puppets devised by: Louis Bunin; set: Howard Bay; original music: Hanns Eisler.

8. In the interview cited in note 5, Robin referred to "the rather innovative things in the soundtrack" of *Pete Roleum and His Cousins* as follows: "In the course of one sequence a character on the screen was interrupted by a voice from the audience. A conversation ensued between the character on screen and the voice in the audience which was done by synchronous projection which I worked out. It worked very well." Curiously, Joseph Losey, the director of *Pete Roleum and His Cousins*, pointed out the same innovative "heckler voice from the audience," but recalled that the film sponsors ultimately ordered this costly sound effect to be omitted and the

scene shown "as a straight film." Michel Ciment, *Conversations with Losey* (London & New York: Methuen, 1985), 57.

9. On the American Film Center and its director Donald Slesinger, see William J. Buxton, "Rockefeller Support for Projects on the Use of Motion Pictures for Educational and Public Purposes, 1935–1954," *Rockefeller Archive Center Research Reports Online* 1 (2001): 5–7.

10. On this Visual Education Unit, which was supported by the General Education Board (hereafter GEB) between 1937 and 1941, see Buxton, "Rockefeller Support for Projects on the Use of Motion Pictures," and his "Reaching Human Minds: Rockefeller Philanthropy and Communications, 1935–1939," in *The Development of the Social Sciences in the United States and Canada: The Role of Philanthropy*, eds. Theresa Richardson and Donald Fisher (Stamford, CT: Ablex, 1999), 185.

11. On 8 December, 1938, the RF awarded a grant-in-aid of $500 to the Stevens Institute of Technology in Hoboken, New Jersey, for Professor Harold Burris-Meyer to compile "a digest of materials on the use of sound effects in dramatic production." The resulting digest proved so promising with regard to further research that half a year later, on June 9, 1939, the trustees of the RF agreed to appropriate another $30,000 to the Stevens Institute of Technology for Burris-Meyer to conduct a three-year project on "the control of sound and light for dramatic purposes." Conditional on the success of the project, it would be supported for two more years up to a term of five years, as requested by the Stevens Institute. "The project was interrupted in 1942, however, when the director was called by the Navy for research work which also required use of the Stevens Institute equipment." RAC, RF, RG 1.1, Series 200, Box 282, Folder 3351. Thus it was only in late 1947 when the RF made an additional grant of $9,600 toward Burris-Meyer concluding the work of the project within fourteen months. The publications in which he summarized the results of his RF-funded work include: coauthored with Edward C. Cole, *Theatres and Auditoriums* (New York: Reinhold, 1949); coauthored with Lewis S. Goodfriend, *Acoustics for the Architect* (New York: Reinhold, 1957); coauthored with Vincent Mallory, *Sound in the Theatre* (Mineola, NY: Radio Magazines, 1959).

12. The same building close to Times Square, the old Studebaker Building of 1902, continued to be in use for various film, video, and recording studios, until it was demolished in late 2004. See David W. Dunlap, "Change, as It Does, Returns to Times Square," *New York Times*, 8 November, 2004, B6.

13. Released in 1940 by Frontier Films; directors, script: Lionel Berman, David Wolff, Robert Stebbins; photography: William O. Field Jr., Sherman Pratt; narrator: Colfax Sanderson.

14. During their five years of existence (1937), Frontier Films released the following motion pictures: *Heart of Spain* (1937), *China Strikes Back* (1937), *People of the Cumberland* (1938), *Return to Life* (1938), *History and Romance of Transportation* (1939), *White Flood* (1940), and *Native Land* (1942). For the most comprehensive account of the history and work of Frontier Films, see Russell Campbell, *Cinema Strikes Back: Radical Filmmaking in the United States 1930–1942* (Ann Arbor: UMI Research Press, 1982), 145–274.

15. On Eisler's score for *White Flood* see Tobias Faßhauer, "Hanns Eisler's *Chamber Symphony* op. 69 as Film Music for *White Flood* (1940)," *Historical Journal of Film,*

Radio and Television 18, no. 4 (1998): 509–19; see also Tobias Faßhauer, "Hanns Eislers Kammersymphonie als Filmmusik zu White Flood (1940)," Musik & Ästhetik 8, no. 31 (2004): 30–48.

16. Minutes of January 19, 1940, RAC Music Filming 1939–1941.

17. Theodor Adorno and Hanns Eisler, Composing for the Films (London & Atlantic Highlands, NJ: Athlone Press, 1994), 138. For this idea of a gap between the extramusical components of motion pictures and the corresponding music, see also Hanns Eisler, "Film Music—Work in Progress," Modern Music 18, no. 4 (1941): 250: "The succeeding years [after the introduction of the sound film in 1927] cover the entire history of the sound film with all the splendid achievements in camera technic [sic], lighting, sound recording, studio equipment, directing and story writing. But during all that time the position of the movie-music composer has not been appreciably affected." See also "Final Report on the Film Music Project on a Grant by the Rockefeller Foundation," 31 October, 1942, 1. RAC, NSSR, Music Filming 1942–1962, RF, RG 1.1, Series 200R, Box 259 Folder 3096 (hereafter RAC Music Filming 1942–1962). The report was published in Historical Journal of Film, Radio and Television 18, no.4 (1998): 595.

18. In the same year (1940), John Marshall became associate director of the HD, a position he held regardless of the HD's conversion into the Division of Humanities and Social Science until he retired in 1970. From 1959, Marshall was, however, largely committed to establishing and directing the Bellagio Study and Conference Center at the Villa Serbelloni in Italy.

19. William J. Buxton, "John Marshall and the Humanities in Europe: Shifting Patterns of Rockefeller Foundation Support," Minerva 41, no. 2 (2003): 142.

20. Minutes of January 19, 1940, RAC Music Filming 1939–1941; additions in square brackets follow the proposal of the FMP, sent with a letter from Alvin Johnson, 1 November, 1939, RAC Music Filming 1939–1941, published in Hanns Eisler, Musik und Politik: Schriften Addenda, Gesammelte Werke III/3, ed. Günter Mayer (Leipzig: VEB Deutscher Verlag für Musik, 1983): 142–44.

21. Template for press release, February 21, 1940, Agnes de Lima Publicity Files, Raymond Fogelman Library, New School.

22. Minutes of January 19, 1940, RAC Music Filming 1939–1941.

23. Proposal of the FMP, RAC Music Filming 1939–1941.

24. John Marshall to Alvin Johnson, 10 January, 1940, RAC Music Filming 1939–1941. With this letter Marshall already submitted the itemization of the grant he intended to recommend at the next meeting of the RF executive committee so that Johnson could "ascertain if it [was] acceptable from the point of view of the School."

25. Minutes of January 19, 1940, RAC Music Filming 1939–1941.

26. See Buxton, "John Marshall and the Humanities in Europe," 135–36. Losey had also been a Delta Upsilon fraternity brother (and 1929 classmate) of Nelson Rockefeller at Dartmouth College, which was likely how he became known to Rockefeller officers. See David Caute, Joseph Losey: A Revenge on Life (London: Faber & Faber, 1994), 29.

27. Caute, Joseph Losey, 45.

28. Letter from Joseph Losey to Alvin Johnson, 26 September, 1939, quoted in Hearings regarding Hanns Eisler: Hearings before the House Committee on Un-American

Activities, House of Representatives, 80th Cong., 1st Sess. (Washington, D.C.: Government Printing Office, 1947), 84.

  29. On the basis of this suggestion of Johnson, it has generally been assumed that, in 1939, Eisler was "armed with a commission from Oxford University Press for a book on music in movies," which was a decisive factor in him winning "a grant . . . from the [RF]." Graham McCann, "New Introduction," in Adorno and Eisler, *Composing for the Films*, xxxiii. Both assumptions, however, are ill-founded. In fact, while Johnson did bring up the contract with Oxford University Press to portray Eisler as a scholar deserving support, the eventual FMP did not correspond to the book Eisler had originally been contracted to deliver. As Philip Vaudrin, editor at Oxford University Press in New York, wrote to Eisler on February 23, 1940: "I was delighted to see in the *Times* this morning that you have received the grant from the [RF]. At the same time, however, I must confess to a slight disappointment, since this does of course postpone your writing of the book you are to do for us" (AdK, HEA 4183). To bridge this gap between Eisler's research and the book he was commissioned to write, it was eventually arranged that the focus of the book would be redefined. As Vaudrin recorded the revised arrangement with Eisler: "The research project on the relation between films and music, which you are carrying out under a Rockefeller grant, will be the basis for a general book on the same subject, and we agree to accept this as a substitute for the book you are at present under contract with us to write" (AdK, HEA 4183).

  30. RAC Music Filming 1939–1941, published in Eisler, *Musik und Politik*, 137–40.

  31. RAC Music Filming 1939–1941, 134–36.

  32. "Research Program on the Relation between Music and Films," RAC Music Filming 1939–1941; see also Eisler, *Musik und Politik, Schriften Addenda*, 138.

  33. Interoffice note from John Marshall to David Stevens, 2 November, 1939, RAC Music Filming 1939–1941. On the RF support of Burris-Meyer's research at Stevens Institute of Technology, see note 11.

  34. Marshall to Stevens, 2 November, 1939. This was a major program of the RF, as shown by the amount totaling $1,410,778 that was granted to altogether 303 displaced or deposed scholars between 1933 and 1945. Claus-Dieter Krohn, "American Foundations and Refugee Scholars between the Two Wars," in *The "Unacceptables": American Foundations and Refugee Scholars Between the Two Wars and After*, ed. Giuliana Gemelli (Brussels, New York: P.I.E.—Peter Lang S.A., 2000), 47–48.

  35. See John Marshall to Alvin Johnson, 13 November, 1939: "I may add—though perhaps for you alone—that our present feeling is that, if anything could be considered for Eisler, it should be more on the basis of the intrinsic interest and value of his work than as assistance for a deposed scholar," and Marshall to Johnson, 26 November, 1939: "Evidently this looks . . . like something which might develop into a small project." RAC Music Filming 1939–1941.

  36. Marshall to Johnson, 20 November, 1939, RAC Music Filming 1939–1941.

  37. On the work of the CHR project, see, for example, Buxton, "Reaching Human Minds," 185; also Buxton, "Rockefeller Support for Projects on the Use of Motion Pictures," 3.

  38. Iris Barry to Marshall, 4 January, 1940, RAC Music Filming 1939–1941.

39. Kurt London, *Film Music* (London: Faber & Faber, 1936; reprinted New York: Arno Press & *The New York Times*, 1970).

40. Hanns Eisler, "Music and Film: Illustration or Creation?" *World Film News* 1 (1936): 23.

41. John Marshall (hereafter JM) Interview, 3 January, 1940, RAC Music Filming 1939–1941.

42. Lazarsfeld's answer of 2 January, 1940, was ambiguous. He admitted that he did not know Eisler well personally, but reported—ever the empirical sociologist—that "no one seems to doubt whatever problems on the social aspects of music he would tackle, his work would be worthy of support." Lazarsfeld also recounted that he had heard rumors of Eisler's having "a too-great interest in his own advancement, sometimes at the expense of his associates." Furthermore, Lazarsfeld added, albeit with the apparent purpose of interceding for further support of Adorno's study of music broadcasting: "My general feeling would be that [Eisler] hasn't quite the deep intellectual sincerity and freshness of approach which Dr. Adorno has, but that his interests lie in the same direction and that from a practical point of view he might be easier to handle." As to the possibility of a collaboration between the RRP and the prospective FMP, Lazarsfeld promised to prepare "a short summary of [the] musical experiments" of the RRP so that Marshall would "be able to judge whether [the RRP could] be of any help in developing Dr. [sic] Eisler's plans." Thus it appears somewhat optimistic when on January 3, 1940, Marshall reported to Eisler "Lazarsfeld's willingness to cooperate in any study of the kind Eisler [wished] to undertake." RAC Music Filming 1939–1941. Equally euphemistic is Albrecht Betz's interpretation of Lazarsfeld's letter as "a very positive opinion." Albrecht Betz, *Hanns Eisler: Political Musician*, trans. Bill Hopkins (Cambridge & New York: Cambridge University Press, 1982), 176.

43. JM Interview, 3 January, 1940, RAC Music Filming 1939–1941.

44. Marshall to Eisler, 29 January, 1940, RAC Music Filming 1939–1941.

45. See Jürgen Schebera, "Research Program on the Relations between Music and Films—Hanns Eislers Filmmusikprojekt in den USA, finanziert durch die Rockefeller Foundation 1940–1942: Verlauf und Resultate," in *Emigrierte Komponisten in der Medienlandschaft des Exils 1933–1945*, eds. Nils Grosch, Joachim Lucchesi, and Jürgen Schebera (Stuttgart: M & P Verlag für Wissenschaft und Forschung, 1998), 73.

46. Hanns Eisler, *Composing for the Films* (New York: Oxford University Press, 1947).

47. When Eisler, charged, among other things, with being the "Karl Marx of communism in the musical field," was heard before the HUAC, he sarcastically offered "as evidence [his] book" and advised Robert Stripling, chief investigator, to study it (*Hearings regarding Hanns Eisler*, 22–23 and 56).

48. See Adorno, "Postscript," in Hanns Eisler [sic], *Composing for the Films* (Freeport, NY: Books for Libraries Press, 1971), 167: "In view of the scandal, I withdrew my name from the book."

49. The first German edition was brought out by the East Berlin publishing house Henschel & Sohn: Hanns Eisler, *Komposition für den Film* (Berlin: Henschel & Sohn, 1949). In this edition, certain passages were altered to accommodate a

European readership and, especially, to comply with the official art doctrine of the Eastern bloc.

50. See Adorno, "Postscript," 168: "I consider it legitimate to publish the book in the Federal Republic of Germany, deleting the changes made for the 1949 edition. It is also correct for it to be published under both our names."

51. Adorno moved to Los Angeles in 1941; Eisler followed in 1942. Until his deportation in 1948, Eisler wrote the music for the following Hollywood pictures: *Hangmen Also Die* by Fritz Lang (United Artists/Arnold Productions 1943); *None but the Lonely Heart* by Clifford Odets (RKO 1944); *Jealousy* by Gustav Machaty (Republic Pictures 1945); *The Spanish Main* by Frank Borzage (RKO 1945); *A Scandal in Paris* by Douglas Sirk (United Artists/Arnold Productions 1946); *Deadline at Dawn* by Harold Clurman (RKO 1946); *A Woman on the Beach* by Jean Renoir (RKO 1947); *So Well Remembered* by Edward Dmytryk (RKO 1947). On Eisler's work as Hollywood film composer, see Claudia Gorbman, "Hanns Eisler in Hollywood," *Screen* 32, no. 3 (1991): 272–85; and Horst Weber, "Eisler as Hollywood Film Composer, 1942–1948," *Historical Journal of Film, Radio and Television* 18, no. 4 (1998), 561–66.

52. Adorno and Eisler, *Composing for the Films*, li–liii. It may be noted that the term "cultural industry," which Theodor W. Adorno and Max Horkheimer developed for their *Dialectic of Enlightenment*, was first introduced into the English-language discourse in *Composing for the Films*. In their joint foreword of September 1, 1944, Eisler and Adorno refer to the theoretical background in the chapter "Kulturindustrie" of the book *Philosophische Fragmente*, as the *Dialectic of Enlightenment* was initially titled. However, this foreword was not published before 1969. Theodor W. Adorno and Hanns Eisler: *Komposition für den Film* (München: Rogner & Bernhard, 1969), 9–10.

53. Adorno and Eisler, *Composing for the Films*, liii.

54. Today the model of "dramatic counterpoint" has become particularly famous, although it is often erroneously considered the only method of audiovisual correlation that Eisler and Adorno accepted.

55. Adorno and Eisler, *Composing for the Films*, 32.

56. Hanns Eisler, *Composing for the Films* (London: Dennis Dobson, 1951).

57. Antony Hopkins, "*Composing for the Films* by Hanns Eisler," *Sight and Sound* 21, no. 4 (1952): 183.

58. See Joy Calico, "'The Karl Marx of Music': Hanns Eisler Reception in the United States after 1947," in *Hanns Eisler müßt dem Himmel Höllenangst werden*, ed. Maren Köster (Hofheim: Wolke Verlag, 1998), 120–36.

59. Roy Prendergast's sweeping assessment of *Composing for the Films* being "testy and valueless" may be regarded as typical for the reaction of those who feel personally insulted by the book. Roy M. Prendergast, *Film Music: A Neglected Art—A Critical Study of Music in Films* (New York: Norton, 1977).

60. With the example of Eisler, Peter Schweinhardt expounds the problems of the factually and psychologically multilayered and often infinite process of the "settling" of migrants. Peter Schweinhardt, *Fluchtpunkt Wien: Hanns Eislers Wiener Arbeiten nach der Rückkehr aus dem Exil*, Eisler-Studien, vol. 2, eds. Peter Schweinhardt and Robert Wißmann (Wiesbaden, Leipzig, & Paris: Breitkopf & Härtel, 2006), chapter 2. Put simply, Eisler's life became more and more centered on East Berlin from the

summer of 1949 and, to a greater extent, from the spring of 1950. Still, the city of Vienna continued to be another focal place in Eisler's personal and professional life for many years.

61. Adorno, "Postscript," 168.

62. Hanns Eisler, "Film Music—Work in Progress," *Modern Music* 18, no. 4 (1941): 250–54, also published in Eisler, *Musik und Politik*, 146–50.

63. It has caused confusion among Eisler scholars that in his 1941 interim report, Eisler described in detail the results of film-music experiments that, in reality, he had not yet undertaken and would never realize, that is, two alternate editions of *White Flood* and a rescored excerpt from *The Long Voyage Home*.

64. See Eisler, *Musik und Politik*, 154–57; also published in *Historical Journal of Film, Radio and Television* 18, no. 4 (1998): 595.

65. Released in 1941 by National Association of Nursery Educators; directors, producers: Joseph Losey, John Ferno; script: Joseph Losey; photography: John Ferno; narrator: Lloyd Gough.

66. See Joseph Losey to Hanns Eisler, 16 August, 1941. AdK, HEA 4139.

67. Caute, *Joseph Losey*, 70.

68. Released 1941 by Pan-American Films; producer, director: Herbert Kline; script: John Steinbeck; photography: Alexander Hackensmid; narrator: Burgess Meredith.

69. Adorno and Eisler, *Composing for the Films*, 140.

70. Adorno and Eisler, *Composing for the Films*, 140; "Final Report on the Film Music Project on a Grant by the Rockefeller Foundation," 595–96.

71. The final "Statement of Expenses: Hanns Eisler—Rockefeller Music Fund" has no item that could be assigned to the recording of a score for a newsreel. RAC Music Filming 1942–1962, Folder 3096. A list of works in the handwriting of Louise Eisler contains the entry "Unbegun: March of Time" (my translation, Hanns Eisler Collection, Feuchtwanger Memorial Library [hereafter FML], Specialized Libraries and Archival Collections, University of Southern California).

72. Released 1941 by History Today; producers, directors, photography: Joris Ivens, John Ferno; commentary written by: Dudley Nichols; narrator: Frederic March.

73. Adorno and Eisler, *Composing for the Films*, 117.

74. JM Interview, 29 April, 1940, RAC Music Filming 1939–1941.

75. See Leo C. Rosten, *Hollywood: The Movie Colony—The Movie Makers* (New York: Harcourt, Brace & Co., 1941).

76. See the undated report on these contacts, probably by Harry Robin, in AdK, HEA 4349.

77. The following details are taken from Eisler's FBI file and from the *Hearings regarding Hanns Eisler*.

78. *Hearings regarding Hanns Eisler*, 101.

79. See the Immigration Act of May 26, 1924, Section 4: "When used in this Act the term 'non-quota immigrant' means . . . (d) An immigrant who continuously for at least two years preceding the time of his application for admission to the United States has been, and who seeks to enter the United States solely for the purpose of, carrying on the vocation of . . . professor of a college, academy, seminary, or university; and his wife . . ., if accompanying or following to join him." One might

presume that Eisler and Johnson concealed this visa matter from Marshall upon applying for sponsorship by the RF. This, however, was not the case. Rather, Johnson wrote to Marshall on November 27, 1939: "Formally at least [Eisler] must round out his second year of teaching here, in order to get a permanent non-quota visa." RAC Music Filming 1939–1941.

80. *Hearings regarding Hanns Eisler*, 153.

81. Harry Robin to Marshall, 23 August, 1940, RAC Music Filming 1939–1941.

82. Marshall to Robin, 27 August, 1940, RAC Music Filming 1939–1941.

83. Marshall to Johnson, 27 August, 1940, RAC Music Filming 1939–1941.

84. Memorandum by Eisler, 26 November, 1941, sent with letter from Johnson, 10 December, 1941, RAC Music Filming 1939–1941.

85. Marshall to Johnson, 11 December, 1941, RAC Music Filming 1939–1941.

86. RAC Music Filming 1942–1962, Folder 3096.

87. From February to October 1942, the final "Statement of Expenses: Hanns Eisler—Rockefeller Music Fund" records the payment of an assistant named "L. Gustami" or "L. Gostony," the misspelled maiden name of Eisler's wife. RAC Music Filming 1942–1962, Folder 3096.

88. Released in 1940 by Twentieth Century Fox; producer: Darryl F. Zanuck; director: John Ford; script: Nunnally Johnson; photography: Gregg Toland; original music: Alfred Newman.

89. See Arthur DeBra to Eisler, 16 December, 1940, and DeBra to Eisler, 30 December, 1940 (AdK, HEA 4309). Whereas the organization of the MPPDA is mainly known for its restrictiveness in imposing the production code, it also played an enabling role in the film projects of the RF. For example, the Hollywood footage that the CHR reedited for educational purposes was funneled through the MPPDA. See also Buxton, "Reaching Human Minds," 184–85; Buxton, "Rockefeller Support for Projects on the Use of Motion Pictures," 3. Thus it was a natural idea to proceed analogously with the FMP, even though Eisler was initially skeptical: "Eisler will now take advantage of the offer of DeBra at the Hay Office to give him further assistance in getting the materials he wants. He doubts the ability of the Hays office to do so, but . . . there can be no harm in taking its offer up." JM Interviews, 27 and 29 October, 1940. RAC Music Filming 1939–1941.

90. Adorno and Eisler, *Composing for the Films*, 146.

91. Eisler to Clifford Odets, 18 November, 1942, Indiana University, Bloomington, Lilly Library, Clifford Odets Papers, Box 2. My thanks go to Jürgen Schebera, the editor of a forthcoming publication of Eisler's letters, who allowed me to look at and make use of his transcription of these letters.

92. The final "Statement of Expenses: Hanns Eisler—Rockefeller Music Fund" lists a payment of $19.95 to the MoMA on 9 November, 1941. RAC Music Filming 1942–1962, Folder 3096.

93. Cf. Hans Schoots, *Living Dangerously: A Biography of Joris Ivens*, trans. David Colmer (Amsterdam: Amsterdam University Press, 2000), 115.

94. See the interview with Helen van Dongen by Abé Mark Nornes in *Documentary Box* 17 (June 2001).

95. Adorno and Eisler, *Composing for the Films*, 148.

96. Adorno and Eisler, *Composing for the Films*, 148.

97. In the "Report on the Film Music Project" as appended to *Composing for the Films*, Eisler and Adorno concede that "sociological investigations might have been undertaken in connection with the general plan of the project," for example, by performing sometimes the original films and sometimes the experimentally re-scored versions "for different groups of listeners" and studying "the reactions . . . by means of questionnaires and interviews." Redefining the concept of the FMP after its outcome, Eisler and Adorno claim that "such investigations lay outside the scope of the project," but recognize that "it would be worthwhile to ascertain whether the audience's aversion to modern music is not merely a legend, and whether it would not approve of modern music that adequately fulfilled its dramatic function" (Adorno and Eisler, *Composing for the Films*, 138).

98. JM Interviews, 12 December, 1940. RAC Music Filming 1939–1941.

99. Rudolf Arnheim to Eisler, 3 January, 1941, AdK, HEA 4090.

100. See Adorno to Eisler, 8 January, 1942, in Gabriele Ewenz, Christoph Gödde, Henri Lonitz, and Michael Schwarz, eds., *Adorno: Eine Bildmonographie* (Frankfurt/M.: Suhrkamp, 2003), 180.

101. See the undated letter from Eisler to Adorno, (possibly 21 or 28 January, 1942, or even 4 February, 1942), AdK, HEA 4205, published as "Falsche Flaschen-post?" ed. Johannes C. Gall, *Eisler-Mitteilungen* 32 (June 2003): 11. It is all the more regrettable that a cooperation with Paul Lazarsfeld and his RRP never came about given that there had been concrete ideas about such a cooperation from the start. In his final pre-grant interview of Eisler, Johnson, and Robin (3 January, 1940, RAC Music Filming 1939–1941), John Marshall "expressed a good deal of skepticism" about the audience tests that Eisler had proposed as part of his FMP. Marshall mooted the suggestion of studying the effects of the experimental soundtracks of the FMP "not on a lay audience, but probably on recipients who could be fairly articulate about their reactions. He reported a device for testing by Lazarsfeld and Stanton of the [RRP], the device consisting simply of a small box with two buttons, one to be pressed for a favorable reaction and the other for an unfavorable reaction, these reactions being noted on a moving tape" so that the test subject could later be confronted with his or her likes and dislikes in their relation to the test program and be questioned about their causes. (On this device, the "Lazarsfeld-Stanton Program Analyzer," see Jack N. Peterman, "The 'Program Analyzer': A New Technique in Studying Liked and Disliked Items in Radio Programs," *Journal of Applied Psychology* 24, no. 6 (1940): 728–41; Tore Hollonquist and Edward A. Suchman, "Listening to the Listener. Experiences with the Lazarsfeld-Stanton Program Analyzer," in *Radio Research 1942–43*, eds. Paul F. Lazarsfeld and Frank N. Stanton (New York: Duell, Sloan, & Pearce, 1944, reprinted New York: Arno Press, 1979), 265–334. In the pre-grant interview, "Eisler was much engaged with the possibility of utilizing" the Program Analyzer. Whereas this possibility did not materialize, Adolf Sturmthal and Alberta Curtis did later apply the Program Analyzer to studying audience reactions to films, namely in the two educational films *Valley Town* and *What So Proudly We Hail*, the first film with a score by the Eisler-influenced composer Marc Blitzstein. (See Adolf Sturmthal and Alberta Curtis, "Program Analyzer Tests of Two Educa-tional Films," in *Radio Research 1942–43*, 485–506). However, the conclusions drawn in this study about the effects of Blitzstein's score are not very far-reaching.

Also, the likes and dislikes of the test subjects are generally all too directly equated with specific strengths and weaknesses of the films.

102. On the screening of 16 September, 1944, within the scope of the symposium "Music in Contemporary Life," (before some 1,500 people) at Royce Hall, University of California Los Angeles, see, for example, the undated letter from Eisler to Louise Eisler (FML Eisler Collection); Walter H. Rubsamen, "A Modern Approach to Film Music: Hanns Eisler Rejects the Clichés," *Arts and Architecture* 41, no. 11 (1944): 38; Naomi Reynolds, "An Institute of Music in Contemporary Life," *Film Music Notes*, December 1944; Alfred Frankenstein, "Triumph of the 12-Tone System," undated newspaper clipping from the *San Francisco Chronicle*. On Eisler's and Adorno's general contributions to the symposium "Music in Contemporary Life," see Albrecht Dümling, "Zeitgenössische Musik im Dritten Reich: Die Beiträge Hanns Eislers und Theodor W. Adornos zur Konferenz 'Music in Contemporary Life' (Los Angeles 1944)," in *Komposition als Kommunikation: Zur Musik des 20. Jahrhunderts* (Festschrift Peter Petersen), eds. Constantin Floros, Friedrich Geiger, and Thomas Schäfer (Frankfurt/M. & Oxford: Peter Lang, 2000), 155–64.

103. "Final Report on the Film Music Project on a Grant by the Rockefeller Foundation," 595.

104. George Beal to Johnson, 23 May, 1944, RAC Music Filming 1942–1962, Folder 3096.

105. The gap that John Marshall's record of his 1944 interviews shows from 28 July, 1944, to 6 September, 1944, suggests that he was away just at the time when, effectively, the course was set for the preservation and future whereabouts of the artistic results of the FMP. Still, it certainly would have been possible for Marshall to intervene after his return to his office. See RAC, RF, RG 12.1, John Marshall diaries, 1944 (microfilmed).

106. Clara Mayer to Hanns Eisler, 17 June, 1947, FML Eisler Collection.

107. See Johannes C. Gall, "Hanns Eislers Musik zu Sequenzen aus *The Grapes of Wrath*: Eine unbeachtete Filmpartitur," *Archiv für Musikwissenschaft* 59, nos. 1 and 2 (2002): 60–77, 81–103; Breixo Viejo, "Disonancias revolucionarias: La música alternativa de Hanns Eisler para *Las uvas de la ira* (1940) de John Ford," *Archivos de la Filmoteca* 47 (June 2004): 128–41.

108. See Johannes C. Gall, "A Rediscovered Way to Describe Rain: New Paths to an Elusive Sound Version," in *Kompositionen für den Film: Zu Theorie und Praxis von Hanns Eislers Filmmusik*, ed. Peter Schweinhardt, *Eisler-Studien*, vol. 3, eds. Oliver Dahin, Johannes C. Gall, and Peter Schweinhardt (Wiesbaden, Leipzig, & Paris: Breitkopf & Härtel, 2008), 87–122.

109. Under my direction, the International Hanns Eisler Society, Berlin, has restored Eisler's film-music study and published it on DVD. Besides the original versions of *White Flood* and *A Child Went Forth*, this DVD contains a reproduction of Eisler's 1941 sound version of *Rain* (produced by the Nederlands Filmmuseum, Amsterdam, in 2005), a reconstruction of Eisler's alternative version(s) of an excerpt from *The Grapes of Wrath* (through a synchronous recording by Berndt Heller and the Saarland Rundfunk Orchestra), and, according to Eisler's proposal in "Film Music—Work in Progress," 253 (see note 63), two other editions of *White Flood*, one with abridged commentary (spoken by musical actor Christopher Murray), the other only with subtitles (both alternate editions using a synchronous recording

of Eisler's score of *White Flood* by Roland Kluttig and the Kammerensemble Neue Musik, Berlin, produced in collaboration with DeutschlandRadio Berlin in 2004). The DVD edition was funded by the German Federal Cultural Foundation and is published as Theodor W. Adorno and Hanns Eisler, *Komposition für den Film*, mit einem Nachwort von Johannes C. Gall und einer DVD "Hanns Eislers Rockefeller-Filmmusik-Projekt 1940–1942," im Auftrag der Internationalen Hanns Eisler Gesellschaft herausgegeben von Johannes C. Gall (Frankfurt/M.: Suhrkamp, 2006).

110. Raymond B. Fosdick, *The Story of the Rockefeller Foundation* (New York: Harper & Row, 1952), 247.

111. See, for example, Frank Hughes, "Red Gospel Advanced by Fund Grants: Exempt Trusts Pay Writers," *Chicago Tribune*, 7 November, 1948.

112. RAC, RF, RG 12.1, John Marshall diaries, 1939 (microfilmed).

113. Reply from Raymond B. Fosdick to John Parnell Thomas, chairman of the HUAC, 4 June, 1947, RAC Music Filming 1942–1962, Folder 3096.

114. See, for example, Brett Gary, "Communication Research, the Rockefeller Foundation, and Mobilization for the War on Words, 1938–1944," *Journal of Communication* 46, no. 3 (1996): 124–47.

115. Eisler himself recognized the precedence of research pertaining to national-security objectives. As Marshall recorded, the composer called on December 18, 1941, "to say that it should be noted that his request for further support for his study of film music was put in before the outbreak of war. He would not have put it in after the war began, since he could appreciate that work of this kind might have to yield to other more urgent demands in war time." John Marshall, Interviews 1941, RAC Music Filming 1939–1941. Adorno also showed awareness of the priorities established by the RF, when, in his letter to Eisler of January 8, 1942, he advised his friend soon to move to Los Angeles and earn a livelihood in the Hollywood film industry: "What is the situation with the prolongation of your project? Since I imagine Rockefeller now focusing only on defense research, you will probably want to pursue your own film plans and I presume that you are going to come out here soon." Ewenz, Gödde, Lonitz, and Schwarz, *Adorno*, 180 (my translation).

8

"Sugar-coating the Educational Pill": Rockefeller Support for the Communicative Turn in Science Museums

Manon Niquette and William J. Buxton

In 1939 the Rockefeller Foundation funded a survey of the exhibition methods used in two great world's fairs of the time, New York and San Francisco. This project served as the basis for *East is East and West in West*, written by Carlos Cummings, curator of the Buffalo Museum of Science, with the assistance of a group of young professionals who had been selected from other museums. This venture was undertaken in conjunction with the New York Museum of Science and Industry, which also produced its own book, *Exhibition Techniques: A Summary of Exhibition Practice*.[1]

Cummings's study is often described as a turning point because it was also the first work to stress the importance of a storyline for communicating the message of exhibits.[2] The previous surveys done by Edward S. Robinson and his collaborators[3] focused more on the behavior of the museum visitors than on the exhibitions per se. The idea of studying two world expositions—both of which were highly permeated by advertising—allowed Cummings to make a radical change in how the interest of visitors was assessed. For the first time, researchers studied how an exhibit, in the same manner as a printed document, could influence attitudes.[4] Reflecting the insight that "education can entertain," an exhibit's ability to arouse and maintain the interest of the crowd was seen as a factor of great importance.

Commentators tend to attribute the relation between museology and communications studies to the far-reaching influence of Paul Lazarsfeld's research on audiences and media efficacy.[5] While in some respect our work shows this to be true, it brings empirical evidence to bear on the fact that Cummings' study and Lazarsfeld's work were interconnected as parts of the program in communication supported by the General Education Board (GEB), in conjunction with the Division of Humanities (HD) of the Rockefeller Foundation (RF) under the directorship of David H. Stevens and his assistant director, John Marshall. This venture, which began to take shape in the mid-1930s, represented the abandonment of the HD's previous emphasis upon underwriting classical scholarly work in the humanities, in favor of support for the theory and practice of how the new media could help disseminate culture to a mass public.[6] The HD, as it announced in 1935, had the aim of giving aid "to selected community institutions in demonstrating methods for widening the field of public appreciation."[7] To this end, the program in communication was directed toward a broadly conceived range of media, which included not only motion pictures, radio, theater, microphotography, and libraries, but also museums. The HD saw the latter as community institutions capable of reaching a public comparable in size to that reached by theater, film, or radio broadcasting. Like these "other instructional and amusement agencies," museums were "reaching out incessantly for the citizen's time," making it necessary to "recanvass the methods of presentations, to develop means of making its exhibits more arresting, more telling, more effective."[8] Moreover, museums were listed as one of the means of oral and visual communication of thought and feeling. It was believed that "though the power of the printed word is not to be minimized, large sections of the public now derive as much from what they hear and see as from what they read."[9]

Focusing on the cases of the Brooklyn Museum, the New York Museum of Science and Industry (NYMSI), and the Buffalo Museum of Science (BMS), the aim of this paper is to show how the modern museums' communicative turn was closely linked to the early media studies funded by Rockefeller philanthropy. In doing so, it will address the moral consequences of this new communicative approach in an era of persuasion, propaganda, and social control. Specifically, in the case of mixed museums of arts and science, this involves the diffusion of ideologies of the time, such as racial hygiene, evolutionism, and eugenics. For museums of industry, this set of ideas was conjoined to commercialism, industrialism, and corporate interests.

ROCKEFELLER SUPPORT FOR THE COMMUNICATIVE TURN IN MUSEUMS

Although museums were considered to be important sites of community influence, relatively few grants were made to them during the 1930s. The RF provided support only for those museums whose practices were consciously communicative in nature. It was believed that the educational power and social values of museums could be improved through a program in training personnel outside the traditional lines of operation. This involved giving interns the opportunity to learn new methods of display and to disseminate their newly acquired knowledge through leadership positions as museum professionals. The HD also thought it important to support initiatives that would allow one to know more about the public response to various types of exhibit. The Buffalo Museum of Science, along with the Brooklyn Museum and the New York Museum of Science and Industry, were seen as being quite innovative in this respect. Therefore, $44,000 was appropriated to the Brooklyn Museum for the training of museum personnel,[10] the NYMSI received $50,000 for the development of new methods of exhibition[11] (as well as $25,000 for the museum's general budget),[12] and the BMS was provided with a sum of $68,500, $50,000 of which was for the training of museum personnel[13] and $6,000 for the study of the exhibits at the two 1939 world's fairs.[14] Later on (in 1941), a final portion of $12,500 was given in order to advise various museums of South and Central America.[15]

LEONARD OUTHWAITE: SCIENCE MUSEUMS AS VANGUARD COMMUNICATORS

The first stage of the HD's museum program came in 1935. Leonard Outhwaite—a former staff member and anthropology consultant of the Laura Spelman Rockefeller Memorial—was commissioned to prepare a report on the educational programs of American museums, the first of its kind in the United States. Above all, Outhwaite's inquiry[16] was oriented toward the place of art museums in the field of popular adult education. Nevertheless, he thought that museums of natural science—and of science and industry—were much more advanced in terms of the development of exhibition techniques that were at once both popular and educational. It seemed possible to apply to the art museum the same principles developed in other kinds of museums. In this sense, the Brooklyn Museum and the BMS were evaluated as doing useful and innovative work. The Brooklyn Museum, which had formerly been a general museum covering the fields of archaeology, anthropology, natural history, and the arts, was said to be "the center of a number of experiments in special museum techniques and educational activities." Further on in his report, Outhwaite included a note on the so-called mixed museum, which he thought had great advantages. In his view, pure art museums had been confined to the outlook and prejudices of European canons. Moreover, the tendency toward remoteness and abstraction made for a separation of art from the emotional appeal and the intellectual judgment of the general public. By contrast, the artistic objects exhibited in the mixed museum were more grounded in the social life of the community that had created them.

Outhwaite had a particular fascination for the period-room type of installation and, even more so, for the use of a chronological order in the
general arrangement of the museum.[17] The Buffalo Museum of Science was
described as "one of the most alert and progressive institutions of its kind
in the country," especially because of its exhibit halls, which were arranged
in systematic and logical sequence.[18] The so-called storyline technique,
developed by the BMS, involved arranging the exhibits to tell a continuous
story, comparable to moving through the chapters of a book. According
to the president of the BMS, Chauncey J. Hamlin, the main inspiration
for the notion of a museum as a book was a comment made by author
H. G. Wells,[19] who had taken the science museum as a model for *The Work,
Wealth & Happiness of Mankind*, which was published in 1932:

> An ever-growing series of industrial developments was sketched out. We
> should have, we thought, to tell the history of steam from Hero's engine to
> the latest turbine. We should have to trace the development of the metal-
> lurgy of every sort of metal. We should have to tell the full story of electrical
> development. . . . We should have accomplished in a book what the Science
> Museum at South Kensington and—more explicitly and fully—its daughter the
> Deutsches Museum at Munich—set out to do.[20]

It is well known today that after World War I, European technological
museums, such as the Deutsches Museum, served as a model for how
sequential displays could be used.[21] In fact, the representation of chronol-
ogy in museums dates as far back as the French Revolution and the invention of democratic culture. This was particularly true in the case of art
museums, in which the notion of change and successive identities could
find a means of expression.[22] The development of ideas of progress and
the emergence of historical disciplines in the nineteenth century engaged
European modern museums into linear, didactic, and evolutionary representations of the past.[23] The taxonomic enterprise of natural history set
the tone. In the United States, the BMS was not the only museum to make
use of what may be called "narrative techniques": it was also the case for
the Smithsonian Institution,[24] the American Museum of Natural History,[25]
the Newark Museum,[26] and as it will be explained further, the Brooklyn
Museum and the NYMSI.

The use of chronological exhibits may not have really been a groundbreaking practice, but the idea that the whole museum should be conceived
as *a story teller* was definitely seen by Outhwaite as innovative. His fascination for sequential displays was in line with his great interest in the themes
of evolution and heredity, which he saw as having played a major role in
the evolution of the Modern Museum. In a report[27] he wrote in 1936 for the
Academy of Natural Sciences of Philadelphia, he cited the study of evolution and the development of "the sciences of heredity and genetics" as ex-

amples of new sciences that had led to "newer and, we hope, more vital and more realistic collections and descriptions of the objects of nature." Because these new sciences had offered "vital explanations *of nature in action*,"[28] this led to what he considered to be a new stage of museum development: the "Functional and Educational Museum." Outhwaite thought there were very few museums "that really understand their responsibility in this regard or have faced the issues with which they are dealing." Museums had opened their doors to the public and put material on display but this was seen as different from really serving the public's needs. Rather than being the specialist's paradise where the visitor was treated in a technical and authoritarian manner, museums had to find ways for their research to become known about and made useful, to make simple and popular exposition of their material, and to study new methods of display in order to get "trained men to mediate between the scientist and the public visitor."[29] Advertising had created standards for color, form display, value, typography, and succinctness. Outhwaite didn't think that the museum should compete with this field, but he was convinced that it had to offer a product, if not with the same methods, at least with "the same spirit." If the museum had to say something, it should be a place where not only objects were on display, but rather where ideas were conveyed. The RF consultant thought it legitimate for the museum to utilize "wonders, curiosities, and the extraordinary perplexities of nature in reaching the public and in dramatizing knowledge," but he also believed that it would be a mistake if these would be the end products of its activity.

THE MUSEUM AS COMMUNICATOR AND STORYTELLER

As it will be shown in this chapter, what the museums supported by the RF had in common was to make extensive use of "the storyline technique"; this was much before the curator of the BMS, Carlos Cummings, had stressed the importance of this exhibition method in his survey of the two world's fairs. The use of a chronological order in the general arrangement of the museum was actually the key feature that aroused the interest of the officers of the Humanities Division of the Rockefeller Foundation, right at the beginning of its communicative venture. Given that the narrative mode is central to every discursive apparatus, and that "making museum histories" presupposes a commitment to fundamental values such as truth, intellectual honesty, and social responsibility,[30] it is deserving of closer attention.

The European museums' approach to chronological exhibits based itself on the accuracy of well-established facts, which became embodied in an internalist view of scientific development. Exhibits were used as visual supports for what students learned from lectures and textbooks. The emergent paradigm in the use of narratives in museums was hence one of education. This phase differed from a later one that we may call "interpretive," which is characterized by the idea that stories have a constructed nature and that alternative narratives are conceivable. Post and Molella attribute this awareness of relativism to a more contextual approach to exhibition.[31] According to these authors, the emphasis upon context in the planning of exhibits implied a radical change in the relations between museums and their audiences; the values of truth and objectivity had to be defended on a different ground, namely that of a perpetual confrontation between celebratory attitudes and a more critical perspective rooted in social history. This approach inevitably led to politicization in the form of an ongoing negotiation of historical representations between museums and parties with an interest in museum content.

We argue that between the earlier educational approach and the more recent interpretive orientation lies another mode of conceiving the so-called museum of ideas, namely that based on communication. What was new about the storyline technique developed by museums such as the BMS was the conception of the *whole museum* as a story, and one might even say, as *a storyteller*—hence, as a communicator. Little attention has been given to the fact that the main inspiration for the exacerbation of teleological progressivist representations in American museums was the extensively used storytelling formula from advertising.[32] The most effective advertisement was thought to be the one that told a moving human story filled with symbols that were familiar to the public. A storytelling technique of this kind was evident in what Marchand called *social tableaux*.[33] The comic-strip style of advertising was one of its most popular forms and saw its best-known application in an exhibit during the world's fairs of the 1930s.

Keeping in mind this close connection between advertising and museum narratives, the fact (as suggested by Post and Molella) that museums felt more obliged to negotiate their historical representations with outsiders cannot be explained by their having a more contextual approach alone. In the 1930s what was at issue, rather, is the deep and abiding relationship between museological practices and audiences that has become second nature, as was the case for other forms of modern mass media, such as radio, film, and mass magazines, all of which have recast the connection to their audiences through marketing techniques. Preparatory research in identifying customers and pretesting their reaction to campaigns were just two examples of the know-how that was transferred from advertising to museums. Window-display design, whose sophistication had been increased by the multiplication of chain stores, became a great source of influence through various aspects of three-dimensional exhibits, such as motion, form and shape, flexibility, color and radiance, the use of flashing lights and animate figures, and so forth.

By the 1930s a whole school of thought concerned with the evaluation of visitors' reactions had already begun to develop through the work of Edward S. Robinson and his co-workers. One of their most notable series of studies was undertaken at the Buffalo Museum of Science, in order to discover methods for making museums "into more effective educational centers."[34] Because this period was one of transition, the vocabulary used to describe the new communicative nature of museums was still derived from education in that the development of a number of media—radio, films, as well as museums—and the reorientation of the adult-education movement—were mutually implicated. Hence, the report written by Robinson's co-workers describes museums as being part of the so-called visual education movement and thereby becoming "media of visual education equal in importance to the cinema and other educational aids used in the classroom." Although children's education was still the focus of this particular series—in opposition to most of Robinson's studies—it was said to be complementary "to the effectiveness of various methods of installation and labeling for the education of adult visitors." The adoption of a new communication vocabulary within the realm of adult education appears clearly in Robinson's collaborators' report: "In the case of adult visitors, the major educational problem as currently phrased is that of determining the most effective indirect or impersonal methods for increasing attention, interest, and knowledge."[35] The inverse was also true. Advertising in the 1930s was described as "one of the great educational forces."[36] The democratizing influence of mass media (which were largely supported by advertising) coupled with the fact that many advertisements in the 1920s had emphasized the themes of science and technology, contributed to the blurring of the boundaries between education and commercialism, as well as between knowledge and propaganda.

THE BROOKLYN MUSEUM:
INTRODUCING TECHNIQUES OF COMMERCIAL
DISPLAYS IN A NEW "SOCIALLY ORIENTED MUSEUM"

Following Outhwaite's report, the officers of the Rockefeller Foundation came to view the Brooklyn Museum, the Buffalo Museum of Science, and the New York Museum of Science and Industry as providing unusual opportunities for experiments in training personnel and testing methods of display. They agreed that university training in art and museum work did not prepare workers "in display methods or in analysis of public interest." Because the background values of those recruited by science museums were to be rooted in industry, the RF officers believed they would have "some clearer idea of popular demonstration."[37]

In September 1935 an initial grant of $44,000 for the training of personnel was allocated to the Brooklyn Museum. The Central Museum of the Brooklyn Institute of Arts and Sciences at that time was undergoing a thorough remodeling. The fondness for industrial design of the new director, architect Philip Newell Youtz, was perfectly suited to the use of art in the dissemination of messages.[38] In the eyes of the RF, the greatest asset of the Brooklyn Museum was that its new policy was oriented toward the perceived needs of the public.[39] The RF officers expressed the same fascination as Outhwaite for the arrangement of the material in a chronological, geographical, or technological order. As noted by a BMS Rockefeller intern:

> An outstanding feature about the Institute is the pre-arranged plan of exhibition. Starting from the lowest level, which is supposed to impart to the visitor the idea that he is looking in on "[40]the early and primitive cultures, and that as he climbs to the upper floor levels he keeps step with the chronological sequence in the development of civilization all over the world. . . . Each period, and occasionally collections, has its key color, and the room devoted to the expression of the subject is painted in the chosen color. This arrangement is supposed to exist through the entire museum.[41]

As arrogant as this representation of Western civilization's supremacy might appear, it was meant to transform the museum into an active agency of adult education. Obviously, the use of a chronological order in the arrangement of the whole museum was not exclusive to the BMS; the Brooklyn museum was also seen as quite inventive in this respect.

The Brooklyn museum was also said to be experimenting with "new ways of utilizing the dramatic." Techniques of commercial display were closely studied and adapted, another good point in the eyes of the RF.[42] The idea was to organize what was to be shown to the visitors in a manner corresponding to their own experience. This could be done, for instance, by emphasizing some aspects of the objects exhibited and by comparing them to objects in everyday use. A store-window dresser from a Fifth Avenue shop had been hired to assist in arranging the exhibits, an initiative that was praised by the RF. According to Youtz, this was, above all, a way of democratizing the museum, so it could be intelligible to the average person.[43] He even had it in mind to undertake a "sociological museum program."[44] He found it unfortunate that, in the United States, the methods of visual presentation had been left to the advertiser and to the cinema while in Russia, the Soviet government had found museums were one of its most effective means of educational practice.[45] Criticizing the fact that art in the United States tended to be the exclusive property of the wealthy, Youtz had in mind the transformation of the Brooklyn museum into a "socially oriented museum":[46] "A museum . . . is a collection of people surrounded by objects, not a collection of objects surrounded by people."[47] Disappointed by the work of the first group of Rockefeller appointees, Youtz thought that they had to learn not only methods of displaying material to the public, but above all they had to become "acutely conscious of their obligation to the public."[48] In Youtz's opinion, university training had done little or nothing to develop "their idea of the social responsibilities of a museum."[49] This problem was also that of the Brooklyn Museum since the experience of the older museum staff was all the same tainted by an "anti-social point of view."[50] In effect, the interests of the Brooklyn Museum and the HD coincided, in that each sought to challenge a particular "monopoly of knowledge" that had become predominant in museum circles. According to John Marshall, assistant director of the HD, museums had largely been in the hands of people who had undergone scholarly training at institutions such as the Fogg Museum at Harvard, at Yale, and at Princeton. He viewed them as a "pretty stodgy" group, who dismissed the HD's interest in improving the techniques of museum display as mere "showmanship." Mirroring the concern of Youtz to present museum objects to the public "in ways which would make them more significant and intelligible," the HD supported the Brooklyn Museum's proposal to "bring to the museum younger museum personnel who shared this interest in more effective visual presentation."[51]

Indeed, Youtz's use of the equation "advertising-education" within the context of the social democratization of knowledge was perfectly in tune with the tendency of the RF to support projects that took the commercial framework as a point of reference. For instance, a number of the projects in motion pictures and radio supported by the HD were marked by an effort to further educational goals within the system of Hollywood film production and private broadcasting, respectively. This "tension between accepting the commercial framework and moving beyond it" characterized the Rockefeller programs in communication.[52]

THE NEW YORK MUSEUM OF SCIENCE AND INDUSTRY: AN EDUCATIONAL WAY OF DOING CORPORATE PUBLIC RELATIONS

The acceptance of a commercial framework is even more evident in the case of the New York Museum of Science and Industry. Support from the RF came at a moment when the NYMSI was in the process of reorganizing its staff in preparation to move to the newly constructed RCA building located in Rockefeller Center.[53] In September 1935 the chairman of the museum's board, Frank B. Jewett, vice president of the American Telephone & Telegraph Company and president of Bell Telephone Laboratories, wrote to RF president Max Mason, asking for his help in keeping the NYMSI in operation. The RF made two appropriations to the NYMSI, totaling

$75,000. The first grant of $50,000 was made in September 1935 for the development of new methods of museum exhibition (1936–1938), and the second in December 1939 (totaling $25,000) was to be used for the museum's general budget.

As was the case for the Brooklyn Museum, the RF saw in the reorganization of the NYMSI an opportunity to develop a new field of experimental display and to improve methods of exhibition and demonstration in different kinds of museums. These included the museums of science and industry, the small museums attached to particular industries, the expositions of applied science, and scientific demonstrations of general museums.[54] The new director of the NYMSI, Robert P. Shaw, had a vision of the communicative functions of museums that was also consonant with that of the RF. One of his mottoes was that the exhibition had to "sugar-coat the educational pill," which could be done by entertaining museum visitors. As was the case with other museums supported by the HD, the use of sequential displays was also a hallmark of the NYMSI. As Shaw expressed it in an issue of *Scientific Monthly*, museum presentation techniques have "progressed a long way since the days when 'half a mile of canned tomatoes' represented a high point in exhibition ideas."[55] In Shaw's opinion, the Chicago Century-of-Progress exposition had played an important part in the raising of the level of exhibition techniques. Since that time, an exhibit dealing with canned tomatoes, instead of piling up cans row upon row, would rather present the product in its historical context and then explain where it belonged in people's everyday life. Shaw described the storyline technique as one of a number of progressive exhibit methods developed at the NYMSI and applied most intensively in the electro-technology division: the story of electricity was told "in a series of exhibit units, each one of which deals with an outstanding phase of that story and leaves it ready to be taken up by the next unit."[56]

In order to redefine the museum as a medium, reference to other communicative practices helped Shaw to make his case. With his emphasis upon dramatization, he used the metaphor of theatrical presentation. He explicitly suggested that "a good plan would be to try to arrange the divisions, sections and groups of exhibits in the form of a running story, with all work based on the script, as in a play, each exhibit advancing the story one step further."[57] Moreover, he saw in the musical show *The Laughing Chevalier* the keynote of the museum idea. The performance begins with a couple in front of a painting titled *The Laughing Chevalier*; visitors say they would like to know how the picture happened to be painted. The scene changes and the audience is taken back to Holland in 1624, where Franz Hals is painting the picture. In Shaw's view, the use of an entertaining story served to "humanize" the painting and to arouse the audience interest, yet the play was fictitious. This technique could then be applied to a museum.[58]

Wherever the idea that *the whole museum should tell a story* came from—a book, a musical, a play, or the science museum itself—the question of the origin of the use of the storyline technique is not the most pertinent. Actually, the notion of storytelling appears to have been the common denominator of all forms of cultural mediation in the new emergent communication society, including educational museums and advertising. Therefore, the tendency to frame the museum as a medium through reference to various narrative forms may be seen as the glimmerings of media convergence.[59]

The fact that Shaw was more inclined to think in theatrical terms and to put more emphasis on dramatization whereas Chauncey J. Hamlin, president of the BMS, favored a more literary metaphor (the museum as a book) was mirrored in a joint venture they undertook. The common interest of the NYMSI and the BMS in new presentation techniques led them to collaborate in collecting data of value in museum displays from the two world's fairs of 1939. On January 19, 1939, HD director David H. Stevens met with Shaw, Hamlin, and BMS curator Carlos E. Cummings to discuss the idea of conducting a survey of the two 1939 World's Fairs, and their potential application to museums. Stevens thought that the data collected could be "a great resource of all museums" and that it would also "lead to the location of some of these fair exhibits at proper museums for permanent installation."[60] By this time, the RF had already allocated a grant to the BMS for a museum-training program similar to that of the Brooklyn Museum. Following the January meeting, a special grant of $6,000 was made by the RF to the BMS for the study of the exhibits at the two World's Fairs. This study was to be made with the RF interns under the direction of Cummings, in cooperation with Shaw. On its side, the NYMSI was appropriated the sum of $25,000 to its general budget.

Even though the New York World's Fair adversely affected NYMSI's attendance, the survey work proved beneficial to the museum in its program for developing industrial cooperation.[61] As part of its plan of industrial cooperation the NYMSI invited private corporations to put in representative exhibits "done in a educational manner as part of a long-range public-relations activity."[62] In this sense, the survey work was helpful in that it put the museum staff in touch with potential exhibitors. Indeed, the book produced by the NYMSI, *Exhibition Techniques: A Summary of Exhibition Practice*, appeared at the same time as the book published by the BMS, namely *East is East and West is West*. While the latter was entirely qualitative, *Exhibition Techniques* devoted an entire chapter to the statistical analysis of various phenomena. The remainder of the work focused on individual exhibits and was mainly descriptive. *Exhibit News Letter*, a monthly bulletin published by the NYMSI, which was designated primarily for executives of business and industrial corporations, described the book as "an invaluable aid to every executive concerned with advertising, promotion, exhibits or public relations in any of their multitudinous phases."[63]

The primary concern of the NYMSI staff was to make detailed analyses of exhibits that might themselves be shown in museums of science and industry. Therefore, it would be an exaggeration to say that the NYMSI wanted to transform itself into a rental space for public-relation exhibits. The RF emphasized that modern museums such as the NYMSI could be, at least in part, self-supporting, and that this was to be done with the cooperation of industry. But at the same time, the officers also praised the fact that the museum kept full control of methods for displaying publicity—in those instances when large industries were given or rented space—and that it determined the amount of time and space in each allotment. Consequently, what the NYMSI offered to companies in exchange for their pledges was its help in bringing their stories to the public.[64] This corresponded closely to the museum's educational purpose which, according to a statement made by Frank B. Jewett, president of the NYMSI, and quoted approvingly by the RF Board of Trustees as reflective of its beliefs, "is to give to lay people and technical people a comprehensive view of the development of scientific and industrial skills from their first primitive appearance to their present state, and to indicate clearly that the present state is but the latest step in a continuously expanding evolution."[65] Therefore, the use of the storyline technique in the context of a museum of science and industry was obviously more than merely an effective and modern method of display: as for the evolutionary representations in nineteenth-century European modern museums, the narrative turn in the diffusion of industrial culture appears to have been the perfect vehicle for ideas of progress, the essence of American confidence in its commercial development. In point of fact, the use of a narrative was seen as both an excellent educational device and an effective tool for public relations. It allowed for the reconciliation of the two antagonistic tendencies that lay at the heart of the Rockefeller Foundation, education and profitability, without falling pray to the vulgarity of advertising and commercial domination.[66]

THE NEW EXHIBITION TECHNIQUES
OF THE BUFFALO MUSEUM OF SCIENCE

In any event, the application of the storyline technique to a series of anthropological exhibits had an entirely different dimension as well. The idea that museums should tell a story in order to be more attractive was entirely consistent with the evolutionist view of civilizations. As we saw, this was the case for the Brooklyn Museum; it was even more striking in the Buffalo Museum of Science. The Rockefeller officers described this approach as "a view to the vivid illustration of ideas rather than the display of a multitude of objects." They saw the museum as "primarily a museum of ideas" whose "exhibits aim above all to give visitors a concrete exemplification of principles and influences."[67] David H. Stevens maintained that the BMS was chosen "on account of the distinction of its present exhibits" and underlined the fact that at the BMS "Science is thought (of?) as an inclusive item."[68] The RF officers' enthusiasm for the BMS evolutionist perspective is evident in the 1937 *Annual Report* that quotes Hamlin's scheme of presentation:

> What we are doing is to try to write and illustrate the whole fascinating story of modern science in our document—our museum—chapter by chapter, in our various exhibit halls, each exhibit leading naturally into the next, and each forming a part of a logical whole. We start the story with an account of the essential unity of different forms of matter, and conclude it with a demonstration of the final goal of civilization, the essential unity of mankind in our interdependent complex of modern life.[69]

Beyond this very general account, there is not much information available at the Rockefeller Archive Center on the specifics of the evolutionist scheme of presentation that the RF officers had acclaimed. Material located at the archives of the BMS provides a more accurate sense of the ideas put forward by the new methods of exhibition. In a letter Chauncey J. Hamlin wrote in March 1937 to Frederick P. Keppel, president of the Carnegie Corporation of New York, he provides more details about the plan behind the BMS's sequential arrangement of halls.[70] The first two chapters of the BMS story, in the Hall of Physics and Chemistry and the Hall of Astronomy respectively, were about the elements constituting the universe and the story of the formation of chemical compounds and minerals. The next chapters, those of Earth Science, the Hall of Life, and the Hall of Invertebrates, Plant Life and Vertebrate Life, carried the story of the formation of the earth and of the coming of life. These halls were followed by the Hall of Evolution and Genetics[71] in which the theory of evolution was presented, in turn, "leading up to the evolution of man itself as illustrated by a splendid series of bronzes" (depicting the so-called primitive man) and "the modern science of genetics as illustrated through a series of exhibits demonstrating the operation of the Mendelian Law" (mostly eugenic exhibits, as will be discussed further). The chapter that followed, in the Cabana Hall of Man, was about human physiological functions. It contained a number of working models from the Deutsches Museum of Hygiene in Dresden, among which was the famous Transparent Man. The last chapters took up the story of the "societal evolution" by showing first, in the Halls of Primitive Man and of Primitive Races, the life of "primitive" and nomad people, and then, in the Hall of Civilization—the last of the whole story—the development of "modern civilization."

In line with Outhwaite's report, John Marshall was particularly impressed by the museum's "exceptional" success "in organizing its exhibits with a view to conveying to its public certain important underlying ideas, not only in the fields of the natural sciences, but of social science, and of general culture as well."[72] He emphasized the museum's "attempt to trace the developing course of civilization . . . up to the final displays dealing with contemporary civilization in which the underlying themes are still made evident."[73] As Hamlin emphasized, the museum's success was "witnessed by the steady growth in attendance."[74] Marshall thought that the establishment of internships, as had been the case with the Brooklyn Museum, would have the effect of carrying to other museums "a direct acquaintance with the rather unusual methods of visual presentation" developed at the BMS.[75] As the internship program was the HD's primary interest, it was resolved to appropriate the sum of $50,000 to the BMS for the period from 1937 to 1940 toward expenses of training museum personnel in the use of new techniques in the visual presentation of museum objects.[76] In the end, thirteen men from various museums were selected and worked on the planning and installation of exhibits. Four of them were from China, Australia, Sweden, and Great Britain respectively.[77] Some interns toured other American museums of science to compare methods and to acquaint themselves with their collections. These visits must certainly have helped to publicize the work of the Buffalo Museum of Science. In addition to the subsequent grant for the survey of the two world's fairs, in 1941 the Rockefeller Foundation gave an additional grant of $12,500 for advisory services and training of personnel to the Museu Nacional, Rio de Janeiro, and to other museums of South and Central America. Hamlin's plan for the "Future National Museum of Brasil of Tomorrow" followed exactly the same model as the scheme developed at the BMS, including an exhibit on "the story of heredity," displayed next to stories of "the social evolution of civilization," and of "health."[78]

TOWARD "A NEW RACE NOBILITY"

The BMS was essentially a museum of natural sciences, so its juxtaposition of both cultural and biological evolution into one comprehensive communicative structure paved the way for the inclusion of eugenic principles. In this sense, it represented an aspect of eugenics that, until recently, has received relatively little attention.

Most studies of eugenics tend to concentrate on scientists and the hardcore membership of eugenics societies while largely ignoring the mainstream vehicles for cultural diffusion.[79] Eugenics was above all a popular movement; a greater emphasis on the more popular aspects of culture is essential to explain its widespread appeal. Since the mid-1990s, a growing number of studies have investigated the involvement of leading groups in the popularization of eugenics. Hasian explains how a number of local projects such as better-baby contests, parenthood programs, women's temperance and contraception movements, self-improvement societies, and even the scouting movement, became sites for the circulation of eugenics rhetoric in the first decades of the twentieth century.[80] Selden shows that eugenically-oriented policy recommendations found their way into high school biology textbooks up until the late 1940s.[81] The 1930s and the 1940s marked the emergence of radio, films, and museums as new forces of dissemination and thereby enhanced the reach of eugenic messages. In this respect, Pernick's study of eugenics in motion pictures suggests that, by the mid-1930s, the revival of interest by American newspapers and magazines in covering issues such as the eugenic euthanasia of "defective babies" might be linked to the admiration that key leaders of American eugenics and euthanasia organizations had for the Nazis' use of film to promote killing as a cure, and also was linked to their own program of distributing Nazi eugenic films to high schools.[82] Rosen examines the involvement of religious leaders in the American eugenics movement during the first half of the twentieth century.[83] Maxwell argues for a strong connection between photography as a powerful visual medium and the success of the eugenics movement in Britain, the United States, and Nazi Germany, from 1879 to 1940.[84] This kind of analysis suggests that in order to better understand the process by which eugenics retained its support well into the Second World War, one needs to situate it within the communicative transformation of cultural institutions.

In this respect, Robert Rydell's work on the reception of eugenics by the American public between the wars is a pioneer study.[85] Christina Cogdell's research on the links between streamline design and the formative principles beneath eugenic ideology shows how the exhibits purchased by the BMS from the Chicago World's Fair were still in tune with middle-class American culture well into the 1930s.[86] In another essay (coauthored with Robert Rydell and Mark Largent),[87] Cogdell places particular emphasis on the travel of the Nazi exposition *Eugenics in New Germany*, which also found a home at the BMS from 1935 to 1943. The three authors analyze how this German exposition has been used as a political tool to win public support for forced sterilization and new immigration restriction laws—a "Republican New Deal"—as opposed to health and social reform. Because their investigation ends with the arrival of the material at the BMS, the ensuing history has yet to be written, namely how the officers of Rockefeller philanthropy saw in the display of the Nazi and American eugenic propaganda—as it had been incorporated into the evolutionist museum narrative—a model for increasing the communicative effectiveness of educational and cultural agencies.

The material from the exposition "Eugenics in New Germany" included fifty-one posters and charts that had been produced by the Deutsches Hygiene-Museum. The announcement of this exhibition in the BMS monthly magazine *Hobbies* specified that the posters were displayed "as a matter of public interest, without endorsement." Nevertheless, it touted the "eugenics program upon which Chancellor Hitler has launched the German people" as "astounding," and it concluded by stating the exhibition "gives Americans a graphic explanation of Germany's campaign to rear in posterity 'a new race nobility.'"[88] The poster reproduced in the magazine was explicitly eugenicist: it featured a collage of German asylums with a table comparing the significant amount of money spent on them in 1930 as compared to the smaller amounts spent on other public services. The two main headings proclaimed that "Germany was proud of having the best lunatic asylums [and] she will be proud some day not to need lunatic asylums any longer."[89]

The German exhibit was not the only eugenic material that arrived at the BMS in 1935. The same year the museum purchased a considerable collection of objects and exhibits from the Chicago Century-of-Progress Exposition—many of which were also originally from the Deutsches Hygiene-Museum in Dresden—for its Hall of Man and its Hall of Heredity and Environment. What was later held to be "offending material" was destroyed at the order of the U.S. government in 1943 and in 1950.[90] This makes it very difficult to uncover evidence of eugenicist propaganda in American museums. Fortuitously, photographs taken before the destruction of the material are still available at the BMS archives. Within the BMS heredity and environment collection can be found four charts prepared by Harry Hamilton Laughlin, superintendent of the Eugenics Record Office at Cold Spring Harbor, Long Island, New York.[91] Specifically these charts consisted of the following: number 1 described "the relation between racial and family-stocks, national welfare and happiness generally."[92] It featured a tree on which "Eugenics" is superimposed in large capital letters between the branches and the trunk. The roots are formed by the bodies of knowledge upon which eugenics supposedly draws. Among them are statistics, anthropology, psychology, heredity, law, genealogy, applied eugenics, and mate selection.[93] Number 2 was a "statistical account of population turn-over with reference to quality."[94] It was titled "How families, communities, races and nations may change greatly in capacity within a few generations."[95] Number 3 showed "an inferior family which, despite opportunity, could never get on."[96] The chart was based on the erroneous interpretation given by Arthur Estabrook (for the Eugenics Record Office) of Richard Dugdale's original study of the Jukes family.[97] Within the BMS exhibit, it was coupled with a display on the supposedly superior Edwards family (see below). Number 4 was another "superior family,"[98] namely the Roosevelts, whose distinguished "family stock" was revealed though a chart showing the distribution of inborn qualities that produced two presidents of the United States.[99]

Most of the other exhibits had already circulated quite widely as staples of eugenics exhibitions. They included:

- A "three-dimensional device" that sought to illustrate the main principles of the Mendelian Law of Heredity. It featured various picture of baby creatures, animals, and humans together.[100]
- A chart in the form of a trellis bearing the title "What you are (inheritance) you acquired from your ancestors." The main message is that "your social worth depends upon the response of your heredity to your environmental opportunities."[101]
- A display with dolls in a case illustrating how physical features such as eye and hair color are inherited, drawing on Mendelian principles of "dominant" and "hidden" factors.[102]
- A poster with close-up pictures of a dozen young people of mixed racial origin. Below each of the pictures was a designation of the ethnic origin of the father and, in smaller letters, the ethnic origin of the mother. Besides "Japanese," "Chinese," "Spanish," and "Portuguese," "American" is given as an ethnic origin. The costumes of the persons suggest that they were considered to be exotic or akin to rare animal specimens. The men's chests are completely naked; the women are displayed with their shoulders exposed or dressed in a low-necked blouse (exposing their cleavages) partially covered by a shawl.[103]
- A poster, the aim of which is to "teach young men and women the immense bearing of a wise or unwise marriage" and to bring "determination to rise and master handicaps by the exercise of his utmost intelligence."[104]

The "great interest"[105] and spirit of "delight"[106] expressed by Hamlin[107] for Laughlin's four "splendid charts" shows the intensity of the BMS's adherence to eugenicist principles.[108] Although no mention of the eugenics exhibits can be found in the RF archives, the information on the museum's exhibits located in the BMS archives leads one to think that Outhwaite's enthusiasm for the themes of evolution and heredity was based on the eugenicist and evolutionist material displayed at the Buffalo Museum of Science. If John Marshall's positive reaction to these specific exhibits is not quite as explicit, his appreciation of the whole scheme of presentation of the museum speaks for itself. The fact that he reported on the BMS having funds in hand to complete the exhibits in the Hall of Genetics and the fact that it would be discussing its aim "with specialists such as those at Cold Spring Harbor"[109] also reveals the RF's tacit endorsement of the diffusion of eugenicist ideas. This is at odds with George Stocking's affirmation that Rockefeller philanthropy played a determining role in the *post-evolutionary* reorientation of Anglo-American anthropology,[110] and more specifically, that Outhwaite's ties to the Boasian tradition gave a special character to its study. However, the evolutionary viewpoint on culture had by no means disappeared; it was still very much present in the American museums of the early 1940s—at least in those of the natural sciences—and the RF was very much inclined to support this perspective. Furthermore, the fact that through the storyline technique, the BMS defined itself as a museum of ideas rather than as a museum of objects calls into question Stocking's claim that the object orientation of museum workers can be responsible for the objectification of those who had made the objects. Such objectification appears to have been more related to the communicative process inherent in museum display: the more the museum defined itself as bearing meanings, the more it produced images of identity and of colonial otherness that revealed the assumption of an American racialized society. In this sense, the big mass media event surrounding the arrival of the most important exhibit that had ever been shown at the Buffalo Museum—during the months the RF was considering giving it a grant—epitomizes how the emergence of a new museum of ideas, through the systematic use of a narrative structure, produced a comprehensive racial discourse of exclusion.

THE TRANSPARENT WOMAN UNVEILED

In April 1937 a major public-relations event took place: the Buffalo Museum of Science welcomed a very special woman from Germany. Nearly 60,000 visitors came to see her during the six weeks she stayed in Buffalo.[111] The Sunday following her arrival, 6,207 persons visited the museum during the three-hour period that it was open.[112] The big event celebrated was the fact that for the first time, she had been given the chance to meet one of her "four brothers." In a special radio broadcast in honor of her arrival in Buffalo, the physician Francis E. Fronczak, health commissioner of the city of Buffalo and president of the American Association of Hygiene, presented her as a welcome departure from the women of the day, who were obsessed with fashions such as

> "la pompadour," or the bird-of-paradise plumage, or the permanent wave, and in external appearance, in all the variations from the sylphlike or the stream-line in some countries, to the well-rounded, sometimes almost elephantine size so preferred in certain parts of the globe.[113]

On the contrary, this "very distinguished guest" was trumpeted as

> the only woman who is not only completely stripped of all decorative append-ages, but is introduced to the public, not only in the nude, but in crystal-like transparency, without withholding from view any anatomical mysteries or secrets.[114]

The guest in question became known as the "Transparent Woman." Cast in a "heroic pose,"[115] she was made of an actual skeleton with artificial internal organs, blue veins and red arteries. Each of the organs listed on the pedestal could be illuminated one at a time. The outside covering was molded from cell horn, a material similar to celluloid in that it could be pliable, transparent, but unlike this material it was practically unbreakable and nonflammable.[116]

The first and only Transparent Woman—who had been fabricated in the Deutsches Hygiene-Museum—was loaned to the BMS by S. H. Camp & Company of Jackson, Michigan, a producer of surgical supplies. In 1935 the BMS had already purchased an exact copy of the Transparent Man—which had previously been exhibited at the 1933 Chicago Century-of-Progress Exposition—along with the collection of objects mentioned earlier.[117] Right after the opening of the BMS Hall of Man, an advertising agency representing the Camp Company conceived the idea of giving the Transparent Man a mate. Negotiations between the BMS and the Deutsches Hygiene-Museum eventually led to "the birth" of the Transparent Woman. In 1936 she made her debut at the New York Museum of Science and Industry and she was then sent to various other places, including the BMS. Exploited by Mr. Camp "as a form of indirect advertising,"[118] she represented what he saw as "his contribution to public health education in America."[119]

In America, as in pre-Nazi Germany, the material from the Deutsches Hygiene-Museum was used for propagandizing eugenicist principles. Some exhibits may indeed have appeared "neutral," such as the Transparent Man or Woman. [120] But the culturally biased physiognomy of these two creations all the same had significant implications for the production of meaning. One can argue about what meaning the figures conveyed. Of greater interest, however, is that they had been produced *to mean something*. Echoing McLuhan, one can say the meanings of the transparent figures are to be found in their constitution as media.

The Transparent Man, which has been seen by millions of people, continues to be one of the main attractions of the Deutsches Hygiene-Museum. According to the official public history of this institution, "the museum's ideas of popular health education and highly developed modern communication methods had been placed in the service of Nazi racist ideology."[121] In the same vein, a 1980s replica of the Transparent Man is currently displayed at the entrance of the traveling exhibition *Deadly Medicine*, mounted by the U.S. Holocaust Memorial Museum in order to recount the history of German racial health policies. As part of the exposition, a text referring to the cover of a brochure for an exhibition presented during the Nazi period states:

> The Hitler regime adopted the scientific "transparent man" to promote the racist goal of creating a genetically "healthy" and "pure" Germanic Volk (people),

which excluded Jews and other minorities. This is the brochure of the exhibition *Eternal People* mounted in 1939 by the German Hygiene Museum in Dresden.[122]

In the catalog of the exhibition, it is explained that the BMS donated the Transparent Man back to the Deutsches Hygiene-Museum "considering the object tainted by its Nazi associations."[123] This interpretation provided by both museums—the Deutsches Hygiene-Museum and the U.S. Holocaust Memorial Museum—tends to belie the fact that the "birth" of the Transparent Man had taken place as part of the development of visual communication within Weimar eugenic culture. In an attempt to trace the historical significance of the Transparent Man, the director of the Deutsches Hygiene-Museum, Klaus Vogel, briefly discusses the origins of the *Gläserner Mensch* in relation to the emergent ideology of racial hygiene in the 1920s.[124] However, his focus is on how one can understand the figure aesthetically—more particularly on the context of its reception as a new form of art—rather than as a vehicle for white supremacist political statements.

Our contention is that the meaning of the Transparent Man and Woman cannot be reduced to a matter of reappropriation. Since they were made to attract and educate people, they must be seen above all as three-dimensional electronic media. They were an embodiment of the eugenic culture in which they were created; racial supremacy was deeply inscribed within the curves that defined their shape.[125] The "transparent" figures could be used to represent the "eternal" people, only if it were understood that the "eternity" of a superior race could be possible through the man-made construction of a perfect being rendered transparent—by electricity—for all to see. Transparency, in this case, implied not only visibility, but also universality, illumination, purity, and chastity.

As Rydell argues, the exposition is the best medium for displaying doctrines (such as eugenics) that have been converted into secular faiths.[126] The Transparent Woman, who was worshipped for her crystalline "perfection," inevitably conformed to this tendency.[127] With her five feet, six inches in height, she was described "as a universal Caucasian type of approximately 30 years of age."[128] The impression given was that one could view the interior with X-ray–like vision. For the BMS, the primary purpose of the Transparent Woman was not to teach the details of anatomy; the exhibit was framed as a pure celebratory spectacle in that one could see as a whole the "perfectly functioning mechanism of the female body . . . for the first time in human knowledge."[129] "TO HER HIGHNESS, THE WOMAN!" voiced Fronczak specifying that he raised his glass to the toast "The Woman" and not "A Woman."[130]

The Transparent Woman was not only stripped of her clothes and of her opaque skin, but also of any sign that her faultless anatomy could have been sullied by civilization. Embodying the eugenic ideal of biological perfection, she was not presented as the typical woman on the street, but as a goddess, a lofty ideal for the human race. As the president of the American Association of Hygiene introduced her on air:

> Ethnologically, that is her race, is no doubt of Caucasian type; her nationality probably of Slav or Latin-Celt origin. Personally, I think she represents the beautiful Polish or French-Irish type. She is not as plump as the Venus of Melus or Milo, but has all her limbs properly adjusted, while the arms are missing in that artistic work of the ancient sculptor. Neither has this woman standing beside me the artificial wasplike waist nor the streamlines so affected today by some females. Her skin is perfectly transparent, so that you may see her through and through, which is not the case in most women alive today.[131]

The Transparent Woman might have had her two arms, but since she was meant (at least at the BMS) to be more of a cult object than one of actual scientific education, she had been rendered sexless. As was the case with the Transparent Man, who in conformity with the BMS wishes,[132] was made *"ohne Penis,"*[133] the genitalia of the Transparent Woman was also omitted: only the uterus and the ovaries were present. She could be an incubator—or at the very most an egg producer—but not a sexual being. Accordingly, she had been designated as "the Transparent Man's sister"[134] and not as his mate, as it had initially been conceived by Camp's advertiser. At the time, biological divinities such as the Transparent Man and Woman, despite the pretence of their sponsors that they were scientific artifacts, could not exhibit their genitals to the public. Moreover, beyond matters of decency, the very notion that each could have his or her full reproductive apparatus seemed unthinkable: these godlike creatures were man-made and it was only men who could produce them:

> This man-made copy of the Woman impresses upon me, and I believe upon all of you, more than ever, the unbounded Wisdom and the infinite goodness of the Supreme Scientist, who made "Her Highness, the Woman," beautiful in form, queenly in bearing, mysterious in her life activities, duties and functions, the most important object of His creation.[135]

These lines of Fronczak's discourse, as they appear in the script of the radio broadcast, were planned to end deliberately with the eulogy "Hail, Her Highness the Woman,"[136] followed by a slot for a five-second applause at which point the BMS president was to break in. Underlying the way in which the Transparent Woman was introduced to the public were sentiments not merely confined to Fronczak's sexist and racist dedication to the "purification" of the human body; this outlook reflected the BMS frame of mind of the time (and presumably of other science museums).

Thus, the exchanges between the BMS and the Deutsches Hygiene-Museum around the transparent specimens show how the idealized vision of the body superseded actual human life and experience; they reveal the importance given to the manipulation of human tissue without regard for human living beings.

"FRESH OFF THE CORPSE"

Such a tendency was evident in the case of the Spalteholz transparencies (transparent specimens made with real organs) that began to attract attention in the 1910s. The worldwide infatuation with this material in the first part of the twentieth century is an intriguing issue,[137] yet their initial appearance preceded the Nazi regime.[138] The fact that many exhibits from the Deutsches Hygiene-Museum displayed at the BMS during the period of national socialism were made of actual human remains is indeed quite disturbing. What is at stake is not simply the medical use or the storage of skeletal materials without any consent from the ancestors' progeny.[139] The mortal remains used for the Spalteholz transparencies were removed directly from cadavers and displayed to a broad lay audience without any regard for their context of origin nor for their human meaning. Desecrated and divorced from their symbolic connections to life and death, they were processed to be sanctified as man-made divine objects.[140] Thus, a human arm, which had been made transparent with injected arteries, was ordered by the BMS from the Deutsches Hygiene-Museum, along with the Transparent Man. It was, however, delayed because the Deutsches Hygiene-Museum claimed to have encountered "great difficulty in obtaining the suitable corpse material"[141] and that "in order to perfect the injections to the arm, the original arm must be obtained fresh off the corpse."[142] After nearly three years of insistent letters from the BMS to the Deutsches Hygiene-Museum, the latter finally wrote to the former in 1937 that it was able to send a specimen made from the arm of a ten- or eleven-year-old child.[143] After confirming the authenticity of the item, the BMS accepted.[144] The final transaction of the BMS with the Deutsches Hygiene-Museum was the purchase in June 1939 of a series of nine actual human embryos, of the Spalteholz type, showing the stages of human development at four-week intervals.[145] Like the other Spalteholz transparencies, the embryos were grounded in the notions of control and accessibility. The secrets of life that only scientists had been able to access through their microscope were now made accessible to the general public through an X-ray–like culture of display.[146] Moreover, the fact that "more neutral" specimens such as the Spalteholz transparencies were displayed in the context of pure eugenicist material meant that they derived their meaning from this backdrop.

Within the BMS evolutionist sequence found in its halls, the Deutsches Hygiene-Museum anatomical specimens, sitting cheek and jowl next to the eugenics exhibits, became a standard to which humans could aspire in order to produce the same kind of perfection through practices such as selective breeding and forced sterilization.

IN THE NAME OF PUBLIC HEALTH

The pattern established by the Chicago Century-of-Progress Exposition, where anatomical and eugenic exhibits were part of an embracing gospel of cultural and industrial progress, definitely inspired the BMS scheme of presentation in which "the story of human biology" is coupled with "the story of civilization." Conversely, the BMS scheme had a widespread influence on the 1939 New York World's Fair and other museums.

A survey conducted by the New York Museum of Science and Industry for the Transparent Woman exhibit in 1937 (which had migrated from the BMS) had shown "that the hygienic field offered the best material" to reach this objective. Akin to the BMS's exhibit, the New York Museum of Science and Industry consequently displayed a collection of Dresden items loaned by the Oberlaender Trust of the Carl Schurz Memorial Foundation in Philadelphia. To what extent this material overlapped with the BMS collection is difficult to know. It was said to constitute "the hygiene exhibit" of the NYMSI. Its objective was "to develop a large spectacular and educational exhibition" that could be used as "a feature attraction for the Museum to interest new groups of people."[147] Not surprisingly, the hygiene exhibit was labeled *The Story of Man*.[148] Another home survey of the New York Museum of Science and Industry showed that it ranked second among the special exhibits the visitors said they came to see in 1938 (after Polaroid and just before the "strip-tease performance"[149] of Miss Anatomy, another full-size female anatomical figure).[150]

Two years later, the same Oberlaender collection was displayed in the Hall of Man of the Medical and Public Health Building at the 1939 New York World's Fair, a venue vaunted by the American Public Health Association as "the best opportunity to initiate a great museum of health," similar to the Deutsches Hygiene-Museum, "modified to fit American conditions and to harmonize with our viewpoint."[151]

Specifically, the Medical and Public Health Building was presented as the new American Museum of Health. It had the financial support of the Carnegie Corporation of New York, the Rockefeller Foundation, the Oberlaender Trust, a number of life insurance companies, many pharmaceutical houses, and various health and medical associations. At the close of the fair, it was estimated that more than 7.5 million visitors had come to the health exhibits. Of these, 5.542 million persons had visited the Hall of Man, with 3.34 million of them viewing the Transparent Man and 2.302 million viewing the Embryo Panel.[152]

Notwithstanding the efforts of the officers of the American Museum of Health to distance themselves from the Nazi race policies, the cathedral-like Hall of Man also displayed a number of exhibits with eugenicist and racist components. Thus, it included an exhibit in the section on reproduction called *The Marvel of Heredity*, with a large map of the chromosomes in the eggs of the fruit fly and heredity charts similar to that of the BMS[153] (the BMS models from the Hall of Heredity and Environment had been loaned to the Golden Gate International Exposition[154]); a section on demography, titled *We, the People*, displaying a large rotating globe showing the distribution of the various races all over the world; a maze of medical superstitions where a mechanical native man described as a "savage medicine man . . . a mad mechanical dervish decked in gauds, charms, mystic numbers, and other insignia of his craft"[155] showed the visitors in a mirror and asked them, "Are you a medicine man?" and so on.

The BMS, the New York Museum of Science and Industry, and the 1930s World's Fairs—along with the museums in South and Central America who received advice from the BMS—were not the only institutions to combine the stories of human biology and human civilization into one broad narrative. This was also the case for the American Museum of Natural History, through the intermediary of Frederick Osborn, nephew of its eugenicist president, Henry Fairfield Osborn. The younger Osborn had been both vice president of the board of directors of the American Museum of Health and chairman of the coordinating committee of the American Museum of Natural History. In 1941 the latter committee worked on a project for the creation of a new Hall of Man that would incorporate the health exhibits of the soon-to-be defunct American Museum of Health. In the end, the American Museum of Natural History's Council of the Scientific Staff formulated a plan where "the inspiring story of human evolution from its earliest beginnings and at the same time the equally significant unity of all life" would be illustrated. This plan, one copy of which was sent to the BMS, included a section on heredity with the following exhibits: "The Mendelian Principles, Twin Studies, Sibling Studies, Family Records, Race Mixture, and Examples of Various Types of Heredity."[156] Reform eugenicists such as Osborn are commonly viewed as proponents of a new population genetics who desired to distance themselves from racist eugenics. However, the inclusion of exhibits on race mixing placed next to mainline eugenic family charts in the plan of the American Museum of Natural History belies this point of view.

Stefan Kühl explains that two tendencies have been observed in the American eugenicist movement: one in support of Nazi race policies and the other critical of what they represented. Some historians have argued that while the ones who were critical were also conversant with the latest developments in genetics, those who supported Nazi racial hygiene were known to be practitioners of pseudoscience.[157] The details of the relation between the Deutsches Hygiene-Museum and established museums in the United States—with the tacit complicity of the Rockefeller Foundation—shows clearly that the interaction between science and politics, as it concerns the popularization of eugenics, is too complex to serve as a basis for a distinction between scientists and pseudoscientists, between mainline and reform eugenicists, or even between supporters and opponents of Nazi racial hygiene. The case of the German physician Bruno Gebhard, who directed the arrangement of the Hall of Man of the American Museum of Health, exemplifies the blurring that occurred within the last pair of terms. He had been invited by the Oberlaender Trust to help arrange the display of the hygiene exposition at the New York Museum of Science and Industry in 1937. A former curator of the Deutsches Hygiene-Museum who was appointed director of research and planning at the Exhibition Office of Berlin in 1932, he had been in charge of an extensive exhibition, *Eugenics in New Germany* (created at the Deutsches Hygiene-Museum) for the Annual Meeting of the American Public Health Association in Pasadena, and was responsible for the major Berlin Health Exposition *Wunder des Lebens* (Wonder of Life) in 1935. He later founded the Cleveland Health Museum that opened its doors to the public in 1940. He lists himself as one of the cofounders of the International Council of Museums (directed at the time by Chauncey J. Hamlin), and as having been involved with the Museum Section of the United Nations Educational, Scientific, and Cultural Organization (UNESCO).[158] Moreover, Gebhard claimed to have been a left-wing dissenter from the Nazi regime and to have been dismissed from the Deutsches Hygiene-Museum for "political reasons."[159] This is conceivable since, as explained by Proctor, a number of socialist physicians who resisted the Nazis had supported racial eugenic measures during the Weimar period, and some of them even accommodated their views to certain aspects of Nazi racial hygiene. These practices were, however, generally understood as voluntary rather than obligatory, hence the importance of public health education.[160] Therefore, Gebhard could dissociate himself from the Nazis yet keep a strong eugenicist orientation, evident in his praise of the BMS, as late as 1947, for being "with a physician as director . . . one of the first to establish a 'Hall of Man' and to include exhibits on genetics and eugenics."[161]

Gebhard's life history—at least as he recounted it—shows that it might be overstated to affirm that the BMS, the New York Museum of Science and Industry, and the American Museum of Health were in any sense pro-Nazi institutions. Nevertheless, the evidence suggests that they played a key role in the spread of the old mainline eugenics fueled by the ideas of German institutions such as the Deutsches Hygiene-Museum during the Nazi regime. This is particularly true for the BMS, whose integration of eugenic exhibits within an all-encompassing evolutionary narrative became a model for similar ventures in popularization.

AMERICAN SUPPORT FOR THE POPULARIZATION OF EUGENICS: A COMPLEX INTERACTION BETWEEN SCIENCE AND POLITICS

The support by the RF for museums such as the BMS, the New York Museum of Science and Industry, and the American Museum of Health was in line with the longstanding interest of Rockefeller philanthropies in eugenics, evolution, and "race betterment." Through his private philanthropy, John Rockefeller Jr. (Junior) initially underwrote both the Eugenics Records Office (ERO) and the American Eugenics Society, and he later backed eugenically inclined organizations such as Margaret Sanger's American Birth Control League and Dr. Robert Dickinson's Committee on Maternal Health through his private donations and through the Bureau of Social Hygiene.[162] By the 1930s, Junior had largely abandoned his support for eugenics and race-betterment ventures, and he no longer funded the Bureau of Social Hygiene, which closed in 1934. The Rockefeller Divisions that carried on Junior's general interests in this area moved away from direct support of eugenics in the United States (which had become increasingly marginalized and discredited) toward less controversial fields such as genetics, population control, demography, and human biology.

This trajectory has been taken to represent the modernization of eugenics and population studies on an international basis.[163] Yet there is significant evidence that Rockefeller officers in various divisions were quite resistant to "modernizing" or reforming the practice of eugenics in Nazi Germany well into the 1930s and were strikingly quiescent about the activities of the fascist regime. While the RF supported the Emergency Committee in Aid of Displaced German Scholars to help bring Jewish faculty to the United States, its efforts were marred by the "gentile Anti-Semitism" of some of its officers, as evidenced in a general slowness to react, a concern that a backlash would be provoked through the disruption of informal quotas, and the continuation of funding for an institute that practiced anti-Semitic persecution. There was a general sense that fascism was a temporary aberration and would not be of long-term consequence.[164] Despite widespread evidence that German scientific institutions had become highly corrupted by the change in power, Rockefeller officials held to the view that the work in eugenics could be separated from overall fascist racist policies and funded a number of eugenically-oriented studies after the Nuremberg Laws of 1933.

These included support for research at the Kaiser Wilhelm Institute for Psychiatry; the Kaiser Wilhelm Institute for Anthropology, Human Heredity, and Eugenics; the Kaiser Wilhelm Institute for Brain Research at Berlin-Buch, and the University Hospital in Munich, involving racial hygienicists such as Ernst Rüdin, Eugen Fischer, Otto Reche, Hans F. K. Gunther, and Otmar Freiherr von Verschuer.[165]

Rockefeller support for particular initiatives in Denmark reflected a similar orientation. After having provided a fellowship for the Danish geneticist Tage Kemp to visit prominent eugenics researchers, such as Charles Davenport and von Verschuer, the RF, in conjunction with the Danish state government, provided funding support for the Institute for Human Genetics and Eugenics at Copenhagen, which opened in 1938 under Kemp's direction. The Institute bore the promise of making significant contributions, in that "besides the existing advanced laws in Denmark on sterilization and on control of mental disease, there is good expectation that, with the high level of intelligence, future research may lead to improved laws in the broad field of human genetics and eugenics."[166] In all likelihood, the acceptance by John Marshall of HD-supported museums displaying eugenicist and race-betterment exhibits from Germany was reflective of a broader pattern of acquiescence to racial hygienicist views by Rockefeller officers.

In any event, the communicative turn taken by the BMS, supported by the program in communication of the Rockefeller Humanities Division, played a key role in the spread of the old mainline eugenics fueled by the ideas of German institutions such as the Deutsches Hygiene-Museum. During the Nazi regime, its integration of eugenic exhibits within an all-encompassing evolutionary narrative—inspired by the storytelling technique used in advertising—became a model for similar ventures in popularization.

CONCLUSION

The Rockefeller views on the modernization of museums through communication techniques certainly had a far-reaching influence. Already in the 1930s, the Buffalo Museum of Science was considered to be one of the leading innovators in the use of new techniques for museum displays. Its techniques and educational programs were widely emulated. Katz and Katz described the BMS as "so highly regarded that its influence has extended beyond the United States into South America."[167] Indeed, the influence of the BMS extended far beyond the Americas and continued well after the museum's golden years. Its president, Chauncey J. Hamlin, was a leader in museology and was in the vanguard of the museum world. President of the American Museum Association from 1923 to 1929, he was to receive a distinguished service award from this association in 1947. Most significant, he became the principal founder of the International Council of Museums (ICOM) in London, England, in 1946, serving as its first president from then until 1953. He was able to secure recognition of the organization from UNESCO in the form of a cooperation agreement signed in 1947, which allowed ICOM to open a head office in Paris. In recognition of his activities on behalf of ICOM, he was named as an officer of the Legion of Honor by the French Government—one of the many honors that he would receive.[168]

By the same token, Cummings' *East is East and West is West* has become a classic in the field of museology. The chapter about the storyline is certainly the most well-known part of this eminent book. The idea of transforming the museum into a storyteller may not have originated in Cummings' survey of the world's fairs—as is generally thought to be the case—but it is certain that the Rockefeller Foundation, through its museum program, was unabashedly one of its main boosters.

In a report concerning the totality of the financial aid given to museums up to the 1950s, John Marshall evaluates the grants to the Brooklyn Museum and the BMS for "internships" as being the most effective and significant ones. The idea of developing new methods for reaching an audience, which had been ahead of its time, was now prevailing in museum circles, even at the most formerly staid institutions such as the Metropolitan Museum in New York and the Louvre in Paris. Most of the interns, who had remained in museum work and held important and influential posts, carried out the idea to other museums. Looking back, it seemed amusing for Marshall that the grant to the Brooklyn Museum was said to provide training in "mere window dressing." Today, museum professionals are still resistant to the idea that their practice might have something to do with advertising. Without knowing about the past, they fear for the future of public education. More than ever, the growing commercialization of museums is still a danger. But the real threat is to ignore how the communicative function has grown out of the commercial realm, and how museum people have themselves built a bridge between education and advertising. In this sense, through recognizing and confronting this historical linkage, they can learn from the past and give a more appropriate orientation to the democratization of knowledge.

NOTES

Unpublished material in this chapter has been quoted courtesy of the following archives: the Rockefeller Archive Center, Sleepy Hollow, New York; the Archives of the Buffalo Museum of Science, Buffalo, New York; and the Pickler Memorial Library, Special Collections, Truman State University, Kirksville, Missouri.

1. Carlos E. Cummings, *East is East and West is West* (Buffalo: Buffalo Museum of Science, 1940); New York Museum of Science and Industry, *Exhibition Techniques:*

A Summary of Exhibition Practice (New York: New York Museum of Science and Industry, 1940).

2. Denis Samson and Bernard Schiele, *Faire voir faire savoir* (Québec: Musée de la civilisation, 1992), 114; Denis Samson, "Les stratégies de lecture des visiteurs d'expositions," in *L'écrit dans le media exposition*, ed. A. Blais (Québec: Musée de la civilisation, Coll. Museo, 1993), 9.

3. E. S. Robinson, *The Behavior of the Museum Visitor* (Washington, DC: American Association of Museums Monograph, New Series, no. 5, 72: 1928); "Psychological Problems of the Science Museum," *Museum News* 8 (1930): 9–11; "Exit the Typical Visitor," *Journal of Adult Education* 3, no. 4 (1931): 418–23; "Psychology Studies of the Public Museum," *School and Society* 33 (1931): 121–25; "Experimental Education in the Museum: A Perspective," *Museum News* 10 (1933): 6–8; "Psychology and the Public Policy," *School and Society* 37 (1933): 537–43; "The Psychology of Public Education," *American Journal of Public Health* 23, no. 2 (1933): 123–28.

4. Bernard Schiele, "L'invention simultanée du visiteur et de l'exposition," *Publics & Musées* 2 (1992): 71–97.

5. Schiele, "L'invention simultanée du visiteur et de l'exposition."

6. See William J. Buxton, "From Radio Research to Communications Intelligence: Rockefeller Philanthropy, Communications Specialists, and the American Intelligence Community," in *The Political Influence of Ideas: Policy Communities and the Social Sciences*, eds. Alain G. Gagnon and Stephen Brooks (Westport, CT: Praeger, 1994), 187–209.

7. "Work of the Rockefeller Foundation in 1935," *Quarterly Bulletin* 9, no. 3 (January 1936): 8.

8. "New Ideas in Museum Techniques and Training," excerpt from Confidential Monthly Report to Trustees, November, 1935, 12. Rockefeller Archive Center (hereafter RAC), Rockefeller Foundation Archives (hereafter RF), Record Group (hereafter RG) 1.1, Series 200, Box 213, Folder 2556.

9. RAC, RF, Rockefeller Foundation, *Annual Report*, 1935, 261–62.

10. Rockefeller Foundation Resolution 35116. RAC, RF, RG 1.1, Series 200, Box 212, Folder 2546.

11. Rockefeller Foundation Resolution 35151. RAC, RF, RG 1.1, Series 200, Box 262, Folder 3115.

12. Rockefeller Foundation Resolution 39100. RAC, RF, RG 1.1, Series 200, Box 262, Folder 3115.

13. Rockefeller Foundation Resolution 37071, 21 May, 1937. RAC, RF, RG 1.1, Series 200, Box 213, Folder 2555.

14. Grant-in-Aid, Buffalo Museum of Science, 27 February, 1939. RAC, RF, RG 1.1, Series 200, Box 213, Folder 2557.

15. Rockefeller Foundation Resolution 41061. RAC, RF, RG 1.1, Series 200, Box 213, Folder 2561.

16. RAC, RF, Leonard Outhwaite, *Museum Survey: Activity of Museums in Adult Education*, January–March 1935. RAC, RF, RG 1.1, Series 200, Box 252, Folder 3005.

17. RAC, RF, Leonard Outhwaite, "Visits and Interview, Philadelphia," Interview with Fiske Kimball, Director of the Pennsylvania Museum of Art, 20 February, 1935, 1–2. RAC, RF, RG 1.1, Series 200, Box 252, Folder 3005.

18. RAC, RF, Leonard Outhwaite, *A Note on Special Activities of Museums*, 1–2. RAC, RF, RG 1.1, Series 200, Box 252, Folder 3005.

19. It should be noted that Wells advocated the improvement of human genetic stock through selective breeding. Diane Paul, "Eugenics and the Left," *Journal of the History of Ideas* 45, no. 3 (July–September 1984): 568. Moreover, Hamlin had a particular admiration for Wells.

20. Herbert George Wells, *The Work, Wealth and Happiness of Mankind* (London: Heinemann, 1932), 17.

21. From 1923 to 1924, with the financial help of the General Education Board, the director of the American Association of Museums, Charles R. Richard, undertook a survey of museums of industrial art in Europe. The results of the survey were published in a book in which he briefly mentions that at the London Science Museum, "some steps have been taken towards depicting the more elementary phases of industrial methods, but as yet the arrangement of material in progressive series to illustrate industrial evolution is not a conspicuous feature of the museum," and that at the Deutsches Museum, "the typical method that is pursued is to illustrate the development of every art by first showing its primitive beginnings, either through actual apparatus, models or representations. . . . From this starting point the museum shows in sequence the important progressive steps that have taken place." Charles R. Richards, *The Industrial Museum* (New York: Macmillan, 1925), 18, 25. These statements have also been quoted in Kenneth Hudson, *Museums of Influence* (Cambridge: Cambridge University Press, 1987), 95, 99.

22. Eilean Hooper-Greenhill, *Museums and the Shaping of Knowledge* (London & New York: Routledge, 1992), 188.

23. Kevin Walsh, *The Representation of the Past: Museums and Heritage in the Post-Modern World* (London & New York: Routledge, 1992). For an account of how le Palais de le Découverte paved the way for a museological paradigm that was in line with a new system of cultural legitimation in France, see Jacqueline Eidelman, "La création du Palais de la Découverte: Professionalisation de la recherche et culture scientifique dans l'entre-deux-guerres" (Ph.D. diss., University of Paris V, René Descartes, 1988).

24. Arthur Molella explains that as early as 1881 in the United States, Smithsonian Institution official George Brown Goode had elaborated a teleological conceptual scheme for a new technological museum according to which human culture and industry would be illustrated in all its phases. Inspired by the taxonomic enterprise of natural history and the evolutionary arrangements found in some other European modes of display, Goode proposed a way of exhibiting artifacts that would incorporate a progressivist vision of technical evolution. However, his early death kept this project from becoming reality. Goode's plan, nevertheless, became a guiding principle for the subsequent curators of the Smithsonian who also embraced progressivism and wanted to produce an American version of the Deutsches Museum. Arthur P. Molella, "The Museum That Might Have Been: The Smithsonian's National Museum of Engineering and Industry," *Technology and Culture* 32, no. 2, pt. 1 (1991): 237–63.

25. Donna Haraway, in her study of taxidermic representations at the American Museum of Natural History, claims that the African Hall, opened in 1936, "was meant to be a time machine" and that "a diorama is eminently a story." Donna Haraway, *Primate Visions: Gender, Race, and Nature in the World of Modern Science* (New York & London: Routledge, 1989), 29. Her observation is, however, largely based on impressionistic thoughts of what the viewer may have experienced when

viewing these scenes. Each separate anthropocentric tableau depicting animal groups was obviously made to stimulate an epic imaginary narration in the mind of the viewer. But lacking other evidence, it is difficult to conclude that the whole set of dioramas was deliberately made up of closed, logically saturated sequences that could syntagmatically keep together what Vladimir Propp called "narrative functions." For some reflections on how the discourse of history differs from imaginary narration, see Roland Barthes, "Le Discours de l'histoire," *Information sur les sciences socials* 6, no. 4 (1967): 65–70.

26. In an explanatory note, John Cotton Dana refers to the exhibition titled "The Story of the Mollusks and the Shells They Live In" as a "new form of story." It was prepared by Margaret C. Sherman at the Newark Museum and was presented as a "unique method of presenting a story in guide book form." "The Story," *Museum Work* 3, no. 6 (1921): 185–86.

27. Leonard Outhwaite, *The Modern Museum: Its Purposes and Functions*. Report to the Academy of Natural Sciences of Philadelphia, 15 January, 1936. RAC, Special Collections, Leonard Outhwaite Papers, Series 3, Box 6, Folder 66.

28. Underlined in the original text.

29. Outhwaite, *The Modern Museum*, IV–3.

30. See Gaynor Kavanagh, *Making Histories in Museums* (London & New York: Leicester University Press, 1996).

31. Robert C. Post and Arthur Molella, "The Call of Stories at the Smithsonian Institution: History of Technology and Science in Crisis," *Icon: Journal of the International Committee for the History of Technology* 3 (1997): 44–82.

32. Deane Uptegrove, "Advertising Art," in *The Handbook of Advertising*, eds. E. B. Weiss, with F. C. Kendall and Carroll B. Larrabee (New York & London: McGraw-Hill, 1938), 51–55.

33. Roland Marchand, *Advertising the American Dream: Making Way for Modernity, 1920–1940* (Berkeley: University of California Press, 1985).

34. The efforts of museums to try to anticipate audience reception can be traced back to the 1910s. The dire financial circumstances after the crash of 1929 were a catalyst for museums to become more effective at attracting visitors. See Samson and Schiele, *Faire voir faire savoir*, 107–27.

35. Hence, the report written by Robinson's co-workers described museums as being part of the "visual education movement," thereby becoming "media of visual education equal in importance to the cinema and other educational aids used in the classroom." Although children's education was still the focus of this particular series—in opposition to most of Robinson's studies—it was said to be complementary "to the effectiveness of various methods of installation and labeling for the education of adult visitors." Arthur W. Melton, Nina Goldberg-Feldman, and Charles W. Mason, *Experimental Studies of the Education of Children in a Museum of Science* (Washington, D.C.: AAM, 1936), 1–2.

36. Earnest Elmo Calkins, "Introduction," in Weiss, Kendall, and Larrabee, *Handbook of Advertising*, 10–11.

37. Rockefeller Foundation, "Brooklyn Museum-Training Personnel," 1. RAC, RF, RG 1.1, Series 200, Box 212, Folder 2548.

38. Not surprisingly, Youtz later became director of the Pacific Area at the Golden Gate International Exposition, where the joint use of art and anthropology gave a racial inflection to representations of Pacific Rim history. This account embodied

the patronizing outlook of European and U.S. expansionism. Robert Rydell, *World of Fairs: The Century-of-Progress Expositions* (Chicago: University of Chicago Press, 1993), 88–89.

39. Rockefeller Foundation Resolution 35116, "Brooklyn Museum-Training of Museum Personnel," 21 June, 1935, 2. RAC, RF, RG 1.1, Series 200, Box 212, Folder 2546.

40. Only the quotation mark indicating the beginning of the quotation appears in the original text.

41. Rockefeller Interns, Harry N. Geiger Report, "The Brooklyn Institute of Arts and Sciences," in *Report of Eastern Trip*, December 27, 1938 to February 1, 1939, 12. Archives of the Buffalo Museum of Science, (hereafter ABMS), A–017 (03) F08.

42. "New Ideas in Museum Techniques and Training," 2.

43. Philip Youtz to Edward C. Blum, 11 April, 1938, 1. RAC, RF, RG 1.1, Series 200, Box 212, Folder 2548.

44. Youtz to David Stevens, 1 June, 1936. RAC, RF, RG 1.1, Series 200, Box 212, Folder 2547.

45. Philip N. Youtz, "Project for Offering Practical Experience in a Socially Oriented Art Museum to Younger Members of the Museum Profession," submitted to the Rockefeller Foundation, 6 May, 1935, in accordance with the recommendations of Dr. David H. Stevens and Mr. John Marshall, 2. RAC, RF, RG 1.1, Series 200, Box 212, Folder 2546. Youtz knew of Soviet museum practice through a visit of his wife to Russia in 1934. John Marshall (hereafter JM) Interview with Philip N. Youtz, 11 April, 1935, 3. RAC, RF, RG 1.1, Series 200, Box 212, Folder 2546.

46. Rockefeller Foundation Resolution 35116, 2. RAC, RF, RG 1.1, Series 200, Box 212, Folder 2546.

47. Philip N. Youtz, quoted in unsigned article, "The Living Museum," *Brooklyn Museum Quarterly* 21, no. 3 (1934): 99.

48. Youtz, "Project for Offering Practical Experience," 2.

49. JM Interview with Youtz, 11 April, 1935.

50. Youtz to David Stevens, 16 May, 1935, 1. RAC, RF, RG 1.1, Series 200, Box 212, Folder 2546.

51. Oral history of John Marshall, Interview #6, 12 February, 1973, 202–203. RAC, RF, RG II–13, Box 1, Folder 2.

52. William J. Buxton, "Reaching Human Minds: Rockefeller Philanthropy and Communications, 1935–1939," in *The Development of Social Sciences in the United States and Canada*, eds. Theresa Richardson and Donald Fisher (Stamford, CT: Ablex, 1998), 184.

53. Prior to 1933, the NYMSI was the only museum of its kind in North America. It was the brainchild of Henry R. Towne who left a bequest earmarked for the creation of a museum of industrial arts, somewhat along the lines of the Deutsches Museum of Munich and the South Kensington Science Museum of London. First called "the Museum of the Peaceful Arts," it changed its name to "the New York Museum of Science and Industry" and moved in 1936 to the Rockefeller Center. Under the terms of the lease, the Rockefeller administration would accept as rent all admission fees up to $37,500, after which the gate receipts would be divided between the landlord and the tenant. The RF officers found favor with the unusual decision to charge an admission fee as a source of income for a public institution.

See New York Museum of Science and Industry, *Newest in the Family of Museums,* 4–5, Annex to Frank B. Jewett to Robert P. Shaw, 20 October, 1939. RAC, RF, RG 1.1, Series 200, Box 262, Folder 3116; Frank B. Jewett to Max Mason, 13 September, 1935, 3; RAC, RF, RG 1.1, Series 200, Box 262, Folder 3115; Rockefeller Foundation appraisal of the New York Museum of Science and Industry, September 1938, 1. RAC, RF, RG 1.1, Series 200, Box 262, Folder 3116.

54. Rockefeller Foundation Resolution 35151, 27 September, 1935, 2. RAC, RF, RG 1.1, Series 200, Box 262, Folder 3115.

55. Robert P. Shaw, "New Developments in Science Museum Techniques and Procedures," *Scientific Monthly* 48 (May 1939): 443.

56. Shaw, "New Developments," 445.

57. Robert Shaw, *Report on Studies of Palace of Discovery, Paris International Exposition, Museums of Science and Industry and Other Exhibitions in Europe,* 22 November, 1937, 80. RAC, RF, RG 1.1, Series 200, Box 262, Folder 3119.

58. Shaw, *Report on Studies,* 82–83.

59. Indeed, in furthering the theory and practice within a broad range of technologies conceived of as variants of "mass communications," the Humanities Division arguably helped to clear common ground for the old and new media of the day. See William Buxton, "The Political Economy of Communications Research," in *Information and Communication in Economics,* ed. Robert E. Babe (Boston/Dordrecht/London: Kluwer, 1994), 147–75.

60. David H. Stevens interview with Chauncey Hamlin, Carlos E. Cummings, and R. P. Shaw, 19 January, 1939. RAC, RF, RG 1.1, Series 200, Box 213, Folder 2557.

61. Robert P. Shaw, Report on Activities of the New York Museum of Science and Industry from January 1, 1939 through December 31, 1939, 4. RAC, RF, RG 1.1, Series 200, Box 262, Folder 3118.

62. Frank B. Jewett to Edward R. Stettinius Jr., 20 October, 1939, 2. RAC, RF, RG 1.1, Series 200, Box 262, Folder 3116.

63. *Exhibit News Letter,* April, 1940, "Survey of World's Fair Exhibition Techniques," 1–4. RAC, RF, RG 1.1, Series 200, Box 262, Folder 3120.

64. Jewett to Stettinius, 2.

65. Rockefeller Foundation Resolution 39100, 5–6 December, 1939, 3. RAC, RF, RG 1.1, Series 200, Box 262, Folder 3115.

66. Be this as it may, over the period covered by RF grants the museum reputedly became more commercially oriented, in part because of its dire financial circumstances. It closed in 1949, reopening later that year as the New York Hall of Science with quarters in the Hotel Claridge. The museum shut its doors for good in 1951. JM Interview with S. V. Tursi, Inspector, Food & Drug Administration, New York district, 14 and 17 September, 1951. RAC, RF, RG 1.1, Series 200, Box 262, Folder 3117.

67. Rockefeller Foundation Resolution 37071.

68. David H. Stevens, *Notes for President's Review and Annual Report,* 1937, 4. RAC, RF, RG 3, Series 911, Box 2, Folder 10.

69. Chauncey J. Hamlin to John Marshall, 15 March, 1937, RAC, RF, RG 1.1, Series 200, Box 213, Folder 2555. Quoted in RAC, RF, Rockefeller Foundation *Annual Report,* 1937, 314–15.

70. Hamlin to Frederick P. Keppel, 25 March, 1937. ABMS, Box: Papers of Carlos E. Cummings, Subject Files 1930–1948 E–Z, Manuscripts, Cummings C. E., Rockefeller Interns, Reports, conferences, agendas, correspondence, 1937–1939, A–017 (3) F3.

71. Actually, the so-called Hall of Evolution and Genetics was divided into two different halls: the Schoellkopf Hall of Evolution and the Goodyear Hall of Heredity and Environment. The latter was often simply called "the Hall of Heredity" or "the Hall of Genetics." Hamlin's merging of the two halls illustrates the extent to which the themes of evolution and heredity were bound together.

72. JM interview with Chauncey J. Hamlin, 4 March, 1937, 1. RAC, RF, RG 1.1, Series 200, Box 213, Folder 2555.

73. JM Interview with Hamlin, 4 March, 1937, 1.

74. Hamlin to Marshall, 15 March, 1937, 2. RAC, RF, RG 1.1, Series 200, Box 213, Folder 2555.

75. Marshall to E. E. Day and R. J. Havighurst, Inter-office correspondence, 24 March, 1937. RAC, RF, RG 1.1, Series 200, Box 213, Folder 2555.

76. Rockefeller Foundation Resolution 37071.

77. Some interns could be appointed from outside the country, but the training of American museum workers was the priority. Moreover, the BMS deliberately confined the appointments to young men because there was "more assurance of their continuing in museum work than young women who are apt to leave museum service on marriage." See Hamlin to Charles M. B. Cadwalader, president of the Academy of Natural Sciences, 9 April, 1938. ABMS, A–028 (15) F21, Rockefeller Grant 1937–39.

78. Chauncey J. Hamlin, *The Future National Museum of Brasil of Tomorrow: A Report Prepared for the National Museum of Brasil at the Request of its Director, Heloisa Alberto Torres,* Rio de Janeiro, (1941), 58–68. RAC, RF, RG 1.1, Series 200, Box 214, Folder 2565.

79. For a discussion of these issues, see Frank Dikötter, "Race Culture: Recent Perspectives on the History of Eugenics," *American Historical Review* 103, no. 2 (April 1998): 475; Robert N. Proctor, "Eugenics among the Social Sciences: Hereditarian Thought in Germany and the United States," in *The Estate of Social Knowledge,* eds. JoAnne Brown and David K. van Keuren (Baltimore & London: Johns Hopkins University Press, 1991), 180; Garland E. Allen, "Genetics, Eugenics and Class Struggle," *Genetics* 139 (1975): 29–45.

80. Marouf Arif Hasian, *The Rhetoric of Eugenics in Anglo-American Thought* (Athens & London: University of Georgia Press, 1996).

81. Steven Selden, *Inheriting Shame: The Story of Eugenics and Racism in America* (New York & London: Teachers College, Columbia University, 1999).

82. Martin S. Pernick, *The Black Stork: Eugenics and the Death of "Defective" Babies in American Medicine and Motion Pictures Since 1915* (New York & Oxford: Oxford University Press, 1996), 165, 168.

83. Christine Rosen, *Preaching Eugenics: Religious Leaders and the American Eugenics Movement* (Oxford: Oxford University Press, 2004).

84. Anne Maxwell, *Picture Imperfect: Photography and Eugenics, 1879–1940* (Eastbourne, UK: Sussex Academic Press, 2008).

85. Robert W. Rydell, *World of Fairs*, 38–58. His claim is that eugenicist ideas broadened their scope from upper-class culture to a more general audience through the national exhibition culture of the interwar period. More specifically, he argues this development took place through the incorporation of a European "coloniale moderne" sensibility into the vision of America's future championed by the organizers of the 1933 Chicago World's Fair.

86. Christina Cogdell, *Eugenic Design: Streamlining America in the 1930s* (Philadelphia: University of Pennsylvania Press, 2004), 84–98.

87. Robert W. Rydell, Christina Cogdell, and Mark Largent, "The Nazi Eugenics Exhibit in the United States, 1934–43," in *Popular Eugenics: National Efficiency and American Mass Culture in the 1930s*, eds. Susan Currell and Christina Cogdell (Athens: Ohio University Press, 2006), 359–84.

88. "Museum News," *Hobbies* 16, no.1 (October 1935): 14–15.

89. "Museum News," 14.

90. "Museum News," 40–41; Ralph B. Houser to Mrs. Karl E. Wilhelm, 5 May, 1950. ABMS, Registrar, Correspondence, Deutsches Hygiene-Museum, Dresden, 1932–1950.

91. Garland E. Allen, "The Eugenics Record Office at Cold Spring Harbor, 1910–1940: An Essay in Institutional History," *Osiris*, 2nd series 2 (1986): 225–64.

92. Harry H. Laughlin to President Franklin D. Roosevelt Jr., 18 September, 1933. Pickler Memorial Library (hereafter PML), Special Collections, Truman State University, Harry H. Laughlin Papers, C–2–2: 4.

93. ABMS, Exhibit, Heredity & Environment II, P–005 (6) F9.

94. ABMS, Exhibit, Heredity & Environment II.

95. ABMS, Exhibit, Heredity & Environment II.

96. Laughlin to Roosevelt, 18 September, 1933.

97. ABMS, Exhibit, Heredity & Environment II. The chart traces how the relative quality of the members of two families, the Edwards and the Jukes (the former highly successful and the latter largely consisting of misfits and ne'er-do-wells), could be attributed to hereditary factors. Estabrook's chart likely had its origins in his book, *The Jukes in 1915* (Washington, D.C.: Carnegie Institution of Washington, 1916). Among those included in the "superior" Edwards family was George E. Vincent, president of the Rockefeller Foundation at the time.

98. Laughlin to Roosevelt, 18 September, 1933.

99. ABMS, Exhibit, Heredity & Environment II.

100. ABMS, Exhibit, Heredity-Environments Hall 8–Part 1 P–005 (6) F8.

101. ABMS, Exhibit, Heredity & Environment II.

102. ABMS, Exhibit, Heredity & Environment II.

103. ABMS, Exhibit, Heredity & Environment III, P005 (6) F10.

104. ABMS, Exhibit, Heredity & Environment III.

105. Hamlin to John M. Merriam (Carnegie Institute of Washington), 8 November, 1933. ABMS, A–017 (2) F2, General Correspondence 1930–1940 I–L.

106. Hamlin to Harry H. Laughlin, Eugenics Record Office, 29 November, 1933. ABMS, A–017 (2) F2, General Correspondence 1930–1940 I–L.

107. Chauncey J. Hamlin came by his interest in eugenics honestly. He was the grandson of Cicero J. Hamlin, considered one of the most influential harness-racing

breeders of the twentieth century. There was a close relationship between practical breeders and the studies of heredity; see Kathy J. Cooke, "From Science to Practice, or Practice to Science? Chickens and Eggs in Raymond Pearl's Agricultural Breeding Research, 1907–1916," *Isis* 88, no. 1 (1997): 62–86; Barbara A. Kimmelman, "The American Breeders' Association: Genetics and Eugenics in an Agricultural Context, 1903–13," *Social Studies of Science* 13, no. 2 (1983): 163–204. Moreover, the BMS president was Theodore Roosevelt's campaign manager for western New York. It is instructive that Teddy Roosevelt "probably did more than any other individual to bring the views of academic race theorists to ordinary Americans" by initiating a "race-suicide" panic with public declarations on the importance of good breeding for women of "good stock." Diane Paul, *Controlling Human Heredity, 1865 to the Present* (Atlantic Highlands, NJ: Humanities Press, 1995), 102; see also Wendy Kline, *Building a Better Race: Gender, Sexuality, and Eugenics from the Turn of the Century to the Baby Boom* (Berkeley: University of California Press, 2001), 11; Elaine May, *Barren in the Promised Land: Childless Americans and Pursuit of Happiness* (New York: Basic Books, 1995), 92, quoted in Kline, *Building a Better Race*, 189n8.

108. The popularity of Laughlin's charts is also a good example of how powerful the blurring of the boundaries between advertising and museum practices could be. The charts had previously attracted the attention of the Associated Merchandising Corporation of Chicago who wished to circulate two of them among its member stores (such as Bloomingdales and Harrods) over a six-month period. PML, M. N. Strass to Eugenics Record Office, 22 August, 1933. As Laughlin noted in his response to the letter, "We believe that the Merchants Association can do a great deal of good in showing these charts. The principle task of eugenics for the next ten years is popular education. A visitor to one of your stores who reads the two charts which you have selected will be a little more firmly convinced than before that success and achievement in any field of human activity depend to a very special degree upon the hereditary stuff out of which the people are made." PML, Laughlin to Associated Merchandising Corporation, 29 August, 1933. The circulation of the two charts among some of the member stores of the Corporation appeared not to have materialized; Laughlin decided to give the exhibit material to the Buffalo Museum of Science upon the closing of the Chicago World's Fair in the fall of 1934. Nevertheless, the strong interest in the material shown by the corporation reveals the extent to which elites in the business world, in a manner echoing the views of those in the museum, exposition, and philanthropic sectors, embraced the tenets of eugenics well into the 1930s.

109. JM Interview with Chauncey J. Hamlin, 24 March, 1937, 1. RAC, RF, RG 1.1, Series 200, Box 213, Folder 2555.

110. George W. Stocking Jr., "Philanthropoids and Vanishing Cultures. Rockefeller Funding and the End of the Museum Era in Anglo-American Anthropology," in *Objects and Others: Essays on Museums and Material Culture*, History of Anthropology, vol. 3, ed. George W. Stocking Jr. (Madison: University of Wisconsin Press, 1985), 112–45.

111. More precisely, 57,918 visitors came to the exhibition, even though the museum had to reduce its exhibit hours from sixty-one to twenty-five hours a week because of a reduced budget. BMS to S. H. Camp, 9 June, 1937. ABMS, A–043 (1) F20, Exhibits-Transparent Woman 1937.

112. E. C. Barcellona to Frank H. Kaufman, 19 April, 1937. ABMS, A–043 (1) F20, Exhibits-Transparent Woman 1937.

113. Francis E. Fronczak, "Unveiling of the Camp Transparent Woman," Script for Radio Program from the Buffalo Museum of Science, Station WKBW, 14 April, 1937, 2. ABMS, A–043 (1) F20, Exhibits-Transparent Woman 1937.

114. Fronczak, "Unveiling of the Camp Transparent Woman," 2–3.

115. Buffalo Museum of Science, *The Camp Transparent Woman*, no date, 2. ABMS, A–043 (1) F20, Exhibits-Transparent Woman 1937.

116. Insightful commentary on the Transparent specimens can be found in *Der gläserne Mensch—Eine Sensation: Zur Kulturgeschichte eines Ausstellungsobjekts*, eds. Rosmarie Beier and Martin Roth (Stuttgart: Verlag Gerd Hatje, 1990).

117. The Transparent Man, excluded from "the offending material" destroyed during and after the war, was later transferred to the Deutsches Historisches Museum of Berlin in 1989 "as an expression of friendship between the American and the German peoples." George F. Goodyear, with Virginia L. Cummings, Ethel Lee Helffenstein, and Joan G. Manias, "Society and Museum. A History of the Buffalo Society of Natural Sciences 1861–1993 and the Buffalo Museum of Science 1928–1993," *Bulletin of the Buffalo Society of Natural Sciences* 34 (1994): 40–41. Further information can be found in Cogdell, *Eugenic Design*, 87.

118. A. E. Cabana to Chauncey J. Hamlin, Memorandum of 20 July, 1936. ABMS, A–043 (1) F20, Exhibits-Transparent Woman 1937.

119. G. K. Thompson to Chauncey J. Hamlin, 12 August, 1936. ABMS, A–043 (1) F20, Exhibits-Transparent Woman 1937.

120. On this point, Weindling notes that when the exhibits of the Deutsches Hygiene-Museum were first displayed in 1930, they conveyed a rhetoric of the body "as a 'symbol' of national unity and productivity," *Health, Race and German Politics*, 415.

121. See the web site of the Deutsches Hygiene-Museum: http://www.dhmd .de/neu/index.php?id=1144 (French) http://www.dhmd.de/neu/index.php?id=791 (English) (accessed November 18, 2008).

122. *United States Holocaust Memorial Museum, Deadly Medicine: Creating the Master Race*, Traveling Exhibition presented at the Canadian War Museum, Ottawa, Ontario, 12 June, 2008, through 11 November, 2008.

123. Note accompanying a photo showing Carlos Cummings and the Transparent Man, appearing next to the text of Daniel J. Kevles, "International Eugenics," in *Deadly Medicine: Creating the Master Race*, eds. Susan Bachrach and Dieter Kuntz (Washington, D.C.: U.S. Holocaust Museum & Chapel Hill: University of North Carolina Press, 2004), 41.

124. Klaus Vogel, "The Transparent Man—Some Comments on the History of a Symbol," in *Manifesting Medicine*, ed. Robert Bud (London: Board of Trustees of the Science Museum, 2004), 31–61.

125. As McLuhan put it, "We shape our tools, and thereafter our tools shape us." Marshall McLuhan, *Understanding Media: The Extensions of Man* (New York: McGraw-Hill, 1964), xi.

126. Rydell, *World of Fairs: The Century-of-Progress Expositions*, 38–58.

127. This is consistent with Cogdell's discussion of how the Transparent Man and the Transparent Woman conveyed Nazi ideals of human perfection through race hygiene. See *Eugenic Design*, 87, 185–87, 196.

128. Fronczak, "Unveiling of the Camp Transparent Woman," 2.

129. Fronczak, "Unveiling of the Camp Transparent Woman," 1–2.

130. Fronczak, "Unveiling of the Camp Transparent Woman," 3.

131. Fronczak, "Unveiling of the Camp Transparent Woman," 4.

132. The committee in charge of the Cabana Hall of Man felt that "it would be better for their purposes if the external genitalia of the model be omitted," Carlos E. Cummings to Paul R. Ehrke, 20 July, 1933. ABMS, Registrar, Correspondence, Deutsches Hygiene-Museum, Dresden, 1932–1950.

133. Paul R. Ehrke to Hamlin, 27 January, 1934. ABMS, Registrar, Correspondence, Deutsches Hygiene-Museum, Dresden, 1932–1950.

134. Chauncey J. Hamlin, "Unveiling of the Camp Transparent Woman," Script for Radio Program from the Buffalo Museum of Science, Station WKBW, 14 April, 1937, 2; Chauncey J. Hamlin, Invitation to the Buffalo Premiere of the Camp Transparent Woman, 6 April, 1937; E. C. Barcellona to the Board of Managers, 24 March, 1937. ABMS, A–043 (1) F20, Exhibits-Transparent Woman 1937. Nevertheless, the image of a couple maintained a hold on the popular imagination. An article published in the *Buffalo Times* of 2 August, 1936, was titled: "Love is Like a Goldfish Bowl, Perhaps; Transparent Woman to Visit Museum Man." Frank H. Kaufman to A. E. Cabana, 24 August, 1936, ABMS, A–043 (1) F20, Exhibits-Transparent Woman 1937.

135. Fronczak, "Unveiling of the Camp Transparent Woman," 6.

136. Fronczak, "Unveiling of the Camp Transparent Woman," 6.

137. This also holds true for the current fascination for the exhibitions of real human bodies, *Body Worlds*, produced by the German Gunther von Hagens, who developed a technology for preserving anatomical specimens called "plastination."

138. The transparencies were named after their creator, the anatomist Werner Spalteholz (1861–1940), who established the principle that "the transparency of tissues depends first of all on the refraction index of permeating liquid," and began to produce transparent organ specimens. They were first exhibited at the first International Hygiene Exposition held in Dresden in 1911. A special exposition featuring the Spalteholz collection was shown in 1926. The popularity of this exposition led to the creation of the first "Transparent Man" by Franz Tschackert for the second International Hygiene Exposition held in 1930. See Susanne Hahn, "Der Leipziger Anatom Werner Spalteholz (1861–1940) und seine Beziehungen zum Deutschen Hygiene-Museum," *NTM* 7, no. 2 (1999): 105–117; Klaus Vogel, "The Transparent Man—Some Comments on the History of a Symbol," in Bud, *Manifesting Medicine*, 31–61.

139. This is the issue raised by the excavation of native burial sites by museums. Glen W. Davidson, "Human Remains: Issues Confronting Museums and the Scholarly Disciplines," *Caduceus* 7, no. 1 (1991): 18–33.

140. The same can be said about Gunther von Hagens' *Body Worlds* as the primary goal of the exhibition is defined as that of health education; the "individual specimens" are used to help the visitor understand the body and its functions. However, the political context is different, and one can perceive a touch of humanism in the statement: "Humans reveal their individuality not through the visible exterior, but also through the interior of their bodies, as each body is distinctly different from any other."

See http://www.plastination.com/en/exhibitions/mission_exhibitions.html (accessed November 18, 2008). See also Gunther von Hagens, "Anatomy and Plastination," in *Body Worlds—The Anatomical Exhibition of Real Human Bodies*, eds. G. von Hagens and Angelina Whalley (Heidelberg: Institut für Plastination, 2005). Nevertheless, the remains are contemplated as human-made objects, deprived of their personal identity.

141. Translation of letter from W. F. [*sic*] Ehrke to Chauncey J. Hamlin by Mr. Morgenroth Jr., 24 April, 1934. ABMS, Registrar, Correspondence, Deutsches Hygiene-Museum, Dresden, 1932–1950.

142. Translation of a letter from Paul R. Ehrke to Carlos E. Cummings, October, 1936. ABMS, Registrar, Correspondence, Deutsches Hygiene-Museum, Dresden, 1932–1950.

143. Deutsches Hygiene-Museum to the BMS, 6 February, 1937. ABMS, Registrar, Correspondence, Deutsches Hygiene-Museum, Dresden, 1932–1950.

144. When the BMS got the letter translated, the word "Spalteholz" had been mistranslated as "split wood." Hamlin wrote to the Deutsches Hygiene-Museum to say that a wooden hand and arm would not be satisfactory and insisted that the Deutsches Hygiene-Museum fulfill the original order for a real arm made transparent. Translation of the letter from the Deutsches Hygiene-Museum to the BMS, 6 February, 1937; letter from Chauncey J. Hamlin to the Deutsches Hygiene-Museum, 31 March, 1937; letter from the Deutsches Hygiene-Museum to the BMS, 20 April, 1937; letter from Carlos E. Cummings to the Deutsches Hygiene-Museum, 10 May, 1937. ABMS, Registrar, Correspondence, Deutsches Hygiene-Museum, Dresden, 1932–1950.

145. This was the second series of embryo models that the BMS purchased; one had already been acquired from the 1933 Chicago Century-of-Progress Exposition. Carlos E. Cummings to the Deutsches Hygiene-Museum, 6 February, 1937; Deutsches Hygiene-Museum to BMS, 19 April, 1939; Chauncey J. Hamlin to the Deutsches Hygiene-Museum, 9 May, 1939; Invoice from the Deutsches Hygiene-Museum to the BMS, June, 1939. ABMS, Registrar, Correspondence, Deutsches Hygiene-Museum, Dresden, 1932–1950.

146. In 1895 German Wilhelm Conrad Röntgen was the first scientist to publish a paper on X-rays and to systematically study them. The production and exhibition of the Spalteholz transparencies a few years later substantiate the strength of the German expertise.

147 Robert P. Shaw, *Report on Activities of the New York Museum of Science and Industry from January 1, 1937 through December 6, 1937*, 4. RAC, RF, RG 1.1, Series 200, Box 262, Folder 3118.

148. Internal document, *Science Parade in Rockefeller Center*, Excerpt from Trustees' Confidential Bulletin, December 1937, 15. RAC, RF, RG 1.1, Series 200, Box 262, Folder 3115.

149. The expression is from Cummings's *East is East and West is West* (Buffalo, NY: Buffalo Museum of Science, 1940), 302.

150. New York Museum of Science and Industry, "Table Showing Special Exhibits which Visitors Came to See in the Museum," Report on Activities of the New York Museum of Science and Industry from January 1, 1938 through December 31, 1938. RAC, RF, RG 1.1, Series 200, Box 262, Folder 3118.

151. Louis I. Dublin, "Introduction," in *Man and His Health: A Guide to Medical and Public Health Exhibits at the New York World's Fair 1939, together with Information on the Conservation of Health and the Preservation of Life* (New York: Exposition Publications, 1939), 5. Cogdell discusses the planning of the health exhibits in *Eugenic Design*, 118–23.

152. Homer N. Calver, "Health Information, Please," *Journal of the American Medical Association* 115 (October 12, 1940): 1251–53.

153. Cummings, *East is East*, 253.

154. Buffalo Society of Natural Sciences, 1861–1939, *Seventy-Eighth Annual Report, July 1, 1938–June 30, 1939*, 6.

155. Dublin, "Introduction," *Man and His Health*, 6.

156. *Proposed Treatment by American Museum of Natural History of Biological and Health Exhibits Now Owned by the American Museum of Public Health.* ABMS, A–017 (2) F9.

157. Stefan Kühl, *The Nazi Connection: Eugenics, American Racism, and German National Socialism* (Oxford: Oxford University Press, 1994), 65.

158. Gebhard also says that he helped to develop a Health Museum in Mexico City in 1943 and one in Bogotá in 1944. See Bruno Gebhard, "From the Dresden Hygiene Museum to the Cleveland Health Museum," *Ohio State Medical Journal* 514, nos. 9–10 (1969): 1004–1008, 1134–36.

159. Gebhard, "From the Dresden Hygiene Museum," 1134.

160. See Robert N. Proctor, *Racial Hygiene: Medicine Under the Nazis* (Cambridge, MA: Harvard University Press, 1988), 268–75.

161. Bruno Gebhard, "The Origin of Hygiene and Health Museums," *CIBA Symposia* 8, no. 2 (1947): 584–93.

162. John Ensor Harr and Peter J. Johnson, *The Rockefeller Century* (New York: Scribner's, 1988), 454; Raymond B. Fosdick, *John D. Rockefeller: A Portrait* (New York: Harper & Brothers, 1956), 386; Nicole Hahn Rafter, ed., *White Trash: The Eugenic Family Studies, 1877–1919* (Boston: Northeastern University Press, 1988), 12.

163. Paul Weindling, "Modernizing Eugenics: The Role of Foundations in International Population Studies," in *American Foundations in Europe: Grant-Giving Policies, Cultural Diplomacy, and Trans-Atlantic Relations, 1920–1980*, eds. Giuliana Gemelli and Roy McLeod (Brussels: P.I.E. Peter Lang, 2003).

164. Peter M. Rutkoff and William B. Scott, *New School: A History of the New School of Social Research* (New York: Free Press, 1986), 86–101, passim.

165. Proctor, *Racial Hygiene*, 349; Jean-François Picard, *La Fondation Rockefeller et la Recherche Médicale* (Paris: PUF, 1999), 111; Cornelius Borck, "Mediating Philanthropy in Changing Political Circumstances: The Rockefeller Foundation's Funding for Brain Research in Germany, 1930–1950," *Rockefeller Archive Center Newsletter* (Spring 2001): 4–5; Paul Weindling, *Health, Race and German Politics between National Unification and Nazism: 1870–1945* (Cambridge: Cambridge University Press, 1989), 468; Paul Weindling, "The Rockefeller Foundation and German Biomedical Sciences, 1920–40: From Educational Philanthropy to International Science Policy," in *Science, Politics, and the Public Good: Essays in Honor of Margaret Gowing*, ed. Nicholas A. Rupke (Basingstoke, UK: Macmillan, 1988), 119–39; Kühl, *The Nazi Connection*, 20; Diane B. Paul, "The Rockefeller Foundation and the Origin of Behavior Geneticism," *The Expansion of American Biology,*

eds. Keith R. Benson, Jane Maienschein, and Ronald Rainger (New Brunswick, NJ: Rutgers University Press), 268.

166. Daniel O'Brien to Alan Gregg, 14 March, 1935, cited in Alain Drouard, "The Rockefeller Foundation and the Creation of the Institute for Human Genetics in Copenhagen," paper presented at Conference on American Foundations in Europe [1920s–1990s], Amalfi, Italy, 2001.

167. Herbert Katz and Marjorie Katz, *Museums, USA: A History and Guide* (Garden City, NY: Doubleday, 1965), 132.

168. See http://icom.museum/founders.html. Extracts from the biographies written by Sid Ahmed Baghli for the *History of ICOM*, (accessed November 18, 2008). See also Goodyear et al., *"Society and Museum,"* 51–56.

9

The Political Economy of Rockefeller Support for the Humanities in Canada, 1941–1957

Jeffrey Brison

> For these purposes a hundred million dollars were voted to the Council. Unlike most countries where assistance is voted annually, here the Council was entrusted with a capital sum. This has advantages. It makes it possible to plan ahead and to carry out a planned programme. In this respect The Canada Council resembles one of the great American foundations, which have so richly nourished and strengthened the universities in the United States and Canada.[1]
>
> —Brooke Claxton (1957)

> It was Mr. King who led us to this point. And his leadership has been so completely accepted that today only the Communists and a diehard remnant of Tories go about talking of "American Imperialism." Well, no, this isn't quite correct. There are also those academic intellectuals in our universities who are still thinking up nasty wisecracks about American imperialism regardless of the fact that most of their own pet research projects are apt to be financed by money from Rockefeller or Carnegie or Guggenheim.[2]
>
> —Frank H. Underhill, *Canadian Forum* (1950)

The long-awaited opening for business of the Canada Council for the Encouragement of the Arts, Letters, Humanities and Social Sciences in the spring of 1957 marked the end of one era and the beginning of another for the arts and letters in Canada. Since the early 1920s private American philanthropy had been an important contributor to the making of Canadian culture. The Rockefeller Foundation (RF) and the Carnegie

Corporation of New York (CC), in particular, made substantial grants to Canadian universities, to public and private galleries, and to libraries and museums. They supported individual Canadian artists and scholars directly with grants and fellowships, by sponsoring art associations and research councils, and by funding special projects that enabled recipients to carry out their research and to publish their work. Together, the American foundations contributed almost $20 million to the economy of Canadian culture. After its formation, it was the new federal-state–funded Canada Council that provided the lifeblood for Canadian cultural and intellectual endeavors. In this new era, in the new environment of public patronage, the Canada Council reigned supreme.

The shift in the political economy of Canadian culture cannot be overstated. To begin with, the formation of the Canada Council brought with it a tremendous increase in cultural funding. The new council boasted an initial endowment exceeding $100 million, the sum realized from succession duties on the estates of Izaak Walton Killam and Sir James Dunn and passed on, in turn, by the federal government.[3] Of the 7,300 foundations in the United States at the time, only seven—Ford, Rockefeller, Carnegie, Duke, Kellogg, Pew, and Harkness—could boast of larger endowments. Speaking at the combined meeting of the Empire Club of Canada and the Canadian Club on October 17, 1957, Brooke Claxton, the first chairman of the Canada Council, proudly pointed out that "even measured in American terms" his organization, was "a sizable operation."[4] And as Dean Rusk, president of the Rockefeller Foundation, observed in the first meeting of the Canada Council, the new body had at its disposal the resources to spend as much in its first four years on the arts, humanities, and social sciences in Canada as the Rockefeller Foundation had spent in the previous forty-five years in these areas.[5]

To those who had been lobbying the federal state for support for the arts and letters for decades, it was an even more substantial alteration to the architecture of Canadian culture that the "power of the purse" now resided in Canada. It had long been a source of embarrassment to cultural nationalists that the likes of the Carnegie Corporation, the Rockefeller Foundation, and, of late, the Ford Foundation were, as one British commentator put it in 1933, "paying the shot"[6] for the development of Canadian culture. As Maurice Lebel and J. F. Leddy, leaders of the Humanities Research Council of Canada (HRCC), advised the Canadian government's Royal Commission on National Development in the Arts, Letters and Sciences (popularly known as the Massey Commission after its chairman, Vincent Massey) in the summer of 1949, "It is significant commentary on the maturity of our culture, that . . . [the HRCC] should have been financed almost entirely by grants from the United States."[7] Echoing this message nearly a decade later,

Prime Minister Louis St. Laurent told his fellow parliamentarians that the time had come to nationalize support for the arts and letters:

> Up to the present time little relatively has been done in Canada in the form of financial contributions from governments or from munificent individuals for the encouragement of the arts, the humanities and social sciences. . . . The main source of such encouragement in Canada has come from other countries. In this respect I think many of us share the view expressed in the Massey report that "we have not much right to be proud of our record as patrons of the arts."[8]

CANADA AND AMERICAN PHILANTHROPY

Even today, as public support for culture and scholarship in Canada is coming under attack, when increasingly we speak of a new public-private mixed economy of culture, "new managerialism," the "free market," and "value for money," and when Canadian universities vie for the title of "the Harvard of the North," the idea of private American wealth contributing so heavily to the fabric of Canadian culture seems, well, a little bit "foreign." That both the HRCC and its sister council, the Canadian Social Science Research Council (CSSRC)—forerunners to today's apparently almighty state-funded Social Science and Humanities Research Council of Canada (SSHRCC)—were not only funded almost exclusively by private American foundations for their first twenty years or so, but were also directly modeled after such American research councils as the Social Science Research Council and the American Council of Learned Societies would, I suspect, shock most Canadian scholars.[9] Equally puzzling to Canadians brought up in an environment of government-funded arts councils, research councils, museums, and galleries is talk of the Canada Council as a foundation patterned after the "big" private American foundations—bigger, better, Canadian, and publicly funded to be sure—but a foundation nonetheless. Adding insult to Canadian nationalist injury was the presence of Dean Rusk, one of the "Deans" of what sociologist C. Wright Mills coined the American "Power Elite,"[10] and a number of other leaders of American philanthropy as honored guests at the first meeting of the Canada Council—their attendance in recognition both of past contributions to the making of Canadian culture and of their knowledge of culture-making generally. After all, historians and cultural commentators, not to mention what has been so thoroughly naturalized as our own Canadian "common sense," all tell us that such organizations as the Canada Council and SSHRCC are the cornerstones of the federal infrastructure which, since the late 1950s, has been so carefully constructed to protect Canadian culture against incursions from the south. As Jody Berland succinctly summarizes, key to the mythology of Canadian identity "is a complex apparatus of agencies and institutions [nurtured as part of a paternalistic federal-state] which for over half a century has sought to administer culture as part of the larger enterprise of defining the nation's borders."[11] Surely, the contributions of private American philanthropy to the making of Canadian culture should serve to complicate our essentialistic and (largely) ahistorical notions of contrasting national identities and cultural economies. Where does this fit, for instance, in the matrix of Canadian-American difference—in the now mythologized juxtaposition of an American culture fueled by the free market and a Canadian one sustained by state support?

In the broader study from which this chapter is drawn[12] I look back through the clouds of what I suspect is a nationalist-inspired historiographical amnesia to an era when the Canadian state's involvement in culture was still fairly limited and when there were few alternative sources of funding—to a period during which the contribution of private American philanthropy to Canadian culture and higher education was of a formative and essential nature. There I argue that, in many ways, the national-elite consolidation that reached a high point with the formation of the Canada Council, and with the establishment of other means of state support for culture following the Massey Report, was facilitated by the American foundations' support of the efforts of Canadian artists and intellectuals to organize and rationalize the cultural sphere. Viewed in this light, the system of state support for the arts and letters that emerged in Canada from the late 1950s through the 1960s—a system that included as its prime components the Canada Council, federal funding for higher education across Canada, and a greatly enhanced commitment to the Canadian Broadcasting Corporation, the National Film Board, and to the national museum complex—must be conceptualized not simply as a Canadian rejection of the American model of private philanthropy but as the product of a mixed economy of culture and, specifically, of partnerships between American foundations and a Canadian cultural elite.

In this chapter I focus on the involvement of the RF's Humanities Division in Canadian projects from the early 1930s to the late 1950s. I briefly survey the broad range of Rockefeller involvement in the humanities at the local, regional, and national levels, suggesting both the motivation for a Canadian program, as well the long-term impact on the rationalization and professionalization of the humanities in Canada. For the sake of clarity, I divide my summary discussion of the Foundation's Canadian program into two categories: (1) support for research infrastructure aimed at fostering cultural interpretation of Canadian locales and regions and (2) support for nationally focused research and for national research infrastructure in the social sciences and the humanities. History on the ground, of course, is never so neat and tidy—these tendencies were just that. The Foundation's goal was to sponsor social research in Canada and to integrate Canadian scholars and cultural producers into broader regional, national, continental, even trans-Atlantic systems of intellectual production.

"CULTURAL INTERPRETATION"

In the early 1930s, in the midst of the Great Depression, the leaders of the RF began to express their concern about the social and cultural implications of the boom-and-bust rhythm of industrial capitalism. Able to provide leadership in the development of public health, medical education, and scientific knowledge generally, RF officers realized they were losing ground in the free market of ideas.[13] At a time of extreme economic crisis, they feared that unregulated mass production of information posed a grave challenge to the moral and spiritual health of the American nation and, in particular, to older, "traditional" notions of community. While Rockefeller philanthropy through the General Education Board (GEB) and the Laura Spellman Rockefeller Memorial (LSRM) had played a fundamental role in establishing the prominence of the humanities disciplines in North American universities, it had done little, one officer noted, to bring the "humanities from books, seminars and museums into the currents of modern life."[14]

In 1935, in an effort to address this situation, Rockefeller Foundation director for the humanities David Stevens and his assistant director John Marshall established a new program in what they referred to as "cultural interpretation." Stevens and Marshall looked to reach deeper into American society, not to operate "above" the emerging mass culture, but rather to bring the Foundation's work in the humanities "more directly into contact with daily living" and to gain a clearer idea of "the ways in which the American public now gains its culture."[15] The officers saw as their target nothing less than a reformulation of the humanist tradition that would make it directly relevant in Depression-era America. As cultural leaders who wanted to maintain the existing social hierarchy, men like Marshall and Stevens saw humanism as a way of thought that could be used to combat the sense of rootlessness and the accompanying crisis of authority brought on by the tragedy of the Great Depression. The resulting program was designed to influence how Americans created, as Stevens put it, their "own forms of mental, emotional and spiritual freedom."[16] By funding artists and intellectuals engaged in community theater, educational film and radio, and in the collection of regional folklore, the Foundation attempted to combat the assumption that "culture was something foreign" and to foster "a larger appreciation of those elements in American life that constitute our national heritage."[17] The primary concern was for the survival (or indeed the re-creation) of a cultural identity at a time when older notions of community were being challenged by great social, economic, and technological change. In taking measures to create or re-create local, regional, and national heritages, of course, the Foundation and the cultural producers it supported were engaging in the selection and ordering of the elements of that heritage.

Two primary objectives of the new Rockefeller humanities program of cultural interpretation paradoxically led to its exportation to Canada. On the one hand, to Marshall and Stevens, "American life" was not restricted to territory within the political boundaries of the nation-state. In their eyes culture flowed freely across the American-Canadian border. As Marshall later observed, "If the cultural history of the United States were to be studied, the basis had to be not political units, not the nation, but the human regions that made up North America."[18] In this they reflected the attitudes of most representatives of American corporate philanthropy of the era. Indeed, for much of the interwar period the Rockefeller Foundation and its New York City neighbor, the CC, treated Canadian intellectual and cultural infrastructure as part of a broader North American network. Examples of this sort of continental cultural integration abound and include both foundations' support for Canadian universities; the Carnegie Endowment for International Peace's funding for texts and conferences on relations between Canada and the United States; the RF's backing (through the American SSRC) of the Frontiers of Settlement studies in the early 1930s, the CC's support for Canadian museums and galleries (most prominently the National Gallery of Canada and the Art Gallery of Toronto); and its sponsorship of the first national meeting of Canadian artists in Kingston in 1941 and the resulting formation of the Federation of Canadian Artists.[19]

In many respects, this program of North American–cultural consolidation also paralleled the American state's reading of the essential military-strategic reality of North American nationalities facing the perils of world conflict. Speaking at Queen's University in Kingston, Ontario, on August 18, 1938, American president Franklin D. Roosevelt warned his audience that a European war might eventually pose a threat to freedoms and values shared by the peoples of Canada and the United States. After paying homage to Canada's British heritage and its membership in the British Empire, Roosevelt invoked the Monroe Doctrine, assuring Canadians "that the people of the United States will not stand idly by if domination of Canadian soil is threatened by any other empire."[20] Two years later, in August 1940, Roosevelt and Canadian prime minister William Lyon Mackenzie King signed the Ogdensburg Agreement and thereby established a Permanent Joint Board on Defence for the purpose of coordinating continental defense.

Many Canadian nationalists at that time and since have viewed these developments as less the products of binational cooperation and more the result of American imperialism. According to Donald Creighton, the Ogdensburg Agreement, along with the Hyde Park Declaration of April 20, 1941, in which King and Roosevelt agreed to cooperate in the production and purchasing of military equipment, were key moments in Canada's absorption into the American empire.[21] In an ironic twist of Arthur Lower's title for his 1946 survey of Canadian history, *Colony to Nation: A History of Canada*, Harold Innis reflected on what he saw as a fundamental shift in orientation when he concluded that, by the end of the first half of the twentieth century, Canada had merely substituted one metropolitan force for another and thus had been transformed from "colony to nation to colony."[22]

But other Canadians, Marshall was to discover, saw possibilities in the new alignment—possibilities far more in keeping with the Foundation's agendas. In 1941 McGill University law professor F. R. Scott, who at that time was holding a Guggenheim Fellowship and conducting research at the Harvard Law School, published the short book, *Canada and the United States*,[23] in the World Peace Foundation series "America Looks Ahead." In it Scott discussed liberal democratic values and the "unity of historical origin and purpose" shared by the two nations.[24] Scott, Marshall later noted, was "convinced that some North American or North Atlantic organization should prevail in post-war reconstruction."[25] Indeed, Scott theorized how military cooperation and the coordination of continental defense might profitably lead to a greater level of political and economic integration following the war. Under the surface of discussions of defense, Scott noted, there was "a more fundamental process at work":

> Mass production, the industrialization of warfare, the perfection of the internal combustion engine, the science of planning—these basic factors have rendered obsolete the anarchic world of small national sovereignties in which we used to live. A supra-nationalism, a higher federalism, seems to be developing.[26]

In a passage that seemed to confirm the validity of Donald Creighton's worst fears of American empire, Scott even queried his readers whether the defense agreement announced at Ogdensburg might prove to be "the first clause of a North American constitution."[27]

On the other hand, Canada's status as an independent nation made it an object of the Foundation's desire to improve "cultural understanding amongst nations."[28] Marshall, Stevens, and other members of the American philanthropic elite believed that military, economic, and, above all, cultural consolidation could and should be accomplished without undermining Canadian sovereignty. The RF's Humanities Division's turn to Canada was, moreover, a product of a more generalized internationalist perspective that was pervasive in the higher echelons of Rockefeller philanthropy—a perspective that not only fostered the sense of common continental cultures but was responsible at the same time, as William Buxton puts it, for the project of "forging a new transatlantic community on a cultural basis."[29] Ironically, however, the Foundation's efforts at continental and hemispheric consolidation moved to front stage with the retrenchment from its European activities, which necessarily followed the outbreak of war in September 1939.[30] As had been the case earlier in the century when the Foundation had extended its public health and medical education programs north of the border,[31] Canada was thus treated both as a collection of northern regions of a continental culture and as a foreign nation.

JOHN MARSHALL'S CANADIAN TOUR

Between September 1941 and November 1942, Marshall toured Canadian cultural centers, engaging in a search, he later noted in his diary, for individuals and institutions that could, with the helping hand of his organization, contribute to "a better interpretation of Canadian tradition."[32] Marshall's tour was a key part of a broader inventory taking by the Rockefeller Foundation's Humanities and Social Science divisions that also included Associate Director Anne Bezanson's surveys of the social sciences in Canada and Charles McCombs's study of Canadian library facilities.[33] As was the case with the Foundation's efforts to fertilize traditions in the United States, the building blocks of a Canadian national tradition were thought to be "the rich regional cultures" of North America.[34] In keeping with the metropolitanism that infused all Rockefeller philanthropy, each of these "human regions" was seen to emanate from a metropolitan base that served as the center of overlapping transportation, economic, and educational systems. Paradoxically, these regional cultures—while, apparently the components of North American "national" cultures—were not necessarily bounded by the political border that formally separated Canada and the United States. In other words, Marshall came to Canada with the expectation that the Foundation's Humanities Division would expand its program in cultural interpretation of American regions into a broader regional analysis of the North American continent. This desire not only reflected the way Rockefeller Foundation officers perceived the broad sweep of North American history, but also their reading of the present geopolitical situation—a situation marked by an ever-increasing economic and military-strategic integration of Canada and the United States.

Marshall, however, came away from his fact-finding mission with a very different and far more complex analysis of the Canadian scene. In each of the cities and universities he toured, the officer discovered thinkers who, though clearly in need of financial backing for their projects and willing to discuss his ideas about North American cultural regions, had a variety of agendas of their own to pursue. The existence of these elite networks and the strengths and variety of ideas expressed by their members caused Marshall to reconsider the Humanities Division's approach to Canadian development. According to Charles Acland and William Buxton, he concluded that Canada could not be "viewed as a horizontal mosaic extending northwards from the United States." Canada, these writers observe, "was now considered as a distinct region of its own whose metropolitan elites were to receive and administer the largesse of the Rockefeller Foundation."[35]

Clearly, Marshall was impressed by the men he spoke with on his Canadian mission. This was not surprising given the nature of his tours. As was the case with all surveys conducted by Rockefeller philanthropies, the process of cultural selection began long before the officer actually set foot in Canada. Following the (by this time) well-established pattern of the Foundation survey, Marshall set his itinerary in a manner that ensured he spoke with people who would listen. With very few exceptions, all of Marshall's contacts were men.[36] All, moreover, were members of an urban-based national elite, which had been coalescing since the early 1920s. While Raleigh Parkin—Vincent Massey's brother-in-law, an executive of the Sun Life Assurance Company, and a trustee of New York's Crane Foundation—was a key contact and had provided a list of people Marshall should speak to,[37] his business background was the exception that proved the rule. Almost all of Marshall's other hosts were employed at major Canadian universities or cultural institutions. Members of this elite, like the managers of American philanthropy in their own country, nonetheless enjoyed firm connections to the state and business elites. They, like Marshall, assumed that it was their right and duty to lead. In addition, almost every one of Marshall's contacts had some previous exposure, however indirect, to American corporate philanthropy. Most were employed at institutions that had received major contributions from American foundations in the 1920s and 1930s and many had been the recipients of Carnegie, Rockefeller, or Guggenheim awards.

In addition to the social composition of the group and the previous contacts its members had had with American philanthropy, there were other compelling explanations for the generally warm reception Marshall received on his mission. Canadian intellectuals may have been suspicious of Marshall's sense of the precise sources and parameters of North American regional cultures, but most shared the Rockefeller officer's zeal for imagining, defining, and structuring cultural spaces in North America. In a rapidly changing modern environment altered by continual waves of immigration, by urbanization, by economic depression and by war, Canadian intellectuals were also struggling to maintain or reformulate the foundations of community and identity. Many of Marshall's Canadian contacts had been involved in the Royal Commission on Dominion-Provincial Relations (the

Rowell-Sirois Commission of 1937), were currently involved in the Advisory Committee on Reconstruction chaired by McGill University principal Cyril James, and—or would be—involved in the Massey Commission.

Marshall's positive impressions echoed those of Rockefeller Foundation Social Science Division officers, particularly those of Canadian-born Bezanson, who, since the late 1930s, had been working closely with a group led by University of Toronto economist Harold Innis, Queen's historian Reginald Trotter, and John Robbins, chief of the education branch of the Dominion Bureau of Statistics to establish the Foundation-sponsored Canadian Social Science Research Council (CSSRC) as the dominant force in the development of the social sciences in Canada.[38] Given positive assessments by the likes of Marshall and Bezanson, both the Social Science and the Humanities Divisions increasingly attempted to work with and through national bodies in much the same way as they had been doing in the United States since the early 1920s.

It would be a mistake, however, to assume that Marshall gave up on his idea of cross-border regionality or of the importance of cultural regions within larger political units. Marshall's evaluation of Canadian culture and of Canadian metropolitan elites led him and the Foundation to a variety of conclusions about how to approach the Canadian scene. In the provinces of western Canada, in the Maritimes, and in French-speaking Quebec, Marshall discovered what he perceived to be cultural regions—regions that to varying degrees shared attributes with and could benefit from contacts with geographically contingent American regions, but that were distinct regions nonetheless. In these areas, Marshall believed, the Foundation would do well to fund and encourage projects—much like those already established south of the border—aimed at sharpening the collective awareness of regional heritage, tradition, and identity. In contrast, in the metropolitan centers of central Canada, Marshall discerned the heart of a nation.

THE MARITIMES AND WESTERN CANADA

Ideally, influence in the "regions" was exerted simply by privileging Canadian individuals whose approaches already meshed well with Foundation objectives. Canadians who fit the bill were given support for their projects and often fellowships for study at American projects sponsored by the Foundation. Even before Marshall's tour to western Canada, the Rockefeller Foundation funded Alberta playwright and Banff School of Fine Arts instructor Gwen Pharis[39] to study community theater at the Rockefeller-sponsored Department of Dramatic Art at the University of North Carolina headed by Frederick Koch.[40] Following Marshall's visit, the Foundation supported historian A. S. Morton's efforts to create a provincial archive at the University of Saskatchewan. Under Morton's direction, the primary research materials he had gathered for his history of western Canada[41] and for his history of the fur trade[42] were organized and cataloged for use by future scholars. In addition, Morton contributed rich collections of business records and pioneer narratives and helped retrieve from Ottawa copies of public documents from the province's territorial period (1870–1905).[43] As Acland and Buxton point out in their work about the Rockefeller Foundation's program of support for Canadian libraries and archives, this intervention was critically linked "with the writing of regional history and the sense of cultural definition that was to follow from this."[44]

Marshall was equally impressed by the potential of the Canadian Maritime region for cultural interpretation. There the Foundation supported Nova Scotia folklorist Helen Creighton, providing her with a fellowship to attend the Summer Institute of Folklore at Indiana University and to visit the Library of Congress's Archive of American Folk Song in Washington during the summer of 1942. In addition to arguing about the pronunciation of "zees" and "zeds" with preeminent American folklorists, including Alan Lomax, Stith Thompson, and John Jacob Niles,[45] it was during this summer that Creighton began her transformation, as Ian McKay puts it, from "a British-style 'Ballad Stalker' . . . [to] an American-style folklorist."[46] With further Foundation support over the next few years, Creighton conducted research for a book, *Folklore of Lunenburg County*, she published with the National Museum of Canada in 1950.[47] Also in the summer of 1942 the Foundation awarded Clyde Nunn, the director of St. Francis Xavier University radio station CJFX, a grant-in-aid to fund visits to Rockefeller-sponsored projects at the University of Iowa, the Rocky Mountain Radio Council in Denver, and Paul Lazarsfeld's Columbia University Office of Radio Research.[48] Although the size of the grant was relatively small, its influence was enhanced by the relationship of Nunn's project to previous initiatives undertaken by American foundations. Throughout the 1930s St. Francis Xavier's renowned Antigonish experiment in adult education depended on the Carnegie Corporation for the majority of its operating revenue.[49] Under Nunn, CJFX became a leader in the field of educational broadcasting. Its operations coordinated with St. Francis Xavier University's extension program to promote adult education in rural Nova Scotia.[50]

At a conference organized by Marshall for the Humanities Division to investigate possibilities for cross-border cultural interpretation of an Eastern Maritime Region held in Rockland, Maine, in August 1942, the officer was most impressed with Alfred Bailey, a young historian from the University of New Brunswick. In the immediate aftermath of the conference, Marshall wrote University of New Brunswick president N. A. M. MacKenzie and noted that "everyone went away with the feeling that Bailey was a man of unusual promise who ought to get all possible support and encouragement."[51] Keeping Bailey in New Brunswick—"a place," Marshall had previously noted, "where he in many ways belongs"—to develop a regional-studies program became a top priority in Rockefeller Foundation humanities program.[52] Foundation support for Bailey was given not only to help the historian establish his career, but also to entrench the study of regional history at the University of New Brunswick.

Responding to what Marshall had perceived to be the "lack of institutional bases"[53] on which to establish Canadian cultural interpretations, the Foundation also funded limited-term appointments of American scholars at Canadian universities for the purpose of establishing new programs or strengthening existing ones. While Marshall had not perceived a strong sense of Canadian national identity in the northwest, there was, in his assessment, great interest in regional identity. He was particularly intrigued with the uniquely varied arts program at the University of Alberta's Banff School of Fine Arts. Founded with the support of the Carnegie Corporation of New York in 1933, and administered through the University's Department of Extension, the school's mandate was, in the words of its director Donald Cameron, "to simulate the cultivation of drama and the appreciation of music and art in the rural districts of the province."[54] At Banff, writers including Pharis, Elsie Park Gowan, Rowena Hawkings, and John MacLaren were successfully developing a western Canadian literature and theater based on local history and folklore. Similarly, painters W. J. Phillips, H. G. Glyde, and André Biéler were engaging the physical environment of the mountain west as subject matter for instruction and in their own practice. What made the situation at Banff unique—and distinct from Rockefeller-sponsored projects in the United States—was the manner in which the visual and theater arts were meshed in a broader program of regional interpretation. Their efforts, which in this sense shared so much with the Rockefeller Foundation's new program of cultural interpretation, had been encouraged by Frederick Koch, who served as the school's director of creative writing from 1935 to 1941. He was brought to Banff by Cameron precisely because of his proven ability to "inspire the students with a new sense of the milieu in which they lived and with a new sense of its richness from the standpoint of dramatic material."[55] Koch had extensive experience with community theater. From his base in Chapel Hill he had founded the Carolina Players with the support of the Rockefeller Foundation. Perhaps more significant for the future prospects of the Banff School, Koch was also one of the primary architects of the Rockefeller Foundation's drama program.[56]

To further encourage the growth of this program both at Banff and at the university's home campus in Edmonton, American folklorist Robert Gard, a veteran of the Rockefeller-sponsored New York State Play Project at Cornell University, was brought to the University of Alberta to direct the Alberta

Folklore and Local History Project in 1943. While in Alberta, Humanities Division director David Stevens later noted, Gard

> showed his ideas on drama so successfully that an entire province of Canada gained an enduring awareness of its place in a living world. I know of no demonstration more swiftly executed in a merging of history, folklore, and people for a unique expressiveness of an environment.[57]

"FRENCH CANADA"

In approaching the region he called "French Canada," Marshall perceived a society that in some senses was a model for his concept of North American region. Here was a community with a deeply rooted sense of cultural heritage and a clear self-consciousness. "There is among [French Canadians]," Marshall noted,

> still something of 18th century cultural tradition in which every scholar remained in part a humanist. Their own voluminous literature about themselves, though perhaps diffuse and impressionistic in many instances, manifests this bias. More than any other group in Canada, they have interpreted themselves and as a result have a self-consciousness of their own life and the problems it involves, which proves a good base at least for creating understanding of them elsewhere.[58]

Clearly, the Foundation's assistance was not required—as it had allegedly been in Alberta—to make citizens aware of their common cultural inheritance. What was lacking in the region, Marshall felt, was exposure to the rest of the continent. And this was an area—particularly where it concerned the relationship of the province to the United States—in which the Rockefeller Foundation had a vital interest.

At the suggestion of Marine Leland of the Department of French Language and Literature at Smith College in Northampton, Massachusetts, Marshall decided initially to channel Foundation Humanities Division interest in French Canada through the newly established North American French section of the Rockefeller-sponsored Modern Language Association (MLA).[59] Bringing "French Canada" into the continental mainstream, Leland felt, was necessary to eliminating the obstacle of isolation: "If only French Canadian writers can get some means of coming in contact with other Americans who are interested in this continent, they will get greater confidence in themselves and produce more solid works."[60] Accordingly, shortly after his visit to Quebec in January 1942, Marshall convened a conference in New York City to bring together scholars and intellectuals from Quebec with their American counterparts.

Partly as a result of this conference, Marshall and Stevens sent Everett C. Hughes, professor of sociology at the University of Chicago and a former member of the sociology department at McGill University, to teach in the School of Social Science at Laval University for the 1942–1943 academic year. Hughes's tenure at Laval was subsequently extended to include the next academic year. At Laval, Hughes did his best to bring to the study of Quebec's culture "some closer knowledge of certain methods of study developed by sociologists and social anthropologists of the English-speaking world." In return, he hoped he would gain "some further understanding of the role of the intellectuals in a rich, traditional culture such as yours."[61] Participating in seminars and directing individual studies, Hughes felt he would be in a good position "to diplomatically present to students, staff, et al. some American methods, ideas, literature etc."[62] Working with Father Georges-Henri Lévesque, director of the School of Social Science at Laval, Hughes created a program for future research and instruction at the school. Published in the form of a pamphlet at the end of Hughes's stay, the Programme de recherches sociales pour le Québec[63] directed faculty and students to sociological research at the grassroots level. After Hughes's return to Chicago in 1944, the research program he established was continued under the direction of his former student at the University of Chicago, Jean-Charles Falardeau.[64]

The tangible results of the interaction between Canadian cultural producers and academics and the Rockefeller Foundation during the 1930s, 1940s, and 1950s are impressive. The Foundation's support for Gard's Alberta folklore project contributed to the already impressive growth of the Banff School at a critical stage in its development and brought the school that much closer to realizing the goal of establishing the arts as a vital component of regional life. The flurry of activity that surrounded the folklore project also provided the impetus for the creation of the University of Alberta's new department of fine arts—a department that, like no other in Canada at the time, included divisions in visual arts, music, and drama. Encouraged by the success of community drama in Alberta, the Rockefeller Foundation also sponsored a chair of drama at the University of Saskatchewan in 1945. The original Alberta Writers' Conference—initially an offshoot of the folklore project—had, by 1948, evolved into a permanent institution, the Western Writers' Conference.[65] Intent on fostering "a National People's Theatre in Canada," and promoting drama as a means of education at the secondary and postsecondary levels, the Rockefeller Foundation provided funds to bring together individuals from the four western provinces to take part in the Western Canadian Theatre Conference.[66] It, in turn, became a permanent fixture on the western landscape.

The extent to which the Alberta Folklore and Local History Project stimulated and empowered individual cultural producers is more difficult to trace, but should not discounted. At the age of nineteen, Colin Low, who studied at Banff and at the Calgary Institute of Technology and Art under Glyde and Phillips, was selected to draw cover sketches for the first two issues of Gard's newsletter, the *Alberta Folklore Quarterly*. The resulting sketches—the first depicting a bunkhouse scene on the resource frontier, the second an "Indian folk legend about two lovers escaping from the wrath of the thunder god"[67]—visually articulated the literary content of the journal. It is worth pointing out the thematic similarities between these early productions, the aims and objectives of the Alberta Folklore Project, and Low's later work as a producer and director at the National Film Board (NFB).[68] Two of Low's more important early films at the NFB in particular—*Corral* (1954) and *City Of Gold* (1957)—are nostalgic portrayals of the western Canadian frontier.[69] *Corral*, which won first place at the Venice Film Festival the year it was released, shows a cowboy at work breaking in a horse on his ranch in southwest Alberta. Like the folklore Gard collected and disseminated, the film is, in the words of film historian Peter Harcourt, "less [a re-creation] of an actual event than of an atmosphere that has vanished." Harcourt continues his analysis of the film by observing that, like many of Low's movies, there is "a sense of something lost. . . . [an] atmosphere of events more deeply felt than understood. . . ."[70] Low's Academy Award–winning documentary short *City of Gold* recalls the early days of Dawson City, the town at the heart of the Klondike Gold Rush of 1897. Narrated by Pierre Berton, who recalls his early years in the city, the film also uses a series of still photographs to depict the rough and tumble of the gold rush. The women of Paradise Alley, the seemingly "endless human chain" of men climbing the 45-degree ice slope in the Chilkoot Pass, are but a few of the subjects of these photographs. These are juxtaposed with photographs at the film's beginning and end of the present-day city now desolate and grown-over with grass. The film, as Harcourt points out, "while superficially about a gold rush, becomes an emblem of the incomprehensible motivation of man."[71]

More immediately representative of the symbiotic relationship between Gard's brand of folklore and an emerging regional art of western Canada was the performance of Gwen Pharis Ringwood's three-act play *Stampede*, which opened at the University of Alberta's Convocation Hall on March 4, 1946. Commissioned by the Alberta Folklore and Local History Project, it was directed by Sydney Risk and performed by students in the program. Centered on the Calgary Stampede of 1912, the play, according to Cameron, was "a sort of Canadian Oklahoma . . . [which] caught the romance of the rangelands and is one of the most authentic pieces of dramatization of that colourful period in Western Canada when the cowman was king."[72] To a writer who reviewed the production for the *Alberta Folklore Quarterly*, it was "a colourful panoramic of crowds, music, cowboys,

Mounties, Indians, and horse rangers—in fact, it embodies everyone and everything found at the Stampede."[73]

The collaboration between the Rockefeller Foundation Humanities Division and Helen Creighton also proved enormously fruitful for all involved. As so often is the case with Canadian cultural producers, status and recognition received outside Canada led to greater acceptance in Canada.[74] At least partially as a result of the Rockefeller Foundation's and the Library of Congress's stamps of endorsement, the National Museum of Canada not only published Creighton's volume on Lunenburg,[75] but also hired her to continue work on her various collections. Nova Scotia's Department of Education helped her publish a second volume of songs and ballads of Nova Scotia.[76] In the decades that followed, Creighton's flame burned ever brighter. On permanent staff at the National Museum in Ottawa by early 1949, she published numerous scholarly and popular articles on folklore. In 1964, benefiting from the Canadian federal-state's commitment to cultural funding—a commitment that not coincidentally resembled that exhibited by American foundations in an earlier era—she received a Canada Council grant to help her record and transcribe her entire collection of folk songs and tunes.[77] If the Foundation's goal was to subtly foster the growth of a common scholarly community in North America and to thus create common cultural practices, attitudes, and policies, then, as Ian McKay suggests, "Helen Creighton's file can only be regarded as an outstanding success story."[78]

The Laval intervention had both short- and long-term implications. Jean-Charles Falardeau, left in charge of the School of Social Science following Hughes's departure, later emerged as a crucial figure in the development of a French-Canadian sociology. The department at Laval, in turn, was at the center of that evolution until well into the 1960s.[79] In a broader sense, Laval was at the heart of the development of the postwar generation of Quebec City intellectuals.[80] As important, the Hughes exchange cemented the relationship between the Foundation and Father Georges-Henri Lévesque. During his stay at Laval, Hughes had advised Marshall that the Foundation should "continue to work with Père Lévesque . . . on the ground that his activities, and all that they stand for, will have increasing importance in the life of the province."[81] Hughes's prediction was an accurate one. Not only was Lévesque to play a large role in the development of the province, but, as one of five members of the Royal Commission on National Development in the Arts and Letters (the Massey Commission) and, later, the first vice chairman of the Canada Council, he was an important figure in the cultural and intellectual life of postwar Canada. The inclusion of Lévesque in the Foundation's ever-expanding network of influence may well have been the most significant aspect of Hughes's visit to Laval.

The ambitious regional and provincial studies program Bailey envisioned for the University of New Brunswick did not become a reality, at least not in the short term. Bailey remained at Fredericton, as MacKenzie and Marshall had hoped he would, and enjoyed a long and distinguished career as an administrator and teacher at the University of New Brunswick. Although Bailey subsequently published more poetry than ethno history, he was, nonetheless, an early and vigorous proponent of both regional and social history in Canada.[82] Funding for Bailey should also be considered support for N. A. M. MacKenzie's leadership and for an effort to further solidify an already strong relationship with an important figure on the Canadian scene. In 1944 MacKenzie left New Brunswick, as Marshall expected he might, to take up the presidency of the University of British Columbia (UBC). The move extended the Rockefeller Foundation's influence at the increasingly important west coast university, although, for a number reasons, UBC was never successful in winning the type of support some of its prominent eastern counterparts garnered. The enhancement of the relationship between MacKenzie—like Lévesque a future member of the Massey Commission and, later still, a key member of the Canada Council—and the Rockefeller Foundation is one of many examples of how the Foundation was woven into the fabric of Canadian culture and power.

It would be a gross exaggeration to claim that support for projects of local and regional interpretation alone constituted even an attempt by the Foundation at the scientific management of Canadian culture. In conjunction with the activities of the Carnegie Corporation in Canada and with the Foundation's efforts to organize the humanities and social sciences in Canada in the 1940s, however, the support for regional studies and for the creation of regional infrastructure was a significant intervention in Canadian culture. This was particularly true at a time when, due to the constraints, first, of economic depression and, then, of the war effort, there was much talk but very little action on the need to support culture and scholarship in Canada.

The financial backing and access to American expertise the Rockefeller Foundation provided were invaluable to Canadians who were in the process of defining Canadian local and regional traditions and cultures. Foundation initiatives designed to develop the study of cultural history, sociology, and folklore had a lasting impact in Canada, both in terms of making the work of Creighton, Bailey, and others possible and by influencing how these individuals approached their areas of specialization. In negotiating this support, the Foundation was also involving itself in, and lending its support to, the emerging network of Canadian institutions, associations, and individuals coalescing around the impulse to structure and lead Canadian culture. In this manner, the Rockefeller Foundation contributed, in no small way, to the emergence of MacKenzie, Lévesque, Bailey, and Creighton as cultural authorities—thus helping them in their ascension to positions of leadership and influence.

"NATION"

On the one hand, Marshall discovered cultural regions in "French Canada," the Maritimes, and the Canadian Northwest. Though, in the case of the latter two, the regions he imagined spanned the American-Canadian border, all three, he felt sure, fit his and Steven's definition of "rich regional cultures." In the metropolitan centers of central Canada, on the other hand, Marshall found a nation. In Montreal, Toronto, Ottawa, and even Kingston, Marshall immediately assessed his hosts as being of "national" stature. These men, it went almost without saying, were too busy with existing research and matters of national or even international administration to be concerned with local and regional matters. Playing the part of a cultural diplomat, Marshall treated F. R. Scott, S. D. Clark, Raleigh Parkin, and, particularly, Donald Creighton and Harold Innis as important members of a friendly, but foreign, national elite. They, to be sure, were worthy of support. But their concerns and their research were not exclusively "regional" in nature. These men, it seemed, to Marshall, had the "stuff" to build a national culture.

There are a number of possible explanations for this contrast. In a simple sense it can be explained as a reflection of the realities and disparities of Canadian Confederation. Needier individuals from newer and/or less financially secure institutions were willing to do more to attract the support of the American foundation. Marshall's presence undoubtedly provoked—as the visit of a foundation officer invariably would—energetic attempts by university officials and scholars to ascertain what he wanted to hear and what sort of projects he would recommend for support. If regional analysis and regionally-based projects were important parts of the Rockefeller Foundation Humanities Division's program, many Canadians may accordingly have surmised that these were worth pursuing. Considering the history of regional discontent with central Canadian dominance, it is also likely that exploring regional histories and traditions and even accepting a greater north-south orientation was considered a small price to pay to win Rockefeller support. Indeed, as I have argued elsewhere, the support of American foundations for regional cultural producers and their institutions was a critical stimulus and an empowering agent in the construction of strong regional cultures that stood as counterforces to a hegemonic central Canadian–based nationalism.[83]

Marshall's perceptions, however, were also influenced by the history of Rockefeller Foundation involvement in Canada and by the ideological position of the Foundation. Since the beginning, Rockefeller officers had assumed that Toronto and Montreal occupied positions of dominance roughly equivalent to those of the metropolitan centers of the northeastern United States. This assumption represented not only an acceptance of how things were, but also an evaluation of how they should be. For the big-city philanthropoids in Manhattan, interest in cultural regions did not negate the hold of the metropolitan center. Since the early 1920s the Foundation had relied on the advice of such national leaders as Vincent Massey, later chair of the Royal Commission on National Development in the Arts and Letters and, later still, first Canadian-born governor general, and William Lyon Mackenzie King, Canada's longest-serving prime minister, and had deemed central Canadian institutions such as McGill University and the University of Toronto as truly national centers of education and research. With large contributions to their general endowment funds and medical schools, the Foundation made a concerted effort to strengthen the positions of these two institutions at the top of the hierarchy of Canadian higher education. To the Rockefeller Foundation, Ontario and English-speaking Montreal were not regions; they were, simply, "Canada." So while the Foundation contributed significantly and vitally to specific regional projects in drama, local history, and folklore, it, nonetheless, treated Toronto, Montreal, and Ottawa as the cultural capitols of the emerging nation. Of course in advancing this hierarchy the Foundation was naturalizing the dominance of the central-Canadian elite and thus contributing to the institutionalization of a central-Canadian regional ideology of Canadian nationality.

As crucial to Foundation strategy as the development of national "centres of excellence" in central Canada was the focus on the development of national research councils in the social sciences and the humanities. Since the early 1920s Rockefeller philanthropies had channeled much of their support in these fields through such American research councils as the Social Science Research Council and the American Council of Learned Societies. From the late 1930s to 1957, when the Canada Council was formed and the principal of federal-state support for scholarship in the Humanities and the Social Sciences was realized, the officers of both the Rockefeller Foundation and the Carnegie Corporation worked with Canadian scholars to build national councils consciously modeled on American precedents and designed to support scholarship. In addition to funding the daily operations of both the Humanities Research Council of Canada (HRCC) and the Canadian Social Science Research Council (CSSRC), American foundations covered the bill for the councils' scholarly aid programs.[84]

The impact of both the operating funds and the foundations' support for research and publication was nothing less than astounding. Such large-scale research and publishing initiatives as the Canadian Frontiers of Settlement studies and the Carnegie Endowment for International Peace conference and text series on Canadian-American relations, which were both funded directly by American foundations in the 1930s, and the CSSRC's multi-volume study of social credit in the Canadian west set the tone for an era of social research in Canada.[85] It is not an exaggeration to say that works published with the aid of American philanthropy established canons in several academic disciplines. In my own discipline of history, the narrative of national development, which remained orthodoxy until well into the 1970s, was established in this period. A short list suggesting the magnitude as well as the disciplinary and ideological range of works funded by the foundations includes J. Bartlett Brebner's *North Atlantic Triangle: The Interplay of Canada, the United States and Great Britain*; Harold Innis's *The Cod Fisheries: The History of an International Economy*; Donald Creighton's *The Commercial Empire of the St. Lawrence, 1760–1850, Dominion of the North*, his two-part biography of Sir John A. Macdonald,[86] and his tribute to Innis[87]; Arthur Lower's *The North American Assault on the Canadian Forest*, as well as his *Colony to Nation: A History of Canada*; Innis's and Lower's, *Settlement and the Forest and Mining Frontiers*; W. L Morton's *The Progressive Party of Canada*; C. B. Macpherson's *Democracy in Alberta: The Theory and Practice of a Quasi-Party System*; several volumes related to the official William Lyon Mackenzie King biography project[88]; and S. D. Clark's *Movements of Political Protest in Canada, 1640–1840*.[89] It would be difficult to think of a major work in the social sciences and humanities that did not receive foundation support either directly or via the Canadian research councils. Speaking about the Carnegie series, historian Carl Berger notes that it involved almost "every Canadian historian . . . at one time or another,"[90] and "functioned as a combined Social Science Research Council and Canada Council to Canadian scholars in the 1930s and early 1940s."[91] Even a cursory glance at this list reveals the importance of foundation funding to the emergence of a national leadership group in the social sciences and the humanities, which included such disciplinary and interdisciplinary "founding fathers" as economic historian Innis, historians Creighton, Morton, and Lower, and sociologist Clarke.

Particularly privileged in the division of spoils were members of the University of Toronto's Department of Political Economy, which was led by Innis until his death in 1952. This was, of course, no accident. Very early in the process, Rockefeller officers from both the Humanities and Social Sciences Divisions had decided that this unusual grouping of scholars was Canada's primary "centre of excellence" for social, economic, and political research. In addition to privileging the "men of Toronto" in the distribution of grants and supporting their efforts to build national research infrastructure in the form of the HRCC and the CSSRC, following Innis's death, the Rockefeller Foundation favored the department with sizable legacy grants to honor the man its officers knew simply as "Innis of Canada."[92] It was these Toronto scholars, particularly Innis himself and Creighton, that their colleague in political science, Frank Underhill, had in mind when he referred to those "academic intellectuals . . . who are still thinking up nasty wisecracks about American imperialism regardless of the fact that most of their own pet research projects are apt to be financed by money from Rockefeller or Carnegie or Guggenheim."[93]

CONCLUSION

In a lot of ways it is the bigger picture of the impact of private American philanthropy on the Canadian cultural scene that concerns me, not merely the activities of the Rockefeller Foundation Humanities Division, or even the entire Canadian operations of the Foundation, but the broader scope of American philanthropic activity in Canada, including interventions by the Carnegie Corporation of New York, the Carnegie Endowment for International Peace, the Guggenheim Foundation, and by the 1950s, the Ford Foundation. This broader influence—as I have suggested elsewhere, and as Buxton and Acland have also argued—has not been given the scholarly attention it warrants in the historiography of Canadian cultural and intellectual development.

For non-Canadianists I will summarize the established orthodox narrative of Canadian cultural policy in a nutshell paragraph. The story goes something like this: The development of federal-state support for arts and scholarship in the 1950s and 1960s was the culmination of a long, quintessentially Canadian (tinged, of course with an appropriate measure of British Toryism) fight to beat back the incursions of American culture—cultural incursions that went hand in hand with a century of increased continental economic integration and the tightening of a wartime military-strategic relationship between Canada and the United States that was cemented and symbolized with the defense agreements at Ogdensburg and Hyde Park in 1941 and 1942 respectively. The Massey Commission and the formation of the Canada Council to fund artistic production and scholarship in the humanities and the social sciences were crowning moments of retaliation and defense in a glorious fight for Canadian cultural sovereignty and survival.

There is some truth in this grand narrative of Canadian cultural survival. That Innis, Donald Creighton, and scores of other Canadian academics relied heavily on the support of the Rockefeller Foundation and the Carnegie Corporation does not, of course, make them "puppets" whose work was "animated" by American wealth. Certainly, in Creighton's case, the fact that most of his important work was assisted by Carnegie Corporation and Rockefeller Foundation grants for publication, for research, and for release time from teaching commitments did not in any simple or obvious manner bias his analysis.[94] In his later years he made very sure that his reputation for anti-American sentiment was unquestioned and well deserved. The same might be said of the manner in which Innis had used his role as the Rockefeller Foundation's adviser on the social sciences and the humanities in Canada.

It is quite possible that, particularly in Creighton's case, the dependence on American philanthropy only enhanced the sense of urgency to find Canadian sources of support. Nonetheless, as Frank Underhill reminded readers of the *Canadian Forum* in 1950, these men and the structures they helped establish depended on American support in this critical era of development, and that irony is too tantalizing to ignore. With needed funds and with the knowledge to build research councils and research centers, the foundations set the parameters for Canadian development in the days before the creation of the Canada Council. Even the council itself—that supposed bulwark against the negative influence of American-centered mass culture—was patterned after models built in New York City. It is not an exaggeration to argue, as does Paul Litt, that "the Canadian cultural elite was as much affected by American high culture as the general population was by American mass culture."[95] It is a testament both to the desire and ability of the American foundations to embed their influence within such mediating bodies as the research councils and to the chauvinism of nationalist historians that the history of Canadian cultural structures has been so effectively "cleansed" of this element of American cultural imperialism. It is as if the "arts and letters" was the one aspect of Canadian culture too pure to be sullied by American influence.

In making the case for the significant role played by the Carnegie Corporation and the Rockefeller Foundation in the making of modern Canada, I have tried to interrogate and transcend simplistic notions both of American-Canadian difference and of the border between the "public" and "private" spheres. From a narrow cultural nationalist perspective it would have been appealing to add American philanthropy to the colony-to-nation narrative of Canadian history by telling a glorious tale of Canadian agency and resistance to American cultural imperialism. In such an epic, Donald Creighton, Bailey, Innis, Helen Creighton, Lévesque, MacKenzie, and all the rest took the wealth of the Carnegie Corporation and the Rockefeller Foundation and "ran with it" to strengthen the foundations of the Dominion. Elements of this story ring true. Members of the Canadian elite did use their ties to American philanthropy to pursue their own agendas and to supplement their power. It is equally true that aspects of the cultural policies that emerged in the 1950s and 1960s did not greatly resemble the politics of culture in the United States. The system that emerged was, as a whole, unique to Canada. The reality of the matter, however, was that there was no fundamental contradiction between the agendas pursued by the Canadian cultural elite and the foundations' pursuit of the scientific management of culture.

In the larger project from which this paper is drawn I discuss the relationship between American philanthropy and Canadian culture in terms of cultural and intellectual hegemony. I am not arguing, in other words, that this was ever a case of the RF forcing Canadians to do research or establish programs of study. This is not a story of a crude brand of cultural imperialism. Instead my research indicates a case of providing support for those who wanted the same things and who thought, or who were willing to think, the same way as the foundations' leadership. In this way, intellectual freedom was not threatened by coercion but, more specifically, by an unequal distribution of rewards and benefits. As sociologist Clyde Barrow observes, "Research grants, stipends, and consultantships in turn play a significant role in the opportunities for publication, promotion, and tenure that influence individual positions within the university."[96] An "unequal system of rewards and incentives," Barrow continues, may not formally prevent radical research and teaching, but does serve to authorize the ideas of individuals who choose to "play the game."[97] In extolling the virtues of intellectual freedom in a liberal society we would do well to heed one Canadian historian's recent reminder that "not all 'discourses' circulate equally."[98]

Barrow's warnings about the limited parameters of intellectual activity sanctioned by the foundations inform my discussion here. I take the position that within the academy there existed what Barrow refers to as a "negotiated range of theoretical free space between absolute autonomy and totalitarian control [that] is real and substantial."[99] Scholars existing in the environment created in large part by the big foundations labored in this "theoretical free space" and were thus "relatively autonomous." They were not, however, free to pursue the full range of intellectual curiosity. And all ideas, moreover, did not receive equal support and sanction.

What is even clearer is that "private" foundation funding bought influence in an area all agree is in the "public" domain. In doing so, private foundations provided leadership in what Raymond Williams refers to as a "central system of practices, meanings and values, which we can properly call dominant and effective."[100] In the process, American foundations were exerting power over cultural expression in Canada at least equal to that contained within the formal political structures of the state at the time. Don't get me wrong. If I am to assess the products of the collaborations between American foundations and Canadian intellectuals in terms of "good" and "bad," I would say that the overall influence was extremely positive. Put simply, I believe in university departments, research councils, and support for scholarship, artist associations, museums, and galleries. But this doesn't mean that the existence of these has nothing to do with the relative cultural power of donors and recipients. To function, hegemony requires the active consent of the "client"—or the receiver of patronage in this case. The relationship of influence and consent must be constantly renegotiated for hegemony to exist. Thus, a hegemonic relationship not only allows for but, in fact, requires that the "client" continually benefits from the patron-client relationship. This central fact should not, however, obscure the fundamentally undemocratic nature of the system or of the society it produced.

That an ardent Canadian nationalist such as Donald Creighton (to choose just one prominent example) skillfully gained from the support provided by the foundations does not negate the fact that during the pre-Canada Council era Americans held the "power of the purse" in such pivotal Canadian projects as the Canadian Social Science Research Council, the Humanities Research Council of Canada, the (Carnegie Corporation's) Canadian Museums Committee, and the Federation of Canadian Artists. Creighton recognized the benefits to Canadian researchers and their associations, as well as the negative aspects of dependency on foundation funds when, in 1955, as chair of the Humanities Research Council of Canada, he pleaded with Rockefeller officials for an extension of a Foundation grant. The historian knew all too well that Americans held all the "carrots" and "sticks" and that intellectual production in the humanities depended on their wishes and whims. Stating that the loss of funding would mean an "abrupt break in the continuity of the work upon which our academic community has come to rely" and noting that his position was "a very embarrassing one," Creighton asked Marshall whether the Foundation could "help us out for another year." When the initial response was no, Creighton wrote to Foundation president Dean Rusk and observed that he fully understood Rusk's "reluctance to do once more what the Canadians apparently refuse to do themselves."[101]

Creighton, the Massey commissioners, Prime Minister Louis St. Laurent, and host of others recognized the positive impact of American philanthropic activities on the Canadian arts and letters. At the same time, however, they also recognized the troubling nature of being dependent on private American foundations. Of course, they did not use the term "cultural hegemony" to characterize the source of their ambivalence to foundation support for the arts and letters in Canada. They spoke instead of their concerns for Canadian cultural sovereignty and self-determination. But the message was clear. The products of the relationship—arts councils, publications, artists' conferences, research councils, and support for scholarship in the humanities and social sciences—were all to the good. The dependence on American foundations and the associated infringement on intellectual freedom and cultural sovereignty was not.

NOTES

Unpublished material in this chapter has been quoted courtesy of the following archives: Library and Archives Canada, Ottawa; the Carnegie Corporation of New York, New York City; and the Rockefeller Archive Center, Sleepy Hollow, New York.

1. Brooke Claxton, "One Hundred Million Dollars for What?" Presented to the Empire Club of Canada, joint meeting with Canadian Club, 17 October, 1957, 8. Canada Council of the Arts Records (hereafter CCR), Claxton file, memoranda.

2. "Concerning Mr. King," *Canadian Forum* (September 1950): 122. A short version of this quotation is included in the conclusion of Kenneth McNaught, "Frank Underhill: A Personal Interpretation," *Queen's Quarterly* 79 (Summer 1972): 134–35.

3. Claxton, "The Canada Council," 3. CCR, Claxton file, memoranda. For an excellent discussion of the Canada Council's formation see J. L. Granatstein, "Culture and Scholarship: The First Ten Years of the Canada Council," *Canadian Historical Review* 65, no. 4 (December 1984): 441–74.

4. Claxton, "One Hundred Million Dollars for What?" 8.

5. "The Canada Council: Minutes of the First Meeting," 19–20. CCR.

6. S. F. Markham to H. O. McCurry, 11 August, 1933. National Gallery of Canada Archives (hereafter NGCA), Record Group (hereafter RG) 7.4 C, File: December 1932–August 31, 1933.

7. "A Brief Presented by the Humanities Research Council of Canada to the Royal Commission on National Development in the Arts, Letters and Sciences," 15 July, 1949, 2–3, Sent by Stephen Stackpole to John Robbins, 10 October, 1949. Carnegie Corporation of New York Records, Columbia University Rare Book and Manuscript Library (hereafter CCNYA), Series III.A, Box 175, Folder 1 ("Humanities Research Council of Canada, 1944–1955).

8. House of Commons, *Debates*, 18 January, 1957, 393.

9. See Donald Fisher, *The Social Sciences in Canada: 50 Years of National Activity by the Social Science Federation of Canada* (Waterloo: Wilfrid Laurier University Press in collaboration with the Social Sciences Federation of Canada, 1991); and Jeffrey D. Brison, *Rockefeller, Carnegie, and Canada: American Philanthropy and the Arts and Letters in Canada* (Montreal: McGill-Queen's University Press, 2005).

10. C. Wright Mills, *The Power Elite* (New York: Oxford University Press, 1956); Leonard Silk and Mark Silk, *The American Establishment* (New York: Basic Books, 1980).

11. "Politics After Nationalism, Culture After 'Culture,'" *Canadian Review of American Studies* 27, 3 (1997): 40.

12. Brison, *Rockefeller, Carnegie, and Canada.*

13. David H. Stevens, "The Humanities in Theory and Policy," 31 March, 1937, 2. Rockefeller Archive Center (hereafter RAC), Rockefeller Foundation Archives (hereafter RF), RG 3, Series 911, Box 2, Folder 10.

14. "Humanities—Program and Policy: Extract from DR 486, Report of the Committee on Appraisal and Plan, December 11, 1934," 72.

15. "New Program in the Humanities," 10 April, 1935, i–ii. RAC, RF, RG 3, Series 911, Box 2, Folder 10.

16. Stevens, "The Humanities in Theory and Policy," 1.

17. "Program in the Humanities," March 1934. "RAC, RF, RG 3, Series 911, Box 2, Folder 9.

18. Quoted in Charles R. Acland and William J. Buxton, "Continentalism and Philanthropy: A Rockefeller Officer's Impressions of the Humanities in the Maritimes," *Acadiensis* 23 (Spring 1994): 75.

19. See Brison, *Rockefeller, Carnegie, and Canada*; Fisher, *The Social Sciences in Canada*; Charles R. Acland, "Mapping the Serious and the Dangerous: Film and the National Council of Education, 1920–1939," *Cinema(s)* 5 (Fall 1995): 101–18; Acland, "National Dreams, International Encounters: The Formation of Canadian Film Culture in the 1930s," *Canadian Journal of Film Studies* 3 (Spring 1994): 4–26; Acland and Buxton, "Continentalism and Philanthropy," 72–93; William J. Buxton and Charles R. Acland, *American Philanthropy and Canadian Libraries: The Politics of Knowledge and Information* (Montreal: Graduate School of Library and Information Studies and the Centre for Research on Canadian Cultural Industries and Institutions, McGill University, 1998); Maria Tippett, *Making Culture: English-Canadian Institutions and the Arts before the Massey Commission* (Toronto: University of Toronto Press, 1990); Michael Bell, "The Welfare of Art in Canada," introduction to *The Kingston Conference Proceedings: A Reprint of the Proceedings of the 1941 Kingston Artists' Conference* (Kingston: Agnes Etherington Art Centre, 1983); Jeffrey Brison, "The Kingston Conference, The Carnegie Corporation and a New Deal for the Arts in Canada," *American Review of Canadian Studies* 23 (Winter 1993): 503–22; Jeffrey Brison, "The Rockefeller Foundation and Cultural Policy on the North Western Frontier," *Journal of Canadian Art History* 23, nos. 1 and 2 (2002): 66–90; Carl Berger, "The Conferences on Canadian-American Affairs, 1935–1941: An Overview," in *The Road to Ogdensburg: The Queen's/St. Lawrence Conferences on Canadian-American Affairs, 1935–1941*, eds. Frederick W. Gibson and Jonathan G. Rossie (East Lansing: Michigan State University Press, 1993), 11–35; Carl Berger, "Internationalism, Continentalism, and the Writing of History: Comments on the Carnegie Series on the Relations of Canada and the United States," in *The Influence of the United States on Canadian Development: Eleven Case Studies*, ed. Richard Preston (Durham, NC: Duke University Press, 1972), 32–55; Paul Litt "The Massey Commission, Americanization, and Canadian Cultural Nationalism," *Queen's Quarterly* 98 (Summer 1991): 375–87.

20. J. L. Granatstein and Norman Hillmer, *For Better or for Worse: Canada and the United States to the 1990s* (Toronto: Copp Clark Pitman, 1991), 103–4; J. L. Granatstein, *How Britain's Economic, Political, and Economic Weakness Forced Canada into the Arms of the United States: A Melodrama in Three Acts*: The 1988 Joanne Goodman Lectures (Toronto: University of Toronto Press, 1989), 24; and John Herd Thompson and Stephen J. Randall, *Canada and the United States: Ambivalent Allies* (Montreal: McGill-Queen's University Press, 1994), 147. For a detailed analysis of the development of continental defense arrangements, see Galen Roger Perras, *Franklin Roosevelt and the Origin of the Canadian-American Security Alliance, 1933–1945: Necessary But Not Necessary Enough* (Westport, CT: Praeger, 1998).

21. Donald Creighton, *The Forked Road: Canada 1939–1957* (Toronto: McClelland & Stewart Ltd., 1976). For discussions of William Lyon Mackenzie King, the Ogdensburg Agreement, the Hyde Park Declaration, and what Carl Berger describes as "the demonology of [Canadian] nationalism," see Berger, "The Conferences on

Canadian-American Affairs, 1935–1941: An Overview," in Gibson and Rossie, eds. *The Road to Ogdensburg*, 29; Thompson and Randall, *Ambivalent Allies*, 155; and Granatstein, *How Britain's Weakness*, 24–26.

22. A. R. M. (Arthur) Lower, *Colony to Nation: A History of Canada* (Toronto: Longmans & Green, 1946); Harold A. Innis, "Great Britain, the United States, and Canada," in *Essays in Canadian Economic History*, ed. Mary Q. Innis (Toronto: University of Toronto Press, 1956), 405, cited by Paul Litt, "The Massey Commission, Americanization, and Canadian Cultural Nationalism," 376.

23. Boston: World Peace Foundation, 1941.

24. F. R. Scott, *Canada and the United States* (Boston: World Peace Foundation), 11.

25. Marshall, "Canada: Diary of Visit," "Third Part: French Canada—Montreal and Quebec, January 12–16, 1942," p. 12, RG 1.1, Series 427R, Box 27, Folder 264, RF, RAC.

26. Scott, *Canada and the United States*, 64.

27. Scott, *Canada and the United States*, 7.

28. "Program in the Humanities, March 1934."

29. William J. Buxton, "John Marshall and the Humanities in Europe: Shifting Patterns of Rockefeller Foundation Support," *Minerva* 41, no. 2 (2003): 152. Buxton traces the Foundation's internationalist position to Rockefeller Foundation director Raymond Fosdick's early involvement in and support for the League of Nations. Fosdick served under Woodrow Wilson as senior American representative to the League. Although he resigned the post after the U.S. Senate refused to ratify the Treaty of Versailles, Fosdick continued to promote the League. He also convinced John Rockefeller Jr. of its value and Rockefeller later provided valuable financial support to the League. See Buxton, "John Marshall," 149, n65.

30. See Buxton, "John Marshall," 152.

31. Brison, *Rockefeller, Carnegie, and Canada*, 56–62; see also William B. Spaulding, "Why Rockefeller Supported Medical Education in Canada: The William Lyon Mackenzie King Connection," *Canadian Bulletin of Medical History* 10 (1993): 67–76; and Marianne P. Stevens, "The Rockefeller Foundation and Canadian Medical Education," *Research Reports from the Rockefeller Archive Center* (Spring 1999): 14–16.

32. John Marshall, "Canada: Diary of Visit," "First Part: Quebec and Ontario, September 29–October 3, 1941," 1A. RAC, RF, RG 1.1, Series 427R, Box 27, Folder 264.

33. Bezanson visited Canada during the spring of 1941 while McComb conducted his research in the summer and autumn of that year. See Acland and Buxton, *American Philanthropy and Canadian Libraries*; and Brison, *Rockefeller, Carnegie, and Canada*, 169–71.

34. Fosdick, *The Story of the Rockefeller Foundation*, 256.

35. Acland and Buxton, "Continentalism and Philanthropy," 92.

36. Acland and Buxton correctly attribute this to the "largely unstated masculinist assumptions that underpinned the philanthropic and academic practices of the period." See "Continentalism and Philanthropy," 84, n63.

37. Acland and Buxton, *American Philanthropy and Canadian Libraries*, 10.

38. See Brison, *Rockefeller, Carnegie, and Canada*, 165–74; Donald Fisher, *The Social Sciences in Canada*; and Fisher, "Harold Innis and the Canadian Social Science Research Council: An Experiment in Boundary Work," in *Harold Innis in the New*

Century: Reflections and Refractions, eds. Charles R. Acland and William J. Buxton (Montreal: McGill-Queen's University Press, 1999): 135–58.

39. After her marriage in September 1939 to Dr. John Brian Ringwood, Pharis used her married name, Gwen Pharis Ringwood.

40. Brison, "The Rockefeller Foundation and Cultural Policy on the North Western Frontier," 71.

41. Arthur S. Morton, *A History of the Canadian West to 1870–1871: Being a History of Rupert's Land (the Hudson's Bay Company's territory) and of the North-West Territory (including the Pacific slope),* ed. Lewis G. Thomas (Toronto: Thomas Nelson, 1939).

42. See *David Thompson* (Toronto: Ryerson Press, 1930); *The North West Company* (Toronto: Ryerson Press, 1930); *Sir George Simpson, Overseas Governor of the Hudson's Bay Company; A Pen Picture of a Man of Action* (Toronto: J. M. Dent & Sons, 1944); *The Journal of Duncan McGillivray of the North West Company at Fort George on the Saskatchewan, 1794-5, with introduction, notes and appendix by Arthur S. Morton* (Toronto: Macmillan, 1929); *Under Western Skies, Being a Series of Pen-Pictures of the Canadian West in Early Fur Trade Times* (Toronto: T. Nelson & Sons, 1937); and *Five Fur Trade Posts on the Lower Qu'Appelle River, 1787-1819* (Ottawa: Royal Society of Canada, 1941).

43. Marshall, "Canada: Diary of Visit," "Second Part: Manitoba, Saskatchewan, Alberta, and Vancouver, October 20–30, 1941," pp. 12–14. RAC, RF, RG 1.1, Series 427R, Box 27, Folder 264.

44. Buxton and Acland, *American Philanthropy and Canadian Libraries,* 27–8.

45. Helen Creighton, *A Life in Folklore: Helen Creighton* (Toronto: McGraw-Hill Ryerson, 1975), 131.

46. Ian McKay, *Quest of the Folk: Antimodernism and Cultural Selection in Twentieth-Century Nova Scotia* (Kingston: McGill-Queen's University Press, 1994), 78.

47. Helen Creighton, *Folklore of Lunenburg County, Nova Scotia* (Ottawa: National Museum of Canada, 1950).

48. Acland and Buxton, "Continentalism and Philanthropy," 86.

49. John G. Reid, "Health, Education, Economy: Philanthropic Foundations in the Atlantic Region in the 1920s and 1930s," *Acadiensis* 14 (Autumn 1984): 75.

50. Acland and Buxton, "Continentalism and Philanthropy," 86.

51. Marshall to MacKenzie, 2 September, 1942, cited in Acland and Buxton, "Continentalism and Philanthropy," 84.

52. Marshall, "Canada: Diary of Visit," "Fourth Part: The Maritime Provinces, April 22–30, 1942," p. 28. RAC, RF, RG 1.1, Series 427R, Box 27, Folder 264. This was not the first time that officers of an American foundation worked with local officials to make the environment in Fredericton more attractive for Bailey. In the mid-1930s the Carnegie Corporation provided the New Brunswick Museum (located near Fredericton in St. John) with several grants to support Bailey's employment at the institution. See Ernest R. Forbes, *Challenging the Regional Stereotype: Essays on the 20th Century Maritimes* (Halifax: Acadiensis Press, 1989), 56.

53. Marshall, "Canada: Diary of Visit," "First Part: Quebec and Ontario, September 29–October 3, 1941," p. a. RAC, RF, RG 1.1, Series 427R, Box 27, Folder 264.

54. Donald Cameron, *The Campus in the Clouds* (Toronto: McClelland & Stewart Ltd., 1956), 123–24.

55. Cameron, *The Campus in the Clouds,* 22. For a discussion of Koch's influence on local playwrights see Cameron, *The Campus in the Clouds,* 21.

56. In early 1934 Koch, Arthur Quinn (University of Pennsylvania), Allardyce Nicoll (Yale University), A. M. Drummond (Cornell University), and E. C. Mabie (University of Iowa) were involved in discussions with the directors of the Rockefeller Foundation's Humanities Division. Out of these meetings emerged the guiding principals of the Foundation's support of community theater in North America. See William J. Buxton, "RF Support for Non-Professional Drama, 1933–1950," *Research Reports from the Rockefeller Archive Center* (Spring 1999): 2.

57. David H. Stevens, foreword to Robert Gard, *Grassroots Theater: A Search for Regional Arts in America* (Madison: University of Wisconsin Press, 1955), ix.

58. Marshall, "Canada: Diary of Visit," "Third Part: French Canada—Montreal and Quebec, January 19–23, 1942," p. 25. RAC, RF, RG 1.1, Series 427R, Box 27, Folder 264.

59. Marine Leland to John Marshall, 20 December, 1941. RAC, RF, RG 2, Series 427R, Box 222, Folder 1545.

60. Leland to John Marshall, 20 December, 1941.

61. Hughes to Lévesque, 4 August, 1942. RAC, RF, RG 1.1, Series 427R, Box 26, Folder 259.

62. Hughes to David Stevens, 20 May, 1942. RAC, RF, RG 1.1, Series 427R, Box 26, Folder 259.

63. Everett Hughes, "Programme de recherches sociales pour le Québec," *Cahiers de l'Ecole des Sciences Sociales, Politiques et Economiques de Laval* 2, no. 4 (1943).

64. Alain-G. Gagnon and Sarah Fortin, "Innis in Quebec: Conjectures and Conjunctures," in Acland and Buxton, *Harold Innis in the New Century*, 217.

65. Newton to Stevens, 28 November, 1946, p. 1. RAC, RF, RG 1.1, Series 427R, Box 29, Folder 288.

66. Newton to Stevens, 28 November, 1946.

67. *Alberta Folklore Quarterly* 1, no. 2 (June 1945): 1.

68. Low joined the NFB in 1945 to work, principally, as an animator. In 1950 he was appointed the head of the animation unit at the NFB. During his long career he directed and produced numerous titles for the film board, including *The Romance of Transportation*, winner of the 1953 Prix du film d'animation at Cannes, and *City of Gold*, which won the 1957 Academy Award for best documentary short. In all, Low has been nominated for nine Academy Awards. See Peter Harcourt, "The Innocent Eye: An Aspect of the Work of the National Film Board of Canada," in *The Canadian Film Reader*, eds. Seth Feldman and Joyce Nelson (Toronto: Peter Martin Associates Ltd., 1977), 74–75; For summaries of Low's career see http://www.nfb.ca/portraits/colin_low/en/ (accessed November 1, 2008).

69. Harcourt, "The Innocent Eye," 74.

70. Harcourt, "The Innocent Eye," 74.

71. Harcourt, "The Innocent Eye," 75.

72. Cameron, *The Campus in the Clouds*, 30.

73. *Alberta Folklore Quarterly* 2, no. 1 (March 1946): 39.

74. McKay, *The Quest of the Folk*, 76.

75. Helen Creighton, *Folklore of Lunenburg County, Nova Scotia.* Nova Scotia National Museum of Canada, Bulletin No. 117, Anthropological Series No. 29 (Ottawa: Canada Department of Resources & Development, 1950).

76. Helen Creighton with Doreen Senior, *Traditional Folksongs from Nova Scotia* (Toronto: Ryerson Press, 1950).

77. Fellowship Cards: Creighton, 4–5. RAC, RF.

78. McKay, *The Quest of the Folk*, 78.

79. Marlene Shore, *The Science of Social Redemption: McGill, the Chicago School, and the Origins of Social Research in Canada* (Toronto: University of Toronto Press, 1987), 270. See also David Nock, "History and Evolution of French Canadian Sociology," *Insurgent Sociologist* 4 (Summer 1974): 21.

80. Michael D. Behiels, *Prelude to Quebec's Quiet Revolution Liberalism Versus Neo-Nationalism, 1945–1960* (Montreal: McGill-Queen's University Press, 1985), 34.

81. John Marshall Interviews, Laval University, Quebec, 30–31, December, 1942. RAC, RF, RG2, Series 427, Box 239, Folder 1655.

82. P. A. Buckner, "'Limited Identities' and Canadian Historical Scholarship: An Atlantic Provinces Perspective," *Journal of Canadian Studies* 23 (Spring–Summer 1988): 179. Bailey's published collections of poetry include *Thanks for a Drowned Island* (Toronto: McClelland & Stewart Ltd., 1973); *Miramachi Lightning: The Collected Poems of Alfred Bailey* (Fredericton, New Brunswick: Fiddlehead Poetry Books, 1981); and *The Sun, the Wind, the Summer Field* (Fredericton, New Brunswick: Goose Lane Publishing, 1996).

83. Brison, "The Rockefeller Foundation and Cultural Policy on the North Western Frontier," 67.

84. Brison, *Rockefeller, Carnegie, and Canada*, 165–74; Donald Fisher, *The Social Sciences in Canada*.

85. For a thorough discussion of Frontiers studies see Marlene Shore, *The Science of Social Redemption*, 162–94. On the Carnegie Series, see chapter 6, "A North American Nation," in Carl Berger, *The Writing of Canadian History: Aspects of English-Canadian Historical Writing Since 1900*, 2nd ed. (Toronto: University of Toronto Press, 1986), 137–59; Berger, "Internationalism, Continentalism, and the Writing of History"; and Robin S. Harris, *A History of Higher Education in Canada, 1663–1960* (Toronto: University of Toronto Press, 1976), 339–44. The most recent work on the conferences is Gibson and Rossie, *The Road to Ogdensburg*. This volume, which is an edited collection of selected papers from each of the four conferences, includes an introductory essay by Berger: "The Conferences on Canadian-American Affairs." See also Brison, *Rockefeller, Carnegie, and Canada*, 155–86.

86. Donald Creighton, *John A. Macdonald: The Young Politician* (Toronto: Macmillan, 1952); and Donald Creighton, *John A. Macdonald: The Old Chieftain* (Toronto: Macmillan, 1955).

87. Donald Creighton, *Harold Adams Innis: Portrait of a Scholar* (Toronto: University of Toronto Press, 1957).

88. See Brison, "The Memory of Mackenzie King: American Philanthropy, 'a Canadian biography and Canadian History'" (unpublished paper, presented in "Mackenzie King: Contested Legacy," Queen's University, Kingston, Ontario, 8 November, 2001).

89. J. Bartlett Brebner, *North Atlantic Triangle: The Interplay of Canada, the United States and Great Britain* (Toronto: Ryerson Press, 1945); Harold Innis, *The Cod Fisheries: The History of an International Economy* (Toronto: Ryerson Press, 1940); and Donald Creighton, *Commercial Empire of the St. Lawrence, 1760–1850* (Toronto: Ryerson Press, 1937).

90. Berger, *The Writing of Canadian History*, 151.

91. Berger, "Internationalism, Continentalism, and the Writing of History," 43–44.

92. Bezanson to Willits, 18 November, 1952. RAC, RF' RG 1.2, Series 427S, Box 16, Folder 160. See also Brison, *Rockefeller, Carnegie, and Canada*, 186–94.

93. Underhill, "Concerning Mr. King," 122.

94. In addition to receiving Rockefeller and Carnegie support, Creighton held a Guggenheim fellowship in 1941. He used this fellowship to work on *Dominion of the North*.

95. Litt, "The Massey Commission, Americanization, and Canadian Cultural Nationalism," 383.

96. Clyde Barrow, *Universities and the Capitalist State: Corporate Liberalism and the Reconstruction of American Higher Education, 1894–1928* (Madison: University of Wisconsin Press, 1990), 252.

97. Barrow, *Universities and the Capitalist State*.

98. Ian McKay, "Introduction: All that is Solid Melts into Air," in *The Challenge of Modernity: A Reader on Post-Confederation Canada*, ed. I. McKay (Toronto: McGraw-Hill Ryerson Ltd., 1992), xxiii.

99. Barrow, *Universities and the Capitalist State*, 252.

100. Raymond Williams, "Base and Superstructure in Marxist Cultural Theory," in *Rethinking Popular Culture: Contemporary Perspectives in Cultural Studies*, eds. Chandra Mukerji and Michael Schudson (Berkeley: University of California Press, 1991), 413.

101. Creighton to Rusk, 15 June, 1955. RAC, RF, RG 1.1, Series 427S, Box 32, Folder 325.

10

Inadvertent Architects of Twentieth-Century Media Convergence: Private Foundations and the Reorientation of Foreign Journalists

Marion Wrenn

INTRODUCTION

When Jeremy Tunstall famously claimed "the media are American" in the late 1970s he voiced what had by then become a truism. Consider his book's eponymous opening lines: "'The media are American. And Vodka is Russian. So what?'" commented one American. It is hard to miss the shrugging apathy implied in that sentence. With the flip "So what?" tagged on to the end of the supposedly overheard phrase, Tunstall telegraphs that the American belief about the nation's media power had by then become common sense, so natural seeming as to be dismissed. But Tunstall unpacks this conventional wisdom by working in two ways—he hoped to show more jaded readers that such a state of affairs was "neither obvious nor inevitable" and to convince dubious readers that though seemingly "far-fetched" the claim was "nevertheless true."[1]

Read as an artifact of its time, his book signals an era in which empirical evidence of homogeneous global media cultures became fodder for the burgeoning critique of what had previously been a de facto presumption that the dominance of Anglo-American media content and production practices was basically a good thing for all involved. The appearance of *The Media Are American* in the late 1970s stoked the era's radical critique of the status quo; it became a major part of the discourse on how cultural imperialism was enacted via media dominance. His book appeared as the idea of a New World Information Order, one which would not exacerbate the gap between the developed and developing worlds, dominated the discourse of the media imperialism debate.[2] Intellectuals, policy makers, media professionals, and institutions like UNESCO began to shift away from technocratic neutrality, questioned the dominant rhetorical paradigm of modernization theory, and adapted a critical approach to the dominance of the Anglo-American media model.

By the 1970s utopian modernization theory gave way to the "media imperialism" critique.[3] Tunstall's description of the increasing hegemony of American media patterns underpinned this critique of American media influence: The American media empire fostered dependence, was built on a unidirectional flow of technology and content, and cinched the erasure of extant or potential media diversity. At the core of this critique lay the belief that the world's media systems were converging.[4] But modernization theory and the media imperialism critique were two sides of the same coin; both presumed that the media were powerful and were, ultimately, "American."[5]

Though current comparative media scholars deem Tunstall's early argument overly simplistic, the widespread presumption of such homogeneity is an artifact of the era, bearing traces of the optimism of modernization theory and its opposite, the media-imperialism critique.[6] It is also, I would argue, a central myth of the golden age of American journalism. In the following pages, I delve into the prehistory of the media-imperialism debate in order to partially reconstruct the ways certain widely held beliefs about American journalism reinforced ideas of American media power. This connection between the presumption of American media power and the history of American journalism is at the heart of the following case study of a project designed to foster the global spread of democracy via mass communication and journalist training. This chapter focuses on a little-known mechanism of the diffusion of the *belief* in the inevitability of such power—post–World War II international journalist-reorientation programs.

Media scholars have long been interested in the social forces that influence news production, and much has been written about the effect of media ownership and multinational corporations on news production, aesthetics, and values. Relatively less has been written about the way other institutions have influenced the journalistic profession on a national or international scale.[7] An important story of media influence within the history of American journalism emerges if we shift focus from the impact of multinational corporations and corporate ownership on news production to account instead for the relationship between private foundations, universities, and the state, particularly as this triumvirate attempted to influence news values and production internationally in the aftermath of World War II.

Part of a larger study of foundation-funded journalist-training seminars that explores the impact of the way private foundations, universities, and the U.S. government conceived of, and assumed a role in, shaping national news cultures outside of its borders, this article focuses on the Rockefeller

Foundation's early and pivotal role in fostering the development of such seminars. In the following pages I will describe the way the United States—through the collaboration of its occupying forces in Japan and Germany, Columbia University, and the Rockefeller Foundation (RF)—was involved in the reorientation of foreign journalists to the values of a free press and the free flow of information beginning in the wake of World War II. Such reorientation seminars form a fascinating optic through which to see the embrace of journalism, democracy, national security, propaganda worries, and communication research—not to mention the genealogy of the belief that the world's media and press cultures were (or should be) homogeneous. I argue that private foundations—and the institutions with which they collaborated—were the inadvertent architects of the myth of the inevitability of global media convergence.

THE SEMINARS IN CONTEXT

Media historians describe the years spanning the aftermath of World War II to the late 1970s as a unique era in the history of American journalism.[8] During these decades there was a proliferation of professional associations, news organizations, professional training, and professional norms. Hallin calls this period the high-modernist age of American journalism and describes how

> the historically troubled role of the journalist seemed fully rationalized . . . it seemed possible for the journalist to be powerful and prosperous and at the same time independent, disinterested, public-spirited, and trusted and beloved by everyone, from the corridors of power around the world to the ordinary citizen and consumer.[9]

Elite journalists shared a strong orientation toward public service and formed a relatively tightly knit, highly socialized professional discourse community. Hallin attributes two major social conditions to the development of this particular image of the professional journalist: (1) New Deal–cold war political consensus and (2) economic security (both for American society as a whole and for the media industries in particular).[10]

These macrolevel conditions make sense, but they render certain microlevel triggers invisible. One such apparatus for the diffusion of this professional ethos is the focus of this chapter—postwar international-journalist-training seminars hosted by Columbia University, seminars funded by the Ford and Rockefeller Foundations. American journalists were invited to "reorient" German and Japanese journalists by discussing common problems, articulating their news values and practices, and inviting their guests to hometown newspapers and radio stations for behind-the-scenes access.

Though charged to avoid the appearance of cultural indoctrination, seminar leaders conveyed the implicit message that the American way was the best way. Sitting at the intersection of journalism history and media hegemony, such projects contributed to the conventional wisdom that the world's media were American and helped drive that truism home.

Well into the pages of *The Media Are American*, Tunstall claims the age of "American media conquest" begins in 1945, the aftermath of World War II. In the crucial years from 1947 to 1948 "American media reached their highest point in terms of direct dominance of the media in other countries."[11] The little-known American project to reorient international journalists by bringing them to the United States began in this period. In the wake of World War II, Columbia University trained German and Japanese radio and newspaper personnel through a series of grant-funded projects at the Bureau of Applied Social Research (BASR) and the newly founded American Press Institute (API).[12] Starting in 1947, particularly through John Marshall and program officers Edward F. D'Arms and Charles B. Fahs, and under the advisement and approval of the U.S. Army, the Rockefeller Foundation supported a series of seminars and training programs for journalists, editors, and broadcasters from these war-torn countries. According to the grant files at the Rockefeller Archive Center and Ford Foundation, these projects were explicitly designed to "reorient" participants to the values of a "free and democratic press," terms reverberating not only with Anglo-American press values, but also with wartime propaganda worries and with the 1940s-era U.S. debates over freedom of the press signaled by the Hutchins Commission and the so-called "free press crusades."

The oft-repeated ideal of a "free and democratic press" found throughout the letters and memos exchanged among journalism professionals, foundation officers, or military officials appears at first to be an example of a seeming doxic American belief in press freedom. But such rhetoric should be understood as an allusion to a number of important phenomena in the history of American journalism; for instance, it is a nod to the 1940s-era Commission on the Freedom of the Press, also known as the Hutchins Commission. Rooted in debates around New Deal policies and changes in the journalism industry during the 1930s, the Commission was assembled in the 1940s to assess the state of journalism in the United States. Funded by Henry Luce and chaired by Luce's former Yale classmate Robert Maynard Hutchins, the Commission was particularly interested in the function of the press in a capitalist mass society, and it pursued this question by focusing on, among other things, the practice of objectivity and fundamental questions about journalism and democracy.

But the postwar mission to "reorient" press practitioners to the value of a free and democratic press also alludes to the free-flow doctrine and the "free press crusade" of the 1940s and 1950s. An integrated push for the free flow of information on an international scale, the crusade was first aligned with antifascism and then aligned with cold war containment policies. As Blanchard notes, with its roots in the propaganda worries of World War I and the 1927 International Conference of Press Experts (where U.S. journalists extolled the virtues American domestic news practices), the idea that a free and democratic press would lead to world peace and should be a basic right of all human beings lived on between the wars through the League of Nations and increased in fervor with World War II. By the early 1940s, press associations had the support of powerful figures in the U.S. government who, "from Franklin D. Roosevelt on down, adopted freedom of information as a war aim."[13] But, as Hallin and Mancini point out, the crusade "enjoyed limited success, in the sense that American proposals were often rejected."[14] Nonetheless, the crusade "contributed to the dissemination of liberal media principles that were indeed becoming increasingly hegemonic."[15]

Largely because the movement was led by the American Society of Newspaper Editors (ASNE) and the U.S. Department of State and focused on international agencies like the UN and United Nations Educational, Scientific and Cultural Organization (UNESCO), Blanchard's extensive study does not linger over the role of U.S. private foundations in the free-press crusade.[16] However, if we take these international journalist seminars into full account, foundations played a crucial role. The seminars were both a strategic reaction to the problem of postwar reconstruction and an extension of the logic of the free-press crusades.[17] With foundation monies, foreign journalists and broadcasters from vanquished nations were brought into the United States, participated in discussions and seminars at Columbia University, visited broadcast stations and newspaper operations across the country on their own or in small groups, reconvened to share their findings with other participants, and were then sent back to their home countries. The hope, as articulated by the Rockefeller Foundation, was that "a little leaven" would "leaveneth the whole loaf."[18] These seminars are a fine-grain illustration of what Tunstall means when he describes the way "this period provides the most unambiguous examples of American military force and political strength being used to impose media on other countries. Generals did quite literally set up newspapers, license radio stations, select certain senior personnel, and veto everyone else."[19] But the military was only a part of the matrix of institutions involved in the creation of the reorientation programs. Seminar participants were handpicked by military officers of the occupying forces, program officers from donor foundations, and senior staff of the American Press Institute. And, as we shall see, the seminars are not quite the "unambiguous examples" of American military, political, or media power that they might at first appear to be.

The story of the international reorientation seminars can be tracked in local newspapers of the cities visited by seminar participants. While local papers were fascinated by their visitors and their visitors' perception of the United States, national coverage was slim.[20] Scant coverage of the first few seminars appeared in the national press. The seminars did, however, catch the attention of trade publications like *Printer's Ink, Editor and Publisher*, and *Variety*. For example, in March 1949, *Variety* ran a very brief article on a special program to be run by Columbia University: a total of ten Asian radio broadcasters (four Koreans and six Japanese) were to be brought into the United States, provided with intensive seminars, discussion, and training in New York, and were then to travel to various local and network stations across the country.

The program announced in *Variety* was merely the tip of the iceberg. In 1947 and 1948 there was a German radio personnel project, followed closely by a German journalism project (both made up of fifteen participants).[21] In 1949 there was a radio broadcasters' project for Korean and Japanese participants, dedicated to training radio personnel. There was also a Japanese journalism project in the same year. During these early years the Rockefeller Foundation contributed over $140,000:

1947–1948	German Radio Personnel	($25,000)
	German Journalists and News Personnel	($40,246)[22]
1948–1949	Korean Radio Personnel	($21,000)
	Japanese Radio Personnel	($29,000)
	Japanese Journalists and News Personnel	($25,000)

By today's standard, the foundation's three-year contribution would be equivalent to more than $1 million. No small investment for a fledgling project.

Arguably part of what Tunstall calls the "high tide of American media," from 1943 to 1953, these early seminars were also clearly part of the U.S. postwar reconstruction strategy. World War II was a brutal war waged by totalitarian forces whose domination of their national media made communications a crucial site of reconstructive action. The state had had total control over the content, form, and technologies of communication in Germany and Japan, and the political climate in these countries had a profound impact on journalism as a profession. American anxieties—as well as those of the French and British, for that matter—hinged on how important a different system of media communication would be to denazification in Germany and demilitarization in Japan. Understood thus, it is important to note the overlap between newspaper-journalist and radio-broadcaster reorientation. The medium did not matter; the goal was to reorient news professionals, whether they worked in radio or print, to the democratic principles of a free press and the free flow of information.[23]

Under the auspices of Columbia's Bureau of Applied Social Research (BASR), Robert K. Merton and Paul F. Lazersfeld administered the radio projects.[24] BASR's pioneering research in communication studies (from consumer behavior to voting habits to radio-audience analyses) and its genealogy (having originated as the RF-funded Radio Research Project) made BASR the logical venue for the radio seminars. As Merton, who administered the Korean-Japanese broadcasting seminars, noted, the grant made by the Rockefeller Foundation in support of Columbia's training seminar for six German radio program directors was based "on the premise that mass communications can play a strategic role in furthering both intercultural relations and democratically organized society."[25] Merton's words stop far short of claiming that mass communications can mold the hearts and minds of audiences; instead, the goal was to create international understanding (more on this distinction shortly).

But the military demanded tangible results. A key player among the U.S. military personnel involved in designing the seminars was Brigadier General Robert McClure of the Civil Affairs Division of the War Department. Serving in Germany McClure wrote urgently about the lack of trained German media professionals "retarding" his division's "first objective": to establish properly licensed "competing newspapers in every city of 100,000 or over" in occupied Germany.[26] So thorough had been Hitler's subjugation of the press that Allied authorities struggled to find seasoned press personnel who did not bear the stigma of Nazism or who were young enough to have entire careers ahead of them. "There are no government funds available for training German personnel," wrote McClure in a letter to the Rockefeller's Edward F. D'Arms.[27] He turned to the Foundation for financial support and got it. McClure's persistence triggered meetings and correspondence among program officers at the Rockefeller and Ford Foundations and with elite journalists at API and the *New York Times*, discussions that brought about the stateside reorientation of international journalists for decades to come.[28]

The lockstep progression of the concurrent radio- and news-personnel seminars held at Columbia also echoes the rhizomatic development of several key institutions in the journalistic field. Whereas BASR administered radio sessions, newspaper seminars were under the direction of Carl Ackerman, dean of Columbia's School of Journalism, and conducted by Floyd Taylor and J. Montgomery Curtis at API, also housed at Columbia. API served a crucial function in the development of these seminars and others like them. Established in 1946, API was founded by American newspaper publishers for "the purpose of raising the level of the American press" by offering mid-career training programs for U.S. journalists. From the outset, API conducted "seminars covering all phases of American journalism."[29] It is interesting to note that a fledgling institution designed to serve American news professionals was mobilized in the service of the postwar reconstruction effort.

But API was not the military's first choice for the postwar reorientation seminars. There was initially much interest on the part of the Office of the Military Government, United States (OMGUS), as well as the Rockefeller Foundation's program officers, in an association with Harvard, not Columbia: "The possibility of association between the German personnel and the Nieman Fellows at Harvard seemed highly desirable to all."[30] As discussions progressed, OMGUS produced a detailed outline of what the seminar program might look like if the well-established journalism institute at Harvard undertook the project.[31] However, there was some confusion about the tenor of the army document outlining goals and outcomes; the Nieman Fellows took the inquiry as a command, not a suggestion, and balked. Responding to their anxiety with blunt clarity, the Rockefeller's John Marshall pointed out that OMGUS did not have the power to design the program; OMGUS's suggestions were to be seen as just that, suggestions. Despite this reassurance (and citing an already overextended faculty plus the difficulties of administering the program over the summer), Harvard declined the project.

This opened up an opportunity for API. Founding director Floyd Taylor and his team at Columbia were eager to take on the project, saw the army's goals as consistent with their own, considered the memo from Colonel Textor, the director of the Information Control Division in Germany, a legitimate outline, and applied for a Rockefeller grant via General Eisenhower's formal request on behalf of Columbia University, where he then served as university president.[32] Not only were they enthusiastic about the opportunity to serve the nation, they were also eager for the financial solvency foundation monies would offer API in its cash-strapped early years.[33] As one-time API director J. Montgomery Curtis recalls in his memoir, "An idealistic purpose led API to the foreign work. But there was a bonus. Floyd Taylor insisted that no money provided by U.S. newspapers should finance foreign seminars. The foundations covered in their grants API's expenses, including staff salaries. API socked salary allowances in the bank."[34]

Still, API's interests were not merely mercenary. Traces of the organization's sense of a free press as a potential tool for the development of democratic culture can be found in its early formulation of the international seminars' mission: "The first purpose of an API foreign seminar is to provide professional information helpful in building responsible, independent and economically strong newspapers—newspapers which better serve their readers and their countries."[35] In the American version of press freedom, autonomy fuses with economic security. A "free and democratic press" meant an economically solvent press, wholly free of government intervention. API's mission fit the military's agenda quite well.

Wartime collaboration between the academy and the military was certainly not a new phenomenon in the 1940s. With World War I as precedent, historians were mobilized by the War Department, linguists served as spies, and physicists continued to serve the war effort during World War II. The U.S. press also found itself in collaboration with Washington during both wars. But the postwar mobilization of professional journalism contradicts the widely held belief in American journalism's autonomy, particularly since 1945 marked a significant reversal of the profession's trend of wartime collaboration.[36] In the midst of the profession's efforts to reassert independence in the Second World War's aftermath, API brought the State Department, the U.S. Army, the U.S. Office of Education, Columbia University, the Carnegie Corporation, and the Ford and Rockefeller Foundations together in a collaborative project of training and reorienting foreign journalists.[37]

This collaborative network fostered the formation of yet another important international organization in the field of journalism, the International Press Institute (IPI). In 1950 the Rockefeller Foundation and the Carnegie Corporation supported a seminar for journalists from fourteen countries, a program that directly resulted in the creation of IPI, an institution that in turn nurtured the development of national press institutes in a number of the countries of its members—such as India, Turkey, and the Philippines—over the course of several decades. To date, IPI remains a vital professional organization for journalists across the globe. Despite IPI's international status, its early funds came primarily from U.S. foundations. The Rockefeller Foundation demonstrated an early interest in IPI, an interest picked up and extended by the Ford Foundation's International Affairs Program and its director, Shepard Stone.[38] The Ford Foundation eventually became IPI's primary funding source in an unprecedented series of grants.[39]

Thus, though Tunstall calls the decade from 1943 through 1953 "the high tide of American media," the early seminars of the late 1940s through the early 1950s are part of a much larger series of projects designed to train, reorient, and familiarize foreign broadcasters, journalists, and editors with American news practices and principles, particularly a professional (or better, a passionate) commitment to the value of a "free and democratic press," programs which extended through the 1960s and into the 1970s.[40]

Interestingly, these dates—from the aftermath of World War II through the end of the 1970s—are in synch with the decades Hallin calls American journalism's "high modern era." The dominant professional norms of American journalism—such as the rhetorical norms of objectivity and press autonomy, for example—coalesced in the years after World War II and continued to dominate the profession during the middle of the century.[41] It is a safe bet to assume that the opportunity given certain elite American journalists to host foreign journalists, articulate their own homegrown values and practices to their foreign guests, and provide these international visitors with insider access to the culture of production of American news likely helped crystallize and diffuse dominant professional norms among the Americans themselves. These postwar seminars may have been designed to influence the international participants but they had an effect on the Americans as well. For instance, articulating rhetorical norms at home yielded the unintended consequence of further ensconcing the rhetorical norm of objectivity in the American press during the era.[42] What is more, articulating these norms and imagining what amounted to a global fraternity of like-minded professionals likely stoked what must have seemed like the inevitable logic of global convergence. The so-called "high tide" of American media influenced American journalism's "high modern era"—and the belief that the "media are American" became more firmly entrenched.

MOTIVES AND METAPHORS

Despite the intricate network of grants for the reorientation of international media professionals, the institutional relationships that helped foster them, and decades-long foundation support, the Rockefeller Foundation's early and influential funding of the German and Japanese reorientation seminars is of particular interest.[43] The early foundation-funded post-war-journalist-training seminars reveal culturally held ideas about the role of the press, the role of the journalist, and the institutional arrangements involved in the tricky project of instilling democratic values in previously (and potentially) totalitarian states. As illustrated above, multiple institutions worked in concert as they strove to shape the media systems of war-torn countries in the service of a free press and the spread of democratic institutions. The nature of their interrelationship has challenged critics and historians of the era to develop an accurate descriptive language. The State Department, the occupying governments of Germany and Japan, Columbia University, and the Rockefeller Foundation were enmeshed in what might be called the academic national-security complex.[44] Olivier Zunz, on the other hand, calls relationships such as these an "institutional matrix"—a web of institutes, research universities, corporations, foundations, and government agencies, a network with roots in the early part of the twentieth century.[45] Whereas the term "complex" conjures an image of a structure built of various interrelated parts, the term "matrix" suggests the atmosphere or environment in which objects or institutions are embedded. Both metaphors work here: the seminars fit inside the institutional architecture of the postwar era, and they were simultaneously a product of this environment and its intellectual atmosphere. By deciphering the intentions of these early seminars and the institutional relationships that ensured their development, we might better apprehend the motives and tensions found in the nexus of democracy, journalism, global media flows, and postwar reconstruction.

REORIENTATION AND RECONSTRUCTION

To study the early training seminars is to study media systems during and after political and military crisis, raising the issue of media influence via reconstruction and reorientation. Throughout the letters, memos, proposals, and year-end reports, "reorienting" postwar media cultures to the functions of a "free and democratic press" became the oft-cited motive for both radio and journalism projects. But that begs the question: from what were they being oriented away and to what were they being reoriented? Granted occupation meant that the press cultures of Germany and Japan were "forcibly reshaped along Anglo-American lines" in the aftermath of the war, but their reinvention was not utter; rather, as Tunstall argues, they were "forcibly jerked back to patterns of influence which . . . derive from the nineteenth century."[46] Returning to these nineteenth-century roots meant that Germany and Japan reverted to "importing Anglo-American media products and styles."[47] Even though Tunstall rightly points to the evolution of national media systems over time, his description naturalizes the Anglo-American media model as a normative model. But, as Orwell reminds us, how we frame the past influences the way we see the present and the future. In 1945 the postwar present of Germany and Japan represented different challenges vis-à-vis reconstruction, occupation, and reorientation of their national media.

THE JAPANESE PRESS

Similar to the United States, Japan had had a longstanding press tradition, one which, from its advent, had been influenced by the British.[48] Having industrialized in the early nineteenth century, Japan "had considerably Americanized their business systems by the 1920s."[49] Despite a parallel emphasis on commercialism, the history of Japanese press autonomy is complex. The relationship between the media and the state in Japan can be summarized in four stages: first, the state encouraged the growth of the press by funding and sponsoring papers; second, the state also imposed strict censorship and police control; third, despite these regulations there was a de facto liberal attitude toward press control; then, in an era of military domination, the state exerted direct control over all means of expression.[50] By 1937, when the state imposed draconian control of the press, there was a virtual merger of the media and the state. Since the 1860s, the Japanese press moved from state sponsorship, to state control, to censorship, to its current status as a free press in an industrial democracy.[51]

As this brief overview suggests, there are two press traditions that can be traced in the history of Japanese journalism: the press was the servant of the state—especially in the 1930s and 1940s—but it also had a watchdog function as part of its legacy (a tradition that persisted in press efforts to resist censorship measures). As Pharr points out, the Allied Occupation, beginning in 1945, "carried forth both these legacies" by actively supporting the media and encouraging newspapers to reestablish themselves and by perceiving of the media as a tool to convey its own policies and foster public understanding and acceptance of these policies.[52] During the U.S. occupation of Japan, the extant Japanese press remained intact, was shifted away from the imperial-militaristic censorship of the press (a condition that had existed since the early 1900s), and placed under the double bind of an imposed democracy and the postwar censorship of the occupying forces.[53]

The paradoxical phenomenon of a "revolution from above" (the imposition of democracy on the vanquished Japanese empire), raised a series of strategic problems for the occupying forces. Postwar reconstruction highlighted the paradox of "an authoritarianism that offered the promise of democracy."[54] Led by MacArthur, the American occupying government sought to impose, nurture, and institutionalize democratic values of equality and freedom on a culture whose members saw themselves as imperial subjects, not as democratic citizens. MacArthur's forces (Supreme Command Allied Powers or SCAP) conceived of the press as a tool to effect this change from passive subject to active, engaged citizen. In the service of this belief, SCAP provided travel funds for journalists and broadcasters they selected to participate in the Rockefeller-supported API seminars at Columbia University.[55]

THE GERMAN PRESS

Like the presses of the United States and Japan, the German press had been developing throughout the late nineteenth and early twentieth centuries. However, when the Nazis seized power in 1933, they completely restructured the German media system.[56] Access to the profession was controlled; for the first time in German history a law prescribing "professional education" (defined as a year's worth of training) was implemented. By 1935 training contracts were overseen by the National Federation of the German Press, which was under the control of the minister of propaganda. As Frohlich and Holtz-Bacha (2003) note, "The young discipline, only recently established at universities, enjoyed the regime's support at the price of ideological instrumentalization."[57] The Nazis eventually set up their own school of journalism in Berlin in 1935; its courses "primarily served as ideological instruction for future journalists."[58]

It is part of common German cultural knowledge that OMGUS, and later the High Commission of Germany (HICOG), along with the three other occupying forces in Germany, were extremely influential in shaping the country's media and journalistic field.[59] But what exactly were the American occupying forces' goals? The postwar German press was in a tenuous position, and OMGUS sought to protect its status as a free press. American Press Control Officers in Germany had a clear mission:

> Because of the extreme vulnerability of the newly-licensed democratic German press to pressure from the German government and from vested interests, Press Control Officers must be continuously vigilant to guard and fortify the press' hard-won independence. In close cooperation with the Fiscal Branch of ICD, Press Control Officers at Land level will seek to reveal and correct cases of discrimination against the new press, and to help its members to become economically self-sufficient. Press Control will encourage and cooperate with associations of press publishers in order to enable them to defend the legitimate rights of an independent press.[60]

Press freedom demanded economic security and meant freedom from (German) government intervention or from pressure from powerful political parties (the "vested interests" referred to above). On the surface this excerpt is further illustration of the paradox of imposing freedom from above, but this document also outlines how the Information Control Division of OMGUS designed an apparatus to ensure the growth of democratic institutions like a free press and nurtured the professional ideal of journalistic independence and autonomy.

A passionate commitment to supposedly value-neutral ideals like press freedom was common among officials in the occupying governments and was persuasively articulated by Colonel Gordon Textor, the director of the Information Control Division in Germany. So compelled by the case Textor made, the program officers at the Rockefeller Foundation used his language verbatim in their report to their Trustees:

> German publishers here are now engaged in a fight with German governmental officials and political party leaders to force acceptance in Germany of the well-established American principle that what officials do is the business of the public and news and information about government must never be channeled through a censorship. German officials are attempting to do just that.[61]

Wary of the way German officials seemed to be compromising the progress toward a free press the postwar German media had made, Textor sketched an image of the German press as on the verge of backsliding into the familiar habits of totalitarianism and of being victimized by censorship and partisan politics. The Rockefeller Trustees were persuaded, earmarking funds to extend the Germans' stay in the United States so that they might observe the American press in action. The military and the philanthropies were tightly connected as they sought to institute and preserve a version of Anglo-American press freedom in Germany.

The seminars held in New York City were part and parcel of the larger reconstructive effort, an effort that included journalist reorientation on the ground in occupied countries. A key text in the literature on the postwar German press is Jessica Gienow-Hecht's *Transmission Impossible*, a study of the U.S. government's role in restructuring and "reorienting" the German press in the decade following World War II. She addresses the implications of the U.S. practice of training and reorienting journalists in Germany and focuses on the U.S. government's involvement in mass communications in postwar Germany.[62] She carefully explains that the military offices involved in these training efforts—as dispersed and inconsistent as they were—were directly associated with the Psychological Warfare Division.[63] Despite this association, a rigorous or consistent propaganda drive did not emerge. Noting this lack, Gienow-Hecht raises a point which might very well articulate a basic motive for the stateside reeducation of foreign journalists: "*One wonders if the transmitters of U.S. values should never be American-born. Perhaps they should preferably be natives of the target country with fairly recent exposure to U.S. culture.*"[64] With this last-minute aside, Gienow-Hecht points to the niche the story of stateside postwar press seminars fills. The New York seminars sought the reorientation of foreign broadcasters by exposing them to the beliefs and lived practices of U.S. news professionals. The seminars helped spread a faith in the mission of a free and democratic press, creating an international network of news practitioners who would return home and "transmit" an understanding of American culture and American journalism's values perhaps more efficiently than Americans could themselves.

PROPAGANDA WORRIES

Whereas foreign participants in the seminars held in the late 1950s and 1960s were regularly interviewed by local media in the United States, German members of the first seminars were not allowed to speak to the press. Yet some of them were approached by the U.S. press and accepted fees for radio and newspaper work, to the chagrin of API.[65] The practice was stopped immediately. Technically, the members of the first group of visit-ing Germans were considered "enemy aliens" during their U.S. stay. Swiftly silenced stateside the Germans were nonetheless encouraged to write about their experiences upon their return home. They wrote letters of thanks and praise to the foundations, claiming a genuine understanding of Ameri-can culture, an understanding, many promised, that would influence the way they covered America in their presses at home.[66] Strident boundaries around opportunities to communicate imposed on the early international seminar participants allude to the era's core anxieties regarding communi-cation and propaganda.

The field of communications research, a field in whose development the Rockefeller Foundation played a major role, formed the intellectual backdrop of the impulse to reorient media professionals from Japan and Germany in the wake of World War II.[67] Influenced by World War I and World War II, communications research took shape around questions of propaganda, mass persuasion, and the role of the mass media. The foreign-journalist-training programs under consideration here are directly related to the development of this academic field not only at the level of shared concerns and issues but also in terms of the presence of key individuals and the development of key institutions.

According to historian Brett Gary, the Rockefeller Foundation's John Marshall, along with other "key players . . . from diverse fields and institu-tions, including journalism, philosophy, the social sciences, mass commu-nications research, philanthropy, law, literature, and government service" helped build the "backbone of the United States' propaganda defense," an ideological infrastructure, I would argue, that framed the conception of the training seminars under consideration here:

> Long before it was clear that the United States would be a belligerent in WWII, John Marshall recognized that communications research was essential for national security purposes and that the Roosevelt administration was un-equipped and politically indisposed to carry out that work. Marshall combined the Rockefeller Foundation's concerns about science and public obligation to give direction to the incipient field of mass communications.[68]

Gary's history of the development of the communications field re-counts the strategies devised and deployed by academics, private founda-tions, and the U.S. government to thwart the perceived threat of foreign propaganda techniques—what he calls a "propaganda prophylaxis." One such strategy was the use of private monies to support and develop seminars designed to bring together the brightest minds in the field of communications research. The Communications Group (or the Com-munications Research Seminar), founded and funded by the Rockefeller Foundation, embodied the kind of interpenetration of private monies, universities, and theories of the public that marked the first part of the twentieth century and the developing field of communications research.[69] Noting the neglected role of the Rockefeller Foundation's John Marshall in the "intellectual and institutional history of U.S. mass communications research," Gary describes the way Marshall brought together a cadre of communications scholars in a monthly seminar.

The meetings and exchanges of the Communications Group contributed to the study of media effects in several ways: from the "who said what to whom?" model of media effects to, with the advent of World War II, research into the relationship among propaganda, communication, national security, and the role of experts.[70] "From its outset," writes Gary, "the Communications Seminar was decidedly interventionist and policy oriented, and its purposes were clearly shaped by Marshall's perceptions of the Rockefeller Foundation's social responsibilities."[71] But their ideas and recommendations were also marked by "a deep intellectual and ideological ambivalence about democratic and authoritarian implications of their applied social science orientation."[72] The postwar reorientation seminars of foreign media professionals operationalized the ideas—and the anxieties—of the Communications Group.

The rhetoric of the grant proposals and memoranda reveals an earnest impulse to deliver humanitarian aid to countries affected by the war, as well as emerging anxieties regarding propaganda and cultural imperialism. The American fear of empire manifested itself in antifascism and anticommunism. But "cultural imperialism" was a slippery term. The grant proposals and correspondences housed at the Rockefeller Archive Center—written by John Marshall, Charles B. Fahs, Edward F. D'Arms, and Floyd Taylor, as well as key players in the U.S. Army and at Columbia University—present a kaleidoscopic range of concerns: denazification, propaganda worries, and an explicit humanitarian impulse shifted into anxieties about the appearance of indoctrination and cultural imperialism. This nexus of concerns suggests the unsteady embrace of national security and liberal democracy.

In conceiving of the role of the journalist and the function of news coverage and the press, program coordinators and grants officers seem to have been engaged in conceptualizing national journalistic fields and, arguably, imagining, shaping, and conceiving of a global journalistic field as well. The seminars were a means to institute enduring democratic values via the spread of the seemingly value-neutral rhetoric of journalistic professionalism among potentially influential international journalists. But it is important to note the care with which the foreign news and radio personnel seminars crafted their message. Responding to the lengthy description put together by API's Floyd Taylor of the Japanese journalism project and its pedagogy, Fahs of the Rockefeller Foundation writes, "My hunch would be that the better psychological approach is to consider the project as a means by which American newspaper men and Japanese newspaper men may discuss common problems, rather than a means by which the former may teach the latter."[73] The Rockefeller Foundation and Columbia University sought to foster a culture of exchange and empathy, partly because Japan had an advanced commercial newspaper system but also because the Americans did not want to alienate sophisticated European journalists with a didactic or dismissive emphasis on American superiority. Foreign participants, perceived to be (potential) victims of totalitarian states, were brought to the United States and encouraged—via seminars and tours, social networking, and insider access—to feel into the American journalist's professional and cultural position. The one-time "enemy other," or the potential cold war pawn, was encouraged to empathize with his American professional counterpart. The "best psychological approach" for "reorientation" would cultivate an atmosphere of engaged debate and discussion among professionals.

The archival record of the German journalism project depicts similarly complex impulses. In a letter to John Marshall, API's Floyd Taylor describes the outline for a program that will focus on the "function of the press in a democratic society," and writes an itemized list of goals, which includes, "#7. We should do our utmost to avoid the appearance of blatant indoctrination or of what is sometimes called 'cultural imperialism.'"[74] The self-consciousness with which the seminars were planned is compelling, and this reference to "cultural imperialism" is particularly interesting; it sheds light on the development of the discourse of cultural imperialism during an important historical moment when the term was used as a loaded catchphrase rather than a consolidated theory critical of modernization. But in his effort to distance the project from taint of cultural imperialism and indoctrination, Taylor tips his hand; even though he does not describe API's international work as "media imperialism," Taylor enacts a belief in media power by disavowing cultural imperialism. He implies that mass media bear weighty cultural significance. A free press staffed by passionate advocates of press freedom and objectivity would buttress fledgling liberal democratic institutions and nurture democratic civil society in postwar Germany and Japan.

Hence Merton's comments in reference to the BASR-administered radio reorientation seminars cited in the section above, where he emphasized "intercultural relations" as opposed to explicit propaganda, bear further consideration here. Merton's position must be understood in light of the intellectual debate about audiences and their capacities unfolding in the young field of communications research. For example, Paul F. Lazarsfeld, director of BASR and Merton's close colleague, was one of the regular members of the Rockefeller Communications Group. In the years before World War II, Lazarsfeld, along with other members of the group, were skeptical of the supposedly unlimited power of propaganda. In the postwar years, their skepticism crystallized in the "limited effects" thesis. As articulated by Katz and Lazarsfeld, the argument held that individuals were less susceptible to media influence than intuitive folk wisdom or European theorists charged.[75] Countering the twin beliefs that the media were either all-powerful and malevolent or all-powerful and able to trigger a "new dawn for democracy," Katz and Lazarsfeld tempered such rhetoric with a more rational, scientific appraisal.[76] Merton had been thinking along similar lines and had written about obstinate audiences and the difficulties of mass persuasion as early as 1943.[77] Thus, it makes sense that Merton would emphasize "intercultural relations"—international understanding—not an injection of pro-American propaganda or a magic bullet approach to the project of reorienting international communicators.

In lieu of disseminating propagandistic pro-American content, the journalism seminars emphasized the discussion of common problems among professionals; in short, they were designed to foster empathy among international professionals. This strategy contributed to both intra- and international understanding. One effect of the seminars was mutual understanding among foreign visitors themselves; a second was interaction with and understanding of their American counterparts. For example, as one of the participants in the German seminars reported to the program officers of the Rockefeller foundation, "One of the most potentially valuable parts of the program [is] the fact that most of the Germans had not known each other in Germany and now have the opportunity of becoming acquainted and exchanging ideas. Furthermore, it is believed that they will be able to work out a program of action and continued contact after their return to Germany."[78] Seminar-forged friendships helped create an informal international network of like-minded news professionals; such connections would ensure national and international interpretive communities (or, for that matter, "primary groups") with which individual journalists would feel a strong affiliation. As IPI's director E. J. Rose wrote some years later, describing similar seminars then held in Europe, "Something magical has taken place on these occasions which never ceases to astonish me. Those taking part almost forget that they are nationals of different countries and feel bound to one another by the fellowship of their common profession."[79]

HABITUS AND HEGEMONY

Rose's delight in the budding sense of fraternity he saw among participating journalists masks the deeper logic of media-training seminars such as these—the relationship between habitus and hegemony. Questions of cultural domination are often actually questions of structure and agency and critical social theory offers a rich vocabulary for the nuances and shadings of the perceived power of social actors and social structures. Habitus, for example, as Pierre Bourdieu deploys it, signals the "orchestrated improvisation of common dispositions," the regulated improvization experienced by social actors in their specific social settings.[80] But Bourdieu's theory wears its structuralism with a difference. What feels most natural, most original—as improvised as a conversation, for example, or a choice of wine with dinner—is in fact the result of social forces (education, class, family background, etc.) that limit the range of possibilities.

The enduring dispositions of social actors, the beliefs and actions that keep them engaged in the game of the dominant ideology, the dominant culture, reproducing those values via their actions and interactions—this is an apt description of hegemony. Todd Gitlin explains Gramsci's concept by pointing out that "hegemony operates through a complex web of social activities and institutional procedures. Hegemony is done by the dominant and collaborated in by the dominated."[81] Social theorists and historians writing about the role of foundations in spreading American cultural values abroad, however, tend to use the concept of hegemony with a heavy hand.[82] In this literature, the term "hegemony" has often been used synonymously with explicit and intentional cultural domination.

David Altheide's critique of the media-hegemony perspective is thus instructive. He argues that, despite some basic shared values and norms, "Journalists are not uniformly socialized into the dominant ideology, nor are most elite journalists supportive of conservative values and ideology."[83] Media hegemonists would argue the opposite. But what of the Rockefeller-funded seminars? They seem to confirm one of the basic assumptions held by media-hegemony theorists about the "socialization and ideology of journalists."[84] But the subtleties of reeducation projects built around the paradoxical mission of distancing themselves from cultural imperialism, while spreading a faith in the value of a free press, demand a more nuanced description. The seminars do not wholly undermine Altheide's position; they suggest the complex relationship between habitus and hegemony—a connection based on difference.

Citing Golding and Murdoch, Altheide claims that media hegemonists "contend that the work routines and bureaucratic procedures used by journalists are imbued with implicit and explicit ideological referents which consistently lead to the production of messages emphasizing particular norms, values, and sanctions."[85] Does the dominant ideology "sufficiently influence" work routines as to "negate any journalistic independence"?[86] Altheide calls this the "critical question"; but this question reifies the term "dominant ideology" as if it were a thing that exists outside of individuals, a tool used to coerce consent. Further, the question is in keeping with a use of the term "hegemony," which implies that hegemony is a special "extra" process of securing compliance. Such use suggests that hegemony is at least largely the result of intentional projects to achieve it. Bourdieu, for example, would not deny that elite projects that try to shape dominant culture exist, and thereby secure compliance with unequal social orders, but he would argue that these self-conscious projects were only part of the way in which domination is achieved.[87]

The institutional matrix comprised of philanthropic foundations, the U.S. military, the academy, news professionals, and professional news organizations suggests the "complex web" in which individual social actors are always already caught. Postwar political consensus helped to rationalize the coordinated efforts of key institutions so that key members could serve the nation's goals and simultaneously claim their autonomy from the state. Despite their explicit agenda to reorient international journalists, the seminars reveal the fluidity of consensus among institutions.

As outlined in the grant proposal to the Rockefeller Foundation, the Foundation and MacArthur's forces shared common goals. The Civil Information and Education Section of the Supreme Command Allied Powers described the expectations of the Japanese program this way:

> Whatever the details of the program, it would be hoped that members of the group would return to Japan with:
>
> 1. Heightened professional self-consciousness, enabling them to perceive, analyze and stimulate action on the problem of Japanese journalism.
> 2. Appreciation of why, even in a democracy like the United States, it is imperative for the press to be vigilant against encroachments on its freedom by all levels of government and private pressure groups.
> 3. Realization that beneath the many variations in the attitudes and techniques of American newspapers and despite aberrations of a few newspapers there is a substantial body of principles and practices, still in evolution, worthy of adoption or adaptation in Japan.[88]

The military framed American journalism as an evolving institution in flux which nonetheless has "a substantial body of principles and practices" deemed "worthy of adoption or adaptation." Postwar journalistic professionalism was seen as a legitimate tool in the reconstruction process. And, as the second item notes, press freedom is understood to be freedom from government intervention and from "private pressure groups." The excerpt illustrates the way the seminars' goals—regardless of the "details" of their daily agenda—explicitly yoked "professional self-consciousness" with the vigilant preservation of press freedom.

Thus the seminars render several valences of habitus legible. For instance, American program officers, news professionals, and military personnel shared certain enduring dispositions that helped unify their sense of purpose and their belief in the potential of a free press to be the architect of democracy abroad. Their professional habitus thus shaped the way they responded to the postwar challenge of media reconstruction. Their professional habitus led them to imagine the spread of American journalism's professional ethos as an efficient reconstructive strategy. That is to say they believed that the best approach to securing faith in a free press was to spread the professional ethos associated with one: discussion, rational debate, the free flow of information, and the rhetorical norm of objectivity. Seen this way, the seminars are a fascinating attempt by certain cultural elites from a range of interrelated institutions to spread a particular cultural and professional habitus.

Media-training programs have long preoccupied media scholars. Peter Golding, for example, critiqued the way training and professionalization fit into larger patterns of domination and social control in the context of the expansion of American media.[89] Based on his assessment of the way the national media of developing nations was derivative of advanced industrialized nations, Golding claims that media professionalism should not be understood outside of the "context of cultural dependence, of the ways in which professionalism ensures the reproduction of institutions and practices from the advanced industrial societies."[90] With a focus on training programs in England and France for media professionals from less developed nations, Golding notes that "large numbers of students from the Third World come to study in industrialized nations. Those that return take with them not only skills, but values and attitudes, and not least a receptivity to the men and the machines they have learned to work with."[91] These "values and attitudes" can be read as the durable dispositions Bourdieu had in mind when he wrote of habitus.[92]

If "professionalization," as Golding argues, is understood "as the acquisition not merely of competence, but also of values and attitudes thought appropriate to the implementation of media skills," his claims echo the dilemmas of the post–World War II era.[93] Decades earlier than Golding's study, the Occupying Authorities in Germany and Japan saw a definite need for trained personnel in the press and broadcast fields. OMGUS was involved in restructuring the presses in these countries so that they would be less centralized, encouraging objectivity and an absence of apparent propaganda. Between the intervention of the occupying forces in the culture of media production in key cities abroad and the training of international journalists in the states, a system was designed that was favorable to the transfer of liberal values and the occupational ideologies of American news coverage.[94]

Compared to the training programs for Africans Golding considers, the postwar reorientation seminars possessed the same potential as conduits for skills, values, attitudes, and receptivity. With their two-week stay in

New York City, and their one-on-one interaction with local newspaper operations and broadcast stations throughout the country, postwar foreign-media professionals experienced American news making—and American life—firsthand.[95] In important ways the seminars soldered cultural under-standing with professional empathy and, perhaps more important, fused discussion with desire.[96] For visiting Germans and Japanese, American wealth and consumer largesse must have appeared otherworldly and con-firmed the authority of American abundance. For Americans, victory and economic well-being helped consolidate a pluralist vision that celebrated the average citizen's individual self-realization, democratic political institu-tions, and mass-scale consumer culture. Prosperity and freedom existed in a mutually reinforcing embrace. Along with the empirical fact of America's postwar dominance, a presumption of media power derived from U.S. victory, prosperity, and a vision of progress that suffused projects like the reorientation programs funded by the Rockefeller Foundation.

This vision of progress is part and parcel of modernization theory, the dominant paradigm haunting the postwar institutional matrix, or military-academic complex. Without denying the privileged place assumed by the United States, modernization theorists nonetheless denied anything uniquely American or European in the notion of progress; it was instead a move away from magical-religious social frameworks toward rational, economically-driven arrangements. As Ron Robin notes,

> Given the ability to develop without artificial hindrance—the intervention of subversive, foreign ideologies such as communism, for example—moderniza-tion theorists assumed that all societies would eventually converge toward a singular modular format.[97]

Modernization theorists claimed convergence as progress rather than the spread of ideology. And Anglo-American journalism—with its rhetorical norms of objectivity and autonomy—served as a technique of moderniza-tion. American journalists were mobilized in the postwar era to present, debate, and discuss their practices with handpicked international journal-ists. The seemingly value-free conventions of their professional ethos, along with the seemingly transparent technologies of mass communication them-selves, contributed to the capacity of those engaged in reconstructive efforts to reject the notion that they were "indoctrinating" postwar cultures.

By the mid-1970s modernization theory was deemed suspect by critics like Schiller, Golding, and Tunstall, who considered it an excuse for cul-tural domination. Nonetheless, the seeming rupture in the 1970s between modernization theory and its critique, the cultural-imperialism thesis, can be reread as a continuity of ideas about media power. The two sides of the debate about American media hegemony—champions of modernization as opposed to critics of cultural imperialism—can be traced in the archival record of the grants to support international-journalist-reorientation seminars. Even as the seminar designers sought to distance themselves from the appearance of cultural imperialism, they arguably enacted a version of media imperialism by intervening in the development of media cultures of vanquished nations and engaging in a global project to create a relatively tightly socialized professional community. This paradox reveals the underlying anxieties provoked by the complicated project of imposing liberal democratic institutions on postwar cultures.

CONCLUSION: CONVERGENCE AND ITS DISCONTENTS

In 1941 Henry Luce penned "The American Century," urging his readers to abandon their isolationism and "export democratic principles throughout the world."[98] The Rockefeller-funded international-journalist-reorientation seminars seem to perform that mission. If, in the aftermath of World War II, Americans believed that a free press would build strong democratic institutions at home and abroad, then these seminars, their designers, advocates, and participants are the early inadvertent architects of the belief in the natural dominance of liberal media values on the global stage. The early seminars—as well as those of the 1950s and 1960s—helped disseminate the values of the liberal-media model by circulating the language of the free flow of information, objectivity, and an independent press among the world's media professionals. Inside the United States and out, media professionals were encouraged to believe that the free flow of information and the professional norms of a free press would ensure worldwide peace and prosperity. The spread of such discourse did not necessarily cause the mid-century homogeneity of global media patterns and practices, but it certainly helped create the sense of a shared professional value system among press practitioners worldwide. What flourished was the way media professionals talked about their practices.

Over the course of the twentieth century, liberal media principles have become increasingly hegemonic.[99] Granted many of the Western world's national news cultures share an intellectual heritage that includes Enlightenment values of rationality, values that led to a belief in a marketplace of ideas, a free press, and, arguably, the ideal of objectivity, but that does not mean that all countries "do" news in the same fashion.[100] As recent work in comparative media studies has shown, particular press practices in various news cultures contradict their practitioners' expressed values. While newsmakers from other nations preach their faith in the principle of an independent press and the ideal of objectivity, their practices have been shown to challenge, if not contradict, traditional notions of these values, revealing, for instance, a different understanding of the concept of objectivity.[101] Yet, despite this seeming disconnect between belief and practice, the fact remains that the discourse of the values of openness, the free flow of information, and the rhetorical norm of objectivity circulate among professional journalists across nations.

But the disconnect between belief and practice can also be seen in the United States. As recent controversies in American news making indicate, the news values expressed by U.S. audiences and journalists seem out of synch with news-making practice. Evidence of this disconnect can be seen in the travesty of Jayson Blair's stint at the *New York Times* or the Judith Miller debacle. To illustrate the U.S. predicament, consider, for example, the case of Al Jazeera, as presented in the recent documentary film *Control Room*.

Banned in several Arab countries because of its critique of their regimes, and described as "the mouthpiece of Bin Laden" by the Bush administration, the popular and controversial Arab satellite network sees its work as fundamentally democratic. According to Senior Producer Samir Khader,

> The job of Al Jazeera is first of all educational, to educate the Arab masses on something called democracy, respect of the other opinion, the free debate, really free debate, no taboos, everything should be dealt with intelligently, with openness, and to try, using all of these things, to shake up these rigid societies.[102]

Khader's comments uncannily echo not only the rhetoric of the 1940s-era crusade for the free flow of information but also the expressed motives of the postwar seminars.[103]

But when Al Jazeera broadcast images of American POWs captured by Iraqis, as well as dead U.S. soldiers behind Iraqi lines, the network drew the ire of the Bush administration and world news outlets. Asked to defend the network's policy of releasing such images, to explain whether Al Jazeera's journalists are "capable of being objective" since "they have an opinion about the war," Joanne Tucker, manager of Al Jazeera.net, responds

> Are any U.S. journalists objective about this war? Are any of the news broadcasts that I tune into not taking a position? . . . I'm just trying to show this word objectivity is almost a mirage. If there was true neutrality there would be a welcoming of any and all information from all sides.[104]

Tucker uses the language of Anglo-American journalism's rhetorical norms—objectivity and openness. She invokes the core of the liberal media model's professional ethos. Objectivity and the free flow of information are the shimmering ideal, but such things are verboten when they expose facts that run counter to a nation's interests or idea of itself.

In light of the history of post–World War II training seminars and the present global diffusion of American concepts of press freedom and journalistic professionalization, news outlets like Al Jazeera offer us a deeper understanding of the consequences of perceived media homogeneity, not to mention the utopian potential of comparative media studies. Convergence does not merely describe the erasure of difference, of the growing and fundamental similarities among media systems, it is a process that also has the potential to reveal *differences*.

Perhaps the message the seminars of the late 1940s send to the future is this: the dissemination of American values on a global scale should force reflexive self-conscious comparison. By listening to an "enemy other" discuss news values and practices, we might achieve the mutual understanding that Merton, Lazarsfeld, Marshall, and others imagined. Such understanding might prompt U.S. press practitioners to interrogate the present disconnect between their own beliefs and practices; then, perhaps, media convergence might yield media reform. Or, better yet, such understanding might foster peace.

NOTES

Unpublished material in this chapter has been quoted courtesy of the Rockefeller Archive Center, Sleepy Hollow, New York, and of the Ford Foundation Archives, New York City.

1. Jeremy Tunstall, *The Media Are American* (London: Constable, 1977), 19.

2. See, for example, Sean MacBride, *Many Voices, One World: Report by the International Commission for the Study of Communication Problems* (Paris: UNESCO, 1980). The MacBride report famously called for democratization of media, critiqued the concentration of media ownership, and argued for strengthened national medias in lieu of dependence from outside sources. The Americans and the British were not happy with its findings and withdrew from UNESCO in protest. The MacBride report was also known by its title "*Many Voices, One World.*"

3. For an overview of the relationship between cultural imperialism and media imperialism see John Tomlinson, *Cultural Imperialism: A Critical Introduction* (Baltimore: Johns Hopkins University Press, 1991). See also Herbert I. Schiller, *Communication and Cultural Domination* (White Plains, NY: International Arts & Sciences Press, 1976); Fred Fejes, "Media Imperialism: An Assessment," in *Media, Culture and Society* 3, no. 3 (1981): 281–89; and Chin Chuan Lee, *Media Imperialism Reconsidered* (Beverly Hills: Sage, 1979).

4. I do not refer to the twenty-first century notion of "convergence theory," which describes how distinct mass media will converge to become one medium due to the advent of new technologies. I use the term "convergence" as comparative media scholars tend to use the term, as a synonym for the homogeneity of national media patterns, models, and practices.

5. Media scholars have since noted the limitations of Tunstall's claim that American media patterns have been copied by the rest of the world. Advocates of the

media imperialism thesis, like Tunstall, fail to imagine the fine-grain particularities of the way media cultures appropriate, ignore, adapt, adopt, and transform hegemonic Western media practices. In fact, Tunstall himself has since refined his argument. See Tunstall's recent *The Media Were American* (New York: Oxford University Press, 2007) where he accounts for the massive changes in global media during the last four decades and makes the case for the reemergence of stronger national media systems and a world media structure comprised of interlocking cultural, regional, and national systems. Nonetheless, the seriousness with which his original ideas were initially met warrants our attention.

6. The debate about the degree to which "the media are American" continues. In their *Comparing Media Systems: Three Models of Media and Politics* (Cambridge: Cambridge University Press, 2004), Daniel C. Hallin and Paolo Mancini not only illustrate the empirical limitations of the classic *Four Theories of the Press* thesis, they revise Tunstall's claim: yes, most Western media are "American," but only partially. The Anglo liberal-media model triumphed in the West, but not solely because of media or cultural imperialism. The authors instead credit a range of diverse factors—from commercialization, technology, and the gap between political parties and the media, to the dominance of the United States in the production of information.

7. For accounts of MNC and corporate ownership see Robert McChesney, *Rich Media. Poor Democracy* (Urbana: University of Illinois Press, 1999); Ben Bagdikian, *The Media Monopoly* (Boston: Beacon, 1983); Noam Chomsky and Edward S. Herman, *Manufacturing Consent: The Political Economy of the Mass Media* (New York: Pantheon, 1988); and Schiller, *Communication and Cultural Domination*. Regarding noncorporate funding, see Margaret Blanchard's *Exporting the First Amendment. The Press-Government Crusade of 1945–1952* (New York: Longman, 1986), which focuses on the free-press crusades of the postwar era by tracing its roots back to earlier decades. Further, in *Foundations and Public Policy: The Mask of Pluralism* (Albany: SUNY Press, 2003), Joan Roelofs writes about philanthropies and NGOs. Regarding university influence in the postwar intellectual milieu see Christopher Simpson, ed., *Universities and Empire. Money and Politics in the Social Sciences During the Cold War* (New York: New Press, 1998).

8. See Michael Schudson, *Discovering the News. A Social History of American Newspapers* (New York: Basic Books, 1978), and his later text, *The Sociology of the News* (New York: W. W. Norton, 2003). See also Daniel Hallin, "The Passing of the 'High Modernism' of American Journalism," *Journal of Communication* 42, no. 3 (1992): 14–25.

9. Daniel C. Hallin, *We Keep America on Top of the World: Television Journalism and the Public Sphere* (London: Routledge, 1994), 172.

10. See Daniel C. Hallin, "The Passing of the 'High Modernism' of American Journalism Revisited," *Political Communication Report of the International Communication Association & American Political Science Association* 16, no. 1 (Winter 2006) http://frank.mtsu.edu/~pcr/1601_2005_winter/commentary_hallin.htm (accessed October 23, 2008), in which he writes: "These conditions had to do in part with specific political economy of media industries in this period which reduced commercial pressures and allowed professional autonomy and the ethic of social responsibility to prosper."

11. Tunstall, *The Media Are American*, 141.

12. Materials at the Rockefeller Archive Center (hereafter RAC) and at the Ford Foundation Archives (hereafter FF) form the basis of this research. At the RAC see RAC, RF, RG 1.2, Series 625 R for the Japanese seminars and RAC, RF, RG 1.2, Series 717R for the German seminars. The materials at the Ford Foundation Archives include files for Grant 0560–0013, Grant 60–164, and Grant 58–121 (hereafter 0560–0013, 60–164, 58–121).

13. Blanchard, *Exporting the First Amendment*, 17. Whereas the UN was not ready to consider any fundamental press freedoms until 1946, which saw the first General Conference of UNESCO, the United States was taking steps. Note, for example, that the U.S. State Department partially funded the reorientation seminars under consideration here with grants to cover the overseas travel of seminar participants.

14. Hallin and Mancini, *Comparing Media Systems*, 256.

15. Hallin and Mancini, *Comparing Media Systems*, 256.

16. In fact, neither Roelofs (*Foundations and Public Policy*) nor Hallin and Mancini (*Comparing Media Systems*) specifically refer to these seminars even as they discuss the "crusades" for a free press, the increasing hegemony of American news values, and the spread of the liberal model respectively. However, Blanchard (*Exporting the First Amendment*) does, in fact, briefly reference these seminars when she refers to the history of the American Press Institute and the International Press Institute.

17. Carl Ackerman, for example, not only served as dean of Columbia's School of Journalism in the 1940s, he was a member of the American Society of Newspaper Editors (ASNE) and was directly involved in the free press crusade. In 1944 ASNE, the Associated Press, and United Press International, sent a delegation of U.S. press representatives abroad on a global expedition to spread the message of international press freedom to friendly capitals. Ackerman, like many of his contemporaries, believed in the direct relationship between freedom of the press and peace between nations. By 1947 Ackerman helped direct the German journalist-training program. Less than two years after ASNE's expedition the Columbia projects invert this structure, bringing delegations of foreign broadcasters and journalists into the country; even though the pattern is inverted, the result—the spread of the doctrine of a free press and the free flow of information—is the same.

18. The Trustees Bulletin, 1 April, 1949. RAC, RF 1.2, Series 717R, Box 11, Folder 116.

19. Tunstall, *The Media Are American*, 137.

20. The Ford, Rockefeller, and API archives are replete with clippings for each of the programs from participating papers. All years are covered. However, a ProQuest search of historical archives of the *New York Times*, *New York Tribune*, *Christian Science Monitor*, and *Washington Post*, for instance, yielded less than twenty articles for the period from 1945 to 1995.

21. All references to the German Radio Project are from the German Journalists grant file: RAC, RF, RG 1.2, Series 717R, Box 11, Folder 114. However, the project was clearly distinct and independent from the journalism project as it is separately referenced in the annual report and minutes, which lists the $25,000 grant.

22. The original grant (RF 48079) was for the sum of $36,246. A request for an extra $4,000 grant-in-aid was made (RF 47141) so that the German journalists could spend an extra two weeks in the United States in order make professional

connections and see the country. This extended stay became part of the fundamental design of the seminar programs from then on.

23. In "Americanization, Globalization and Secularization: Understanding the Convergence of Media Systems and Political Communication in the U.S. and Western Europe," in *Comparing Political Communication. Theories, Cases, and Challenges*, eds. Frank Esser and Barbara Pfestch (Cambridge: Cambridge University Press, 2004), 25–45, Dan Hallin and Paolo Mancini write: "American concepts of journalistic professionalism and press freedom based in privately owned media, for example, were actively spread by the government-sponsored free press crusade of the early Cold War period . . . and reinforced in later years by a variety of cultural influences, ranging from professional education and academic research in U.S. universities and private research institutes."

24. See RAC, RF, RG 1.2, Series 717R, Box 11, Folder 114.

25. Robert Merton to Provost Albert C. Jacobs, Columbia University, 28 December, 1948. RAC, RF, RG 1.2, Series 717R, Box 11, Folder 114.

26. Goals are outlined in "Excerpt from Information Control Functional Program dated 19 April, 1947." The document describes the proposed support and scrutiny of DENA, the licensed German News Agency: "Press Control will encourage and cooperate with associations of press publishers in order to enable them to defend the legitimate right of the independent press." RAC, RF, RG 1.2, Series 717R, Box 11, Folder 114.

27. Brigadier General Robert McClure, Civil Affairs Division, War Department, to Edward F. D'Arms, 12 January, 1948. RAC, RF, RG 1.2, Series 717R, Box 11, Folder 114. It is important to note that by the late 1950s, Charles B. Fahs served as director of humanities at the Rockefeller Foundation and played a pivotal role in funding initiatives for foreign journalists from 1955 to 1960. Fahs "originated the five-year series after testing the idea with earlier seminars" from the dedication page of the "report on Two Seminars for Asian Journalists, 1957–1958." FF 56–0013, Section 3.

28. As noted in the grant overview, "The present proposal has been developed with the advice of Mr. Shepard Stone of the *New York Times*, and inquiries by Mr. Stone and General McClure give assurances of the interest of American newspaper publishers and of their willingness to receive these German journalists for observation and experience in their offices." RAC, RF, RG 1.2, Series 717R, Box 11, Folder 114. Stone went on to serve as director of the International Affairs Program at the Ford Foundation where he continued to support international journalist training programs.

29. From a memo titled "International Programs, International Affairs: Columbia University and the American Press Institute." FF, 56–0013, Section 1.

30. Excerpt for Interview-EFD and DHS with McClure and Richard Condon 12/11/47. RAC, RF, RG 1.2, Series 717R, Box 11, Folder 114.

31. See Textor's suggestions. RAC, RF, RG 1.2, Series 717R, Box 11, Folder 114.

32. There was only one hitch. API's founding director, Floyd Taylor, was reluctant to set up the part of the proposed project that would put visitors to work for the presses. John Marshall called a meeting with Stone (who was currently at the *New York Times*) and McClure, who both agreed with Marshall that such direct experience of American journalism would be vital to the success of the program, and they decided that Stone would "discuss the matter" with Taylor. Taylor was persuaded,

and this component of the program was included ever after. John Marshall (hereafter JM) Interview with Stone and McClure, 1 June, 1948. RAC, RF, RG, 1.2, Series 717R, Box 11, Folder 114.

33. API was founded with an initial $250,000 raised by Sevellon Brown from colleagues and associates (among them Arthur Hays Sulzberger, Joseph Pulitzer, and thirty-six others). No official record of start-up monies raised exists. See J. Montgomery Curtis, *API: A Personal Remembrance* (Reston, VA: API, 1980), 5–6.

34. Curtis, *API*, 47.

35. From page 5 of the grant proposal report. Ford Foundation Grant 60–164, Sec. 3.

36. For a more detailed account see, for example, Tunstall, *The Media Are American*, 224.

37. The 1948 German journalist seminar was the first foreign press personnel seminar held by API. By 1951 API had conducted four seminars for journalists from Germany, three for Japanese journalists, and one for Southeast Asian journalists. J. Montgomery Curtis to Shepard Stone, 26 September, 1955. FF, 0560–0013, Section 1. These seminars were supported by grants from the Rockefeller Foundation, the Carnegie Corporation, the U.S. Department of State, the U.S. Army, and the U.S Office of Education. (See the attachment to Curtis's letter to Stone, 26 September, 1955. FF, 0560–0013, Section 1.)

38. For a thorough discussion of Shepard Stone's pivotal role in postwar Germany and at the Ford Foundation see Volker R. Berghahn, *America and the Intellectual Cold Wars in Europe* (Princeton, NJ: Princeton University Press, 2001).

39. From 1955 through 1960, for example, the Rockefeller Foundation and the Ford Foundation jointly funded a series of five seminars for foreign journalists from Latin America and Asia. Such collaborative funding also occurred throughout the 1960s. See, for example, FF, 60–164, Section 3. See especially the following correspondence: John A. Krout, Vice-President of Columbia University, to Shepard Stone on March 8, 1960: "It is requested that funds for the first five seminars be provided 60 per cent by The Ford Foundation and 40 per cent by the Rockefeller Foundation. Funds for the sixth seminar, for European journalists, are sought from the Ford Foundation without participation by The Rockefeller Foundation."

40. Attachment to Inter-office memo from Moselle Kimbler to Swearer, 28 October, 1969. FF, 60–164, Section 4.

41. See Schudson, *Discovering the News* and *The Sociology of the News*, also "The Objectivity Norm in American Journalism," *Journalism* 2, no. 2 (August 2001): 149–70. See also Hallin, "The Passing of the 'High Modernism' of American Journalism."

42. See Schudson, "The Objectivity Norm."

43. My research has shown that the Ford Foundation not only collaborated with the Rockefeller Foundation, providing API with added support, but went on to fund API and IPI international seminars until the 1970s. Shepard Stone, director of the Ford Foundation's International Affairs Program, was a staunch advocate of seminars such as these.

44. See Simpson, *Universities and Empire.*

45. Olivier Zunz, *Why the American Century?* (Chicago: University of Chicago Press, 1998).

46. Tunstall, *The Media are American*, 145. There were notable differences between the media cultures of occupied Germany and occupied Japan. Vanquished Germany was divided among the Allied victors in 1945. British, French, American, and Soviet troops occupied different regions of the country. In Japan the Allied Occupation forces were solely American. This difference is important for several reasons, not the least of which is that the postwar occupied German press reflected the full range of media models of the occupying forces, with American-run papers competing with other Allied presses and occupied German papers. This diversity was not the case for Japan.

47. Tunstall, *The Media are American*, 164.

48. See Tunstall, *The Media are American*, 147; see also Grace Fox, *Britain and Japan, 1858–1883* (Oxford: Clarendon Press, 1969).

49. Zunz, *Why the American Century?* 163.

50. See Susan Pharr, "Media and Politics in Japan: Historical and Contemporary Perspectives," in *Media and Politics in Japan*, eds. Susan J. Pharr and Ellis Krauss (Honolulu: University of Hawaii Press, 1996), 11.

51. Occupied until 1952, the Japanese media system ultimately emerged "for the first time into an environment with basic freedoms in place and no censorship laws of any kind in force" (Pharr and Krauss, *Media and Politics in Japan*, 12). By 1952 API had conducted four seminars in which Japanese broadcasters and news professionals were participants. Over sixty media professionals—selected on the basis of their potential as change agents and the potential trajectory of their careers—had been "reoriented" at API.

52. Susan Pharr, "Media and Politics in Japan: Historical and Contemporary Perspectives," in *Media and Politics in Japan*, 3–17.

53. Echoing earlier state censorship, OMGUS instituted measures to thwart any critique of its policies. For instance, the occupying forces censored any reporting critical of their policies and limited any references to the bombings of Hiroshima and Nagasaki.

54. John Dower, *Embracing Defeat. Japan in the Wake of World War II* (New York: Norton, 1999), 229.

55. J. Montgomery Curtis to Shepard Stone, 26 September, 1955. FF, 0560–0013, Section 1.

56. Similar to the Japanese constitution, which had freedom of the press embedded in it as of 1947, press freedom was also embedded in the postwar German constitution after World War II under the Basic Law; press freedom and open access to the profession has been in effect since 1949.

57. Romy Frohlich and Christina Holtz-Bacha, *Journalism Education in Europe and North America. An International Comparison* (Cresskill, NJ: Hampton Press, 2003), 191.

58. Frohlich and Holtz-Bacha, *Journalism Education*, 191.

59. It is also interesting to note that the military-sponsored papers failed after the occupation.

60. An excerpt from an Information Control Functional Program, 19 April, 1947, called "Measures to Ensure Independence of Press." RAC, RF, RG 1.2, Series 717R, Box 11, Folder 114.

61. RAC, RF, RG 1.2, Series 717R, Box 11, Folder 114.

62. Jessica Gienow-Hecht, *Transmission Impossible: American Journalism as Cultural Diplomacy in Postwar Germany 1945–1955* (Baton Rouge: Louisiana State University Press, 1999).

63. Crucially, it was Brigadier General Robert McClure of OMGUS Germany (and earlier of Psychological Operations or "PSYOPS"), who is cited as the person who conceived of the seminars for the reorientation of foreign media professionals in the first place.

64. Gienow-Hecht, *Transmission Impossible*, 186 (my emphasis).

65. Edward D'Arms Interview with Floyd Taylor, 17 September, 1948. RAC, RF, RG 1.2, Series 717R, Box 11, Folder 114.

66. See, for example, the Ford Foundation's grant to support a twelve-day tour of the United States for one hundred international journalists and editors, members of the International Press Institute, in April 1958. The gratitude expressed by participants included in the project's final report show that if the Americans had intended to foster a worldwide fraternity of like-minded professionals, then their mission was successful: "I feel convinced that the picture we brought back from America and the slant we obtained on so many controversial subjects has helped to clarify the thoughts of many of us. Certainly it has made all the firmer the close ties between us." See six-page narrative report: FF, 58–121, Section 1.

67. See Brett Gary, *The Nervous Liberals: Propaganda Anxieties from World War I to the Cold War* (New York: Columbia University Press, 1999); and Ron Robin, *The Making of the Cold War Enemy* (Princeton, NJ: Princeton University Press, 2001).

68. Gary, *Nervous Liberals*, 6, 125.

69. The 1930s-era Lippmann-Dewey debate about the public and its relative (in) competence, the Hutchins Commission of the 1940s, and the later publication of Fred S. Siebert's, Theodore Peterson's, and Wilbur Schramm's classic *Four Theories of the Press. The Authoritarian, Libertarian, Social Responsibility and Soviet Communist Concepts of What the Press Should Be and Do* (Chicago: University of Illinois Press, 1963) form the backdrop of early- through mid-twentieth-century debates about the press and its function in the United States.

70. Gary, *Nervous Liberals*, 88.

71. Gary, *Nervous Liberals*, 88.

72. Gary, *Nervous Liberals*, 90.

73. RAC, RF, RG 1.2, Series 609R, Box 43, Folder 479.

74. RAC, RF, RG 1.2, Series 717R, Box 11, Folder 114.

75. Echoes here of the fundamental perceived debate between Dewey and Lippmann, for example, regarding the capacity (or impossibility) of the omnicompetent citizen in modern industrial culture. European theorists contributed to the image of a dominated, passive mass audience; Theodor Adorner's and Max Horkheimer's, *Dialectic of Enlightenment*, trans. John Cumming (New York: Continuum, 1982) theorized a vulnerable viewer when they argued that film-going audiences in the first part of the century were reduced to uncritical distraction, complicit in their own exploitation under capitalism, as a result of the mass-produced industrial art of the Hollywood studio system and similarly reduced to passive listening due to "pre-digested," standardized songs within popular music.

76. See Elihu Katz and Paul F. Lazarsfeld, *Personal Influence: The Part Played by People in the Flow of Mass Communications* (Glencoe, IL: Free Press, 1955), 15–42.

77. See, for example, Paul Lazarsfeld and Robert Merton, "Studies in Radio and Film Propaganda," in *Transactions of the New York Academy of Sciences* 6, no. 2 (1943). The piece was modified slightly and reappeared in Merton's *Social Theory and Social Structure: Toward the Codification of Theory and Research* (Glencoe, IL: Free Press, 1949/1968).

78. Taken from Edward F. D'Arms's Interview with Wilhelm von Cornides, 29 September, 1948. RAC, RF. 1.2, Series 717R, Box 11, Folder 115.

79. Rose to Shepard Stone, 25 April, 1956. FF, 56–302, Section 4.

80. Craig Calhoun, *Critical Social Theory. Culture, History, and the Challenge of Difference* (Cambridge, MA: Blackwell, 1995), 143.

81. Todd Gitlin, *The Whole World is Watching: Mass Media in the Making and Unmaking of the New Left* (Berkeley, Los Angeles, London: University of California Press, 1980), 10.

82. See, for example, Roelofs, *Foundations and Public Policy*, as well as Robert F. Arnove, *Philanthropy and Cultural Imperialism: The Foundations at Home and Abroad* (Boston: G. K. Hall, 1980).

83. David Altheide, "Media Hegemony: A Failure of Perspective," *Public Opinion Quarterly* 48, no. 2 (Summer 1984): 477.

84. Altheide, "Media Hegemony," 476. See also Herbert Gans, *Deciding What's News. A Study of CBS Evening News, NBC Nightly News, Newsweek and Time* (New York: Pantheon, 1979) for a careful description of U.S. journalism's "paraideology."

85. Altheide, "Media Hegemony," 480. See also Graham Murdoch and Peter Golding, Capitalism, Communication, and Class Relations, in *Mass Communication and Society*, eds. James Curran, Michael Gurevitch, and Janet Woolacott (London: Edward Arnold, 1977), 12–43.

86. Altheide, "Media Hegemony," 479.

87. See, for instance, Pierre Bourdieu, *The Logic of Practice* (Stanford, CA: Stanford University Press, 1992).

88. This is an abbreviated list of goals; see the further items 4–6 listed in the grant proposal. RAC, RF, RG 1.2, Series 609R, Box 43, Folder 479.

89. Peter Golding, "Media Professionalism in the Third World: The Transfer of an Ideology," in *Mass Communication and Society*.

90. Golding, "Media Professionalism in the Third World," 305.

91. Golding, "Media Professionalism in the Third World," 295.

92. Calhoun, *Critical Social Theory*.

93. Golding, "Media Professionalism in the Third World," 292.

94. Bourdieu would call the acquisition of such technical, professional, and cultural competencies a form of regulated improvisation, of habitus. In more strident terms than Bourdieu would use, Peter Golding, in "Media Professionalism," reads the impact that the training programs run by the BBC or France's SOROFAM had on African broadcasters and journalists as an explicit form of domination: Is professionalism, he asks, "merely the ideological Trojan horse for the commercial expansion of technological enterprise in the developed world?" (304–5). For a discussion of professional ideologies in the field of U.S. journalism see Gaye Tuchman, "Objectivity as a Strategic Ritual: An Examination of Newsmen's Notions of Objectivity," *American Journal of Sociology* 77, no. 4 (January 1972): 660–79; Schudson, *Discovering the News*,

The Sociology of the News, and "The Objectivity Norm": Hallin, "The Passing of the 'High Modernism' of American Journalism"; and Gans, *Deciding What's News.*

95. See McClure's January 12, 1948, letter to D'Arms: "The persons selected should be key operating editorial personnel who, when they return to their jobs in Germany, could put into practice what they have learned here and pass that along to others with whom they are working. (These individuals upon their return, or at stated periods thereafter, might very properly hold Seminars for other journalists from the various zones in Germany.)" RAC, RF, RG 1.2, Series 717R, Box 11, Folder 114.

96. See, for example, the Ford Foundation's 1958 grant (58–121) to the American Committee of IPI to support a twelve-day tour of America for one hundred international editors (see note 66). The entourage traveled on a chartered flight dubbed "Gutenberg's Folly" for the occasion and visited agricultural, industrial, and entertainment sites throughout the country. For a complete discussion of the expansion of American consumer culture across Europe, see Victoria de Grazia, *Irresistible Empire: America's Advance through 20th-Century Europe* (Cambridge, MA: Harvard University Press, 2005).

97. Robin, *The Making of the Cold War Enemy.*

98. See *Life,* February 17, 1941, 61–65.

99. See, for instance, Hallin and Mancini, *Comparing Media Systems,* "Americanization, Globalization and Secularization."

100. See Paolo Mancini, "Political Complexity and Alternative Models of Journalism: The Italian Case," in *De-Westernizing Media Studies,* eds. J. Curran and M-J. Park (London: Routledge, 2000); Rodney Benson and Daniel C. Hallin, "How States, Markets and Globalization Shape the News: The French and U.S. National Press, 1965–97," *European Journal of Communication* 22, no. 1 (March 2007): 27–48; J. K. Chalaby, "Journalism as an Anglo-American Invention: A Comparison of the Development of French and Anglo-American Journalism, 1830s–1920s," *European Journal of Communication* 11, no. 3 (September 1996): 303–26.

101. See Mancini, "Political Complexity and Alternative Models of Journalism."

102. *Control Room* (2004), Jehane Noujaim, director.

103. "The first purpose of an API foreign seminar is to provide professional information helpful in building responsible, independent and economically strong newspapers—newspapers which better serve their readers and their countries." FF, 60–164, Section 3 (from page 5 of the grant proposal report).

104. *Control Room.*

11

Screen Technology, Mobilization, and Adult Education in the 1950s

Charles R. Acland

Assessing the cultural impact of philanthropic organizations upon the immediate post–World War II period is a tricky task, one that confronts us with the ambiguities inherent in the reigning liberal ideals of the time. The political and ideological matrix in which bodies like the Ford and Rockefeller Foundations operated appears to be hopelessly contradictory from our vantage point. In the cold war climate of accusation, Congressman Carroll Reece chaired a congressional investigation into use of philanthropic tax exemptions, eventually targeting the Foundations as fronts for subversives. This, for instance, resulted in a Rotary Club ban of Ford Foundation programs, as the leadership of this organization worried about a tainted relationship with potentially un-American operations. In many ways, adult education, a developing area of support for several of the larger foundations, carried a whiff of suspicion through the 1950s as a creator of venues for anti-American sentiment and as a vaguely socialistic idea unto itself. And yet, as has subsequently come to light, the Ford Foundation participated in joint CIA enterprises, including the Congress for Cultural Freedom, to ship U.S. worldviews and to promote U.S. foreign policy abroad. What follows is an attempt to work through these somewhat contradictory cold war ideological forces by examining specific philanthropic initiatives in the domains of culture and education. To that end, I examine the Ford Foundation's support, through its Fund for Adult Education (1951–1961), of the national educational film organization, the Film Council of America (1946–1957).

As a point of departure, we should note that the history and influence of nontheatrical film remains underappreciated. Among nontheatrical genres, educational or instructional film—sometimes appearing under the even less appealing term "functional film"—has been almost entirely neglected.[1] To be sure, the often authoritative voice-overs, cheap sets, dreary composition, and wooden dramatizations of the films we remember from our own school days are not inspiring invitations to passionate close examination. Nonetheless, their newly ubiquitous presence, in the post–WWII period, and the massive amount of resources poured into their circulation, indicate that educational film cannot be dismissed as marginal to our culture. Indeed, I suggest that educational-film agendas set the stage for the current era of "technologizing the classroom." The efforts of organizations like the Fund for Adult Education and the Film Council of America had a lasting impact upon presumptions about the integration of media into curricula and, moreover, about where education takes place. In general, they assisted in the establishment of a critical vocabulary for cultural technologies, one that aided in the dispersal of classroom activity to locations beyond the walls of the brick schoolhouse. That historical moment in the development of media-assisted education calls us to confront the complex relationship between developing media forms and uses, new pedagogical methods, and the expansion of educational sites and institutions.

ORGANIZING NONTHEATRICAL FILM

Well into the 1950s, nontheatrical film was still being described as a wild field without central organizing institutional entities and without clear differences between producers, distributors, and exhibitors. Indeed, the very nature of "nontheatrical" reworked taken-for-granted definitions and categories of the dominant commercial motion-picture industry. This influence was most pronounced in exhibition, where the possible locations for cinematic and instructional spectatorship included department stores, churches, community clubs, schools, museums, libraries, and sporting venues. Concentrating upon the 1940s and 1950s and specifically on nonfiction film, as I do here, is not to say that there were no precursors, and certainly the developments chronicled here are direct continuations of the impact of 16 mm film, introduced in the 1920s. However, in the post–WWII period we begin to see the normalization of the place and operations of nontheatrical film on a mass basis. In the United States, national agencies emerge to attempt to coordinate this arena of exhibition and distribution, and it is here that the influence of philanthropies is most evident.

Driving the emerging visual educational procedures of the first half of the twentieth century were a number of initiatives that took place under the umbrella of philanthropic—and at times industrial—support. Beginning in 1935 several Rockefeller Foundation grants established the Motion Picture

Project of the American Council on Education (ACE), which produced several important publications on education and film.[2] The same agency offered substantial support to the American Film Center (AFC) from 1938 until its demise in 1946. In an effort to coordinate the growing number of organizations, a further grant financed the Joint Committee on Educational Films, formed in 1940, with involvement from the American Library Association (ALA), the Association of School Film Libraries (ASFL), the Motion Picture Project of the ACE, and the AFC.[3] In 1943 the Educational Film Library Association (EFLA) was launched.

I make mention of the establishment of these organizations, if only in a cursory fashion, to indicate the presence of an agreement concerning the film's potential as an educational instrument as we enter the 1940s. What continued to spark debate and study was the mode of its implementation, and here, the activities of funding agencies and the organizations they established show three general priorities. First and foremost was the need for coordination among producers, distributors, and users of educational film. This priority may have been in the name of efficiency, assuring that funding dollars were spent effectively. But industry observers saw the informational and educational film scene as startlingly disorganized, with too many small participants and with inadequate market information. There seemed to be little accounting of whether or not educators and community leaders were being served with films they actually wanted and found beneficial. Increasing coordination among the principal parties became a central funding target and a primary focus of energy.

Second, it was felt that potential users of educational film were lost in a new environment of pedagogical options without training in how to acquire and select appropriate materials. Teachers and group leaders confronted an array of films, some easily accessible and others not, without ready selection criteria to assist them. Even more rudimentary, some were without a basic idea of how to borrow a film and how to thread a projector, let alone how to incorporate it into a lesson. It followed that a key priority would be the circulation of information about new audiovisual education methods. To be part of this informational network, interested agencies placed an emphasis on systems of evaluation of AV material. Sometimes this involved establishing preview centers that would write synopses, assess the functionality of films, and compile catalogs. Sometimes this involved elaborate surveys and postscreening reports. But the aim remained set on constructing an efficient film user, knowledgeable about the implementation of film-aided lessons. One might think of this priority as the expansion and coordination of educational-film expertise.

Third, the thousands of pages studying instructional uses of motion pictures generally zeroed in on a balance between the selection of the title and its incorporation in the service of an educational goal. Invariably, the preferred method involved an orchestration of screening followed by leader-guided discussion. This approach was in contrast to film as an illustration of a lecture and to film as a self-contained educational technology that one passively witnesses. This may seem somewhat obvious and common sense to us today. However, with the sustained attention this received for several decades, not to mention the massive amount of funding it attracted for testing and assessment, I am convinced that the screening-discussion method was far from taken for granted as the best pedagogical approach (or, possibly, that a good portion of educators needed concrete evidence to be reassured that they, as teachers, were not being replaced).

EMERGENCE OF THE FILM COUNCIL OF AMERICA

The most visible and influential U.S. film education organization of the 1940s and 1950s, the Film Council of America (FCA), illustrates these claims.[4] The FCA was a product of widespread interest in the educational uses of new technological forms, one that encompasses the aforementioned three dimensions. The FCA's work helped to settle decades of attempts to negotiate the educational challenges posed by new media, film in particular. It drew from both the earlier "better films" movement and had links with its contemporaries, the more aesthetically invested film-appreciation societies. But it displayed its own character, particularly in the realm of education, new teaching methods, and mass mobilization.

The origins of the FCA were in the Office of War Information's (OWI) plans to mobilize the U.S. population in service of the war effort. One central program relied on film's effectiveness in explaining world events and in outlining the patriotic contribution individuals could make. The government's wartime-film program encompassed distribution as much as it did the production of ideologically appropriate informational shorts. Beginning in 1943, one of the OWI's film objectives was to capitalize upon and expand existing school- and community-media facilities, helping to orchestrate channels through which government information could reach local audiences. The committee created to achieve this acted to gain access to established resources, most important the more than 25,000 16 mm sound projectors held in educational and community institutions, according to estimates used at the time.[5] The head of the National 16 mm Advisory Committee was C. R. Reagan, of Visual Education, Inc., in Austin, Texas, and with the National Association of Visual Education Dealers (NAVED). The Advisory Committee coordinated the work, and relied upon the resources, of seven commercial and educational organizations active in 16 mm informational film: ALA, EFLA, NAVED, the National University Extension Association (NUEA), the National Education Association (NEA), the Allied Non-Theatrical Film Association (ANTFA), and the Visual Equipment Manufacturers Council (VEMC). With their assistance, volunteers organized film screenings and war-related film programs thus reached labor unions, church groups, women's clubs, schools, and other community organizations. In essence, the OWI opened up both public and private materials to designated community leaders, all in the service of the nation in a state of emergency. By the end of the war two years later, the OWI estimated its audience to have been 300 million.[6]

After the cessation of hostilities in Europe, and the disbanding of the OWI, their evident success encouraged those at its final meeting in early 1946 to transform the Committee into a civilian operation, one that would continue to promote film as a catalyst to community action and instruction, and one that could be called upon to mobilize people should the government require it.[7] With the termination of federal support at the war's conclusion, a largely voluntary film-education movement stepped in to fill that void. The members formed the Film Council of America on January 17, 1946. The Council remained a joint effort on the part of the original seven member organizations of the OWI Committee, with Reagan still in charge once elected as the first FCA president.[8] According to its constitution, the FCA was a nonprofit educational association whose mission was "to increase the information and work toward the general welfare of all people by fostering, improving and promoting the production, the distribution, and the effective use of audio-visual materials."[9] It was to pursue these ideals by coordinating and supporting the activities of community-based councils and national AV organizations, whether commercial or not.[10] Its main function over the years was to be a clearinghouse for information about film, its availability, and its classroom and community use. By early 1951, it had affiliations with thirty national organizations and, counting the membership of each, the FCA claimed to have access to 13,000 chapters and 17 million members.[11] It and its supporters reasoned that this put the FCA in a unique position of being able to reach the estimated potential market of 2 million programmers of nontheatrical film.[12] More concretely, by June 1951 the FCA had more than 150 local councils and had developed film information centers in more than 1,200 towns.[13]

The national umbrella organization received funding support from its institutional members and industrial donations. The local chapters collected membership fees and relied upon their own fundraising to survive. The sale of publications covered their production costs and little else. From 1954 to 1957, the FCA collected registration fees from the American Film Assembly festival, which they ran. Still, as with most voluntary societies of its kind, it operated very close to the line. Their first fundraising coup came from the Carnegie Corporation of New York (CC), which after several years of assessing the educational-film scene offered support. The

CC saw its 1948 grant of $10,000 per year for two years as complimentary to one given to the ALA for facilitating distribution. The FCA's grant was for garnering audiences and using film "intelligently."[14] As such, the CC divided its funding intentions between the coordination of film circulation, performed by the ALA, and the coordination of film expertise and promotion, performed by the FCA (though the CC was well aware that FCA activities encompassed the former too). The Carnegie grant was for the executive director's salary, which at the time would go to the newly elected Glen Burch.[15] The CC followed this with a final grant of $16,000 allocated from 1950 to 1952.[16]

THE FORMATION OF THE FUND FOR ADULT EDUCATION

Just as these funds were coming to a close, and there were no prospects for renewal, the Ford Foundation was in the midst of launching its Fund for Adult Education (FAE).[17] A philanthropic upstart, the Ford Foundation seemed to have lavish resources beyond its own imagination. Dean Rusk described it as "the fat boy in the philanthropic canoe."[18] Dwight Macdonald called it "a large body of money completely surrounded by people who want some."[19] Snobbishly seen as the "new money" of the philanthropic scene, its massive boost in funds arguably stemmed from an apparent postwar tax dodge involving the passing of the Ford fortune from one generation to the next and incidentally sparking the accusations that led to the Reece Commission investigations. As these congressional hearings got underway, the Foundation dispensed its riches domestically, giving special attention to adult education.

The FAE initially ran its operations from Pasadena before moving to New York in the mid-1950s. The FCA, strictly speaking, did not focus on adult education, instead serving all manners of audiovisual instruction. But adult education benefited from a broad definition and encompassed formal university extensions and informal programs of continuing instruction as conducted by social clubs, religious organizations, and community-based groups. It seemed opportune, then, to highlight the work the FCA could feasibly undertake in this area, whether expanding their status as a clearinghouse for film information, as a preview center for film programs, or as a promoter of the proper deployment of films. As its grant request was about to be reviewed by the Ford Foundation, Scott Fletcher—who was head of the FAE, an active and founding FCA board member and former president of Encyclopaedia Britannica Films—estimated that the chances were nine to one that the FCA would receive funds.[20] Some machinations had to have been in motion, for within a few weeks the Fund for Adult Education announced awards of $20,000, then $30,000 for 1951 and 1952 respectively, and outgoing FCA executive director Glen Burch had been hired to work for the FAE.[21] The FCA's work in promoting film in adult education secured it the more substantial sums of $75,000 for 1952–1953, $180,000 in 1953–1954, and $220,000 in 1954–1955 from the same agency. Using the FCA to conduct a variety of educational experiments and to prepare and publish written material on educational film usage, the total amount of FAE support for the FCA was $738,500.[22]

The FAE declared its purpose as resolutely liberal, emphasizing the individual as a unique, self-contained person and citizen. Its guiding policy stated that "as a citizen of a free society the individual is the means for the preservation and continual improvement of the kind of society which makes possible the fullest development of his own capacities and those of his fellow citizens."[23] To achieve this lofty goal, the FAE promoted reflection and moral concern through a liberal-arts education, as distinct from the repetitive procedures of training and the "inculcation of beliefs" of indoctrination.[24] While privileging the lifelong and informal nature of learning—as its policy proclaimed, "Education terminates only with death"—mass media and communication channels appear as essential elements to this modern liberal education. Of special note was the balance to be struck between the wide and easy diffusion of mass media and the requirement of individual study and discussion.[25] Describing the approach as new, though with roots in the Socratic tradition, the FAE reasoned that "liberal education through the study-discussion method has three principal characteristics: adults coming together to discuss a particular subject; a common body of knowledge in the form of assigned study materials; and informed and trained leaders."[26] By design, the FAE championed the study-discussion method as the properly liberal path to contemporary citizenship: "Study-discussion programs in the liberal arts and sciences are aimed at improving the ability of participants to make independent judgments on critical issues, to develop their intellectual faculties and aesthetic sensibilities and to encourage sustained intellectual curiosity."[27] In this the role of the leader was explicitly a facilitator rather than topic expert, which in theory was a "challenge to the participant to seek out knowledge and expand his appreciation and critical ability."[28] Leaders were to be concerned with, and knowledgeable about, group dynamics and not dominating authorities on subject matter. Accordingly, one of its first initiatives was to fund the production of three films with a grant to Encyclopaedia Britannica Films, through the University of Chicago, on the mechanics of adult group discussion. They were *Room for Discussion* (1953), *How to Organize a Discussion Group* (1954), and *How to Conduct a Discussion Group* (1954). Intended for distribution through film councils and libraries, television was an equally desired platform for these films.[29]

The FCA fit neatly into these plans. Arguing for FCA funding, the FAE concluded that film service specifically for adult education was "practically zero," and that most attention has been on existing school and future television venues. FCA was seen as the body that could initiate national coordination between users and producers of adult-education film material. Mindful of the international implications of such actions, the FAE hoped that this would not only support the domestic situation, but "show world leadership in the use of high quality motion pictures."[30]

In an early cooperative endeavor, the FCA and the FAE orchestrated the making of a film depicting an informal adult film discussion. Louis de Rochemont produced *Cleveland Council for World Affairs* (1951), which demonstrated the work of a local film council and highlighted film-discussion techniques.[31] The Fund's grant to increase local councils and film-information centers and to conduct experiments in distribution to adult-education users came at virtually the same time that the FCA promised to put all of its resources at the disposal of training and informing citizens about the looming international crisis, again a holdover activity from the FCA's wartime predecessor. While the agendas of community service and adult education are not mutually exclusive, they are also not equivalent. In fact, representatives of some local council affiliates began to complain that there was too little attention to them, too much attention to adult education, and not enough "safeguarding against infiltration by undesirable persons."[32] This comment was an oblique reference to the Reece Commission and its questioning of the patriotic pedigree of the Foundation.

THE EXPERIMENTAL DISCUSSION PROJECT

Pursuing the procedural connection between film screening and guided discussion, one of the FAE's major initiatives was its Experimental Discussion Project (EDP), which received more than $2.1 million in its first five years (1951–1956).[33] The EDP was "designed to prepare a substantial number of study-discussion programs in areas of world, political, economic and cultural affairs. All of these programs used selected readings and some used supplementary properties, such as films, recordings, film-strips, charts and maps. These programs were then tested in discussion groups that used a wide range of methods to train lay leaders. The final phase of the EDP project was to use the best of the programs in a test of distribution, use, and financing."[34] Discussion emerged from a multimedia encounter, involving reading, watching, and talking, with the project initially called the Experimental Film Discussion Project. A 1952 *New York Times* article on it—a point at which the Experimental Film Discussion Project spanned fifty-nine groups and over 2,000 people—put the guiding query as follows: "Will the development of a combination of materials—films, essays, guides and posters—used together in a series of programs, help relatively untrained discussion leaders and inexperienced adult groups get more out of the discussion of some of the important problems of our time?"[35] Glen Burch was the director of the EDP through to its cessation of activity, ultimately writing its final report in 1960.[36]

The FAE did some of its own promotion for its first two series, "World Affairs are Your Affairs" (see table 11.1) and "Great Men and Great Issues," and it began by testing its programs.[37] The former, internationalist in design, consisted of ten films, corresponding essays, and discussion manuals, each taking on a different "tension area." While the principles included world peace and democracy, groups were to understand the importance of "the economic foundations of the free world" and "the threat of totalitarian communism."[38] Of the test programs assembled, "World Affairs are Your Affairs" had perhaps the greatest longevity and viewership. As its leader's manual indicates, participating groups were to meet weekly over three months to "read about it, see it happen, talk it over."[39] Scholars prepared essays of about 2,000 words in length for each of the ten weeks, while the films were already in circulation, some of which were several years old. "Great Men and Great Issues," a series of nine film packages, was nationalist in intent, presenting American heritage through historical figures like Benjamin Franklin and Abraham Lincoln.[40] As the promotional material reiterates and reassures again and again, essays and discussion questions—and in some cases the films themselves—were prepared by a qualified authority on the subject. Evident is the core liberal-democratic idea of bringing "ordinary" people together and encouraging them through free exchange to work through complex political and historical problems. The EDP recommended that discussion groups be a maximum of twenty-five people.[41] In actuality, numbers ranged from six to eighty.[42] Though the interest in informal education remained, many of the sponsoring bodies were general-education or extension departments of universities.[43]

Table 11.1.   Films Selected for "World Affairs are Your Affairs" Program[44]

World Trade for Better Living (Encyclopaedia Britannica Films, 1951)
Farmers of India (United World Films, 1949)
Japan and Democracy (March of Time Films, 1950)
Oriental City (United World Films, 1949)
Iran in Crisis (March of Time Films, 1951)
Tropical Mountain Land (United World Films, 1948)
Tito, Our Ally? (March of Time Films, 1951)
Challenge in Nigeria (British Information Services, 1951)
Picture of Britain (British Information Services, 1951)
World Affairs are Your Affairs (Cleveland World Affairs Council, 1952)

The FAE recruited the FCA to distribute the Experimental Film Discussion Project once through the testing phase.[45] The FCA received $88,500 to distribute the first two Experimental Discussion programs, which involved 20,000 participants and 1,000 groups.[46] The FAE handed over the full administration of them in November 1952,[47] and the FCA then handled the distribution of materials, including essays, films, leader's kits, and discussion guides, for these two programs. The first year's evaluations captured a feeling that the "Great Men and Great Issues" films were "too amateurish and shallow" and "too immature for adults."[48] Feedback on "World Affairs are Your Affairs" tended to be more positive, though some felt the films were out-of-date and dealt too much with agrarian societies and "underdeveloped countries."[49] In spite of these criticisms, from November 1952 through the end of June 1953, the FCA distributed 1,394 sets of the "Great Men and Great Issues" essays, and 3,036 of the "World Affairs are Your Affairs" essay sets.[50] In 1953–1954, the FCA distributed 1,412 of the former, and 4,041 of the latter.[51] These numbers do not reflect actual usage as it is unclear how often booklets went unused or were reused, and some councils and societies only made essays available on a lending basis. By the fall of 1954, as the FAE expanded the project to cities rather than programs, the FCA role ended.[52]

The "test cities" phase of the EDP carried forward the guided small-group-discussion idea, though various media were introduced and monitored. The project consisted of twelve city laboratories and a regional community one, in the local conduct of informal adult education.[53] Each test city experimented with the following: (1) harmonization of schools, councils, libraries, and other community groups in the service of a liberal-educational program; (2) development of "lay leadership" skills and interest in adult education; (3) cooperation among existing organizations; (4) examination of the effects of educational materials and methods used; (5) exploitation of mass media to achieve adult-educational objectives; and (6) potential for ongoing, community-based, financing for lifelong learning.[54] The role of mass communication here was to develop "a relationship between liberal adult education programs carried through the mass media and those in face-to-face situations."[55] As a priority, their five-year report claimed that "no educational endeavor on the local level has experimented more and made more significant contributions in the utilization of the mass media for the stimulation of thought and the encouragement of participation in educational activities than have the Test Cities."[56] The integration of television, film, radio, newspapers, group meetings, and essays in pamphlet form not only disseminated an educational program, but also assisted in the gathering of audiences for the formation of discussion groups. "Such integration of the mass media and discussion groups is not only possible but also highly practical and simple. Natural friendship groups seem to offer the best basis for the organization of such discussion nuclei."[57] This sort of "schooling without walls" was said to have transformed the entire San Bernardino Valley "into a 'classroom.'"[58]

Discussion programs moved with increasing rapidity into general circulation and were acquired and implemented by school and community organizations. This was done with the active involvement of traditionally credentialed experts (professors and PhDs), and included people such as Mortimer Adler, Gilbert Seldes, and Harold Lasswell, and organizations like the Brookings Institute. Some program titles were "Your Money and Your Life," "Human Freedom," "You and Modern Art," "Mass Media," "Life Under Communism," "World Affairs (Europe)," and "Discussion Leadership."[59] Apropos of this last program, in 1959 New York University, in its Division of General Education, participated in the training of informal adult-education discussion leaders specially prepared to lead film programs prepared, tested, and promoted by the FAE, including "The Ways of Mankind," "Looking at Modern Poetry," and "World Politics."[60]

The programs and procedures of discussion both reinforced notions of well roundedness acquired through self-motivated learning. This strain of mass education complimented other middlebrow initiatives, from book clubs to the Great Books Foundation, and likewise advanced an ideology of worldly, individual engagement with and resolution of contemporary troubles.[61] The image was of grassroots acquisition of timeless world knowledge and negotiation of contemporary world-historical issues as encountered in a carefully constructed multimedia context and addressed through civil discussion. This model assumed that some sort of collective commonsense could reason out the complexities of any number of topics and questions, if prompted and prepared. Ordinary opinion, properly elicited and directed, would thus amplify the exemplary status of American civility and democracy.

Evident in this array of activities, beyond an interest in discussion and leadership of discussion, we witness the premium placed upon an interaction among media. These educational projects sought out relations among media forms. Though the FCA's direct responsibility for the discussion project ended, FAE support for the association did not stop. The grant renewal in 1955 funded its preview centers, its publication and clearinghouse operations, and the American Film Assembly, a film festival for informational film.[62] The FAE also underwrote the FCA's affiliations with educational television, including televised film discussions. In Chicago the FCA had an agreement with television station WTTW to select and supply films for broadcast.[63]

The growth of what we might call multimedia education through the 1950s was nothing short of astounding. As Fletcher remembered, despite earlier technological capability, "Sound motion pictures for education in schools didn't really come into being until after World War II."[64] But by the start of 1959, there were an estimated 595,000 16 mm projectors in the United States, or one for every 305 persons.[65] Organized around this growth was a twofold configuration of responses: first, that the opening up of far-flung sites of education required monitoring by cultural authorities, and second, that the technologizing of instruction dramatically expanded an educational market. Both responses worried about ethical mismanagement and underexploited potential. For example, after decades of the film-library idea, only 112 of the almost 7,000 U.S. public libraries had circulating nontheatrical film collections in June 1952.[66] With this budding alignment of a dispersed educational market, one can see how the 1958 National Defense Education Act institutionalized and solidified much of the earlier activity of the 1950s. Perhaps it is no wonder that Scott Fletcher became one of twelve appointees to the Act's National Advisory Committee on New Educational Media in January 1959.[67]

CONCLUSION

By way of conclusion, I wish to return to Edward Berman's important 1983 volume, which argues that philanthropic foundations promoted an internationalist liberal agenda in order to smooth the way for imperialist conduct. To make his case, he uses a rather straightforward theory of hegemony to explain the social control and consensus sought by U.S. elites over international ones, all with the ultimate objective of furthering U.S. foreign policy. Much of his study remains instructive, and it is convincing in its documentation of the career trajectories of philanthropic luminaries and key projects. For instance, in 1961 President John F. Kennedy made Philip Coombs (an officer with the FAE from 1952 onward) his assistant secretary of state for education and cultural affairs; Ford Foundation president Paul Hoffman had been director of the Marshall Plan; and the Rockefeller Foundation's and Carnegie Corporation's War-Peace Studies Project, 1939–1945, which recommended access to foreign raw resources and argued that international prosperity makes for better trading partners, became the basis for the World Bank and the International Monetary Fund.[68] More recently, Frances Stonor Saunders reiterates the claim writing, "At times, it seemed as if the Ford Foundation was simply an extension of government in the area of international cultural propaganda . . . working closely with Marshall Plan and CIA officials on specific projects."[69]

Still, I am drawn to wonder about some of the contradictions of what Berman terms an ideology of "democratic elitism."[70] For instance, the book does not contain much detail about what was actually being advanced by philanthropic-foundation activity and instead draws its conclusions from broad ideological assessments of the fact of institutional liaisons. He does emphasize that among their main programs and objectives, the foundations "encouraged experimentation in the fields of teacher education, instructional technology, and nontraditional modes of education."[71] With his focus on foreign policy, he concludes, "Third-World nations, particularly in the 1960s, were frequently laboratories for the application of novel educational techniques imported from the United States and subsidized by the foundations, the Agency for International Development, and the World Bank."[72] However accurate this may be, as the preceding documentation shows, the U.S. population was an earlier laboratory for many of these innovations.

Further, this lab may have brought an agenda of U.S. domestic and foreign policy to the table, but it equally valued a humanist mode of communal assembly and rhetorical exploration, the structure of which is perhaps more telling than the content. Scott Fletcher noted in his oral history that people were very dubious about the study-discussion method and that significant resources had to be devoted to testing in order to demonstrate unambiguously that it was effective and had certain advantages in a multimediated context, which is precisely what the EDP showed.[73] On the same period, Ron Greene and Darrin Hicks make a similar point in their examination of cold war–debate organizations, noting that the processes and rules of decision by debate acted as a cultural technology that meshed moral education with American exceptionalism on the world stage.[74] Likewise, the experiments with media discussion groups were part of an effort to establish regularized procedures and conditions for a particular vision of democratic life, one in which laypeople, guided by a disinterested leader, would come to know and respond to world issues in an informal, locally generated, situation. Here, structured group talk, not formalized debate, was central to this vision of mediated screen democracy.

The post–WWII "messianic liberalism," to use Daniel Yergin's term describing the internationalism of the period,[75] here coincides with other rising ideas about how mass society operates. This cannot be reduced to the more authoritarian plans stemming from psychological-warfare agendas, as documented by Christopher Simpson.[76] These two approaches ran side by side. If we situate initiatives like the Experimental Discussion Project in the context of the emerging media theories of the day, theories that grow out of research funded initially through the Rockefeller Foundation's Humanities Division and the GEB, we see that the two-step flow idea—an idea that "rediscovers" the role of interpersonal dynamics and reference groups in exerting influence in this mass age—was not only a theory: *it was a dominant policy objective.*

As Leon Bramson concluded decades ago, one can see the two-step flow theory as a particularly liberal American reworking of the more dramatically critical European mass-society theorists.[77] The two-step flow model was a direct extension of a Deweyian model of democratic life as well as a product of Kurt Lewin's then newly circulating research on "group dynamics."[78] What I am proposing, though, is that this so-called dominant paradigm of communication studies, as typified by the work of Elihu Katz and Paul Lazarsfeld,[79] operated as a bureaucratic rudder, guiding the functions and decisions of institutional influence as much as it lent coherence to the new pursuit of communication research. The work of the FCA and the FAE was not simply about extending a single ideological case, or representing sanctioned foreign policy only, but of *setting the terms for how a mass public was to be located and engaged,* and who would be in a position to legitimately guide it. This was a truly hegemonic pursuit, insomuch as it is about consent to procedures of public and democratic life rather than coercion, in this instance involving media-generated small group discussion of national and international affairs.

The problem of film education was never just one of how we know film and the information it can impart, but how we know people and communities. This was a question of cultural nationhood and citizenship as linked to media evaluation and usage for social purposes. The concentrated efforts in the arena of film education resulted in the emergence of networks of cultural authorities taking on an organic (which is not to say progressive) intellectual function, emerging from and in contact with localized small groups. For all the emphasis upon the nonexpert group-discussion leader, this did not mean that experts did not figure in the programs. Instead they appeared at the production stage, selecting topics, advising filmmakers, writing essays to accompany films, and composing discussion questions. The media discussion series gave prominent billing to their input, in a sense relying upon the reputation of middlebrow experts and professionals to lend credibility to the programs for, largely though not exclusively, amateur educational operations. This stratum of educationalists succeeded in creating nongovernmental and industrial agencies. The FCA was one force in the initiation and administration of the site and substance of film concerns. Film was seen to act as a catalyst to modern democratic participation in community life poised against film as promoter of social malaise and apathy. It could only be so, however, if managed and guided appropriately, hence the solidification of certain patterns of cultural leadership, selecting, promoting, and guiding activity.

So, the expansion to multiple sites of education—the promises of lifelong learning—unsettled existing social relations, creating a space for nonauthorized leaders to operate. In this staging ground for the delineation of the porous borders between state and civil society, agencies acted to occupy this space with new networks of cultural authorities and instructional agendas. The three broad areas of interest—coordination of the audiovisual industry, the organization of media expertise, and the promotion of cross-media group discussion procedures—all participate in the refinement of this realm of cultural power. Along with a policy instilling and orchestrating a two-step model of mass communication, they helped to install *mobilization*, a term that encompasses both the movement of bodies and ideas, as a dominant concept describing how mass society might be managed.

NOTES

Thanks goes to the people at the Ford Foundation Archives, Butler Library Special Collections at Columbia University, Special Collections at Iowa State University, Manuscript and Archives Division of the New York Public Library, as well as to William Buxton and Haidee Wasson who offered perceptive editorial comments. Research for this chapter was conducted with financial assistance from the Social Science and Humanities Research Council of Canada. Unpublished material in this chapter has been quoted courtesy of the following archives: Manuscripts and Archives Division, New York Public Library, New York City; Iowa State University Library, Special Collections Department; the Carnegie Corporation of New York, New York City; the Ford Foundation Archives, New York City; and the Minnesota State Archives, St. Paul, Minnesota.

1. Exceptions to this include Haidee Wasson, *Museum Movies: MoMA and the Birth of Art Cinema* (Berkeley: University of California Press, 2005); Lea Jacobs, "Reformers and Spectators: The Film Education Movement of the Thirties," *Camera Obscura* 22 (1990): 29–49; Eric Smoodin, *Regarding Frank Capra: Audience, Celebrity, and American Film Studies, 1930–1960* (Berkeley: University of California Press, 2004); Anthony Slide, *Before Video: A History of the Non-Theatrical Film* (New York: Greenwood Press, 1992); Anne Morey, *Hollywood Outsiders: The Adaptation of the Film Industry, 1913–1934* (Minneapolis: University of Minnesota Press, 2003); Charles R. Acland, "Patterns of Cultural Authority: The National Film Society of Canada and the Institutionalization of Film Education, 1938–41," *Canadian Journal of Film Studies* 10, no. 1 (2001): 2–27; Charles R. Acland, "Mapping the Serious and the Dangerous: Film and the National Council of Education, 1920–1939," *Cinéma* 6, no. 1 (Fall 1995): 101–18.

2. For example, Edgar Dale, Fannie W. Dunn, Charles F. Hoban Jr., and Etta Schneider, *Motion Pictures in Education: A Summary of the Literature* (New York: H. W. Wilson Co., 1938); and Charles F. Hoban Jr., *Focus on Learning: Motion Pictures in the School* (Washington, D.C.: American Council on Education, 1942); for a survey of these and other Rockefeller Foundation mass-communications projects, see William J. Buxton, "Reaching Human Minds: Rockefeller Philanthropy and Communications, 1935–1939," in *The Development of the Social Sciences in the United States and Canada: The Role of Philanthropy*, eds. Theresa Richardson and Donald Fisher (Stamford, CT: Ablex, 1999), 177–92.

3. Gerald McDonald, "Libraries and Films," *Film News* 2, no. 6 (June 1941): 2.

4. For a more detailed description and analysis of the FCA, see Charles R. Acland, "Classrooms, Clubs, and Community Circuits: Cultural Authority and the Film Council Movement, 1946–1957," in *Inventing Film Studies*, eds. Lee Grieveson and Haidee Wasson (Durham, NC: Duke University Press, 2008), 149–181.

5. "Government Influence Dominant in 16 mm Field," *Film News* 4, no. 1 (Summer 1943): 1, 14; "Advisory Committee Meets OWI," *Film News* 4, no. 3 (December 1943): 6, 7.

6. Stephen M. Corey, "What is the Film Council of America?" *Film News* 8, nos. 5/6 (November–December 1947): 3.

7. Minutes, "Film Council of America succeeding National 16 mm Film Committee," 16 January, 1946. New York Public Library, Astor, Lenox, and Tilden Foundations, National Board of Review of Motion Pictures Collection, Manuscript and Archives Division (hereafter NBRMPC), Box 26, Folder 2, 1–4. Gordon Adamson, who worked with distribution at the National Film Board of Canada and would soon become the executive secretary of the National Film Society of Canada, delivered an address in November 1945 to the Visual War Workers group in Washington, D.C. There, he laid out activities of the fairly well-coordinated Canadian nontheatrical circuits and, more importantly, presented a complete account of the function of community film councils and community film libraries. Washington Visual War Workers, founded in 1943, would soon after change its name to the Washington Film Council, and be considered the first chapter of the U.S. council movement. Though the audience would have been familiar with the activities Adamson narrated, the timing of and venue for this address make the event one point that coalesced ideas about how community film operations might be redefined for a peacetime context. Gordon Adamson, "The Film and Canadian Communities," 28 November, 1945. Iowa State University Library, Special Collections Department (hereafter ISU), Orville Goldner Papers, Ms. 528, Box 12 Folder 10, 1–17. Scott Fletcher would later claim that at that time U.S. educationalists were keeping tabs on Canadian developments in audiovisual education, which were seen as particularly advanced in the exploring media discussion groups. He commented, "They not only do so much with so little but they know so much about how to combine the media of mass communications with face to face communications for effective information, discussion, and education." Ford Foundation Archives (hereafter FFA), Scott Fletcher Oral History, interviewed by Charles T. Morrissey for the Ford Foundation, 1–3 March, 1973, Stuart, Florida, 154.

8. Other officers were First Vice President David E. Strom (NUEA and A-V Aids Center, University of Connecticut), Second Vice President Irving C. Boerlin (EFLA), Secretary Vernon G. Dameron (NEA), and Treasurer Merriman H. Holtz (ANTFA and the Treasury Department).

9. "FCA Constitution," 4 March, 1947. ISU, FCA, Ms. 351, Box 1, Folder 1, 1.

10. Evans Clark to Carnegie Corporation, 29 March, 1950. Columbia University Rare Book and Manuscript Library, Carnegie Corporation of New York Records (hereafter CC), Series III. A, Box 144, Folder 12, ("Film Council of America, 1947–1957"), 2.

11. Glen Burch to Ford Foundation, 3 April, 1951. FFA, Reel 4736, B1076, FCA, Section 6.

12. Film Council of America, Grant Recommendation, circa 1955. FFA, FAE, Box 2, Folder 15, 43.

13. As a point of comparison, the FCA had 130 affiliated councils in July 1949, while the National Film Society boasted more than 250 councils in Canada; "Summary Report on the Second Annual Meeting of the Film Council of America," *Film Counselor* 3, no. 2 (July–August 1949), np. Though FCA and Ford Foundation executives repeatedly referred to the more highly developed Canadian community film scene, these tallies reflect the more centralized organizational structure of the U.S. agency and not the size of educational film audiences.

14. "Educational Film Projects," circa March 1948. CC, Box 144, Folder 12, ("Film Council of America, 1947–1957"), 14–15.

15. "$20,000 Grant to FCA—Glen Burch, New Director," *Film News* 8, no. 11 (May 1948): 1, 9.

16. "Film Council of America," circa May 1950. CC, Box 144, Folder 12 ("Film Council of America, 1947–1957"), 1–2.

17. See Anna McCarthy's chapter in this volume for an expanded discussion of other media projects pursued by the Ford Foundation in the 1950s, in particular the Fund for the Republic's educational television programs.

18. Quoted in Edward H. Berman, *The Influence of the Carnegie, Ford, and Rockefeller Foundations on American Foreign Policy: The Ideology of Philanthropy* (Albany: State University of New York Press, 1983), 2.

19. Quoted in Frances Stonor Saunders, *The Cultural Cold War: The CIA and the World of Arts and Letters* (New York: New Press, 1999), 139.

20. Record of Interview, "Film Council of America," 1 May, 1951. CC, Box 144, Folder 12, ("Film Council of America"), 1947–1957.

21. "Investing in FCA's Future," *Film Counselor* 2, nos. 5/6, (May/June 1951): 1–2.

22. Minutes, Board of Directors Meeting, Fund for Adult Education, 6 May, 1952, 11. FFA, Box 1, Folder 3; Minutes, Board of Directors Meeting, Fund for Adult Education, 20 January, 1954. FFA, Box 2, Folder 10, 25; "Summary of Activities, April 3, 1951 to February 29, 1956." FFA, FAE, Box 3, Folder 20, April 27, 1956; Fund for Adult Education, *Annual Report, 1953–1954* (New York: Ford Foundation, 1954), 33; Fund for Adult Education, *Annual Report, 1954–1955* (New York: Ford Foundation, 1955), 45.

23. "The Fund for Adult Education: Statement of Purpose and Principles," revised June 1952. FFA, FAE Box 1, Folder 4, 1.

24. "The Fund for Adult Education: Statement of Purpose."

25. "The Fund for Adult Education: Statement of Purpose," 2.

26. Fund for Adult Education, *A Ten Year Report, 1951–1961* (New York: Ford Foundation, 1962), 29.

27. Fund for Adult Education, *A Ten Year Report.*

28. Fund for Adult Education, *A Ten Year Report.*

29. Scott Fletcher to Chancellor Lawrence A. Kimpton, 16 July, 1951. FFA, Reel 4736, B1076, Encyclopaedia Britannica Films Section, 1–2. See also Glen Burch, "F.A.E. and the Mass Media," *Educational Screen* 31 (February 1952): 54–55, 70–71.

30. "Coordination," Docket, January 23–24, 1953, FAE Administrative, Board of Directors Meetings Dockets and Minutes, 1951–1953. FFA, FAE, Box 1, Folder 7, 5.

31. "Of Local Origin," *New York Times*, 12 December, 1951, 50.

32. Tom W. Hope to C. Scott Fletcher, 11 September, 1953. Minnesota State Archives, Minnesota Department of Education Records, Audiovisual Dept., Richard C. Brower Papers, Minnesota Historical Society, Box 105.D.11.9.B, Folder 2, 1–3.

33. "Summary of Activities, April 3, 1951 to February 29, 1956." FFA, FAE, Box 3, Folder 20, April 27, 1956.

34. Fund for Adult Education, *A Ten Year Report*, 34.

35. Benjamin Fine, "Education in Review: Film Discussion Groups are Carrying Out a Novel Experiment in Adult Education," *New York Times*, March 30, 1952, E11.

36. Glen Burch, *Accent on Learning: An Analytical History of the Fund for Adult Education's Experimental Discussion Project, 1951–1959* (Pasadena, CA: Fund for Adult Education, Ford Foundation, 1960).

37. "For Clubwomen," *New York Times*, July 1, 1952, 20.

38. "Statement of the Fund for Adult Education and the Experimental Film Discussion Project," circa 1952. FFA, Reel 4741, 2–3.

39. Promotional Brochure, "World Affairs are Your Affairs," circa 1952. FFA, Reel 4741, np.

40. The other figures included Thomas Jefferson, Alexander Hamilton, George Washington, John Quincy Adams, Andrew Jackson, John C. Calhoun, Daniel Webster, and John Marshall.

41. Gene Currivan, "Education in Review: New Plan for Informal Discussion Groups of Adults to be Tried in New York," *New York Times*, 29 September, 1957, 183.

42. "E.F.D.P. Evaluation," circa 1953. FFA, Reel 4736, B1076, FCA Section, 1, 3.

43. Gene Currivan, "Education in Review," 183.

44. Promotional Brochure, "World Affairs are Your Affairs," circa 1952, np.

45. "Film Council of America," circa May 1952. FFA, FAE, Box 1, Folder 3, 13.

46. Film Council of America, Grant Recommendation, January 20/21, 1955. FFA, FAE, Box 2, Folder 15, 43–46.

47. "Educational Film-Discussion Project," July 1, 1953 to June 30, 1954, Financial Report. FFA, Reel 4736, B1076, FCA Section, n.p.

48. "E.F.D.P. Evaluation," circa 1953, 2.

49. "E.F.D.P. Evaluation," circa 1953, 4.

50. Charles Bushong (FCA) to Robert J. Blakely (FAE) with EFDP report, 9 September, 1953. FFA, Reel 4736, B1076, FCA Section, n.p.

51. "Educational Film-Discussion Project," July 1, 1953 to June 30, 1954, 13.

52. "Agreement Between the Fund for Adult Education and the Film Council of America," 22 October, 1954. FFA, Reel 4736, B1076, FCA Section, 1–5.

53. The test locations were Akron, Bridgeport, Chattanooga, Kansas City, Little Rock, Lubbock, Memphis, Niagara Falls, Racine, San Bernardino, Sioux City, York, and West Texas. "A Report on the Test Cities Project," 15 May, 1956. FFA, FAE, Box 3, Folder 21, 3.

54. "A Report on the Test Cities Project," 3–4.

55. "A Report on the Test Cities Project," 4.

56. "A Report on the Test Cities Project," 17.

57. "A Report on the Test Cities Project," 17.

58. "A Report on the Test Cities Project," 18.

59. "Educational Film-Discussion Project," July 1, 1953 to June 30, 1954, Appendix A.

60. "Discussion Leaders Prepared by NYU," *New York Times*, 18 January, 1959, 80. The FAE adapted "The Ways of Mankind" from Lister Sinclair's CBC radio series, which had received rave reviews when the FAE financed its U.S. broadcast in 1952.

Jack Gould, "Radio and Television: Canadian Network Shows How Broadcasters Can Offer Listenable Programs with Language Study," *New York Times*, December 15, 1952, 33.

61. Other work on middlebrow self-education includes Janice Radway, *A Feeling for Books: The Book-of-the-Month Club, Literary Taste, and Middle-Class Desire* (Chapel Hill: University of North Carolina Press, 1997); Joan Shelley Rubin, *The Making of Middlebrow Culture* (Chapel Hill: University of North Carolina Press, 1992); and for a study that addresses relationship between middlebrow and motion pictures, cf. Dana Polan, *Scenes of Instruction: The Beginnings of the U.S. Study of Film* (Berkeley: University of California Press, 2007).

62. Film Council of America, Grant Recommendation, January 21/22, 1955.

63. "Have You Heard?" *Educational Screen and AV Guide* 35 (November 1956): 394–95.

64. Scott Fletcher, Oral History, 1973, 198.

65. John Flory and Thomas W. Hope, "Scope and Nature of Nontheatrical Films in the United States," *Journal of the Society of Motion Picture and Television Engineers* 68, no. 6 (June 1959): 388.

66. "Progress Reports for Board Meeting, May 28–29, 1953, Film Council of America." FFA, Reel 4736, B1076, FCA Section, 33.

67. "Memorandum to all members of the Board of Directors from C. Scott Fletcher," 19 January, 1959. FFA, FAE, Box 4, Folder 30; and U.S. Department of Health, Education, and Welfare, Press Release, 3 December, 1958. FFA, FAE, Box 4, Folder 30, 1–3.

68. Berman, *The Influence of the Carnegie, Ford, and Rockefeller Foundation*, 12, 47, and 43–51, respectively.

69. Saunders, *The Cultural Cold War*, 139; also instructive on this topic is Volker R. Berghahn, *America and the Intellectual Cold Wars in Europe: Shepard Stone Between Philanthropy, Academy, and Diplomacy* (Princeton: Princeton University Press, 2001), 201.

70. Berman, *The Influence of the Carnegie, Ford, and Rockefeller Foundations*, 27.

71. Berman, *The Influence of the Carnegie, Ford, and Rockefeller Foundations*, 168.

72. Berman, *The Influence of the Carnegie, Ford, and Rockefeller Foundations*, 162.

73. Scott Fletcher, Oral History, 1973, 9.

74. Ron Greene and Darrin Hicks, "Lost Convictions: Debating Both Sides and the Ethical Re-Fashioning of Liberal Citizens," *Cultural Studies* 19, no. 1 (2005): 100–126.

75. Quoted in Berman, *The Influence of the Carnegie, Ford, and Rockefeller Foundations*, 43.

76. Christopher Simpson, *Science of Coercion: Communication Research and Psychological Warfare, 1945–1960* (New York: Oxford University Press, 1994).

77. Leon Bramson, *The Political Context of Sociology* (Princeton, NJ: Princeton University Press, 1961).

78. Cf. Wilbur Schramm, *The Beginnings of Communication Study in America: A Personal Memoir*, eds. Steven H. Chaffee and Everett M. Rogers (Thousand Oaks, CA: Sage Publications, 1997).

79. Elihu Katz and Paul Lazarsfeld, *Personal Influence* (Glencoe, IL: Free Press, 1955).

12

The Television Activities
of the Fund for the Republic

Anna McCarthy

It is by now well known that philanthropic support for mass-media research
and production after World War II was heavily influenced by the cold war
political and cultural milieu. The Ford Foundation and its related subsidiar-
ies, or "Funds," dominated this field, having become the largest foundation
in the world following the deaths of Henry and Edsel Ford in the 1940s.[1]
Ford's unprecedented postwar expansion coincided with a number of
important developments in U.S. political culture: the triangulated threats
of nuclear annihilation, international communism, and anticommunist
hysteria; the civil rights movement; public awareness of decolonization
struggles in regions thus far unaligned within the emerging bilateral world
order; the introduction of new media such as television; and the boom
in communications and media research, a boom fueled by propaganda
production in wartime and mass-consumption politics in peace. A concern
with these cold war–inflected historical contexts is evident in the 1949
mission document outlining the Foundation's funding areas and setting its
agenda for the advancement of humanity.[2] Authored by Rand Corporation
head Rowan Gaither, the so-called Gaither Report defined Ford's funding
priorities in terms of five recommended "programs": "The establishment of
peace, the strengthening of democracy, the strengthening of the economy,
education in a democratic society, and individual behavior and human relations."[3] Although their wording has changed over the years, these catchall
funding areas continue to define the Ford Foundation mission to this day.

Gaither and his committee of investigators identified both mass communications and the arts as crucial funding targets in all of these areas,

but they understood the purpose of such funding in very particular terms. One of the few directives Foundation Chairman Henry Ford II issued in his charge to the committee was that its recommendations should not duplicate funding areas, among them the arts, that were already covered by existing trusts.[4] As a result, media and other forms of expressive culture could not be funded as autonomous creative phenomena deserving of support on "purely" aesthetic grounds—art for art's sake, as it were. Instead, the authors of the Gaither Report approached culture and mass media as *instruments* to be deployed in the service of particular extrinsic goals on a continuum of authoritative uses of media, from education to propaganda. Still, there remained the question of *how* to instrumentalize mass media within the shifting agendas of postwar liberalism. This would become a pressing conundrum for Ford and other organizations seeking to shape civic culture and participate in civil governance at mid-century.

This chapter explores early philanthropic experiments in popular and mass media that attempted to solve this problem, mobilizing television as an instrument for teaching citizenship and aiding the preservation of liberal democracy. It focuses specifically on projects undertaken within the borders of the United States, specifically, on the television-sponsorship activities of the Fund for the Republic. A Ford Foundation subsidiary created in 1952 in response to McCarthyism's incursions on constitutional freedoms, the Fund's dual-pronged mission was to educate Americans about civil liberties and civil rights. These were two issues of central importance among establishment liberal circles at the time. Observing Southern racial conflicts from their Northeastern enclaves with persistent, if detached, outrage, many liberal elites identified affectively and politically with the "vital center," Arthur M. Schlesinger Jr.'s vision of a fair, moderate, and rational leadership bloc composed of humanistic anticommunists (as opposed to hysterical anticommunists like McCarthy).[5] This sense of principled moderation shaped liberal elites' attitudes toward Southern segregation. From the perspective of enlightened businessmen, educators, jurists, and intellectuals outside the South, segregation, like McCarthyism, was not only morally wrong, it was also a regressive element in the national political culture that tarnished the image of the United States abroad. For the establishment liberal of the 1950s, these backward ways of thinking impeded the advancement of western democracy as the basis of global governance in the postwar era. Against such views, David A. Horowitz notes, there emerged insurgent forms of populism at the time spoke in an "antielitist and antirationalist tone" and which challenged a bipartisan political establishment primarily concerned with stability and the orderly conciliation of differences."[6]

Within the establishment, Robert Maynard Hutchins, the head of the Fund for the Republic for most of its lifespan and a controversial figure within educational and political mainstreams, voiced a robust and often uncompromising conceptualization of liberal governance in relationship to the perceived ignorances of segregation and McCarthyism. Hutchins often expressed the sense of superiority associated with the liberal political program with unusual candor. One phrase, variations of which appear in several of his published writings and speeches, encapsulates this stance: "The American people are the most powerful in the world. If they are unenlightened, they will be the most dangerous people in the world."[7] Invoking the ignorance of others as a moral or social threat, a classic trope of American liberalism, Hutchins and other fund officers proposed that mass education of Americans held the key to fully activated national citizenship and indeed global survival. In the years following the end of World War II, when he was converted to the cause of world government, Hutchins lumped technocrats and philistines together, lamenting the "new barbarians . . . who have had no will or no opportunity to develop a system of ideas because they . . . have no conception of the nature of the world or the destiny of man." Isolated from others by their own biases, he wrote, "They cannot be members of a community."[8] Yet in many respects, Hutchins' proposed solution to this problem was the epitome of top-down, technocratic rationality: "If we want world peace, a world community, and a world state that will last, we must promote a moral, intellectual, and spiritual revolution throughout the world."[9] Confusingly, he cautioned that "if you set out to do other people good, it is difficult to avoid the ultimate conclusion that you can do them good because you are better than they are" while arguing that that this revolution should be "led by educated men and women."[10] Such grandiosity, expressed on a global scale yet emanating from the idiosyncratic worldview of a man who had spent most of his life in a university, made Hutchins the frequent target of charges of elitism. In a scathing review of the Great Books series in which Hutchins was deeply involved, Dwight Macdonald declared, "There is a difference between informing the reader and telling him what to think that seems to escape Dr. Hutchins, possibly because in his case there isn't any difference."[11]

As this chapter details, television was a venue in which elite liberal men like Hutchins attempted to stage, and resolve, pressing democratic conflicts, often in the autocratic manner noted by MacDonald. Projecting onto the audience and the medium an idealist model of communicative rationality and didactic persuasion, the Fund officers hoped that TV would reactivate the republican ideals of the U.S. Constitution. In keeping with the values of Cold War liberalism, they understood *freedom* to be the touchstone for these ideals; W. H. "Ping" Ferry, Hutchins' assistant at the Fund, wore a button on his lapel that said "Think Free."[12] In ascribing such power to freedom, Ferry, Hutchins, and others at the Fund approached television as what Nikolas Rose called a technology of "responsibilization," a tool of "government through the inculcation and shaping of private responsibility."[13] Rose's interest lies in those forms of practice separate from the state, from therapy to shopping to schooling, that create an inner self via the power of freedom. But the ethos of responsibilization applies very aptly to techniques of liberal civic education as well, among them the Fund's approach to television, which one of its media workers described as "stimulating discussion of civil liberties matters by aiding their presentation on television."[14] Aiding discussion via such techniques as example-setting through role play, narritives based in parable and allegory, and documentary persuasion, Fund television projects responsibilized the viewer, aiming to instill what Rose defines as "techniques whereby selves would simultaneously practice upon themselves as free individuals and bind them into a civilized polity by means of that freedom and the modes in which it was enacted."[15]

This civilizing project in TV can tell us a great deal about the self-image of what, for want of a better term, we might want to call white liberalism—a racial designation I use in recognition of the degree to which cold war liberalism was organized by questions about what to do about racial struggle and acknowledged, in problematic ways, the contradictions within liberal democracy that racial struggles signified. MacDonald's indictment of Hutchins' inflexible and top-down understanding of education applies in many respects to the television projects of the Fund for the Republic. Many of the Fund's projects, including an extensive operation documenting the successes of Southern civil rights activism for local news stations, were groundbreaking and relevant, although as I will explain, they were ultimately at odds with Hutchins's visions of civic pedagogy and his assessment of the responsive capacities of the television audience.

This vision was congruent with the unswaying belief in the applicability of pedagogical principles on a mass scale espoused since the 1930s by Hutchins' close friend and associate, the popular philosopher and Great Books advocate, Mortimer Adler. Although he referred to television as a "fungus," Hutchins believed the promise of civic education through TV was compelling enough to override the unseemly taint of mass culture that made most establishment liberals recoil from serious involvement in the new medium (with the exception, obviously, of television executives like William L. Paley and Frank Stanton of CBS). Along with Adler, Hutchins envisioned education as a form of secular religion, and he subscribed to a transhistorical understanding of reason as the basis of human nature. Advocating a return to medieval scholasticism's quest for moral certainty, the Great Books program proposed that the development of the intellect through classical texts of Western civilization was the key to civic and, more broadly, global enlightenment.[16] For Hutchins and Adler, the pursuit of reason was a battle not only against backward ways of thinking but also against scientific positivism and pragmatism, which Hutchins saw as false rationalism.[17] As a philosophy of education, this viewpoint infuriated men like John Dewey, who denounced it in 1943 as an "assault against all that is modern and new in education."[18] It also infuriated critics like Macdonald, who charged that the Great Ideas was first and foremost a marketing ploy preying on the cultural aspirations of the lower middle class.[19] Hutchins' interest in television can be seen as a response to John Dewey and others who found his claims for the Great Ideas program to be obfuscatory and idealist at best, false and opportunistic at worst. As will become evident over the course of the following pages, Hutchins' efforts to adapt the rarified methods he had conceived with Adler into a concrete program for civic awakening that could activate awareness of constitutional rights and freedoms were contradictory and imperfect solutions to the problems of democracy and governance that the Fund was trying to reform.

That Hutchins persisted in his pursuit of television airtime despite numerous obstacles reflects not only his native intransigence but also the more general understanding of media as instruments for rebuilding and strengthening democracy that suffused much foundation work in the cultural field during the cold war. This was especially the case for the Ford Foundation, deriving its mission directly from the Gaither Report. Within the broad context of the "cultural cold war" waged by Ford and other foundations, scholarship has focused primarily on funding activities directed toward audiences overseas, activities often carried out in covert collaboration with the CIA. Although these activities used cultural funding as a propaganda tool, as has often been noted, it was the perceived capacity of arts and letters to *resist* instrumentalization that paradoxically proved so useful in these covert projects of cultural diplomacy. Numerous cultural historians have outlined these international activities in some detail, showing how U.S. philanthropies and government agencies enlisted filmmakers, painters, composers, authors, and intellectuals in an anticommunist *Kulturkampf.*[20] Avowing a distinction between art and politics in order to achieve political ends, Foundation cultural activities overseas were congruent with the doctrine of containment advanced by foreign-policy architect George Kennan. And indeed, when Kennan advised the Foundation on how it might implement program 1, "the establishment of peace," he suggested that it focus not on direct expressions of opposition to communism but rather, in one Ford officer's words, on "long range activities (e.g., U.S. self-improvement, promotion of free inquiry and expression throughout the rest of the world.)."[21] Artistic freedom, in short, was a useful vehicle for U.S. statecraft on the international stage because it was disconnected from the forms of governance associated with the exercise of state power.

Containment had a domestic component too, and it is in this category that the Fund's efforts at civic education by television belong. It is useful to think about the domestic politics of containment as a popularized counterpart to the "Marshall plan of the mind" implemented in European intellectual circles through such institutions as the Salzburg Seminar. However, the object being contained through these domestic programs was not totalitarianism, nor even communism, but mass culture. Neutralizing the unruly politics of populism and replacing it with pluralism was, as Andrew Ross notes, central to the liberal project in mass culture in the early cold war: "A long postwar debate among intellectuals about mass culture and mass society . . . is explicitly shot through with a rhetoric about containment."[22] The forms of cultural governance supported by the Ford Foundation on the cold war's home front suggest that the domestic project of containment was more than just rhetoric. Mass-media projects associated with the tenure of Paul Hoffman, the Foundation's first president, attempted to bring about the establishment of peace through highly directive forms of uplift and civic enlightenment. Along with the Fund for the Republic, Ford Foundation agencies such as the Fund for Adult Education, the Fund for the Advancement of Education, and the Television Radio Workshop sponsored television and radio programs that fell into Kennan's category of "U.S. self-improvement." But unlike Ford's *international* arts programs, which enacted a form of cultural containment via the dissemination of highbrow forms seemingly uncontaminated by ideology, the domestic media projects of the Fund for the Republic and other Ford-related groups were more direct, if not propagandistic, in their efforts to reach American citizens. Indeed, the term "self-improvement" is misleading; the various forms of mass-mediated civic education explored by officers at the Fund and other Ford agencies were directed not toward themselves but rather toward those "other" people who comprised the television audience. Not surprisingly, they were largely unsuccessful.

But history loves a failure, and indeed, it is *because of* the failures and contradictions plaguing Fund efforts to enlist television within projects of liberal governance that its forays into popular civic education are so illuminating. Its archives, housed at Princeton University, provide insights into the relationship between media sponsorship and conceptions of political citizenship in the mentality of postwar liberalism. Although the Fund staff's deep ambivalence toward mass media and its audiences was typical of the bipartisan establishment that flourished in the decades before Watergate and the U.S. failures in Vietnam, they were themselves unusual within this elite brotherhood in their persistent efforts to work within the media to teach citizenship.[23] As a technocratic solution to mass culture's corrosions and a fulfillment of the liberal dream of rebuilding the United States as a rational republic of world citizens, postwar experiments with television as a tool of reform are a unique and important window onto the cultural politics of mid-twentieth-century liberalism, particularly the complex relations among liberal intellectuals, media audiences, and corporate media outlets.

It is commonplace to view this relationship as antagonistic, a judgment that certainly holds true when applied to the published opinions of critics such as Leslie Fiedler, Lionel Trilling, and Dwight MacDonald. But the narrative of antagonism leaves out the attitudes and actions of the liberal intellectual popularizers that these men held in such low regard. The practical ventures in mass and middlebrow culture that men like Adler and Hutchins undertook seemed laughable to mass-culture critics. But these critics' crowing dismissal of the popularizers' efforts to administer citizenship in measured doses, through culture and mass media, does not make these efforts irrelevant.

The populizers were far more visible as intellectuals in the postwar mass-cultural field than critics like Fiedler. However clumsy, or even distasteful, their projects may appear today, any attempt to reckon with the liberal relationship to mass culture and politics must take stock of the cultural work they performed, ideally doing so from a viewpoint that stands to the side of postwar critics' contempt for the middlebrow. Resisting the seductively superior certainty of mass-culture critic's makes it easier to look closely at the field of strategies and assumptions in which liberal acts in media took form, approaching middlebrow intellectuals and mainstream liberal media reformers as representatives of a particular disposition within political culture. Their work then becomes an opportunity to examine the political work of mass-media institutions like television in new ways—not simply in terms of their demonstrated or speculated impact on audiences, but also in terms of the coalitions they help build among elites and between corporate leaders, academic administrators, professors, politicians, and jurists.

These networks of establishment figures and middlebrow intellectuals were closely tied to the Ford Foundation, which offered an early and important venue for thinking about the civic role of television sponsorship and viewership under its first president, Paul Hoffman. The projects that emerged from this context were unique among the media efforts of philanthropical organizations.[24] The Fund for the Republic was established at a moment when support for educational broadcasting was by no means Ford's clear priority in mass media. Hoffman advocated the use of both commercial *and* nonprofit media for "the rapid and extensive education of adults about the world situation, the nature of the struggle in which we are engaged, and the heritage we are seeking to defend."[25] And indeed, *Omnibus*, the most lavishly funded Hoffman-era media project, aired not on educational channels but on commercial TV networks.[26] An arts-and-culture television program hosted by Alistair Cooke, *Omnibus*'s reform agenda was, in the words of one Ford media consultant, to "raise the level of American taste." A technocratic solution to cold war liberal fears of entrenched cultural ignorance and isolationism among the U.S. population, the program was also an indirect way of affirming the civic integrity of commercial broadcasting.[27] It was funded in what would now be called a "public-private partnership" between the Foundation and corporate advertisers, an arrangement that embodied the corporate liberal vision associated with Hoffman's short-lived presidency of the Foundation and his previous post as director of the Marshall Plan. Like many of the Ford projects associated with James Webb Young, an advertising executive and close friend of Hoffman, *Omnibus* sought to achieve democratic enlightenment of the masses not simply through funding, but also through the assertion of the moral responsibility and cultural benefits of the free-enterprise system.

Hoffman's fervor for the promotion of capitalism did not have much effect on the Fund for the Republic's television projects, which, as the organization's name might suggest, were more narrowly pitched toward the promotion of Jeffersonian ideals of freedom and justice for all.[28] The Fund's purpose—to investigate, and increase public awareness of, problems surrounding the preservation of civil rights and civil liberties—was far more explicitly activist than Ford's. But the Fund nevertheless adopted Hoffman's ambitious vision of commercial television sponsorship as a form of civic education in which philanthropies might productively engage, even if it approached sponsorship as a type of media *reform* rather than an affirmation of the democratic value of television in its present form. Because of its controversial mandate, the Fund for the Republic was organizationally independent of the Ford Foundation.[29] Indeed, Dwight McDonald quipped that it was a "wholly disowned subsidiary." This focus on political issues that were "hot to handle" reflected the political present of the nation at mid-century. But in its approach to these issues, the Fund looked for inspiration in the republican past. As is evident in its eventual transformation into the centrist liberal think tank, the Center for the Study of Democratic Institutions, the Fund's vision of liberal democratic change had little in common with the materialist redistributive goals of political movements outside the establishment mainstream. Rather, it was confined to the full activation of categories created within liberal political theory, with its emphasis on rights, freedoms, and individual sovereignty. Hutchins and his colleagues saw their task primarily in terms of the democratization of the Constitution, that is, as the unleashing and protection of all the freedoms promised in that document. They saw liberal Supreme Court Justice William O. Douglas as their intellectual leader and constantly tried to popularize his ideas in their television projects.

The narrative of the Fund's media work is in many respects the story of mainstream mid-century American liberalism's search for a popular voice in which to transmit its core values. Perhaps inevitably, the effort to implement these principles in popular media replicated all of the contradictions of liberalism in this period. In calling, like Douglas, for a renewed, inclusive understanding of republican liberties, the Fund articulated a pressing need to affirm *principles* of freedom over the *rhetorics* of freedom associated with popular anticommunism in this period. This somewhat abstracted approach to pressing political problems reflected the pedagogical commitments of Hutchins dating back to his time at the University of Chicago. But it also reflected Treasury Department policy prohibiting advocacy by nonprofit organizations, a policy invoked several times in the 1950s via congressional investigations of both the Ford Foundation and the Fund for the Republic. Increasing public awareness of the founding principles of the nation was, for Fund officers, a neutral and thoroughly defensible educational mission. Yet the Fund's cautious and intellectualized approach to racial injustice and political hysteria was not merely a function of the idiosyncratic convictions of its president, nor indeed a response to the policies governing nonprofit organizations in this period. Rather, as a vision of governance, it was symptomatic of currents in postwar liberal media activism and reform. Sponsorship, from the Fund's perspective, was an ideal technique for teaching citizens how to define the common national interest; in other words, Fund officers saw it as a tool for teaching people how to govern themselves at a crucial and transformative moment in U.S. political history.

GOVERNING BY TELEVISION

The Fund's utopian commitment to the rationalist ethos of classical republicanism was accompanied by a concern with managing what it saw as the irrational impulses of the population at large, making its primary task the discovery of persuasive techniques that could break past emotions to activate the viewing subject's rational, civic-minded core. The tensions between the various elements of the Fund's vision of mass politics were rendered most acutely in the Fund's own television-sponsorship projects, as distinct from those it merely supported with grant money. Archival records of negotiations between Fund officers and media professionals document how Hutchins and his staff translated their class- and culture-bound assumptions about the civic capacities of television audiences into modes of media address. They approached mass media via a familiar liberal dichotomy, as a social relationship promising at once a means for public education and debate and a means for the destruction of civil society altogether through the promotion of triviality and entertainment. In the end, the Fund was largely unsuccessful in using television sponsorship as a form of citizen education. Even after its move to Santa Barbara and its reincarnation as the Center for the Study of Democratic Institutions, Hutchins and his cohort seemed stuck in a loop when it came to the question of how to use mass media to govern others, or more properly, teach others how best to govern themselves.

It was TV's promise as an instrument of mass education that led the Fund to seek a place for its views on the commercial airwaves, rather than any proven capacity of the medium to enhance public life. Accepting the Sidney Hillman Foundation award for public service, Hutchins proclaimed the ideal of mass media as resources for civic self-government that is a cornerstone of liberal media reform: "If our hopes for democracy are to be realized, the media must supply full and accurate information on which the people can base their judgment on public affairs, and they must offer a forum for the discussion of those affairs."[30] Media sponsorship was the Fund's solution to deficiencies in this area. As administrator Hallock Hoffman (Paul's son) explained it in 1954, the Fund "has determined to change bad practices and to instigate good practices in as direct a manner as possible. While some of our projects are studies, we embark upon studies only when this appears to be necessary to action, or the only practicable means of action."[31] When audiences for existing forms of broadcast media proved recalcitrant, Hutchins did not hesitate to invent his own forms. At one point he explored the possibility of sponsoring a national lecture series, transmitted via Theater Television, in which international leaders, among them Charles De Gaulle, Arnold Toynbee, Winston Churchill, and Albert Schweitzer, would address the American people. In typically impulsive fashion, he issued telegrams of invitation asking these and other distinguished figures to participate and "help the American people understand the world and their position in it," without ever checking on whether this patently unfeasible plan would actually be possible.[32]

Hutchins' grandiose and impractical vision of transforming the nation's movie theaters into televisual lyceums was only one of many possibilities for media work explored at the Fund over the course of the 1950s. Most of them took the form of sponsorship. In early television, when presented as educational and offered in the public service, sponsorship was an opportunity to speak politically while seeming to rise above mere "politics." In a sense, it was a form of patronage, a relationship with the public based on shared and unarguable notions of civic good. The most immediately notable aspect of the Fund's various forms of sponsorship is their incoherence. Over the course of its nine-year existence, the Fund hopped, seemingly at random, from one television venture to another. If there was any discernible logic underneath this meandering, it was a sensitivity to scale. Programs developed for the networks or for national syndication, most of which never aired, were more likely to be pitched as popular genres such as situation comedy, anthology drama, and soap opera, although the Fund also tried to get national airtime for more educationally oriented material, from historical biography to documentary films.[33] Its local and syndicated TV and radio programming, in contrast, concentrated almost entirely on public affairs. Mostly sponsored by third parties using Fund-administered grants, these local projects included both individual broadcasts and entire series of programs focusing on civil liberties and civil rights; most prominent among the latter was the Los Angeles–originating *Confidential File*, which covered topics of race relations (and to a lesser extent civil liberties) with a somewhat sensationalist slant.

Most of the programs produced with Fund money aired in low-rated timeslots provided by commercial stations to fulfill federal public service requirements—the sleepy Sunday lineup of religious, educational, and public-affairs programming one critic called an "intellectual ghetto."[34] But despite its educational mission, the Fund constantly sought broader audiences than the miniscule share that Sunday's schedule provided. Indeed, it aimed for the status of "institutional" sponsor, a prestige that Ford enjoyed with *Omnibus*. Institutional advertising was a genre associated with prime-time sponsors like DuPont, which offered the historical-anthology program *Cavalcade of America*. Selling not products but rather ideas, institutional advertising was a form of corporate public relations that exploited potential connections between sponsorship and civic speech by stressing the social beneficence of the sponsoring corporation or, more generally, the free-enterprise system. DuPont and other institutional advertisers frequently depicted their films and television programs about the benefits of unregulated competition as "economic education," a genre of corporate media that flourished after the 1947 Taft-Hartley Act loosened restrictions on management communications to allow for "neutral" and nonthreatening forms.[35]

The institutional advertisement, in the postwar period, was thus a form of neutral advertising that aspired to the status of a reasoned, neutral policy document. Like post Taft-Hartley institutional sponsors, the Fund sought access to this voice, hoping to speak to the public in a manner that the National Association of Manufacturers (NAM) described as "constructively, not argumentatively, and in the public interest."[36] But unlike NAM and other institutional advertisers, the Fund for the Republic had no interest in speaking on matters of economic governance. Rather, Fund officers were attracted to the program genres associated with institutional sponsors and other "prestige" corporate advertisers, like Westinghouse, because of their tendency to tackle social themes from a liberal perspective. However, they did not grasp the basic conditions under which such programming was produced. For corporate advertisers, a "hands-off" approach in the sponsorship of quality programming forms like the anthology drama was perceived as a way of generating "goodwill" for the company—a form of noninterventionist propagandizing that obeyed a logic similar to the products of artistic freedom exploited by foundations and the State Department in overseas cultural diplomacy. This was the economic-ideological contract underlying the so-called "golden age" of television drama, and it was dependent upon the assertion of artistic freedom by auteurs like David Susskind and Paddy Chayevsky.

In contrast to this arrangement, the Fund's officers saw the dramas and comedies they sponsored as an occasion for sending a message. It commissioned *Westinghouse Studio One* veterans Rod Serling and Reginald Rose to script a pilot episode for an anthology drama about civil liberties, a program promoted as the first of several "'open-ended dramas' . . . primarily concerned with freedom in our time, and [which] will present more than one side of situations."[37] But when the Fund sent the resulting script, titled "The Challenge," to several consultants for comment, it was not favorably received. Writer Reggie Schuebel noted that the script was simplistic in its representation of its right-wing characters. "I'm afraid," she wrote, "these disciples of liberalism underrate the brain power of the right wing so that intolerance bounces back upon itself."[38] The Fund was undeterred by Schuebel's criticism. It shot the script, with Sidney Lumet producing and *Studio One* director Worthington Minor directing, then sent it to the networks in the hope that the all-star production team would attract a sponsor for the series. Although CBS was initially interested, no sponsor was forthcoming. The film was eventually reedited as an educational short to be shown locally, to civic groups, in public meetings.[39]

The failure of "The Challenge" calls attention to the shortcomings of centrist liberalism as a political stance within postwar media. On one level, the incoherence and heavy-handedness of the program reflected the Fund's precarious position, caught between the networks and the federal government, each of which sought to circumscribe—for different reasons—the kinds of civic-media pedagogy in which the Fund could engage. But more basically, it reflected the organization's fractured and contradictory relationships with the causes it espoused and the audiences it sought to reach. The next section outlines the ideas about the audience that emerge from the records of the Fund officers' interactions with media professionals both at the networks and on their own staff. After that, I turn to a consideration of the shifting logics of political representation that characterized the two final television projects of the Fund. The first of these was the eighteen-month Newsfilm Project, which worked closely with newsreel cameramen, local-station production staff, and amateur camerapersons gathering footage of civil rights and civil liberties news stories and distributing them via syndicated news services to local stations and network news directors. The second, inaugurated after the Fund changed its mission to focus on sponsoring research on the "Basic Issues" of democracy, was the Fund's final television project, an interview program hosted by Mike Wallace on ABC in 1958. The story of the transition from one to the other is, I shall argue, the story of a shift in the way the Fund imagined its audiences and, along with it, the scale on which it might best effect social change.

IMAGINING THE VIEWER CITIZEN

Untroubled by any apparent contradiction between their paternalistic methods and the freedoms they sought to teach, Fund officers believed they could activate the civic awareness of a national TV audience they saw as a foreign and uneducated "other," doing little to disguise their distaste for the programs they devised to teach principles of civil liberties and civil rights to ordinary Americans. Remarking on a proposed Fund-sponsored TV series about the Stewarts, an American family facing in their daily life "all of those problems brought about by . . . anti-democratic forces," media consultant Howard Chernoff wrote dismissively that the treatment was "corny enough to appeal to the people we are trying to reach."[40] Such characterizations established Fund officers as a group apart from the mass audience, refusing to own television sets or claiming not to watch them—as did Walter Lippman, who kept the TV in the kitchen, to be viewed by the maid.[41] When Fund TV projects foundered or stalled, it was often because of officers' inflexible and one-dimensional preconceptions about the TV audience.

The Fund's limited and contradictory understanding for the audience was particularly pronounced in programs that addressed issues of racial prejudice and attempted to modify both the attitudes and behaviors of viewing subjects perceived to be lacking in civic awareness. Fund officers repeatedly placed their faith in programs that used artificial forms like staged role-playing exercises to show viewers inappropriate civic behaviors, then corrected these behaviors with commentary from an authoritative facilitator. It was a structure of civic engagement comparable to the imagined utility of early human-relations films, produced for screening and discussion in civic groups and schools. Such visions of civic culture were a thriving arena in nontheatrical film production in this period, although they were already being mocked among black intellectuals and radicals in the 1950s.[42] When confronted with pitches for Fund-sponsored civic lessons undertaken in this vein, network executives were appalled. Sylvester "Pat" Weaver, upon viewing the pilot for the Fund's first TV project, reacted with utter distaste at the program's format and its realization: a series of sketches dramatizing civil-liberties violations and incidents of prejudice, interspersed with "humorous" commentary by cartoonist Al Capp (this was prior to Capp's "right turn" in the early 1960s).[43] Summarizing the NBC programming chief's concerns, one staff member wrote that Weaver found the humor inappropriate, questioning whether such direct treatment was wise. He further noted that Weaver advocated NBC's method of liberal representation as an alternative: "in the case of discrimination, for example, to use Negro actors wherever they should be used without any emphasis on the actual fact of their use."[44] Weaver's concern with the advisability of adopting such a didactic voice reflected a sense of the audience and its receptivity more flexible and nuanced than that of the Fund officers. If the Fund saw viewers as open vessels for ideology, Weaver saw the audience as recalcitrant and ultimately resistant to lectures from above.[45]

What is illuminating about Weaver's response to the proposed *Al Capp Show* in the context of postwar establishment liberalism is the way it illustrates both the manifest differences and the underlying similarities between the sensibilities of media professionals who set representational policy at the networks and those of the Fund's officers. Both groups believed in example-setting, but their goals and objects were different. In Weaver's view, social change was best effected through the unremarkable representation of black people. It was a logic of representation without comment, in which black individuals onscreen, by their display of talent and competence, would serve as positive examples of the race as a whole. The unstated, and pathologizing, assumption in his policy was that such treatment would normalize the black other in the white mind. Fund officers, on the other hand, addressed cognition and behavior in the examples they tried to set, seeking to normalize liberal attitudes rather than particular populations in the minds of the average white viewer.

This top-down, didactic understanding of TV's civic capacity was a perpetual point of contention between Fund officers and the media consultants from whom they sought advice. The latter were almost unanimous in their criticisms, focusing like Weaver on the crudeness of the chosen mode of address and the transparency of the Fund's preaching. Astonishingly, Fund officers paid little heed to the advice of others whose knowledge and expertise in media far exceeded their own. The extent of Fund officers' resistance to critical feedback from media experts is evident in the postmortem memoranda that circulated following the airing of a nationally syndicated installment of the local Los Angeles program *Confidential File*, intermittently supported by Fund money. The program in question focused on the plight of black professionals passing as white and featured interviews with, and testimonies of, subjects whose identities were concealed. When one staff member noted that the program was clumsy and stilted, doing little to advance the cause of racial injustice, Hallock Hoffman was outraged: "Let's . . . fire Miss Huling if her opinion is as bad as I think," he wrote in jabbing strokes on the front of the interoffice memorandum transmitting her critique.[46] Such complete rejection of professional opinion suggests that the Fund's arrogance toward media audiences extended to media producers as well, the latter somehow contaminated by their association with the taint of the popular and the mass.

The consequence of this sense of superiority, at once high-handed and idealistic, was that Fund officers not only talked down to their audiences, they also believed naively that viewers would forgive aesthetic shortcomings and weaknesses of form, responding only to the rational-political content of the TV programs they funded. In other words, alongside its condescending image of the collective TV audience as the masses, the Fund's leadership contradictorily presumed an individual spectator-interlocutor that was the embodiment of the ideal liberal subject—a subject capable of knowing the world from an omniscient viewpoint, for whom the basic tenets of republican democracy were transparent, logical, and, once identified, easily differentiated into more or less appropriate forms of action. This understanding of the sovereign viewing individual never quite reconciled itself with the image of the mass audience Hutchins and others held, a suggestible mass seeking entertainment alone. Indeed, when Fund officers saw problems in their projects, their judgments rested on whether or not they recognized an address to this imagined liberal spectator in the program. In a sense, they were looking for an image of themselves, or what they imagined themselves to be, in the programs they sponsored on television.

This method of evaluation, looking to the programs for confirmation of a vision of rational human agency, was at odds with the methods of the Fund's media consultants, all of whom kept in mind the desires and judgments of a spectatorial imago they considered to be the "average" television viewer when they read scripts and viewed films. This was how the unfortunate Miss Huling judged the *Confidential File* episode's shortcomings; the difference between the two positions is evident in Hallock Hoffman's critique of the same show. In a letter to Paul Coates, the producer of the show, Hoffman suggested that although "the feeling of the injustice practiced on the people before your camera was clear and compelling, [t]he other feeling, that the society was denying itself able, creative work from able, creative people by discrimination, was not as clear."[47] The shortcoming, in other words, lay not in the tone or the affective relations between viewer and onscreen subject, but in the way the program failed to lay out a positive course of action for a viewer who was at heart a rational citizen awaiting information that would make him or her aware of the objective social costs of irrational phenomena, such as discrimination.

Dependent on the Fund for their livelihood, media producers the Fund hired as consultants devised program forms that attempted both to bridge the gap between their own experiences and the media visions of their client, and to educate the Fund's officers about the shortcomings of these visions. In 1956, newly hired Newsfilm Project director George Martin attempted to make the translation, pitching a (presumably network) show that would illustrate "what happens to people in conversations on civil liberties and bill of rights that take place by chance in club cars . . . barber shops . . . bars . . . in taxicabs, airplanes and elevators." Everydayness was an important element of Martin's idea. Suggesting the consummate everyman, he proposed that "some sympathetic personality as James Stewart would portray the man with the answers in conversations on specific aspects of the Bill of Rights." Martin's idea seemed to be intended as much as a subtle message to the Fund about how to conceive of its audience as it was a feasible proposal. He stressed that the program should "avoid sterility and preaching and . . . permit viewers to identify themselves with the man asking the questions." Also he indicated that the aesthetic norms of conventional entertainment should predominate: "The films should be so paced that audience conviction will flow naturally from the argument as it develops on the film . . . [they] should each wind up with some kind of affirmation or agreement on the fact that room for differences is the nation's greatest source of strength."[48] Martin's proposal thus impressed upon his supercilious clients that didacticism must be submerged in drama; enlisting the figure of the motion-picture industry's consummate liberal dramatic pedagogue, James Stewart, it encouraged them to identify with the average viewer.

Other Fund media workers, especially those like Martin who had worked in local TV, shared his respect for the audience's political and intellectual curiosity. Summarizing the approach of his news program *Dateline: Freedom*, Edward Howden of the San Francisco Council for Civic Unity suggested that people would not listen to drama or documentary programming on issues like racism unless they are of "the highest quality." Moreover, he contended, they avoided interview or discussion programs "because they are too dry." But "almost everybody listens daily and weekly to some news program," and indeed, this format was particularly effective for educating viewers on racial injustice: "important here, it seems, is the absence of preachment, of an underlying attitude of moral superiority, or of other emotionalized and opinionated approaches commonly associated with the field of intergroup relations."[49] Like Martin, this author cautioned the Fund against sermonizing. Taking this point further, he offered a model of the effects that the Fund might hope to achieve in its sponsorship of local news programs more nuanced than those advanced by Hoffman and Hutchins:

> Our considered view is that gradual, almost imperceptible modification of the outlook of individuals (as distinguished from "conversion") takes place under the impact of the news, fairly presented in context, of both good or bad happenings touching minority groups. . . . It is important to distinguish between merely verbal antagonisms in this field and what individuals actually do in specific problem situations; e.g., a person may continue to state his prejudices, but in many particular situations will refrain from behaving according to those

statements. *Dateline*, we think, encourages growing recognition of, and behavior consistent with, the rights and opportunities to which all are entitled.[50]

Somehow this model of media activism, using diverse forms of information to modify behaviors rather than ideas, must have appealed to Fund officers, one of whom noted that *Dateline: Freedom* was "most promising . . . and might set a model for similar programs in other areas."[51] Indeed, it seems likely that it formed the basis of the project that Martin headed, a newsgathering and distribution service that provided information on civil liberties and civil rights to local stations. The Newsfilm Project, as it was known, had a direct, activist goal: to educate the public about threats to civil liberties across the nation, and to publicize the efforts of desegregationists in the South to local television audiences across the country (although in many cases it did not even try to distribute its newsreels to Southern stations).

This activist agenda put into practice Hallock Hoffman's belief that the constructive representation of action was the best way of reaching viewers, and it did so without the condescending and distracting efforts to entertain that had marred the Fund's efforts to speak to the public within network TV programming. The Newsfilm Project sought to counter sensationalist coverage of desegregation in the South by providing stations with footage of moments of successful integration that were not being covered in the news, as well as iconic moments in the history of the civil rights struggle, such as the Montgomery bus boycott. Newsfilm camera crews recorded desegregation efforts in the Louisville public school system, in Dallas's public transportation, and at the University of North Carolina. They also considered projects that might not seem particularly newsworthy but which affirmed the mainstream liberal creed of the Fund, such as a Yale dermatologist's discovery of "substances which can, with comparative ease, change skin color from light to dark and in many cases from dark to light."[52] These stories were roughly edited into clips and distributed by United Press-Movietone, which recorded the number of stations that used the footage. The project never reached a huge audience—2 million to 3 million viewers for local broadcasts, around 15 million for the occasional network airing.[53] But it was a radical effort given the sorry state of TV coverage of desegregation in 1955.

The suggested scripts submitted to TV stations along with silent footage and brief sound on film segments offer insight on the idea of the viewer on which the Newsfilm Project rested. The scripts generally appealed to viewers' rational faculties, seeming to target those who fell into a fundamentally moderate, though inactive, political majority. As one script for the Montgomery bus boycott asserted, "There is a large group of middle-of-the-road whites in the south, midway between extremists of both sides," and it expressed the hope that the interracial Alabama Council on Human Relations would "provide that bridge that is so greatly needed between our negro and white populations."[54] In its rejection of extremism this sentiment bore more than a passing resemblance to the political subjectivity advocated by Schlesinger Jr.'s *Ur text* of cold war liberal centrism, *The Vital Center*. As an attempt at televisual governance, the Newsfilm Project operated under the assumption that viewing images of orderly liberal conduct (and disorderly extremist conduct) would teach citizens to choose the path toward desegregation, civil rights, and the preservation of civil liberties. For Fund officers, this choice was a self-evidently reasonable and moderate decision. They assumed that viewers, like themselves, would react with distaste rather than sympathy when confronted with segregationist hatred and that they would similarly identify with the dignity, pride, and moral righteousness of civil rights activists and workers depicted onscreen.

This assumed spectatorial relationship suggests an interesting variant of the dominant form of U.S. white liberalism, which Saidaya Hartman and others have incisively criticized for its subjugating dependence upon emotions such as charity, pity, and guilt. As summarized by Julie Ellison, liberal guilt is an emotional performance in public culture "which from the very beginning is bound up with self-conscious racial difference [and] is repeatedly staged through stories of cross-racial spectatorship. It relies on visual practices of seeing pain and being seen to be afflicted by it."[55] Against the guilt-ridden bleeding heart, the Fund for the Republic offered a new organ for liberal affect: the judging mind. Replacing abolitionist sentiment, with republican virtue this alternative strategy was not so much a repudiation of the processes of identification and sympathy on which liberal guilt depended as it was a rewriting of the scenes in which sympathy was staged, orienting the process of sympathetic identification toward uplift rather than abjection. Against network news coverage, which tended toward the display of black subjection, a technique decried by Fund officers as exploitative and sensationalistic, the Newsfilm Project tried to incite sympathetic identification between the imagined rational, moderate viewer and the rational, well-behaved individuals the Newsfilm Project had selected to represent the civil rights and civil liberties causes onscreen. The replacement of banished emotions with a new currency of liberal identification based on viewer recognition of the dignified, orderly, and reasonable nature of the causes portrayed in its footage extended the ethos of "positive images" long advocated by the NAACP from the representation of black people to encompass the representation of progressive causes. In showing that black protesters and civil liberties advocates were decorous and rational, the Newsfilm Project sought to extend these attributes to their causes and, by extension, to the viewer.

As ethical resources, these attributes linked the Newsfilm Project to other forms of liberal political affect in mid-century public culture. *Dignity* was a powerful keyword in public evaluations of affect and politics, used to describe a range of figures and modes of address, from advertisements that didn't belittle the viewer[56] to the "dignified negro" played by Robert Earl Jones in Elia Kazan's film *Wild River*.[57] It was often used in implicit opposition to political affects deemed extremist. As John Nickel points out in his analysis of the disabled black man in racial message films, "Dignity . . . was a catchword in the postwar and civil-rights eras, lavished on those who took persecution on the chin and did not deign to fight back." For the Newsfilm Project, *dignity* did not signify what it signified to those involved in the civil rights struggle, namely, the demand to be recognized respectfully, to have one's human dignity acknowledged.[58] It was, rather, a value to be endowed upon others by the benevolent white liberal. As the next and concluding section argues, the final hours of the Newsfilm Project and the emergence of what would prove to be the last commercial television project of the Fund for the Republic illustrate a shift in perceptions of viewer engagement with liberal causes back to a model with which Hutchins was clearly more comfortable. It indicates the triumph of this white, liberal understanding of dignity over other, potentially more radical, possibilities for activism embodied, if only through implication, in the Newsfilm Project. After all, despite its limited understanding of spectatorial engagement, the idea of a liberal local news distribution service held an unfulfilled promise to use local television news to connect and publicize local struggles across the nation.

SURVIVAL AND FREEDOM

The ostensible motivation for the Fund's abandonment of the Newsfilm Project came from without. Although the project may seem limited or tame today, it nevertheless skirted dangerously close to violating both FCC regulations and the laws governing tax-exempt organizations, specifically the prohibition against "propagandizing" and the exertion of political influence. In the first case, distributing materials for broadcast without identification was a violation of FCC policy on sponsorship, which required that sponsors always be "identified at both beginning and end in case of a controversial program."[59] In the second case, a 1955 appearance by Hutchins on *Meet the Press* led HUAC to instigate a Treasury Department review of the Fund's tax-exempt status and an investigation into the Fund's activities. During the broadcast Hutchins challenged blacklisting as a violation of the Bill of Rights and the principle of Equal Protection, issuing the provocative statement that he would not hesitate to hire a communist at the Fund if he were qualified for the job. This was a position far more principled than the accomodationist concern with false accusation through which many other liberals voiced their opposition to McCarthyism. As the investigation proceeded, pressure on the Newsfilm Project to produce footage that was "balanced," showing both sides of an issue and refraining from advocacy, became particularly intense. Although Martin was careful to avoid stories that might appear to take sides in political campaigns, his work for the Fund was drawn into the investigation in 1956. The Treasury Department found that three pieces of film were possible examples of bias. The first was a report on postal censorship, which detailed the U.S. Postal Service's decision to confiscate copies of the *Moscow Gazette* ordered by a retired schoolteacher trying to learn Russian. The second was footage covering attacks on pacifists protesting war on Armed Forces Day. The third was a report covering a meeting of the Congress of Freedom, which the investigators claimed intentionally sought to make the participants look ridiculous.[60]

The federal investigation and ensuing controversies were the death knell of the Newsfilm Project. Martin, a seasoned professional in broadcast-news production, was vociferous in challenging the Treasury Department's accusations, soliciting testimonials asserting the project's balanced approach from news directors at network-owned-and-operated stations who had used Newsfilm Project material in the past. However, the Fund was not willing to take risks. Its lawyer, Bethuel M. Webster, called Martin to tell him to "play possum . . . and not get engaged in things which our enemies could cite against us as being outside of our charter powers and our tax exemption." Although the investigation had not cited any of the civil rights stories in its investigation, Webster told Martin that the injunction to remain innocuous applied to a planned story he described as "the Fund chaperoning this trip of negroes and whites into Louisiana."[61] When Martin protested that the project would not be chaperoning, but "merely following them and reporting what happened," Webster replied that they could be interpreted as chaperoning, appealing to the broader concern with the safety of the Fund: "It helps not to prejudice our entire program in order to get an exciting picture of race relations in Baton Rouge."[62] In 1957, despite several heartfelt pleas from Martin, the Fund reined in its direct involvement in the Newsfilm Project and other activist media, taking the opportunity to rewrite its mission statement entirely.

The result of this organizational remaking was, in many respects, a matter of *plus ça change*, as it hearkened back to the experiments in educating business leaders inaugurated by Hutchins and Adler in 1943.[63] The centerpiece of the new plan, titled the Basic Issues Program, was a series of small working groups of elite opinion leaders convened to study the "Basic Issues" of constitutional democracy. From that point onward the Fund ceased making grants to small, grassroots activist organizations, such as the San Francisco Council for Civic Unity and its TV program, *Dateline Freedom*. Redefined by this longitudinal project, the Fund became the Center for the Study of Democratic Institutions in 1959, relocating to Santa Barbara, California, under the leadership of Hutchins. With the adoption of the Basic Issues Program, the Fund's trajectory in the 1950s becomes clear. It followed a path that led from an eclectic, multivariant approach engaged in sponsoring small-scale efforts to bring about concrete change on the local level to a more nationally identified and abstract set of discussions staged among elites. The Basic Issues Program mainstreamed the Fund for the Republic into a more centrist advocacy dialogue in postwar culture. The group counted among its founding ideas for discussion "the role of the corporation" and "the role of the trade union" as well as cold war foreign policy. These foci, coupled with the increased involvement of corporate, liberal business leaders and mainstream centrist liberals brought the Fund's projects in line with centrist establishment organizations like the Twentieth Century Fund.

This trajectory away from grassroots was reflected in the Fund's final television project, the interview program officially entitled the *Mike Wallace Interview*, but which Fund officers referred to as *Survival and Freedom*. Hosted by Mike Wallace on ABC, it was intended to serve as publicity for the Basic Issues Program. *The Mike Wallace Interview* drew on Wallace's previous success at the DuMont Network, where he hosted a sensationalist and probing interview show called *Nightbeat*. The program was known for covering controversial figures in the news. In sponsoring it, the Fund sought to capitalize on this notoriety while bringing in a roster of guests whose high profile might encourage "opinion leaders" to watch the show.[64] Hutchins and his staff initially conceived of the program as a seven-hour telethon, an idea that had been raised periodically at the Ford Foundation and that invited a measure of incredulity and horror among every media professional to whom Hutchins and his staff pitched it.[65] Finally dissuaded by journalists Eric Sevareid and Edward R. Murrow, the Fund settled on the interview format, inviting to appear among its guests such well-known liberals as theologian Reinhold Neibuhr and Supreme Court Justice William O. Douglas, public intellectuals such as psychologist Eric Fromm and author Aldous Huxley, liberal business leaders such as Cyrus Eaton of Republic Steel and NBC's Sylvester "Pat" Weaver, and prominent foreign-policy figures like Henry Cabot Lodge Jr. and Henry Kissinger. It did not steer clear of civil rights issues, but it chose to focus on them by inviting Harry Ashmore, a white newspaper editor from Arkansas who was known for his antisegregation stance to discuss the issues, rather than civil rights leaders themselves.

As a network-sanctioned series airing nationally, *Survival and Freedom* was the Fund's most successful foray into network television, but it came at the price of editorial control. Network personnel were suspicious of the Fund's sponsorship, and they were wary that association with Hutchins would expose ABC to charges of bias. When Ted Yates, the show's producer, did try to get the network to approve Martin Luther King Jr. as a guest, ABC refused, arguing that Ashmore had already appeared on the program. Yates protested, pointing out that "in the interests of balanced programming it would seem sensible to me to have an important negro on the series. In the year-plus that we've been on the network we have not interviewed a negro. And in the presentation of the integration issue we have interviewed Governor Orval Faubus, the Imperial Wizard of the Ku Klux Klan, and Senator James Eastland, all segregationists."[66] However, ABC stood firm and refused to sanction the interview. In one highly publicized case, the network refused at the last minute to air Wallace's interview with UN ambassador Henry Cabot Lodge because the Fund had allowed Lodge to edit and reshoot his comments. Hutchins protested, claiming that the program was not news but rather an "educational interview" and that editing merely reflected a desire for conceptual clarity.[67] John Daly, the ABC news director who canceled the broadcast, noted that Hutchins' letter of protest to the network misquoted *New York Times* columnist Jack Gould's assessment of the controversy. As he pointed out, Gould did not support the Fund's position, although Hutchins had claimed he did. Gould, Daly noted, was highly critical of the Fund's description of the programs: "I quote: '(U)nder Dr. Hutchins' novel concept of the educational interview, genuine reportorial independence becomes mere camouflage for a handout.'"[68] Undeterred, the Fund filed a claim against the network with the American Civil Liberties Union (ACLU), but it found no support. Executive Director Patrick Malin and Radio-TV Representative Tom Carskadon reviewed the case for Hutchins and agreed with Daly. In their words, "Since the program is offered to the public as a news interview, the audience assumes it will see the give-and-take of a regular journalistic interview in which the subject presents his opinions in direct response to the questions. This is particularly true in view of the wide and deserved recognition that Mr. Wallace has won because of his penetrating television technique."[69] In its efforts to alter the program against the network's insistence on journalistic freedom, the Fund had, in short, violated the credos of republican free expression the Fund was established to serve.

This episode offers telling insight into the conditions and assumptions on which cold war liberalism rested. It reveals the degree to which the Fund's commitment to free speech was subservient to its broader understanding of television as a tool through which elites might educate the masses—a sensibility not so far removed from that of business organizations using television for purposes of "economic education" in this period. But whereas business groups enjoyed a measure of freedom in defining their sponsored programs as educational, most notably NAM's Peabody Award–winning *Industry on Parade*, the liberal causes of civil liberties and civil rights were implicitly matters of controversy and opinion. This distinction suggests that the task of broadcast professionals in this period was to define, and police, the boundary between opinion and information.

In focusing on "opinion leaders" as a target audience, rather than a broader notion of the American public, the program drew on the two-step flow model of propaganda and influence, a model developed in cold war communications sciences, to describe pathways of information and opinion-making within a mass populace.[70] The Fund's decision to focus on what it perceived as an educated minority within the general population was, in a sense, not so much a switch from one audience to another as it was the recognition that, ultimately, its audience was always elites like itself. Hutchins and Hoffman were never completely comfortable with the Newsfilm Project, as they could never quite trust the opinions of its staff. Fund officers endlessly questioned the amount of time it took to complete the films that were in production, and they refused to believe that the project's editor worked nine hours of overtime in one day.[71] Reading through the Fund's papers, it seems at times that showing other members of the liberal establishment that the Fund was an active grant-funding organization was more important, ultimately, than actually achieving results through local, grassroots work.[72] Even though *Survival and Freedom* was a poorly rated program, with significant restrictions imposed upon it by the cautious network, it was high profile enough to advance Hutchins' Basic Issues Program agenda, generating public responses that could point to the advisability of establishing his longstanding goal: a center devoted to liberal discussion of controversial issues. With the establishment of the Center in 1959, the program's work was done—it would be Hutchins' last attempt to find a sympathetic venue for his ideas in the commercial media.

In their failures and complications, the Fund's diverse techniques for teaching individuals to reap the benefits of democratic rights and freedoms suggest a productive pathway for thinking about the relation between media practices and the effect of liberal government Foucault called *governmentality*. A form of rule defined by the privatized expansion of the powers and obligations of governing beyond the realm of the state, *governmentality* works not through repression or coercion but rather through the creation and protection of individual sovereignty. It is integrated into apparatuses of expertise and social welfare—like philanthropy—that manage populations through an ethos of maximized freedoms and an insistence on the internalization of principles of ethical conduct.[73] The media activities of the Fund for the Republic are a rich source of primary material in which to examine the processes in which governing by television is worked out as a set of techniques and concrete knowledges. What they demonstrate is that the relationship between media and governance in liberal capitalist societies is not a friction-free execution of internally coherent programs of rule. As O'Malley and colleagues note, the governmentality literature tends at times toward an overly idealistic focus on political rationalities rather than their more "messy" implementation, a focus that tends to reward the analytical separation of contest from rule.[74] The Fund for the Republic's experiments in television, circumscribed by the complex relations between networks, philanthropic officers, and media professionals, provide a glimpse of this implementation process across a broad range of social institutions and actors. In them, we can grasp the points of connection and divergence between mainstream liberal republicanism and the corporate liberal ideologies connecting sponsorship and citizenship in early TV. If the latter is an ideology discernible in many institutional and programming forms, from the anthology drama's benevolent institutional messages to the public-service claims of the networks, the checkered history of the Fund's attempts harness this ideology and illustrate the conflicts and obstacles surrounding its implementation in the context of explicit attempts to govern by television.

NOTES

Unpublished material in this chapter has been quoted courtesy of the Princeton University Library, Princeton, New Jersey, and the Ford Foundation Archives, New York City.

1. To avoid selling shares and forfeiting their controlling interest in the Ford Motor Company, the surviving Ford family members moved $417 million of nonvoting stock into the Foundation's coffers, at the time a small Michigan charity. However, estimates of the size of the initial holdings differ. This one comes from Francis X. Sutton, "The Ford Foundation: The Early Years," *Daedalus* 116, no. 1 (Winter 1987): 52.

2. Report of the Study for the Ford Foundation on Policy and Program (Detroit: The Ford Foundation, 1949).

3. *Report of the Study for the Ford Foundation*, table of contents.

4. *Report of the Study for the Ford Foundation*, 47.

5. Arthur M. Schlesinger Jr., *The Vital Center: The Politics of Freedom* (Boston: Houghton Mifflin, 1949).

6. David A. Horowitz, *Beyond Left and Right: Insurgency and the Establishment* (Urbana, IL: University of Illinois Press, 1997), 270.

7. Robert Maynard Hutchins to Jack Skirball, 4 October, 1955. Fund for the Republic Records, Public Policy Papers, Seeley G. Mudd Manuscript Library, Department of Rare Books and Special Collections, Princeton University (hereafter Fund Papers), Box 108 (used by Permission of the Princeton University Library). See James Sloan Allen, *The Romance of Commerce and Culture: Capitalism, Modernism, and the Chicago-Aspen Crusade for Cultural Reform* (Chicago: University of Chicago Press, 1983), 103, and Dwight Macdonald, *Against the American Grain* (New York, Random House: 1952), 257, for very similarly worded quotes from Hutchins on liberal education.

8. Robert Maynard Hutchins, "The Spirit Needed for These Times," *Journal of Higher Education* 18, no. 5 (1947): 237–38.

9. Hutchins, "The Spirit Needed," 280.

10. Hutchins, "The Spirit Needed," 235, 280.

11. MacDonald, *Against the American Grain*, 251.

12. W. H. Ferry Oral History, 112. Ford Foundation Archives (hereafter FF).

13. Nikolas Rose, *Powers of Freedom: Reframing Political Thought* (Cambridge: Cambridge University Press, 1999), 78.

14. George Martin to Joseph Brickley, 14 August, 1956. Fund Papers, Box 110.

15. Rose, *Powers of Freedom*, 78.

16. Adler's television program, *The Great Ideas* (1953–1954) was the most extensive effort to apply the principles of education through reasoned judgment to the new medium of television.

17. Allen, *Romance of Commerce and Culture*, 90.

18. John Dewey, quoted in Allen, *Romance of Commerce and Culture*, 92.

19. This is Macdonald's point in an essay on Adler, *Against the American Grain*, 258–61.

20. See, for example, Frances Stonor Saunders, *The Cultural Cold War: The CIA and the World of Arts and Letters* (New York: New Press, 2000); Volker Berghahn, *America and the Intellectual Cold Wars in Europe* (Princeton, N.J.: Princeton University Press, 2002); Penny von Eschen, *Satchmo Blows Up the World: Jazz Ambassadors Play the Cold War* (Cambridge, MA: Harvard University Press, 2004).

21. Dyke Brown, quoted in Sutton, "The Ford Foundation," 59.

22. Andrew Ross, *No Respect: Intellectuals and Popular Culture* (London: Routledge, 1989), 45.

23. As one *New York Times* book review describes it, the establishment in this period was a group of men who "may have been partisan, but who tried to sound judicious and evenhanded. There was such a thing as consensus, and their job was to find it and speak on its behalf." Alan Wolfe, "The New Pamphleteers," *New York Times*, 11 July, 2004, 13. Wolfe writes nostalgically about the establishment's demise, a move that might classify him among the Boomer Liberals—a group Eric Lott incisively diagnoses as white members of the old New Left for whom a politics organized around culture and identity damages the cause of the left. Lott includes in this group David Hollinger, Richard Rorty, and Todd Gitlin. If it were not for the reactionary nature of Boomer Liberalism, it might serve as a close analogy for the position of the Fund for the Republic in the present day. See Lott, "Boomer Liberalism: When the New Left Was Old," *Transition* 78 (Spring 1999): 24–44; and "After Identity, Politics: The Return of Universalism," *New Literary History* 31, no. 4 (2000): 665–80.

24. In addition to the Fund's TV projects and other Ford Foundation-sponsored programs, the only other program sponsored by a major philanthropy on commercially owned airwaves was the Sloan Foundation's *American Inventory*. Many nonprofit organizations sponsored programs, particularly in the public-service time allotted by commercial stations for community discussion and debate, among them the Advertising Council, the AFL-CIO, the National Association of Manufacturers, and other more local organizations. But these more activist organizations were not part of the network of philanthropic trusts that included Ford, Rockefeller, Sloan, Carnegie, and others.

25. Quoted in C. Scott Fletcher, "For the Board of the Adult Education Fund," FF, Box 2, Folder 24.

26. Ford officers moved to terminate *Omnibus* shortly after Hoffman left the Foundation, although the program continued for a few more seasons, largely because of the tenacity of its producer, Robert Saudek.

27. Transcribed proceedings of the meeting of the board of advisors of the TV-Radio workshop, 6 December, 1953, Box A, Wesleyan Cinema Archives, Wesleyan University, Saudek Collection.

28. Frank Kelly, *Court of Reason: Robert Hutchins and the Fund for the Republic* (New York: Free Press, 1981), 13.

29. Kelly, *Court of Reason*, 15–16.

30. Hutchins, "A Sickness Afflicting Our Country," Speech upon receiving Sidney Tillman Foundation Award, 28 January, 1959. Fund Papers, Box 143.

31. Hallock Hoffman to Edward Howden, 21 October, 1954. Fund Papers, Box 110.

32. Telegrams, 5 May, 1955. Fund papers, Box 111, Folder 3. A few months later, when invitees Arnold Toynbee and Vijayalakshmi Pandit followed up on the project's progress, Hutchins had dropped the project and had nothing to tell them. Telegrams, Fund papers, July and August, Box 108.

33. Like many public-service television films, a number of these unsold Fund TV projects were eventually sent to the armed forces for screenings in bases overseas—the latter a veritable "orphanage" for unwanted and unsellable factual films in this period.

34. Charles A. Siepmann, "Moral Aspects of Television," *Public Opinion Quarterly* 24, no.1 (Spring 1960): 15.

35. On Taft-Hartley speech-code revisions see William L. Bird, *Better Living: Advertising, Media, and the New Vocabulary of Business Leadership, 1935–1955* (Evanston, IL: Northwestern University Press, 1999), chapter 7.

36. National Association of Manufacturers advertisement, quoted in Bird, *Better Living*, 160.

37. "Devoted to the Documentary," *Christian Science Monitor* (23 May, 1955): 6 (clipping). Fund Papers, Box 108.

38. Reggie Schuebel, memorandum, 28 March, 1955. Fund Papers, Box 108.

39. The file for this project includes letters of inquiry from interested organizations. These consisted for the most part of labor groups and liberal churches (Unitarians and Quakers), the latter bulwarks of grassroots liberalism in the mid-century United States and among the Fund's core constituency. Fund Papers, Box 108.

40. Chernoff to Hutchins and Ferry, 8 December, 1954. Fund Papers, Box 110.

41. On Lippman's TV, see Robert Saudek oral history (FF), and Robert Saudek to Walter Lippman, 11 November, 1952. Wesleyan Cinema Archives, Wesleyan Cinema Archives, Series II, Box 6, Folder 305.

42. The 1959 film *The Cry of Jazz* by African American filmmaker Edward O. Bland is a pointed critique of the sanctimonious and smug attitude of the earnest white liberal in the discussion group.

43. This program was based upon an existing program, *The Al Capp Show*, featuring Capp commenting on sketches meant to illustrate the foibles and blind spots of the average American. If the extant copy housed in the Peabody Award archives

at the University of Georgia is any indication, the original was no funnier than the version the Fund attempted to sponsor.

44. Edward Reed Memo to Ping Ferry, 9 January, 1954. Fund Papers, Box 108.

45. This attitude might seem in contradiction with Weaver's famous educational programming strategy, "Operation Frontal Lobes," although as Vance Kepley and others have shown, this strategy was as much a form of public relations for the network as it was a comprehensive program of education by television. Kepley, "From 'Operation Frontal Lobes' to 'The Bob and Bob Show,'" in *Hollywood in the Age of Television*, ed. Tino Balio (Boston: Unwin Hyman, 1990), 41–61.

46. Hallock Hoffman, handwritten response on covering page of memorandum from Edward Reed to Hoffman, 26 January, 1956. Fund Papers, Box 109.

47. Hallock Hoffman to Paul Coates, 8 December, 1955. Fund Papers, Box 109.

48. Martin to Reed, 20 March, 1956. Fund Papers, Box 111. All ellipses save the last one in original.

49. Howden (presumably). "Notes on General Approach and Evaluation of Impact," n.d. (ca. 1954). Fund Papers, Box 110.

50. Howden, "Notes on General Approach."

51. David Freeman, memorandum to Hallock Hoffman, 29 September, 1955. Fund Papers, Box 110.

52. George Martin, Progress Memo to Frank Kelly, 1 August, 1956. Fund Papers, Box 111.

53. These figures are from a memorandum sent by George Martin to Frank Kelly, 3 January, 1957. Fund Papers, Box 111.

54. Suggested Film Script, 16 March, 1956. Fund Papers, Box 111.

55. Julie Ellison "A Short History of Liberal Guilt," *Critical Inquiry* 22, no. 2 (Winter 1996): 344–7, 352.

56. Bird, "Better Living," 167.

57. A. H. Weiler, "Kazan Film Is Drawn From Two Novels," *New York Times*, 27 May, 1960, 22.

58. For an excellent account of how this demand played out in local media activism in Mississippi, see Steven D. Classen, *Watching Jim Crow: The Struggles over Mississippi TV, 1955–1969* (Durham, NC: Duke University Press), 62.

59. It was a policy used effectively by labor leadership following the National Association of Manufacturers distribution of the news film of the McLellan racketeering hearings to stations around the country without identification. "TV Stations Rebuked on Use of NAM films," *AFL-CIO News* (9 August, 1958): 8.

60. Described by producer George Martin as "an extreme right wing group," this was likely not the same as the Congress of Cultural Freedom detailed by Saunders in *The Cultural Cold War*. Martin to Frank L. Kelly, 14 September, 1956. Fund Papers, Box 110.

61. I have not as yet determined to what event this refers.

62. Transcript of telephone conversation between George Martin and Bethuel Webster, 2 August, 1956. Fund Papers, Box 111.

63. Allen, *Romance of Commerce and Culture*, 100.

64. C. H. Percy, president, Bell & Howell Company to Hutchins, 17 June, 1958. Fund Papers, Box 144.

65. Eric Sevareid to Frank Kelly, 10 November, 1958. Fund Papers, Box 143.

66. Ted Yates to Don Coe, 23 June, 1958. Fund Papers, Box 144.

67. Mimeographed statement 15 June, 1958 by Hutchins on ABC's refusal to broadcast the Henry Cabot Lodge interview after it had been edited. Fund Papers, Box 144.

68. John Daly to Robert Hutchins, 24 June, 1958. Fund Papers, Box 144.

69. Malin and Carskadon to Hutchins, 20 June, 1958. Fund papers, Box 144.

70. Paul Lazarsfeld, Bernard Berelson, and Hazel Gaudet, *The People's Choice* (New York: Duell, Sloan & Pearce, 1944).

71. Memorandum, Ping Ferry to Hallock Hoffman, 27 May, 1957. Fund papers, Box 111.

72. This may reflect the fact that the inactivity of the Fund was the subject of a stinging critique of the Fund from New Yorker writer Dwight Macdonald in *The Ford Foundation: The Men and the Millions* (New York: Reynal & Co., 1953).

73. On these principles, see Toby Miller, *The Well-Tempered Self: Citizenship, Culture, and the Postmodern Subject* (Baltimore: Johns Hopkins University Press, 1993).

74. Pat O'Malley, Lorna Weir, and Clifford Shearing, "Governmentality, Criticism, Politics," *Economy and Society* 26, no. 4 (1997): 514.

13

"The Weakest Point in Our Record": Philanthropic Support of Dance and the Arts

Julia L. Foulkes

In the 1920s and 1930s, when philanthropic support enlivened the field of communications, the arts received little attention. For some foundations, like Rockefeller, a conservative underpinning often conflicted with the arts, especially the morally ambiguous endeavors of theater and dance. The mission of the foundation to broaden and organize fields of knowledge was also at odds with the arts, which were more fields of production rather than knowledge per se. In fact, the primary contributor to the arts during this period, the Carnegie Corporation, supported the place where knowledge intersected production: arts education. The recipient of the largest gift from the Carnegie Corporation, the American Federation of the Arts, encouraged the development of art clubs, the study of art in public schools, and the supervision of "beauty" in public parks, buildings, and architecture.[1] This narrow view of the arts, focusing on visual arts and education, remained consistent among philanthropic support before World War II and indicates the tentativeness with which most foundations gazed at the arts. Convinced neither of the worth nor neediness of the arts (which could survive by the whims of individual patronage or commercial taste), foundations gave more readily to other fields such as public health, education, and communications, which had better chances of more obvious, long-term results.

PHILANTHROPY AND THE ARTS

Attention to the arts picked up, however, in the 1930s and, especially, after World War II. The course of the Rockefeller Foundation and the private

philanthropy of John D. Rockefeller 3rd during this period offer a way
in which to trace the changes in attitude toward the importance of the
arts. Moreover, the place of dance within this giving to the arts highlights
both the initial tentativeness on the part of foundations and the eventual
embrace. In general, and still today, dance receives proportionately less
attention from foundations because it faces several limitations: it did not
gather adherents and interest in the United States until the first part of the
twentieth century; it is dependent on intensive training and rehearsal; it is
based on the ephemerality of performance, with no clear means for com-
modification and reproduction in the marketplace; and it is fused to bodies, with all their attendant social neuroses. In the United States, a commitment to confrontational politics by modern dancers added to the troubles.
So, the foundations that did give, particularly Rockefeller and Ford, deserve
attention for what they can tell us about how the arts were perceived, what
interest foundation officers had in respect to dance, and how dance and the
arts were seen in relation to the goals of the foundation.

Giving to the arts caused considerable debate within the Rockefeller
Foundation from the 1930s to the 1950s. Foundation officers questioned
where the arts should be placed, in education or humanities divisions,
and wrote memos to each other defining the arts and humanities and articulating their worthiness. David Stevens, the director of the Humanities
Division in the 1930s and 1940s, and John Marshall, its assistant director,
spent considerable time teasing out the importance of the humanities. In
a 1939 draft about the evolving Humanities Program—begun in 1928—
they offered the definition that "the essential function of the humanities
is perhaps the communication of value. . . . In the humanistic sense value
is the worth the individual can discover in what their own or other cultures offers."[2] To this end, as William Buxton has written, they devoted
attention to libraries, museums, drama (particularly in universities), mi-
crofilm, radio, and film. Marshall made particular note in a draft of the
1939 report that the Foundation had "avoided help to the arts in general,
including particularly help to literature and the dance," apparently from
a lack of knowledge rather than pointed intention. He went on to observe
that this may be at odds with their working definition of the humanities
since, "if we take the arts seriously as a means of communicating what the
culture offers that may be of value to the individual, perhaps this is the
weakest point in our record."[3]

Marshall's observation reflected the rising visibility of the arts that occurred during the 1930s, most obvious in the efforts of the U.S. government
through the Works Progress Administration (WPA). Not only did government fund artists—as unemployed workers—and public works, such as
murals in post offices, theatrical works, and music concerts, it exclaimed
the worth of the arts and their importance in defining and promulgating

a national heritage. In the nascent field of concert dance, for instance, the WPA accorded modern dance a place of priority over ballet because it was an original American art form rather than a European offspring. Similarly, the efforts of the government and artists inspired by socialist and communist theories worked to make the arts accessible to all in the belief that such access and freedom of expression stood as fundamental principles of democracy. So by the World's Fair of 1939, the year of the Rockefeller Foundation report, art assumed a new public role in a pavilion dedicated to European "Masterpieces of Art" and another to contemporary American art, which included folk art and handicrafts, in performances of dance and theater, and even in the planning and design of the site with its large sculptures, a globelike perisphere, and a 700-foot spire called *Trylon*.[4]

The year 1939 marked a high point of government and city giving to the arts, however, as the threat of war became more ominous. The war caused a hiatus in most government and foundation giving to the arts, even though conversations continued among government officials and philanthropists.[5] By the latter half of the 1940s, however, foundations renewed steps to increase attention to the arts. The Rockefeller Foundation started with an overview of its giving to the arts up to that point, noting that drama had been a constant interest and literature a more recent one, with small grants to writers and literary magazines. As with many instances of philanthropy, the particular interests of a foundation donor or officer determined the focus; drama in colleges and universities had been of particular interest to Stevens, the director of the Humanities Division.[6] Support of literature grew out of the concern for drama but also indicated the difficulties in figuring out how to best support the arts. The problem of supporting an individual writer was difficult because who would be the arbiter of artistic success? And what kind of long-term effect could a gift to an individual artist ensure? The report turned, thereby, to institutions, the more traditional recipient of monies. Here lay more challenges: attending to institutions, and the academy in particular, the report went on, may lead to an ignoring of individual artists who work outside institutions and who may indeed be at the forefront of the field and in greater need. Officers described a paradox: the arts suffered from a "lack of responsible institutions," but "unhappily, 'responsible' institutions in the arts tend . . . to become unresponsive to the truly contemporary; and responsive institutions when they exist may seem, and often are, irresponsible."[7] The result had been that giving overwhelmingly went to longstanding institutions or organizations, such as museums, orchestras, college and university art and drama programs, with the struggling, perhaps most innovative, artist rarely supported.

The aid to small literary magazines was one opportunity viewed as a success in getting beyond the paradox of "responsible" institutions. Here, monies were given to increase the rate of pay to contributors by magazines lauded for their role in identifying "contemporary literary significance."[8] So writers themselves benefited from foundation funds, but the money was funneled through a respected institution and resulted in benefiting readers as well. This also bypassed the difficulty of making judgments about artistic merit by foundation officers themselves who had little knowledge of a field. Even so, gathering information about organizations and institutions spawned a reliance on critics, then accorded a great deal of power in this philanthropic scenario. Although the report did not specify or worry over this reliance on critics, it honed in on the dire need of the arts in the United States. The report urged the Foundation to attend to art forms beyond drama and literature, using as examples the deficits that Martha Graham incurred yearly, and the devoted, but exhausted, patron of the Ballet Society—Lincoln Kirstein and his enduring support of the company that later became known as the New York City Ballet. These examples signaled both the new inclusion of dance within the purview of the arts and its desperation relative to other art forms. The first step, quite expectedly, was a series of studies.

SURVEYING THE ARTS

The penchant for studies betrays foundations' need to defend their giving to donors, trustees, and the larger public but also to see more traditional, concrete results, even if those results were academic papers rarely acted upon.[9] The hesitancy of both the Rockefeller and Ford Foundations in giving to the arts—a more risky endeavor both in terms of public support and realizable results—meant that considerable time and money was spent surveying the arts before funding any endeavor more boldly. This surveying, defining, and reporting were impressive, both in the amount of time spent and in the effort by officers to grapple with emerging knowledge and formulate opinions. Within the Rockefeller Foundation, for example, Charles Fahs, who became director of the Humanities Division in 1950, identified three means by which the Foundation could support creative activity "without interference with its freedom": "through direct aid to new *original* work, through the further development of *criticism* of original work new and old, and through the broadening of opportunities for its experience." Fahs's suggestions indicate the depth of thinking about the field—and the apparent need for thorough clarity before donation. Given that, a year later, he reviewed what he called the nonverbal arts—music, the visual and plastic arts, architecture, and dance—that he had left out of the earlier report because the justification for their support could not yet be articulated clearly.[10]

What is interesting to note about these deliberations is that they were prompted by the Foundation officers themselves who had not received trustee authorization to consider specific projects. In fact, in a 1955 survey of foundations, only 54 out of 620 foundations expressed any interest in "esthetics."[11] Officers interested in the field had to expand their knowledge without consideration of specific projects. This often led to abstract and general philosophizing, which in turn led to hesitancy on the part of the trustees. The result: small and erratic funding. In turning to the arts, then, Foundation officers were broad and bold in their investigation of new fields, even if action required thorough defining, on-going defending, and resulted in constrained giving.[12]

In music and dance, the investigation at the Rockefeller Foundation began with critics. In 1949 Virgil Thompson, composer and critic, and two other composers, Quincy Porter and Otto Luening, joined Stevens and Marshall to discuss what the field of music needed. They concluded that the recording and printing of modern American music, as well as copying orchestral scores for performances, would be useful and effective ways of supporting the field. In general, support for specific orchestras, musicians, or composers drew less attention, partly because universities had become the central source of support for contemporary music.[13] As with music, the first forays into the field of dance were conversations with dance critics, including John Martin of the *New York Times* and Walter Terry of the *New York Herald Tribune*, and very modest grants to a book about the history of dance, a bibliography of dance literature, and for cataloging at the Dance Collection of the New York Public Library. Similar to the conversation on music in the attempt to find discrete, nonconfrontational means of support, officers and critics teased out the possibility of recording dance on film for preservation.[14] All these were cautionary steps, within the purview of what the Foundation had supported in the humanities since the 1930s. And the Foundation's giving to music and dance at this time reflected its policy toward the arts in general: support a field of knowledge rather than particular works or inventions.

MODERN DANCE AND BALLET

In gathering information about dance, Foundation officers became attuned to the longstanding rivalry between modern dance and ballet that shaped aesthetic principles, philanthropic support, and audience devotion. Modern dance developed in the United States in the 1920s and 1930s, with many of its main principles—dancing in bare feet, focusing on the gravity and weight of the body, tackling political and philosophical subjects in choreography, claiming itself as an original American art form—created in contrast to ballet. Modern dance followed the precepts of modernism in other genres of art by advocating minimalism in style and adhering to the call of expression rather than beauty. It gained legitimacy in the 1930s, particularly through the support of the WPA, but its audiences were small and almost rabid in their devotion to one choreographer or another. Modern dancers and choreographers struggled to survive and perform, usually subsidizing all their expenses by teaching because patrons remained elusive. Even though philanthropists gave crucial support to modern art, such as Abby Aldrich Rockefeller's role in the building of the Museum of Modern Art in New York City, modern dance elicited no such patronage. Many considered modern dance too dependent on a singular choreographer and believed it would not last beyond that individual talent; it lacked a long tradition in concert dance and derided the one that did exist (ballet). Finally, in its tie to radical politics in its social as well as ideological dimensions, modern dance began to lose its prominence in the dance field by the end of World War II. In the changing cultural and political outlook of the country, ballet, instead, took up the nationalist call, epitomized by the Russian émigré George Balanchine's leadership of the New York City Ballet. In cold war America, the Russian celebrated America's military prowess in works such as Stars and Stripes, set to music by John Philip Sousa. Waging a dance battle on the European turf of ballet—and winning with an aggressive and speedy American style—the success of American ballet became the dominant genre in dance rather than the disparate, experimental, and confrontational style of modern dance.[15]

The turn of foundations to the arts and dance in the 1950s reinforced this trend to support ballet over modern dance. Conversations with dance critics averred that modern dance had declined in recent years, ballet was booming, and George Balanchine and his New York City Ballet led the field. The critic Anatole Chujoy, sponsored by the Rockefeller Foundation to tour the country in 1956 to gather information on dance outside of New York City, thoroughly dismissed modern dance, believing it to be a movement of willful, revolutionary antics. "In Chujoy's view," Marshall noted "little or nothing of significance is happening in the modern dance. In fact, though [Fahs] rather pressed for information, Chujoy came up with nothing in which he evinced any interest."[16] In fact, it was Fahs, rather than dance critics, who insisted that modern dance had made a considerable impact on ballet. Modern dance was still contributing "most in the way of new ideas and originality of interpretation," he wrote in notes about a 1952 performance of José Limón.[17] A few years later, however, another officer remarked on the "almost total lack of beauty" and the sterile, routine choreography in his write-up of a modern dance performance.[18] This reliance on critics, lack of knowledge of the field, and the unevenness of an evolving art form swayed philanthropic support to ballet.

Perhaps one of the most famous grants in giving to the arts is the Ford Foundation's nearly $12 million to ballet in 1963.[19] This grant sealed the ascendancy of Balanchine and his style of ballet by giving exclusively to the New York City Ballet and companies and schools around the country headed by those associated with it. The grant resulted in a "ballet boom" in the 1960s, with many students funneled from regional schools to the School of American Ballet in New York and on to dancing with the New York City Ballet (Suzanne Farrell is the most famous example). This grant doomed the fate of modern dance for the immediate future, and it is often noted as the cause for the dominance of ballet at the expense of modern dance. While the grant certainly aided that dominance, other kinds of philanthropic support during the same period also contributed to the stagnation of modern dance. Less well-known, but perhaps more long-lasting in this escalation of support for ballet, was the inclusion of the New York City Ballet as a resident company of Lincoln Center in the late 1950s and early 1960s. Much of this came about because of the close relationship between Lincoln Kirstein and John D. Rockefeller 3rd.

Lincoln Kirstein, the producer and patron of the New York City Ballet, initiated his consulting with the Rockefeller Foundation in the 1940s.[20] He provided information on the field and often recommended certain small grants, such as the one for a history of dance and, throughout the 1950s, he met regularly with John Marshall, giving him his views of modern dancers and regional ballet companies. At the same time, Kirstein was one of the first people Rockefeller consulted about the building of a performing arts center. Such an idea had been brewing since the early 1950s and came to a head in 1955 by the coincidence of the Metropolitan Opera and Philharmonic Society searching for new homes and the beginning of an urban renewal project, spearheaded by Robert Moses, on the west side of Manhattan. Although not an avid patron of the arts at this point, Rockefeller put his considerable influence behind the project because he was eager to make a contribution to New York City; he believed that Americans now needed balance in their lives by aiding the spirit in addition to the body and mind; and his involvement in international affairs motivated him to better the image of American culture abroad. With these goals in mind, Rockefeller formed an Exploratory Committee for a Musical Arts Center, which included Kirstein, and the committee readily agreed that such a vision needed to go beyond music to include theater and dance.[21]

DANCE AND LINCOLN CENTER

Opera and classical music had clear representation in the center by the companies of the Metropolitan Opera and the New York Philharmonic, but Rockefeller recognized that the place of dance and theater needed more exploration. He appointed a committee for each and, on the dance committee, Kirstein ruled, as the only member from the dance world in these early stages; the critics John Martin and Walter Terry served as consultants. Unequivocal statements from the committee declared that dance not only needed to be included in the project but also to be treated on par with the Metropolitan Opera and Philharmonic rather than folded into constituent branches such as the opera or the Juilliard School. Two options emerged: (1) to bring to the center an existing group as a founding company; or (2) to organize a new group to take on that role in the project.[22] Kirstein effectively ended the debate with a threat. In a letter to Rockefeller, Kirstein accused the board of the Lincoln Center project of having "no interest in or information about" dance. He also derided the idea of "one supergroup" for the complex, claiming that it would be "an amalgam which can be also described as a lowest common denominator." If this were, indeed, the decision, he and Balanchine would likely opt out of the project altogether to "preserve our independence and our integrity . . . rather than to be members of a bureau whose chief aim is to keep everybody, however untalented, happy."[23]

In many ways, a new dance company that featured ballet, modern dance, even popular and Broadway dance styles, would have been an innovative, welcome addition that could have celebrated dance's diversity and broad appeal. Such a company, too, would have suited some of the rhetoric that backers of the Lincoln Center project invoked. Over and over again during the fundraising, construction, and promotion of the project, supporters of Lincoln Center heralded the arrival of the arts for everyone. Promotional efforts for the steep fundraising campaign for the center insisted that Lincoln Center was not a place just for elites. One ad promoting Lincoln Center encapsulated this idea. In a picture of two mimes, the text of the advertisement claimed that Lincoln Center "will be great theater, great music—and great *fun*," a place "to look, to listen, to think, and to *laugh*"; one critic likened this "hawking" of the arts to "a sideshow at the circus."[24]

The reality of such a huge, expensive undertaking coupled with the historic weight of cultural values that reified the arts, however, differed from this rhetoric, and the inclusion of ballet is instructive on this point. The way Lincoln Center promoters envisioned democratizing the "high" arts was to broaden the audience base for opera, symphony, and theater, not change what kind of cultural offerings might be included. In this plan, one kind of dance best fit: ballet. The grand vision of Lincoln Center—the largest home and monument to the performing arts ever constructed at that time—called for a populist appeal in a country dedicated to democratic ideals at a time when the arts were utilized as a weapon in the cold war. Cultural programs financed by the State Department went to countries in Africa and Latin America teetering on the edge of communist rule. Featuring jazz by African Americans and abstract expressionism by visual artists, these programs proclaimed that art flourished in the individual freedom guaranteed by democracies.[25] Lincoln Center played both sides of the cultural cold war, first by claiming "high" culture for everyone, bringing a broader, larger audience base to the highest ideals of beauty. "The arts are not for the privileged few, but for the many," Rockefeller wrote,[26] and, second, by besting European countries, especially Germany and Russia, in their own traditions of opera, classical music, and dance. So ballet was the logical corollary to opera and classical music, and George Balanchine, an émigré from Russia whose choreographic abilities ranged from Broadway shows to story ballets such as *The Nutcracker* to abstract ballet, was the logical choice as the choreographer to trumpet.

The New York City Ballet came to Lincoln Center from City Center, a city-sponsored institution on Fifty-fifth Street. The arrangements were complex and largely driven by the desperate need for funding such a large project. As the years crept on in the search for big-dollar contributions in a fund-raising campaign of over $100 million (the final cost of the project would be $185 million), Rockefeller began to pursue additional support from federal, state, and city sources. Ultimately the state funded one theater in the complex at a cost of $15 million. What became known as the New York State Theater served first as the performing-arts space for the World's Fair of 1964–1965 and, thereafter, as the home of the City Center and two of its resident companies, the New York City Ballet and the New York City Opera. (Under the agreement, City Center also continued its operations on Fifty-fifth Street as independent producers.) The integration of City Center allowed Lincoln Center to herald its goals as a democratic—meaning cost-accessible—home to the arts because the charter of City Center designated a top ticket price and a certain percentage of tickets at low-cost prices.

The inclusion of City Center still resulted in the prominence of ballet and opera, rather than other dance or musical genres and, in this and other ways, Lincoln Center provided wary foundations with an appealing means of generous support to the arts. The Ford Foundation gave a total of $25 million to the construction of the complex, followed by the Rockefeller Foundation with $15.5 million. The gifts from these two foundations represented 90 percent of the $45 million donated by seventy-nine foundations. This massive support provided physical homes for the arts and was independent of other donations by these foundations for programming to specific companies in the complex. The request for a significant grant to Lincoln Center (that would include the expenditure of capital funds) in November 1956 roused dissent within the Rockefeller Foundation, however. Some officers were unconvinced of the main premise of Lincoln Center: that placing music, theater, opera, and dance next to one another would inspire greater creativity; they felt that such placement may, in fact, lead to more competition and hostility. Others questioned the need for

multiple theaters rather than one multiuse hall and the prognosis that audience numbers for the performing arts were increasing steadily and, even,
dramatically. Those dissenting also hinted that treating this request from a
member of the Rockefeller Family with rubber-stamp approval would exert
a heavy toll on trustee and officer morale.[27] Despite these concerns, the
foundation granted $10 million to Lincoln Center at the December 1956
board meeting. In its 1957 *Annual Report* describing the gift to Lincoln
Center, the foundation recognized that "brick and mortar" were not what
it sought to support, believing instead that the "dynamic functioning of the
institution is the important thing." But the foundation believed (or perhaps
more accurately hoped) that "the interplay of related arts at the Center and
the associated education work may well offer a unique stimulus to creative
development."[28] Despite the recognition of the difference between funding
bricks and supporting creativity, gifts to Lincoln Center fit other parameters
set by foundations in avoiding long-term financial commitments and direct
intervention in judging creative production. For the Rockefeller and Ford
foundations, at least, Lincoln Center offered a means of subsidy in a field
difficult to define, know, and support.

Foundations' goals, though, were not as disconnected from aesthetic
judgments as they might have thought, or hoped. The setup of Lincoln
Center as a complex of theaters with constituent companies, for example,
meant that the place of the New York City Ballet as the one dance constituent ruled the dance offerings overall. American Ballet Theatre claimed
that the choice of the New York City Ballet doomed its ability to survive.[29]
(American Ballet Theatre soon found a place in the complex during the off-
season of the Metropolitan Opera's house.) Similarly, in the deliberations
over the inclusion of City Center (and thus the New York City Ballet), William Schuman, the president of Lincoln Center at the time and a composer
who had worked with modern dancers, criticized City Center's lack of attention to modern dance. This resulted in making the deliberations only more
bitter, particularly in the venom it provoked from Lincoln Kirstein and his
compatriots. To Rockefeller, Kirstein threatened to sue for "conspiracy";
Newbold Morris, the head of City Center's board, criticized Schuman for
his "repeated disparagement of the preponderant Balanchine choreography in the Ballet repertoire."[30] In the end, Lincoln Center capitulated
to City Center's demands of control over the theater, booking the empty
weeks of the year and keeping that income. While the cultural politics of
the era made it likely that ballet would be accorded such prominence, the
influence of Kirstein and the difficulties in reconciling the goal of bringing
"high" art at a reasonable price to a large audience pushed the New York
City Ballet into a high-profile position.

Even though ballet ascended in and because of Lincoln Center, foundations consistently returned again to the plight of modern dance. Through the

years of planning Lincoln Center, foundation officers and others involved asked people in the modern-dance world how modern dance could be incorporated into the project. Nobody offered a plan.[31] In the years that followed the formation of Lincoln Center and the large Ford Foundation grant to ballet, the Rockefeller Brothers Fund, led by John D. Rockefeller 3rd, conducted a large study on *The Performing Arts: Problems and Prospects* (published in 1965) that was notable for the full inclusion of ballet and modern dance in the study, and both Rockefeller and Ford Foundations attempted to put together collaborative performances of modern-dance companies in the hope that joining the efforts of small, disparate companies would better boost the art form's visibility and appeal.[32] The arrival in 1963 of Norman Lloyd as director of the Arts Program at the Rockefeller Foundation, in particular, assured attention to modern dance. Lloyd had composed for modern dancers since the 1930s and was an unequivocal rallier of the significant American contribution of modern dance to the world's arts. Soon after his arrival, discussion began about forming a repertory company to be associated with the Juilliard School, run by José Limón, and designed to preserve the classics of modern dance and the challenging works of a variety of current choreographers. The goal was to become a constituent member of Lincoln Center on terms parallel to other constituent members.[33] The American Dance Theatre debuted a week of performances in March 1966, which included works by Merce Cunningham, Doris Humphrey, José Limón, and Alwin Nikolais, among others. Despite that success, the barriers to overcome proved too high. Lincoln Center members had their own battles about the possibility of a new constituent member, particularly the Juilliard School whose facilities and finances would be partially devoted to the new entity; no appropriate leader in modern dance emerged, willing to give up his or her own company to coordinate a repertory company; and a significant amount of foundation support was necessary to ensure a strong start.

Despite these obstacles that faced modern dance, the Ford Foundation tried again to bring some coherence and support to the field a few years later. The foundation agreed to substantially fund separate three-to-four week seasons for modern dance companies from 1968–1969. Three institutions—City Center, Brooklyn Academy of Music, and the Billy Rose Theater in the Lincoln Center complex—would host the performances, choose the companies to perform, and be the recipient of the funds. This scheme furthered the Foundation's belief that the visibility of modern dance would be enhanced by performing on a Broadway-size stage without involving the Foundation in making judgments about particular artists or a commitment to continued support.[34]

The response to the first set of performances at the Billy Rose Theater, in March 1969, highlighted the constant problems in funding modern dance. The performance of Yvonne Rainer, an avant-garde dancer and filmmaker, caused considerable controversy for featuring movies that documented sexual intercourse. Clive Barnes, the dance critic of the *New York Times*, excoriated not just Rainer but the Ford Foundation for sponsoring a performance that he found not only offensive but without any artistic worth. Mrs. Lois Ira, from Spokane, Washington, went further in a letter to the Foundation: "You have . . . caused the general public to wonder if large sums of money are not the breeding pools of obscenities and pornography, of the basest kind—when those same funds could and should be utilized for the betterment of the humanities all around." Another dance critic and the producer of the program who had picked Rainer attempted to undo the damage. The fault or weakness of the performance, they argued, lay not with the Foundation, and just such an attack from an influential critic could diminish or stop altogether any monies to modern dance.[35] The furor demonstrated, once again, the inevitable difficulties in supporting new and evolving genres of art not yet bound to a long tradition or institution.

These failed, or at least only partially successful, attempts to support modern dance–shaped philanthropic support in the following years. Foundation officers focused on setting up university residences for leading choreographers, gave limited money directly to companies, and began to search for arts organizations with educational and social purposes, as cities and campuses erupted around them in the late 1960s and early 1970s. Certainly many of the problems of funding were problems inherent in the art form. Modern dance was confrontational, experimental, fused to the vision of an individual dancer-choreographer, and existed outside of strong institutional structures.[36] The grand vision of dance that suited—and succeeded in—ballet could not be realized in modern dance.

CONCLUSION

In spite of these obstacles, modern dance has slowly found a foothold outside of universities and within communities. Dance historian Sally Banes analyzed the growth and changing definitions of community that shaped the Kitchen Center for Music, Video, and Dance in New York City from the 1970s to the present, and the Kitchen's changes are emblematic of a larger shift in foundations' giving to modern dance.[37] Beginning with a focus on creating a community of artists in the 1970s, the Kitchen moved toward developing a community with its neighbors in the 1980s and then, most recently, in working toward expanding its audience. This turn away from a more exclusive artists' community toward the neighborhood and beyond coincided with the goals of foundations in the 1990s. Dance artists who incorporated nonprofessional community members in their productions, such as Liz Lerman, David Rousseve, Bill T. Jones, and Doug Dorfman, became the repeated recipients of funding in the 1990s. This retreat from the elitism associated with "high" culture was a reaction to the "culture wars." No longer was the aim to popularize "high" culture by means of a grand monument to culture such as Lincoln Center; small, locally defined, process-oriented endeavors were accorded the status of "real" art. As Charles Fahs noted in the early 1950s, expressive participation is the safest, least controversial marker of value in the arts. Attention to building an audience has been an elusive, if constant, goal for foundations, and now the aim is to get the audience involved in the art-making itself rather than building a theater in which to sit.

Philanthropic support to dance, then, has been slow and cautious. A large amount of funding goes to ballet, now alongside well-established modern-dance companies; there has been a wave of building homes for dance companies that began in the 1990s with the flourishing of the Joyce Theater, specifically devoted to dance, and recent building projects for Mark Morris, Alvin Ailey, and the Dance Theatre Workshop; neighborhood or educational efforts still receive a great deal of attention. All this is to the good, but still leaves the confrontational, experimental dancer relatively unsupported; "responsible" institutions, whether they are buildings or established companies, receive the bulk of philanthropic support. As throughout the history of giving to the arts, the difficulty of defining the purposes of dance, its relatively few institutional structures, the dominance of well-established companies, and the prospect of long-term funding causes foundations to be wary. If the arts were the "weakest point in our record" in the Rockefeller Foundation's giving in 1939, they appear slotted to remain in a similar spot today.

NOTES

My thanks to William Buxton for his helpful comments and leadership on this volume and the workshop from which it arose. I am also grateful to the other participants of the workshop for inspiring conversation and questions. The Rockefeller Archive Center, its director, archivists, and staff, deserve special thanks for their unqualified support that goes far beyond their duties. Unpublished material in this chapter has been quoted courtesy of the Rockefeller Archive Center, Sleepy Hollow, New York, and of the Ford Foundation Archives, New York City.

1. Ellen Condliffe Lagemann, *The Politics of Knowledge: The Carnegie Corporation, Philanthropy, and Public Policy* (Middletown, CT: Wesleyan University Press, 1989), 108–11.

2. John Marshall, "DHS's Draft Review of Humanities Program," 19 June, 1939. Rockefeller Archive Center (hereafter RAC), Rockefeller Foundation Archives (hereafter RF), Record Group (hereafter RG) 3.1, Series 911, Box 1, Folder 2.

3. "Humanities grants in 1939," 22 December, RAC, RF, 3.1, Series 911, Box 1. Folder 2; William J. Buxton, "John Marshall and the Humanities in Europe: Shifting Patterns of Rockefeller Support," *Minerva* 41, no. 2 (2003): 133–53.

4. A recent look at the democratization of the arts in the 1930s focuses particularly on the visual arts and includes a review of the 1939 World's Fair: Joan Saab, *Art for the Millions* (Philadelphia: University of Pennsylvania Press, 2004). For an overview of arts and culture in the 1930s, see my "Politics and Culture in the 1930s and 40s," in *A Companion to American Cultural History*, ed. Karen Halttunen (Malden, MA: Blackwell, 2008), 214–29.

5. The most obvious example of the continued conversation is between Mayor Fiorella LaGuardia and the Rockefeller brothers as they worked toward building a cultural center in New York. LaGuardia took advantage of the bankruptcy of the Masonic Auditorium in midtown Manhattan on Fifty-fifth Street between Sixth and Seventh Avenues to found City Center, a theater for the performing arts subsidized by the city. For further discussion of the Rockefeller involvement in these ideas for a cultural center, see my "The Other West Side Story: Urbanization and the Arts Meet at Lincoln Center," *Amerikastudien* 52, no. 2 (2007): 227–47; Murielle Vautrin, "Government and Culture: New York City and its Cultural Institutions, 1870–1965," (Ph.D. diss., Brandeis University, 1997).

6. For an overview of Stevens's view of the humanities, see *A Time of Humanities: An Oral History, Recollections of David H. Stevens as Director in the Division of the Humanities, Rockefeller Foundation, 1930–50*, ed. Robert E. Yahnke (Madison: Wisconsin Academy of Sciences, Arts and Letters, 1976), 80–99.

7. "Old and New Work in the Arts," n.d. RAC, RF, RG 3.1, Series 911, Box 2, Folder 14.

8. "Old and New Work in the Arts."

9. Paul J. DiMaggio, "Support for the Arts from Independent Foundations," in *Nonprofit Enterprise in the Arts: Studies in Mission and Constraint*, ed. P. DiMaggio (New York: Oxford University Press, 1986), 113–39.

10. Charles Fahs, "Defining a Humanities Program (2nd tentative draft)," February 1950. RAC, RF, RG 3.1, Series 911, Box 1, Folder 5 (Emphasis original).

11. *New York Times*, 7 April, 1958.

12. Charles Fahs, "Foundation Program in the Arts," 31 January, 1957. RAC, RF, RG 3.1, Series 911, Box 1, Folder 7.

13. Notes on a Music Conference, 25 February, 1949. RAC, RF, RG 3.1, Series 911, Box 5, Folder 45.

14. John Marshall (hereafter JM), Interview with Walter Terry, 2 March, 1954. RAC, RF, RG 3.1, Series 911, Box 1, Folder 6.

15. For a more thorough treatment of this transformation, see my *Modern Bodies: Dance and American Modernism from Martha Graham to Alvin Ailey* (Chapel Hill: University of North Carolina Press, 2002).

16. JM Interview with Anatole Chujoy, 22 November, 1955. RAC, RF, RG 1.2, Series 200R, Box 309, Folder 2862. For more of Chujoy's views on modern dance, see his notes on Anna Halprin's performance in San Francisco from his cross-country tour and an article from the *Seattle Times*. RAC, RF, RG 1.2, Series 200R, Box 309, Folder 2862. Chujoy also wrote an overview of foundation funding to dance: "Philanthropic Foundations and the Dance," in *U.S. Philanthropic Foundations: Their*

History, Structure, Management, and Record, ed. Warren Weaver (New York: Harper & Row, 1967), 316–28. The article is notable for its continuing disdain of modern dance and for its defense of the large Ford Foundation grant to ballet.

17. Charles Fahs, notes of performance of José Limón and Dance Company, 15 December, 1952. RAC, RF, RG 1.2, Series 200R, Box 320, Folder 2957.

18. Robert W. July, notes on the Ninth American Dance Festival, 16–17 August, 1956. RAC, RF, RG 1.2, Series 200R, Box 320, Folder 2958.

19. For an overview of the Ford Foundation grant, see Elizabeth Kendall, *Dancing: A Ford Foundation Report* (New York: Ford Foundation, 1983).

20. Lynn Garafola provides a good overview of the connections between Kirstein and the Rockefellers in "Dollars for Dance: Lincoln Kirstein, City Center, and the Rockefeller Foundation," *Dance Chronicle* 25, no. 1 (2002): 101–14.

21. For a summary of Rockefeller's reasons for becoming involved in the project, see his address to the 11th Annual "Business Speaks" dinner of the New York Board of Trade, 10 October, 1957; RAC, John D. Rockefeller 3rd Collection (hereafter JDR3), RG 5, Series 1, Subseries 4, Box 76, Folder 655. The most succinct but thorough summary of Rockefeller's involvement in Lincoln Center is chapters 9 and 10 of John Ensor Harr and Peter Johnson, *The Rockefeller Conscience: An American Family in Public and in Private* (New York: Scribner's, 1991). For more on the development of Lincoln Center, see also Edgar B. Young, *Lincoln Center, the Building of an Institution* (New York: New York University Press, 1980); Alan Rich, *The Lincoln Center Story* (New York: American Heritage, 1984); and Julia L. Foulkes, "The Other West Side Story: Urbanization and the Arts Meet at Lincoln Center," *Amerikastudien* 52, no. 1 (2007): 227–47.

22. George Stoddard, "The Dance," 6 March, 1957. RAC, JDR3, RG 5, 1-OMR-Files, Box 3, Folder: Dance Council 1957–58. For even stronger declaration that the status of dance be equal to the other arts in the project, see George Stoddard to John D. Rockefeller 3rd. 16 May, 1957. RAC, JDR3, RG 5, 1-OMR-Files, Box 3, Folder: Dance Council 1957–58.

23. Lincoln Kirstein to John D. Rockefeller 3rd, 29 November, 1957. RAC, JDR3, RG 5, Series 1-OMR, Box 3, Folder: Lincoln Center Dance Council. Kirstein eventually made good on his threat and resigned from the board in 1959, although Rockefeller continued to seek his counsel and Kirstein remained an influential force.

24. *New York Times,* 11 January, 1960. Emphasis original. On the point of not tying the complex to "any form of exclusiveness," see, for example, Fred Palmer to General Maxwell Taylor, 11 March, 1961. RAC, JDR3, RG 17B, Box 62, Folder: 799. On "hawking," see *Economist* (September 22, 1962): 1103.

25. A number of books detail the intersection of culture and the cold war, including Frances Stoner Saunders, *The Cultural Cold War: The CIA and the World of Arts and Letters* (New York: New Press, 2001); David Caute, *The Dancer Defects: The Struggle for Supremacy during the Cold War* (New York: Oxford University Press, 2003); Penny von Eschen, *Satchmo Blows Up the World: Jazz Ambassadors Play the Cold War* (Cambridge, MA: Harvard University Press, 2004); Naima Prevots, *Dance for Export: Cultural Diplomacy and the Cold War* (Middletown, CT.: Wesleyan University Press, 1998); and Lauren E. Brown, "Cultural Czars: American Nationalism, Dance, and Cold War Arts Funding, 1945–89" (PhD diss., Harvard University, 2008).

26. These words of Rockefeller can be found on a plaque at Lincoln Center in honor of his efforts.

27. For the range of opinions of the officers expressing both support and doubt, see RAC, RF, RG 1.2, Series 200R, Box 364, Folder 3291.

28. Excerpts pertaining to Lincoln Center from the *Rockefeller Foundation 1957 Annual Report* in RAC, JDR3, RG 5, Series 1, Subseries 4, Box 77, Folder 656.

29. See, for example, the plea of Alexander Ewing, the Executive Secretary of American Ballet Theatre, to John D. Rockefeller 3rd, 26 November, 1956. RAC, JDR3, RG 5, Series 1, Subseries 4, Box 59, Folder 529.

30. Newbold Morris to William Schuman, 12 November, 1964. RAC, JDR3, RG 5, Series 1, Subseries 4, Box 59, Folder 524. Other letters, notes, and press in this folder detail the battle.

31. Charles Fahs, notes on the Tenth American Dance Festival, 17–18 August, 1957. RAC, RF, RG 1.2, Series 200R, Box 320, Folder 2958.

32. Rockefeller Brothers Fund, *The Performing Arts: Problems and Prospects* (New York: McGraw Hill, 1965).

33. See, for example, the memorandum from William Schuman, 15 June, 1965, which summarizes the conversation up to that point. RAC, RF, RG 1.2, Series 200R, Box 268, Folder 2578.

34. Memorandum from W. McNeil Lowry to McGeorge Bundy, 22 May, 1968. Ford Foundation Archives (hereafter FF), Reel R–2176, Grant #68–620, Section 1.

35. Barnes review, letter from Lois Ira, letter from Charles Reinhart, and review by Marcia B. Siegel. FF, Reel R–2176, Grant #68–620, Section 4.

36. Janice Ross gives a good overview of the impact of academia on the development and institutional structure of modern dance in "Institutional Forces and the Shaping of Dance in the American University," *Dance Chronicle* 25, no. 1 (2002): 115–24.

37. Sally Banes, "Choreographing Community: Dancing in the Kitchen," *Dance Chronicle* 25 no. 1 (2002): 143–61.

Index

About the Contributors

Charles R. Acland is professor and holds the Concordia University Research Chair in Communication Studies at Concordia University, Montreal. He is author of *Youth, Murder, Spectacle: The Cultural Politics of 'Youth in Crisis'* (HarperCollins/Westview, 1995) and *Screen Traffic: Movies, Multiplexes, and Global Culture* (Duke University Press, 2003), which won the 2004 Robinson Book Prize for the best book in communication studies by a Canadian scholar. He is editor of *Residual Media* (University of Minnesota Press, 2007), coeditor of *Harold Innis in the New Century: Reflections and Refractions* (McGill-Queen's University Press, 1999). His current research includes a history of popular ideas about media manipulation in the 1950s and a study of the post–World War II networks of film and media experts.

Jeffrey Brison is an assistant professor in the Department of History at Queen's University in Kingston, Ontario, Canada. In 2005 he published *Rockefeller, Carnegie, and Canada: American Philanthropy and the Arts and Letters in Canada*, a study that explores the influence of private American philanthropy on the making of a national culture in Canada. He is currently working on a project that examines the role private philanthropic foundations played in fostering extranational intellectual networks and infrastructure from the late 1930s to the early years of the cold war. This study aims at deepening understanding of how formal and informal networks of cultural power both facilitated and mediated state-to-state relations between Canada and the United States in an era during which both nations fundamentally redefined their roles in world affairs.

William J. Buxton is professor of communication studies at Concordia University in Montréal. He is author of *Talcott Parsons and the Capitalist Nation-State: Political Sociology as a Strategic Vocation* (University of Toronto Press, 1985), coauthor of *The Politics of Knowledge and Information: American Philanthropy and Canadian Libraries* (McGill University, The Centre for Research on Canadian Cultural Industries and Institutions and the Graduate School of Information and Library Studies, 1998), editor of *Canada's Film Century: Traditions, Transitions, Transgression*, theme issue of volume 6, *Lonergan Review* (Lonergan University College, 2000), and coeditor of *Harold Innis in the New Century: Reflections and Refractions* (McGill-Queen's University Press, 1999). For the summer of 2004 he was the scholar-in-residence at the Rockefeller Archive Center.

Gisela Cramer is associate professor at the history department of the National University of Colombia, Bogotá. She is the author of *Argentinien im Schatten des Zweiten Weltkriegs* (Steiner, 1999) and of various articles focusing on the political economy of Latin America in the twentieth century. Her current research explores the efforts of the U.S. government to influence public opinion in Latin America during the Second World War, particularly through the use of radio and other media to reach and persuade mass audiences. She served as scholar-in-residence at the Rockefeller Archive Center in 2002.

Julia L. Foulkes is an associate professor of history at The New School and the author of *Modern Bodies: Dance and American Modernism from Martha Graham to Alvin Ailey* (2002) and the forthcoming *To the City*, which charts the growth of urbanization in the United States of the 1930s and 1940s through photographs and documents of the New Deal. She has served as an advisor for the documentary *Free to Dance* (2001), been a recipient of two postdoctoral fellowships, and, most recently, was a scholar-in-residence at the Rockefeller Archive Center (2005) and a Fulbright Senior Scholar at Potsdam University in Germany (2005–2006). Her current research examines the intersection of urbanization and the arts in *West Side Story*.

Johannes C. Gall studied music (piano), musicology, philosophy, and German philology in Stuttgart, Tübingen, and Hamburg and was visiting scholar at the University of California Los Angeles. He currently lives and works in Berlin, where he initiated and directed a project to reconstruct and produce a DVD edition of Eisler's Rockefeller film music study (1940–1942), which was released by Suhrkamp in 2006 as part of a special edition he edited of Adorno and Eisler's book *Komposition für den Film*. He is coeditor of the series *Eisler-Studien*, the next volume of which will be his dissertation *Hanns Eisler: Musik für Hollywood*.

Anna McCarthy is associate professor and associate chair of Cinema Studies at New York University. Currently the coeditor of the journal *Social Text*, she is the author of *Ambient Television: Visual Culture and Public Space* (Duke University Press, 2001) and the coeditor of *Media/Space: Place, Scale and Culture in a Media Age* (Routledge, 2004). Her new book about governing by television in the postwar United States will be published by The New Press in 2010.

Manon Niquette is associate professor in the Department of Information and Communication at Laval University (Québec, Canada), and a researcher at the Groupe d'études sur l'interdisciplinarité et les représentations sociales (GEIRSO). She has published on social interaction in science museums and world's fairs, the history of women in public relations, and on social marketing. Her current research is on pharmaceutical advertising and, more specifically, on the representations of uses in drug promotion.

Theresa Richardson is professor of the history and sociology of education and multicultural education at Ball State University. She is a former scholar-in-residence at the Rockefeller Archive Center and has published extensively on the influence of philanthropy on social and educational policy and practice in the United States and Canada. She has four books including *The Century of the Child: The Mental Hygiene Movement and Social Policy in the U.S. and Canada*; *The Development of the Social Sciences in the U.S. and Canada: The Role of Philanthropy* (edited with Donald Fisher); *Race, Ethnicity and Education: What is Taught in School*; and *Educational Research the National Agenda and Educational Reform, A History* (the latter two coauthored with E. V. Johanningmeier).

Haidee Wasson is associate professor, Mel Hoppenheim School of Cinema, Concordia University, Montreal. She is author of *Museum Movies: MoMA and the Birth of Art Cinema* (University of California Press, 2005) and coeditor with Lee Grieveson of *Inventing Film Studies* (Duke University Press, 2008) and with Charles Acland of *Useful Cinema* to be published by Duke University Press. She has previously taught at the University of Minnesota and at Harvard University, publishing widely on topics including American and British film culture, the history of the museum gift shop, and home entertainment and visual technologies. Her current book project investigates the history of mobile film projectors and small screens.

Marion Wrenn earned her PhD from the Department of Media, Culture and Communication at New York University, where her dissertation, *Inventing Warriors: US Philanthropies and the Post-war Reorientation of Foreign Journalists*, was nominated for the Steinhardt School's Outstanding

Dissertation Award. Her work has appeared in *Gamers: Writers, Artists & Programmers on the Pleasures of Pixels* (Soft Skull Press, 2004) and *Practicing Culture* (Richard Sennett and Craig Calhoun, editors). She teaches at Princeton University where she is on the faculty of the undergraduate writing program and is editor of the literary magazine *Painted Bride Quarterly* (pbq.drexel.edu), for which she has received several grants from the National Endowment for the Arts.

About the Cover

From the left, clockwise: Wisdom, Light, and Sound (1934) by Lee Lawrie, located over the main entrance to the GE Building (formerly the RCA Building), 30 Rockefeller Plaza, New York City (copyright Christine Roussel 2009).

Breinigsville, PA USA
23 May 2010
238518BV00002B/3/P